D1450578

Directory of
Contemporary
American
Musical Instrument
Makers

Directory of Contemporary American

University of Missouri Press

Columbia & London   1981

HOWE LIBRARY
SHENANDOAH COLLEGE &
CONSERVATORY OF MUSIC
WINCHESTER, VA.

Musical Instrument Makers

Susan Caust Farrell

Copyright © 1981 by The Curators of the University of Missouri
Library of Congress Catalog Number 80-24924
Printed and bound in the United States of America
University of Missouri Press Columbia, Missouri 65211 All rights reserved
Library of Congress Cataloging in Publication Data
Farrell, Susan Caust, 1944–
Directory of Contemporary American Musical Instrument Makers.

1. Musical instruments—Makers—United States—Directories. I. Title.
ML17.F37   781.91'025'73   80-24924   ISBN 0-8262-0322-1

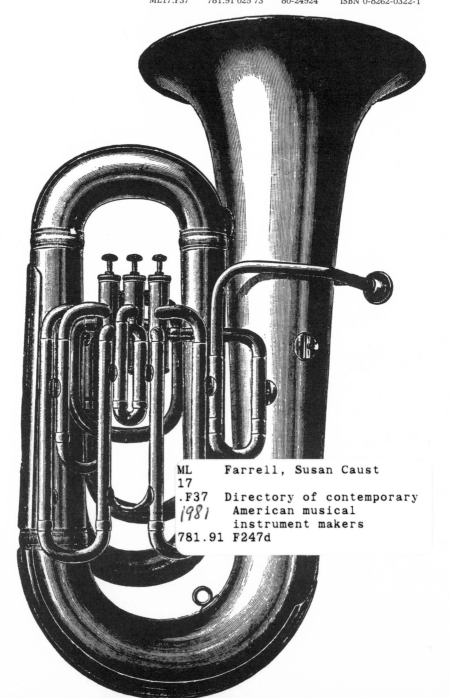

ML   Farrell, Susan Caust
17
.F37   Directory of contemporary
1981   American musical
           instrument makers
781.91 F247d

Contents

HOWE LIBRARY
SHENANDOAH COLLEGE &
CONSERVATORY OF MUSIC
WINCHESTER, VA.

21.60 Goldberg 12-2-81

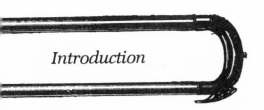

Introduction

In the spring of 1972, the annual meeting of the American Musical Instrument Society, Inc., was held at the Boston Museum of Fine Arts. During one discussion, the question was casually raised whether there existed a complete index of American musical instrument makers. None of the collectors, musicians, organologists, and instrument makers present could remember having seen such a compendium. It was at that point that I began this directory.

The book includes all contemporary American makers of musical instruments, regardless of the number of instruments they produce, the size of their shop, or whether they work full-time or part-time. If there are instruments with the maker's name or label on them, he or she is included in the directory. This book includes instrument makers who work in the fifty states and the District of Columbia. It does not include Canadians or Americans working outside the United States.

The information presented in this directory was obtained primarily through questionnaires sent out from 1974 to 1978. A second mailing to update the information was sent out in 1980. The names came from lists provided by various societies and organizations, advertisements in magazines and journals, from lists of students in schools of instrument making, and, above all, from referrals by other makers. This directory must necessarily be incomplete. The number of makers has been mushrooming in recent years, and it is likely that there are individuals who are not in this directory because they have begun this work too recently. Others may have been unintentionally overlooked because their names never reached me. It is my expectation that there will be periodic updates to this directory and that the information in subsequent editions will reflect the industry even more accurately.

This directory is far more comprehensive than any previous efforts to catalogue America's instrument makers. In March 1979, *The Music Trades* published a report of musical instruments from the 1977 census of manufacturers. The total number of manufacturers given was 427; the number of entries in this directory exceeds 2,500. In the 1977 census, "all manufacturing establishments with one or more paid employees are covered; ... establishments without employees are excluded." This directory covers those individuals who were intentionally excluded from the census as well as the large manufacturers. In fact, nearly three-quarters of all instrument makers work alone (see Figure 1). Not all those who were sent questionnaires responded, but if I was reasonably certain that an individual or firm did make instruments, they have been included with whatever information was available. According to *The Music Trades* report of the 1977 census, more than twenty thousand people were employed in this field. My intent is not to list all those individuals; rather it is to document the number of establishments, whether large or small,

Figure 1. Number of Workers in Shop

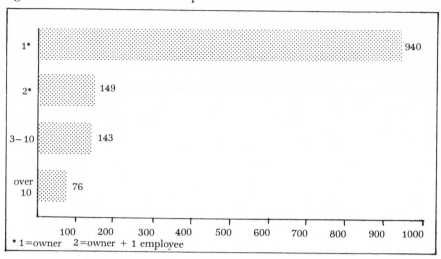

that make instruments. By the same token, I am not attempting to determine the total number of instruments made, as this directory is a study of makers (although it is interesting to note that there are 266 different types of instruments made in the United States today).

While the number of names gathered grew year by year, the purposes of the book have remained unchanged. The first objective is that the relevant information about mid-twentieth-century instruments and their makers be preserved for future reference and use. Historians, organologists, and collectors will have the benefit of these data for reference and scholarship. From a practical point of view, we need only look at the recent and growing activity in musical instruments in the national and international auction houses. In 1976, following the great success of the Sotheby/London auctions, Sotheby Parke Bernet held the first auction of antique musical instruments in the United States. Since then, the number of such sales has increased annually, spreading to PB-84, Christie's, Phillips, and other smaller houses as well. In the future, this directory will be increasingly useful in researching various instruments and in helping to determine their monetary worth. Say, for example, that a hundred years from now someone finds a violin made by John X. By turning to this directory, one may learn, among other things, how many violins John X made. Once discovering how scarce they are, one may then be aided in determining the monetary value of the violin. For the organologist or collector, this information will be helpful in deciding whether it is worthwhile to search for other violins made by John X. On the other hand, we might learn from this directory that he made recorders and oboes in addition to this single violin. In fact, John X was primarily a woodwind maker. This information not only changes our perception of him but probably also changes the value of the violin.

A great many musical instrument makers in this country are known only to a small circle of friends and followers. The second purpose of the directory is to expand that circle. I hope that this directory will increase communication and cooperation among these makers and that musicians and collectors, as well as retailers and wholesalers, will now have a way of knowing about and locating the makers.

The entries should in no way be construed as advertisements or endorsements. This book is strictly a reference work. No judgments are made concerning the quality of the instruments.

The major section of this directory is an alphabetical index of all makers. A key to using this part of the directory follows this introduction.

Following the main alphabetical list of makers are additional secondary lists of makers broken down by instrument and by state. If one wants to know who makes fluegelhorns or who makes instruments in Rhode Island, the information is readily available. In the breakdown of makers by instrument, the total number of names is greater than the number of makers listed by state since one person often makes several types of instruments and is thus counted more than once.

The three appendixes consist of parenthetical bits of information I have collected during the course of this research. The lists of schools of instrument making, societies and organizations, and books are not necessarily comprehensive, but I believe they are substantial and worth sharing. They also give an indication of the blossoming interest in this subject. It should be noted that many of the societies have publications that might extend into the category of books on instrument making but are not listed as such (The Guild of American Luthiers, for example, regularly publishes "Data Sheets" giving tips on instrument making).

Several years ago, a survey published in the *New York Times* rated music as one of the top three personal priorities of adult Americans. *The Music Trades* reported in October 1978 that "the buying public . . . purchased band instruments in record quantities . . . and retailers concur that the instrument sales for 1978 are well ahead of the past several years." Certainly, there is scarcely a household in the United States that does not contain at least one musical instrument. There has been a dramatic increase in the number of people beginning instrument making in the 1960s and 1970s, starting primarily in 1969, when the number rose by almost 50 percent from the previous year (see Figure 2). From my own personal, undocumented observations, many of the new makers were, initially, the same people who were involved in the migration from the cities to the country in the late 1960s. In addition, quite a few people have become involved in instrument making after their retirement from other work. In the last ten years, there has also been a significant increase (to more than fifty) in the number of women making instruments. Societies and periodicals devoted to or emphasizing musical instruments to some degree have burgeoned in this country, as well as in England, where the interest in early music is especially evident. It is, therefore, time to take notice of instrument makers, to credit them for the contribution they are making, and to acknowledge them now and for future generations.

This research was conducted under the auspices of the American Musical

Figure 2. Year Began Making Instruments

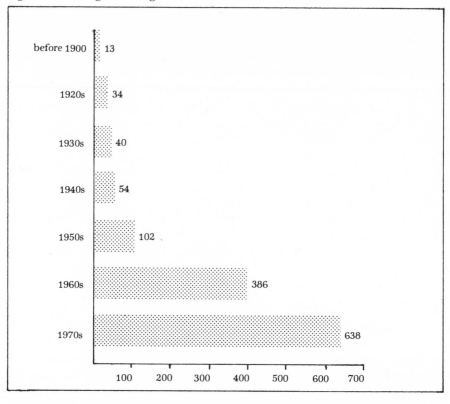

Instrument Society, Inc., and, in part, under a grant from the National Endowment for the Arts. Thanks to Jane Ambrose for the original suggestion, and to Marcia Reisman, Jan Munroe, and Celio for help in organizing and correcting the data. A tremendous boost in computerizing the information was given by Jerry Karush, Sue Ebersten, and Suzy Carlsen. General support and suggestions came from Larraine Brown. A personal and deep thanks to Friedrich Von Huene for his guidance in my early years as a restorer of antique musical instruments. And, above all, I extend my heartfelt thanks, admiration, and respect to Robert M. Rosenbaum, a founder and past president of the American Musical Instrument Society, Inc., who spiritually, financially, and professionally helped to support this project from its inception, and whose all-around confidence is profoundly appreciated.

S. C. F.
Belfast, Maine
October 1980

How to Use the Alphabetical Listing

The alphabetical listing of instrument makers is the major section of this directory. A typical entry might appear as follows:

John Jones Flute Works
4 Tarpit Dr., Floral Park, N.Y. 11427
FT   1971   Active   3 emp.   IA/MTO   Modern and historical
Brochure   9/77 • Modern flute   1–10 to date   1–10 per year • Renaissance flute   1–10 to date   1–10 per year • Also known as: Fred Smith
• *1980: Recorder   1–10 to date   1–10 per year*

First the name of an individual or firm is given. If there are two names for a single entry, there is a cross-reference from one to the other (shown as *Also known as*). A cross-reference is also given from one partner in a firm to the other, between a subsidiary and the parent company, and between the name of the maker and that of the company, if those names differ. The main body of information generally appears under the company name, unless a maker specified a preference for being listed under his or her personal name.

FT or *PT* indicates whether the maker takes part in this occupation full-time or part-time. Some people who have called themselves part-time instrument makers are in fact full-time repairers or restorers. I have taken the liberty of calling them full-time workers, since they are primarily engaged with instruments. Nevertheless, this delineation often changes and should not be considered static.

The year that the individual or company began making instruments is given next. Most of the people responding to my questionnaires were making instruments at that time, although a few have stopped in the meantime. The information as to whether they are still involved in this work is shown as *Active* or *Inactive.*

The number of employees in the firm is given next; *1 emp.* means that the individual is self-employed and works alone; *2 emp.* refers to a shop comprised of one owner and one employee; and so on.

IA and/or *MTO* indicates "instruments available," "made to order," or both. It is followed by the designation *Modern, Historical,* or both to indicate the style of the instruments. If a brochure is available, the word *Brochure* will appear next. (This word is omitted if the maker does not issue a brochure.) The next item in the entry is the date (*month/year*) on which the completed questionnaire was returned to me.

The specific types of instruments and the number made to date (when the questionnaire was filled out) and per year follow. For example, as of September 1977, John Jones Flute Works had made 1–10 modern and Renaissance flutes. The company's yearly output of modern and Renaissance flutes is also 1–10 per year. Following this information, cross-references to makers' names then appear after *Also known as.*

When updated information is available, it appears in italics following *1980.* It is the last section of the entry. In order to make the directory as accurate and as timely as possible, in October 1980 each maker in the directory was sent a copy of his or her entry and given the opportunity to correct and/or update the information. The update section lists only those items that were corrected or updated from the original listing. This information has not been incorporated into the body of the entry because not all makers responded and because the demographic information in the figures, tables, and appendixes was compiled from information gathered in the 1974–1978 questionnaires.

A dagger (†) indicates any information that was requested in 1974–1978 and in 1980 but not provided. Sometimes no information other than the name and address of a maker was provided; other times the information for one or more specific questions was omitted.

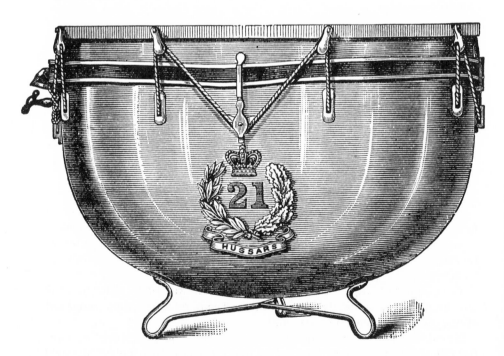

1. Alphabetical Directory of Instrument Makers

A & K Diversified
Also known as: Charles D. Alper

Aardvark Fluteworks
629 N. Linn, Iowa City, Iowa 52240
PT   1972   Active   2 emp.   IA
Historical   Brochure   4/74 • Renaissance
flute   Over 50 to date   Over 50 per year
• Also known as: Robert Paul Block; Peter
Nothnagle

Frank Abbate
33–41 115 St., South Ozone Park, N.Y. 11420†
2/76

Abbott and Sieker
2027 Pontius Ave., Los Angeles, Calif. 90025
FT   1961   Active   5 emp.   MTO
Modern   Brochure   10/75 • Pipe organ
Over 50 to date   1–10 per year

Hank Aberle
885 West End Ave., New York, N.Y. 10025
PT   1971   Active   1 emp.   IA
Modern   9/76 • Classical guitar   1–10 to
date   †

Dr. Peter Abernathy
Dept. of English, Texas Tech University,
Lubbock, Tex. 79409†   2/76

Accorgan Corp.
581 Bergen Blvd., Ridgefield, N.J. 07657†   2/75

Ace Accordion Co.
6324 Fourth Ave., Brooklyn, N.Y. 11232
Maker of accordions†   2/75

Dennis Ackley
1152 N.W. 46, Seattle, Wash. 98107
FT   1976   Active   1 emp.   MTO
Modern   2/78 • Appalachian dulcimer
1–10 to date   1–10 per year •
Monochord   1–10 to date   1–10 per year
• Also known as: Magiworks

Acoustic Music
Also known as: Doug Roomian

Acoustic Stringed Instruments
Also known as: R. Brent Pierce; John R. Snell

Andy Adams
8700 MacArthur Blvd., Cabin John, Md. 20731
FT   1968   Active   2 emp.   MTO
Modern   4/76 • 12-string guitar   10–25
to date • Steel-string guitar   10–25 to
date • Classical guitar   1–10 to
date • Flamenco guitar   1–10 to
date • Lute   †• Viola da gamba   †• All
instruments   1–10 per year

G. F. Adams
204 W. Houston St., New York, N.Y. 10014†
2/76

Jeremy Adams
2A Putnam Ct., Danvers, Mass. 01923
Maker of harpsichords and organs†   2/76

Parker Adams
13701 E. Evans Creek Rd., Rogue River, Ore.
97537
FT   1972   Active   1 emp.   IA
Modern   Brochure   4/76 • Irish harp
Over 50 to date   10–25 per year • Also
known as: New World Harp Co.

Paul Adams
7012 N. Galena, Box 3434, Peoria, Ill. 61614
FT   1974   Active   1 emp.   IA/MTO
Modern and historical   Brochure
4/76 • Appalachian dulcimer   25–50 to
date   †• 5-string banjo   1–10 to date
†• Hammered dulcimer   1–10 to date
†• Kalimba   1–10 to date   †• Also
known as: Lakefront Dulcimore Shoppe

Adams Piano Factory
Box 535, East Dublin, Ga. 31021
Maker of pianos†   2/76

Mark Adler
4617 De Russey Pkwy., Chevy Chase, Md. 20015
PT   1972   Active   1 emp.   MTO
Historical   6/75 • Harpsichord   1–10 to
date   †• Also known as: Cembaloworks of
Washington • *1980: Harpsichord   1–10
per year*

1

Aeolian American Division of Aeolian Corp.
East Rochester, N.Y. 14445
Maker of pianos†   2/76 · *1980: FT*
1823   *Active*   *300 emp.*   *IA/MTO*
Modern and historical   *Brochure*
10/79 · Piano   *Over 50 to date*   *Over 50
per year*

Aeolian Corp.
2722 Pershing Ave., Memphis, Tenn. 38112
FT   1823   Active   300 emp.   IA
Modern   Brochure   4/76 · Piano
†· Also known as: Aeolian American;
Bradbury Piano Co., Inc.; Cable Piano Co.;
A. B. Chase; Chickering & Sons;
Conover-Cable Piano Co.; Duo-Art Player
Piano; Emerson Piano Co.; J. and C. Fischer;
Hallet & Davis Piano Co.; Hardman Peck &
Co.; Ivers & Pond Piano Co.; William Knabe
and Co.; Kranich and Bach; Mason &
Hamlin Co.; Paul G. Mehlin and Sons, Inc.;
Melodigrand Corp.; Henry F. Miller Piano
Co.; Musette Player-Piano; Pianola Player
Piano; Poole Piano Co.; Schiller Pianos;
George Steck and Co., Inc.; Sterling Piano
Co., Inc.; Sting Player Piano; Vose & Sons;
The Weber Piano Co.; Winter & Co.

Aeolian Workshop
1080 Beacon St., Brookline, Mass. 02146†   2/76
1980: FT   *1973*   *Active*   *5 emp.*
IA/MTO   *Historical*   *Brochure*
*10/80 · Wind instruments, organs, and
harpsichords*   †· *Also known as: David H.
Green*

Reginald Aitkins
81 Meadow Ln., North Andover, Mass. 01845
FT   1951   Active   1 emp.   MTO
Modern   Brochure   4/76 · Modern
flute   Over 50 to date   1–10 per year
· Piccolo   10–25 to date   †· Primarily
repairs

James Akright
Silver Spring, Md. 20900
Maker of organs †   1/74

R. Kent Albin
1458 Haight St., #1, San Francisco, Calif. 94117
FT   1959   Active   1 emp.   MTO
Modern and historical   2/75 · Steel-string

guitar   Over 50 to date   1–10 per year
· Classical guitar   1–10 to date   † ·
Appalachian dulcimer   25–50 to date
1–10 per year · Irish harp   10–25 to date
1–10 per year · Electric violin   10–25 to
date   1–10 per year

Alan Albright
R.D. 2, Box 225, Warwick, N.Y. 10990
Also known as: Chardavogne Folk
Instruments

Capt. Cliff Albright
Southern Airways, Memphis Airport, Memphis,
Tenn. 38130 †   12/77

Garett Alden
Musick Shoppe, P.O. Box 197, Point Arena, Calif.
95468
FT   1970   Active   1 emp.   IA/MTO
Modern and historical   11/74 · Strings
25–50 to date   1–10 per year · Flute
over 50 to date   10–25 per year
· Kalimba   Over 50 to date   Over 50 per
year · *1980: c/o S. Freegard, P.O. Box 242,
Arcadia, Mo. 63621 · Brochure · Not making
kalimbas · Carved whistles   10–25 to
date   1–10 per year · Also known as:
Burning Water Instruments; S. Freegard*

Alan Aldridge
Kerhonkson, N.Y. 12446
Maker of flutes †   2/76 · Also known as:
Remarkable Flutes

Alembic, Inc.
Also known as: Rick Turner

Richard Alexander
5719 Keith Ave., Oakland, Calif. 94618
FT   1969   Active   1 emp.   MTO
Historical   2/76 · Harpsichord   10–25 to
date   1–10 per year

Dale Allen
1417 Cedar St. S.E., Roanoke, Va. 24013
PT   1975   Active   1 emp.   MTO
Modern   4/76 · Steel-string guitar   1–10
to date   1–10 per year

John W. Allen
500 Glenway Ave., Bristol, Va. 24201
Maker of harpsichords †   2/76

Laura Rachel Allen
307 E. Blithedale, Mill Valley, Calif. 94941
PT   1970   Inactive   1 emp.   MTO
Modern   4/76 • Zither   1– 10 to date
1– 10 per year • Also known as: Neato
Productions

Richard C. Allen
11224½ Walnut St., El Monte, Calif. 91731
FT   1960   Active   1 emp.   IA/MTO
Modern and historical   5/75 • Electric
guitar   Over 50 to date   1– 10 per year
• 5-string banjo   Over 50 to date   10– 25
per year

Allen Organ Co.
Macungie, Pa. 18062
FT   1945   Active   500 emp.   IA
Modern   Brochure   5/74 • Electronic
organ   Over 50 to date   Over 50 per year
• Electronic piano   Over 50 to date   Over
50 per year

Steven Allerton
827 Forest Ave., Fulton, N.Y. 13067 †   9/76
Also known as: The Magic Flute

Allied Traders of Miami
Also known as: H. E. Huttig

Michael Allison
163 Brook St., Providence, R.I. 02906
FT   1969   Active   1 emp.   IA/MTO
Modern and historical   10/74 • 5-string
banjo   25– 50 to date   10– 25 per year
• Steel-string guitar   1– 10 to date   †
• Electric guitar   25– 50 to date   1– 10
per year • Also known as: Providence Guitar
and Banjo

Allison Stringed Instruments
18926 Knowles Rd., Lake Villa, Ill. 60046
PT   1960   Active   1 emp.   IA/MTO
Modern   5/76 • Classical, flamenco, and
steel-string guitars   † • Also known as:
Jack Woods

Charles D. Alper
P.O. Box 72945, Fairbanks, Alaska 99701
PT   1977   Active   2 emp.   MTO
Modern and historical   2/78 • Electric
guitar   1– 10 to date   † • Also known as:
A & K Diversified

Alpha Omega Corp.
1115 Tower Rd., Schaumburg, Ill. 60195
Maker of electronic organs †   1/78

Alpine Dulcimer Co.
Box 566, Boulder, Colo. 80302
FT   1967   Active   1 emp.   IA
Historical   Brochure   4/76
• Appalachian dulcimer   Over 50 to
date   † • Also known as: William Jones

American Banjo Co.
Also known as: Arthur Gaudette

American Dream Instruments Mfg.
Also known as: Lee Follmer; Bob Morris;
Sam Radding; Taylor Guitars

American Indian Arts
Also known as: Indian Jim

American Plating and Mfg. Co.
2241 S. Indiana Ave., Chicago, Ill. 60616
Maker of fifes †   2/75

Archer Ames
48 Birch Rd., Scarsdale, N.Y. 10585 †   10/74

Ampeg Co.
P.O. Box 310, Elkhart, Ind. 46514
Maker of steel-string guitars, 5-string
banjos, ukuleles, and mandolins †   2/76

Ancient Instruments
Also known as: Jay Witcher

Arnold Dean Anderson
1003 Grove St., Brainerd, Minn.. 56401
FT   Year?   Active   1 emp.   IA/MTO
Modern and historical   11/76 • Violin
25– 50 to date   10– 25 per year • Viola
10– 25 to date   10– 25 per year • Cello
1– 10 to date   1– 10 per year

Arvil Anderson
R.R. 1, Box 49, St. Ignatius, Mont. 59865
FT   1940   Active   1 emp.   IA/MTO
Modern   Brochure   3/78 • Violin   Over
50 to date   1– 10 per year • Viola   10– 25
to date   1– 10 per year • Cello   1– 10 to
date   1– 10 per year • Bass violin   1– 10
to date   1– 10 per year • Steel-string
guitar   1– 10 to date   1– 10 per year

• *1980: Not making bass violins or steel-string guitars • Cello 10–25 to date • Classical guitar 10–25 to date 1–10 per year*

Robert S. Anderson
1752 N.W. Grove Ln., Roseburg, Ore. 97470
PT 1973 Active 1 emp. MTO
Modern 7/74 • Classical guitar 1–10 to date 1–10 per year • Appalachian dulcimer 1–10 to date 1–10 per year

Steven Anderson
5857 E. Thomas Rd., Scottsdale, Ariz. 85251
PT 1975 Active 1 emp. MTO
Modern 12/77 • 12-string guitar 1–10 to date † • Steel-string guitar 1–10 to date † • Appalachian dulcimer 1–10 to date † • Primarily repairs

Andover Organ Co., Inc.
P.O. Box 36, Methuen, Mass. 01844
FT 1948 Active 13 emp. IA/MTO
Modern Brochure 5/74 • Pipe organ 25–50 to date 1–10 per year • Primarily repairs

Andress Mfg. Co.
91 Woodward Ave., Battle Creek, Mich. 49017
FT 1909 Active ? emp. IA
Modern Brochure 12/77 • Snare drum †

Darrol Anger
210 Mission, Suite B, San Rafael, Calif. 94902 † 4/78

Scott E. Antes
236 Lincoln St., Hartville, Ohio 44632
FT 1974 Active 1 emp. MTO
Modern and historical Brochure 12/74 • Appalachian dulcimer 10–25 to date † • Hammered dulcimer 1–10 to date † • Steel-string guitar 1–10 to date † • Electric guitar 1–10 to date † • Also known as: Boulder Junction Stringed Instruments

Apache Guitars
30 Irving Pl., New York, N.Y. 10003
Maker of steel-string guitars † 5/76

Nicholas Apollonio
Tenants Harbor, Maine 04860

FT 1968 Active 1 emp. IA/MTO
Modern Brochure 9/74 • Steel-string guitar Over 50 to date † • Appalachian dulcimer 25–50 to date † • Hammered dulcimer 10–25 to date † • Strings 1–10 to date †

APP Electronics
3109 Timberline Dr., Fort Worth, Tex. 76119 † 2/76

Joan Applequist
1221 State St., Santa Barbara, Calif. 93101 † 9/76
Also known as: Wooden Music

Appleseed John's
Golden, Colo. 80401
Maker of Appalachian dulcimers † 2/76

Apprentice Shop
Box 267, Spring Hill, Tenn. 37174
FT 1976 Active 2 emp. MTO
Modern 2/78 • Steel-string guitar 10–25 to date † • Classical guitar 1–10 to date † • Mandolin 1–10 to date † • Appalachian dulcimer 25–50 to date † • Also known as: Michael Lennon; Bruce Scotten • *1980: Steel-string guitar Over 50 to date • Classical guitar 25–50 to date • Appalachian dulcimer Over 50 to date*

Carlos Arcieri
145 W. 55th St., New York, N.Y. 10019 † 2/76

Ted J. Arensburg
807 Main St., Goodland, Kans. 67735
PT Year? Inactive 1 emp. MTO
Modern 11/74 • Violin 1–10 to date †

James Ariail
1260 Dempsey, Bend, Ore. 97701
PT 1966 Active 1 emp. IA/MTO
Modern 6/74 • Classical guitar 25–50 to date 1–10 per year • Steel-string guitar 1–10 to date 1–10 per year • 5-string banjo 1–10 to date † • Lute-zither 1–10 to date † • Also known as: Old World Guitars

David Akin
Rt. 7, Box 142Q1, Seavy Loop Rd., Eugene, Ore. 97405 † 10/76

John Arkenberg

1748 Atwood, Topeka, Kans. 66604
PT 1972 Active 1 emp. MTO
Modern 7/74 • Classical guitar 1–10 to
date • Flamenco guitar 1–10 to date
• Steel-string guitar 1–10 to date
• Appalachian dulcimer 1–10 to date
• All instruments 1–10 per year • *1980:*
1004 James Dr., Rock Springs, Wyo. 82901

Arlington Stringed Instruments

Also known as: Bernard E. Lehmann

Armadillo Instruments

Also known as: Jay Hardy

Peter A. Armanino

P.O. Box 433, 781 Martin St., Glen Ellen, Calif.
95442
PT 1977 Active 1 emp. MTO
Modern 2/78 • Steel-string guitar 1–10
to date † • Mandolin 1–10 to date †
• Hammered dulcimer 1–10 to date †

Kenneth Armitage

7201 Brennon Ln., Chevy Chase, Md. 20015 †
1/78

Patrick Armstrong

3052 Telegraph Ave., Berkeley, Calif. 94705
Maker of steel-string guitars † 5/74

Tom Armstrong

244 Massachusetts Ave., Arlington, Mass. 02174
† 2/76

W. T. Armstrong Co., Inc.

1000 Industrial Pkwy., Elkhart, Ind. 46514
FT 1931 Active 210 emp. IA
Modern Brochure 6/74 • Modern
flute Over 50 to date Over 50 per year
• Piccolo Over 50 to date Over 50 per
year • Saxophone Over 50 to date Over
50 per year • Clarinet Over 50 to date
Over 50 per year • Also known as: H. Couf;
Linton Mfg. Co.

ARP Instruments, Inc.

320 Needham St., Newton, Mass. 02161
FT 1969 Active 100 emp. IA
Modern Brochure 4/74 • Synthesizer
Over 50 to date Over 50 per year

Arrowhead Music

Also known as: Charles Jirousek

Fred H. Artindale

1243 Palm St., San Luis Obispo, Calif. 93401
FT 1949 Active 1 emp. IA
Modern 11/74 • Violin 25–50 to date
† • Viola 1–10 to date † • Cello 1–10
to date † • Primarily repairs

Artisan Electronics Corp.

5 Eastmans Rd., Parsippany, N.J. 07054
Maker of electric organs † 5/75

Artley, Inc.

P.O. Box 730, Nogales, Ariz. 85621
FT 1939 Active 273 emp. IA
Modern Brochure 6/74 • Clarinet
Over 50 to date † • Modern flute Over
50 to date † • Piccolo Over 50 to
date †

Dan Arvin

7989 Gordean Rd., Jacksonville, Fla. 32205
PT 1977 Active 1 emp. MTO
Modern 2/78 • Steel-string guitar 1–10
to date 1–10 per year

Anthony Ascrizzi

15 Munroe St., Somerville, Mass. 02143 †
11/77

Hammond Ashley Associates

2036 S. 204th St., Seattle, Wash. 98188
FT 1964 Active 6 emp. IA
Modern and historical Brochure 9/75
• New (catgut) violin 10–25 to date †
• Bass violin 1–10 to date † • Vertical
viola 10–25 to date † • Cello 1–10 to
date † • *1980: 19825 Des Moines Way*
South, Seattle, Wash. 98148 • Bass violin
1–10 per year • Vertical viola 1–10 per
year • Cello 1–10 per year

Dan Aslanian

16604 S. Van Ness Ave., Gardena, Calif. 90247
† 2/76

Aspen Guitars

Also known as: International Music Corp.

Associated Luthiers

R.R. 3, Box 395, Sheridan, Ind. 46069
PT 1975 Active 2 emp. IA/MTO
Modern 2/77 • Steel-string guitar 1–10
to date 1–10 per year • 5-string banjo
1–10 to date † • Appalachian dulcimer

25–50 to date　　25–50 per year • Zither
1–10 to date　　1–10 per year • Also known
as: Peter Sean Cooney; Mark Walsh

Astin Weight Pianos
120 W. 3300 South, Salt Lake City, Utah 84115
Maker of pianos †　2/76

E. V. Atchley
5200 Truman Rd., Kansas City, Mo. 64127
FT　1932　Active　2 emp.　MTO
Historical　6/74 • Violin　Over 50 to
date　1–10 per year • Viola　10–25 to
date　1–10 per year • Cello　1–10 to
date　1–10 per year • Bass violin　1–10
to date　1–10 per year • *1980: 1 emp.*

Robert Atwell
Haddam Quarter Rd., Durham, Conn. 06422 †
2/76

Frederick E. Auch
106 N. Orange Ave., Lodi, Calif. 95240
PT　1974　Active　1 emp.　MTO
Historical　10/75 • Baroque flute　1–10
to date　† • Mute cornetto　1–10 to
date　† • Clarinet　1–10 to date　†
• Fife　1–10 to date　† • Alto trombone
1–10 to date　†

Audio Western Corp.
16131-D Gothard St., Huntington Beach, Calif.
92047
Maker of steel-string guitars †　2/76

Augustin Guitar Co.
Also known as: Augustine LoPrinzi

Louis Aull
1347 Chalmette Dr. N.E., Atlanta, Ga. 30306 †
2/76

Austin Organs, Inc.
P.O. Box 365, Hartford, Conn. 06101
FT　1893　Active　70 emp.　MTO
Modern　Brochure　4/75 • Pipe organ
Over 50 to date　10–25 per year

Mike Autorino
R.D. 2, W. Searsville Rd., Montgomery, N.Y.
12549
PT　1965　Active　1 emp.　MTO
Historical　Brochure　6/74 • Psaltery

25–50 to date　　1–10 per year
• Appalachian dulcimer　Over 50 to
date　10–25 per year • Hammered
dulcimer　1–10 to date　1–10 per year

Eugene E. Avery
29 Mechanic St., Hoosick Falls, N.Y. 12090 †
2/76

Victor N. Avila
1156 7th Ave., San Diego, Calif. 92102 †　2/76

Raymond Clifton Aydlett
2210 S. 4th Ave., Tucson, Ariz. 85713
PT　1947　Active　2 emp.　MTO
Modern and historical　10/74
• Steel-string guitar　Over 50 to date
1–10 per year • 5-string banjo　10–25 to
date　† • Mandolin　1–10 to date　†
• Lute　1–10 to date　† • Primarily
repairs • Also known as: Raybern's Music
Co.

Camille Ayoubpour
Also known as: Camille Violin Shop

Vincent Bach
Also known as: Selmer

Bach Piano Co.
6 Greenvale Dr., Rochester, N.Y. 14618
Maker of pianos †　2/76

Lynn Bagley
Acme Music, 1200 Spring St., Santa Rosa, Calif.
95404 †　6/75

Bahr-Schall Music Co.
2309 Central Ave., Kearney, Neb. 68847
Maker of strings †　2/76

Keith Bailey
3457 Evergreen Rd., #101, Pittsburgh, Pa. 15237
PT　1977　Active　1 emp.　IA/MTO
Modern　1/77 • Steel-string guitar　1–10
to date　† • Electric guitar　1–10 to
date　† • Appalachian dulcimer　1–10 to
date　† • Primarily repairs

Q. J. Bailey
9329 Doral Dr., Ingomar North, Pittsburgh, Pa.
15237
PT　1974　Active　1 emp.　MTO

Historical   2/78 • Appalachian
dulcimer   10–25 to date   1–10 per year
• Hammered dulcimer   1–10 to date
1–10 per year • 5-string banjo   1–10 to
date   1–10 per year • Hurdy-gurdy
1–10 to date   1–10 per year • Also known
as: Halcyon Studios

Harry Baily
Vinalhaven, Maine 04863
Maker of strings †   9/76

Thomas C. Baime
1710 Winnebago St., Madison, Wis. 53704
Maker of woodwinds †   3/78

Harvey Baity
Rt. 2, Box 203, Wilksboro, N.C., 28697
Maker of strings †   2/76 • Also known as:
Brushy Mt. Music Co.

Ken Bakeman
11214 N.E. 88th, Kirkland, Wash. 98033
FT   1970   Active   1 emp.   IA
Historical   11/75 • Clavichord   1–10 to
date   1–10 per year • Spinet   1–10 to
date   1–10 per year • Harpsichord
1–10 to date   1–10 per year
• Forte-piano   1–10 to date   1–10 per
year • *1980: MTO • Not making spinets
• Pedal harpsichord   1–10 to date   1–10
per year*

Dennis Baker
R.R. 5, Kenton, Ohio 43326 †   1/78

Ralph W. Baker
P.O. Box 1035, Brattleboro, Vt. 05301 †   2/76

Robert and Janita Baker
Also known as: Blue Lion

George Balderose
1414 Pennsylvania Ave., Pittsburgh, Pa. 15233
FT   1975   Active   1 emp.   MTO
Historical   4/78 • Appalachian
dulcimer   25–50 to date   1–10 per year
• Zither   10–25 to date   1–10 per year
• Xylophone   10–25 to date   1–10 per
year • Hammered dulcimer   1–10 to
date   1–10 per year • *1980: Hammered
dulcimer   10–25 to date*

Baldwin Piano Co.
1801 Gilbert Ave., Cincinnati, Ohio 45202
Maker of pianos †   2/76 • Also known as:
The Fred Gretsch Co.

Geza Balint
10503 Rosehill Ave., Cleveland, Ohio 44104
Maker of bows †   12/77 • *1980: PT
1970   Active   1 emp.   IA/MTO
Modern and historical   10/80 • Bows
Over 50 to date   1–10 per year*

Ernie Ball
Also known as: Earthwood, Inc.

Joan Balter
1725 Carleton St., Berkeley, Calif. 94703
FT   1973   Active   1 emp.   IA
Modern   9/78 • Violin   1–10 to date
1–10 per year • Viola   1–10 to date
1–10 per year • Primarily repairs

B and G Instrument Workshop
318 N. 36th St., Seattle, Wash. 98103
FT   1970   Active   2 emp.   MTO
Historical   Brochure   4/76
• Harpsichord   10–25 to date   1–10 per
year • Clavichord   1–10 to date   1–10
per year • Baroque flute   1–10 to date   †
• Also known as: Lutz Bungart; Alan
Goldstein; Richard Krueger

Bandwagon Repair
Also known as: Jeffrey Lee Smith

Banjo and Fiddle Shop
6229 S.E. Milwaukee Ave., Portland, Ore. 97202
Maker of strings †   2/76

Banjos by Richelieu
786 N. Main St., Box 101, Oregon, Wis. 53575
FT   1923   Active   6 emp.   IA/MTO
Modern and historical   Brochure   10/74
• 5-string banjo   Over 50 to date   Over 50
per year • *1980: 14 emp. • Tenor banjo
Over 50 to date   Over 50 per year • Plectrum
banjo   Over 50 to date   Over 50 per year
• Also known as: C. C. Richelieu*

Banjo Shop
Also known as: Albert W. Worthen, Jr.

Bannister Harpsichords
Spur Rt. 518, P.O. Box 267, Hopewell, N.J. 08525

FT 1959 Active 3 emp. MTO
Historical Brochure 5/74
• Harpsichord Over 50 to date • Spinet
Over 50 to date • Clavichord 1–10 to date
• Forte-piano 1–10 to date • All
instruments 10–25 per year • *1980: 2
emp. • All instruments 1–10 per year*

Barbero Guitars

3145 W. 63 St., Chicago, Ill. 60629
Maker of steel-string guitars † 5/76

Marnie Barbers

Also known as: Westminster Dulcimers

Charles Bardin and Sean Maroney

3120 Broadway, Sacramento, Calif. 95817
FT 1972 Active 3 emp. IA
Modern Brochure 10/75 • Wooden
drum Over 50 to date Over 50 per year
• Marimba Over 50 to date Over 50 per
year • Also known as: Sean Maroney;
Musical Woodcraft

Lester F. Bardin

3688 Donald Ave., Arlington, Calif. 92503 †
2/76

Newcomb Barger

98 Old Long Ridge Rd., Stamford, Conn. 06903
Maker of steel-string guitars † 2/78

Barker Brothers

6100 S. Adam, Box 4020, Bartonville, Ill. 61607
FT 1963 Active 2 emp. MTO
Modern 10/76 • Steel-string guitar
Over 50 to date 10–25 per year • 5-string
banjo 1–10 to date 1–10 per year

Lucien Barnes IV

66 Carmine St., New York, N.Y. 10014
Maker of steel-string guitars † 2/76

Warring Barnes

5305 Iroquois Rd., Glen Echo Heights, Md.
20768 † 2/76

Carl Barney

780 Hancock Ave., Bridgeport, Conn. 06605
FT 1971 Active 1 emp. MTO
Modern 4/74 • Classical guitar 25–50
to date • Steel-string guitar 10–25 to date
• Jazz guitar 1–10 to date • All

instruments 1–10 per year • Also known
as: Guitar Shop

Barrons Harpsichords

7924 Armour, San Deigo, Calif. 92191
FT 1967 Active 1 emp. IA
Modern and historical Brochure 10/74
• Harpsichord 10–25 to date 1–10 per
year • Steel-string guitar 10–25 to
date †

David Barrows

363½ Boulevard, Athens, Ga. 30601 † 2/76

Wilson Barry

P.O. Box 152, Ballardville Station, Andover,
Mass. 01810
FT 1965 Active 6 emp. MTO
Modern and historical Brochure 4/76
• Harpsichord 10–25 to date 1–10 per
year • Organ 1–10 to date 1–10 per
year

Carl Bartolomeo

R.F.D. Box 72-A, Vinalhaven, Maine 04863
PT 1970 Active 1 emp. MTO
Modern and historical 4/78
• Appalachian dulcimer Over 50 to
date 10–25 per year • Steel-string
guitar 10–25 to date 1–10 per year
• Harp 1–10 to date 1–10 per year
• 5-string banjo 1–10 to date 1–10 per
year • Lute 1–10 to date 1–10 per year
• *1980: Northumbrian pipes 1–10 to
date 1–10 per year • Not making banjos*

Clarence Nolan Bartow

329½ S. Washington, Lansing, Mich. 48933
FT 1950 Active 1 emp. IA/MTO
Modern and historical 12/76 • Violin
Over 50 to date † • Viola 25–50 to
date † • Cello 10–25 to date † • Bass
violin 1–10 to date † • Steel-string
guitar 10–25 to date † • Mandolin
1–10 to date † • 5-string banjo 10–25
to date † • *1980: Bows* †

James F. Bartram, Jr.

P.O. Box 239, Bristol, R.I. 02809
FT 1974 Active 1 emp. MTO
Historical Brochure 10/74 • Recorder
25–50 to date † • Renaissance flute
25–50 to date †

Peter Bass
5½ Moulton St., Portland, Maine 04111 †
11/77

Carolyn Bassing
7303 Holly Ave., Takoma Park, Md. 20012
PT   1968   Active   1 emp.   IA/MTO
Modern   Brochure   10/78 • Occarina
Over 50 to date   Over 50 per year

Clarence Bastarache
37168 Norene St., Westland, Mich. 48185
PT   1970   Active   1 emp.   MTO
Historical   4/76 • Viola da gamba   1–10
to date   †

Charles Batchelder
110 Prospect St., East Hartford, Conn. 06108
PT   1975   Active   1 emp.   MTO
Modern   4/76 • Virginal   1–10 to date
† • Spinet   1–10 to date   †
• Harpsichord   1–10 to date   †

Michael Batell
Also known as: Harley A. Day, Jr., and
Michael Batell

Alfio Batelli
119 N. Orange Ave., Monterey Park, Calif. 91754
†   2/76

Frederick Battershell
16412 E. Warren, Detroit, Mich. 48224
FT   1961   Active   1 emp.   IA/MTO
Modern and historical   6/74
• Harpsichord   1–10 to date   †
• Appalachian dulcimer   Over 50 to
date   Over 50 per year • Lute   1–10 to
date   † • Viol   1–10 to date   1–10 per
year • Psaltery   †   1–10 per year • Also
known as: Musical Instrument Workshop

Jack Batts
218 E. Broadway, Johnston City, Ill. 62951
FT   1940   Active   1 emp.   IA/MTO
Modern   6/74 • Violin   Over 50 to date
• Viola   † • All instruments   1–10 per
year

Fred Bauer
47 Rockridge Rd., Box 198, Woodacre, Calif.
94973
PT   1971   Active   1 emp.   MTO

Modern   7/74 • North and South Indian
flute   Over 50 to date   25–50 per year

John Baum
922 El Cajon Way, Palo Alto, Calif. 94303
PT   Year?   1 emp.   MTO   Modern
9/74 • †

Ahmet Baycu
Also known as: Takoma Banjo Works

Baystate Stringed Instrument Co.
3 Parker St., Newburyport, Mass. 01950
Maker of strings †   1/78

Beach Instrument Corp.
Box 246, Lambertville, N.J. 08530 †   2/75

John Beach
908 E. Graybill Dr., Tucson, Ariz. 85719
Maker of strings †   1/78

Beacon Banjo Co., Inc.
32 Fair St., Newburyport, Mass. 01950
Maker of 5-string banjos †   1/78

J. R. Beall
541 Swans Rd. N.E., Newark, Ohio 43055
FT   1970   Active   1 emp.   IA/MTO
Modern and historical   6/74
• Appalachian dulcimer   Over 50 to
date   Over 50 per year • Hammered
dulcimer   1–10 to date   † • Steel-string
guitar   10–25 to date   1–10 per year
• Keyboard   1–10 to date   1–10 per year
• *1980: Inactive • Classical guitar   10–25
to date   1–10 per year • Hammered
dulcimer   Over 50 to date   10–25 per year
• Not making steel-string guitars*

Travis Bean
11671 Sheldon St., Unit J, Sun Valley, Calif.
91352
FT   1974   Active   16 emp.   MTO
Modern   10/75 • Electric guitar   Over 50
to date   †

Sherid Sailer Bearden
Ralston Rd., Box 184, Far Hills, N.J. 07931
PT   1965   Active   1 emp.   IA
Modern   10/74 • Classical guitar   10–25
to date   1–10 per year

Bearden Violin Shop

8787 Lackland Rd., St. Louis, Mo. 63114
FT   1942   Active   7 emp.   MTO
Historical   9/74 • Violin   25–50 to date
• Viola   1–10 to date • Cello   1–10 to
date • All instruments   1–10 per year
• Primarily repairs • Also known as: Lowell
G. Bearden

Philip A. Beaudry Co.

P.O. Box 123, Somerville, Mass. 02145
FT   1966   Active   3 emp.   MTO
Historical   5/74 • Pipe organ   10–25 to
date   1–10 per year

Mr. Beaujolais

7 W. Madison, Chicago, Ill. 60602
Maker of strings †   8/74

John Beck

1137 N. 3d St., Milwaukee, Wis. 53203
FT   1920   Active   8 emp.   IA
Modern   6/75 • Bass violin and cello
†• Primarily repairs • Also known as:
Beck-Beihoff Music

Becker

Chicago, Ill. 60600
Maker of violins †

Carl Becker and Son

Also known as: William Lewis and Son

George Becker

82 S. Broadway, Denver, Colo. 80209
FT   1971   Active   3 emp.   IA/MTO
Modern and historical   8/75 • 5-string
banjo   Over 50 to date   10–25 per year
• Also known as: Ferretta Music Service

Tim Becker

3627 10th Ave., Racine, Wis. 53402
Maker of strings †   1/78

Alan T. Beckman

6309 N. Rosebury, #3, St. Louis, Mo. 63105
Maker of strings †   1/78

Beckman Musical Instrument Co., Inc.

2117 Yates, Los Angeles, Calif. 90040
FT   1972   Active   20 emp.   IA
Modern   Brochure   5/75 • Drum   Over
50 to date   † • Synthesizer   Over 50 to
date   † • Electronic piano   Over 50 to

date   † • Percussion   Over 50 to date   †
• Also known as: Camco Drum &
Accessories Corp.

Wayne Beckman

417 E. Spruce, Missoula, Mont. 59801
FT   1972   Active   1 emp.   IA/MTO
Modern and historical   4/78 • Violin
1–10 to date • Clavichord   1–10 to date
• Harpsichord   1–10 to date • Cello
1–10 to date • All instruments   1–10 per
year • Primarily repairs

Bruce R. Becvar

8864 Old Redwood Hwy., Cotati, Calif. 94928
FT   Year ?   Active   ? emp.   IA/MTO
Modern   Brochure   10/74 • Classical
guitar   1–10 to date   † • Appalachian
dulcimer   25–50 to date   10–25 per year
• 5-string banjo   1–10 to date   †
• Electric guitar   25–50 to date   25–50
per year • Steel-string guitar   25–50 to
date   † • Electric bass guitar   25–50 to
date   25–50 per year

Tom Bednark

Box 13, Centerville, Mass. 02632
PT   1972   Active   1 emp.   IA
Modern   5/74 • Steel-string guitar
10–25 to date   1–10 per year
• Appalachian dulcimer   1–10 to date   †
• *1980: Steel-string guitar   25–50 to date*
• *Appalachian dulcimer   10–25 to date*
†• *Hammered dulcimer 25–50 to date* †

Lee Beeder

1728 N. Vermont Ave., Hollywood, Calif. 90027
FT   1959   Active   1 emp.   IA
Modern   5/74 • Classical guitar   Over 50
to date   † • Flamenco guitar   25–50 to
date   † • *1980: Inactive*

Raymond Beehler

8160 Chaz Pl., La Mesa, Calif. 92041
Maker of strings †   2/76

Thomas Beeston

405 N. Granada, No. 4, Tucson, Ariz. 85705
FT   1969   Active   2 emp.   MTO
Modern and historical   9/74 • Classical
guitar   1–10 to date   1–10 per year
• Flamenco guitar   1–10 to date   1–10
per year • Lute   1–10 to date   1–10 per
year • Steel-string guitar   1–10 to date

1–10 per year • Mandolin 1–10 to date
1–10 per year • Primarily repairs

Stinsen R. Behlen

1010 S. 14th St., Slaton, Tex. 79364
FT 1954 Active 1 emp. IA/MTO
Modern and historical 10/74
• Appalachian dulcimer Over 50 to date
Over 50 per year • Also known as:
Southern-Highland-Dulcimers

Harold E. Behrns

710 9th St., Coronado, Calif. 92118
Maker of strings † 2/76

Bell Accordion Corp.

115 E. 23d St., New York, N.Y. 10010
Maker of accordions † 5/74

Donald Bell

2012 43d Ave. East, #11, Seattle, Wash. 98112
PT 1973 Active 1 emp. IA/MTO
Historical Brochure 2/76
• Harpsichord 1–10 to date 1–10 per
year • Virginal 1–10 to date † • Also
known as: Nota Bene: A Harpsichord
Workshop

William R. Belles

2621 W. 39th St., Anderson, Ind. 46013
PT 1974 Active 1 emp. IA/MTO
Historical 2/76 • Appalachian
dulcimer 1–10 to date † • Balalaika
1–10 to date † • Primarily repairs • Also
known as: The String Shop

Bellville and Hoffman

2219 E. Franklin Ave., Minneapolis, Minn.
55404
FT 1971 Active 5 emp. IA/MTO
Modern Brochure 5/74 • Steel-string
guitar 25–50 to date 10–25 per year
• 5-string banjo 1–10 to date † • Also
known as: Charles A. Hoffman • *1980:
Inactive (Bellville) • Steel-string guitar
Over 50 to date 25–50 per year • Not
making banjos • Also known as: Charles A.
Hoffman, Inc.; Hoffman Guitars*

Philip Belt and Maribel Meisel

19½ Elm St., Stonington, Conn. 06378
FT 1961 Active 2 emp. MTO
Historical Brochure 5/74 • Piano
1–10 to date • Forte-piano 1–10 to date

• Harpsichord 1–10 to date • All
instruments 1–10 per year

Benedetto Guitars

Grover Cleveland Blvd., P.O. Box 1221,
Homosassa Springs, Fla. 32647
FT 1968 Active 1 emp. MTO
Modern Brochure 11/76 • Steel-string
guitar 1–10 to date 1–10 per year

Roger A. Benedict

Water St., Elizabethtown, N.Y. 12932
FT 1975 Active 1 emp. MTO
Modern 2/78 • Classical guitar 1–10 to
date 1–10 per year • Also known as: The
Village Luthier • *1980: IA/MTO • Steel-string
guitar 1–10 to date 1–10 per year
• Electric guitar 1–10 to date 1–10 per
year • Now known as: R. A. Benedict, Luthier*

Benge Trumpet Co.

1640 S. Sinclair, Los Angeles, Calif. 92806 †
*1980: FT 1938 Active 95 emp.
IA/MTO Brochure 10/80 • Trumpet
Over 50 to date Over 50 per year • Cornet
Over 50 to date Over 50 per year
• Fluegelhorn Over 50 to date Over 50
per year • Also known as: Benge Division of
King Musical Instruments*

Bradley W. M. Benn

4424 Judson Ln., Minneapolis, Minn. 55435
FT 1965 Active 2 emp. MTO
Historical Brochure 5/74
• Harpsichord 10–25 to date 1–10 per
year • Spinet 1–10 to date 1–10 per
year • Virginal 1–10 to date 1–10 per
year • Clavichord 1–10 to date 1–10
per year • *1980: IA/MTO • Harpsichord
25–50 to date • Spinet 10–25 to date
• Virginal 10–25 to date*

Dave Bennett

7051 Saulsbury St., Arvada, Colo. 80003
Maker of strings † 3/78

Hans Benning

11336 Ventura Blvd., Studio City, Calif. 91604
FT 1962 Active 1 emp. IA/MTO
Modern and historical 6/76 • Violin,
viola, and viola da gamba † • *1980:
Cello † • All instruments 10–25 per year*

Harold Benson
Rt. 1, Box 84, Bolivar, N.Y. 14715
PT   1954   Active   1 emp.   IA
Historical   10/74 • Violin   25– 50 to
date   1– 10 per year • Electric guitar
1– 10 to date   † • Mandolin   1– 10 to
date   † • Hammered dulcimer   1– 10 to
date   † • *1980: Inactive • Primarily repairs*

Bently Guitars and Banjos
Also known as: St. Louis Music Supply Co.

Berdon Co.
Box 70131C, Seattle, Wash. 98107
Maker of English horns, bassoons,
contrabassoons, and oboes †   1/78

Jon Berg
2632 Hollyridge Dr., Hollywood, Calif. 90068
†   2/76

Paul Berger
30 W. 4th St., Apopka, Fla. 32703
Maker of steel-string guitars †   2/76

Christopher A. Berkov
821 Canyon Rd., Santa Fe., N.M. 87501 †   2/76

Berkshire Organ Co., Inc.
68 South Blvd., West Springfield, Mass. 01089
FT   1954   Active   18 emp.   MTO
Modern   Brochure   12/75 • Pipe organ
25– 50 to date   1– 10 per year

Fred Bernardo
140 N. 9th St., Reading, Pa. 19560 †   1/78

Thomas Bertucca
16 W. 61 St., New York, N.Y. 10023
FT   Year ?   Active   1 emp.   MTO
Historical   6/74 • Violin   1– 10 to date
† • Primarily repairs

John E. Best
6235 Wrightsville Ave., Wilmington, N.C. 28401
Maker of strings †   1/78

Alan Betz
148 Richdale Ave., Cambridge, Mass. 02140
Maker of lutes †   2/76

BFE Guitars
Also known as: Bryan Enright

Bianco Accordions
4019 S.E. Ogden St., Portland, Ore. 97202
Maker of accordions †   5/75

Dr. Stuart Bicknell
1499 Sunset Cliffs Blvd., San Diego, Calif. 92107
PT   1933   Active   1 emp.   IA
Modern and historical   9/74 • Violin
10– 25 to date   1– 10 per year

Leo L. Bidne
2517 E. 106th St., Tacoma, Wash. 98445
FT   1973   Active   3 emp.   MTO
Modern   2/75 • Appalachian dulcimer
1– 10 to date   † • Primarily repairs • Also
known as: Bob Petrulis

Robert Lee Bieker
1632 Cedarwood Ln., Pueblo, Colo. 81005
PT   1968   Active   1 emp.   IA
Historical 4/76 • Hammered dulcimer †

Big Horn Guitars
Also known as: James Newall Hall

Bill Crume Memorial Workshop
Also known as: Lenny Wurtzel

J. Charles Billiris
3004 Pacific Ave., Wildwood, N.J. 08260
Maker of strings †   1/78

Thomas P. Bilyeu
P.O. Box 133, Molalla, Ore. 97038
FT   1967   Active   1 emp.   IA
Historical   Brochure   2/75 • Jew's harp
Over 50 to date   Over 50 per year • Also
known as: Mr. Jew's Harp

Herman Bischofberger
1314 E. John St., Seattle, Wash. 98102
FT   1938   Active   2 emp.   IA/MTO
Historical   Brochure   11/75 • Violin
Over 50 to date   † • Cello   1– 10 to
date   †

Geoffrey Bishop
P.O. Box 874, Danville, Calif. 94526
FT   1974   Active   1 emp.   IA/MTO
Modern   1/75 • Appalachian dulcimer
Over 50 to date   † • Irish harp   1– 10 to
date   † • Psaltery   1– 10 to date   †
• Steel-string guitar   1– 10 to date   †

• Kalimba 1– 10 to date † • Also known as: The Wood Works • *1980: Inactive*

Walter H. Bishop
1859 Westminster Way N.E., Atlanta, Ga. 30307
PT 1967 Active 1 emp. IA/MTO
Modern and historical 9/77 • Viol 1– 10 to date • Division viol 1– 10 to date • Virginal 1– 10 to date • Rebec 1– 10 to date • Harpsichord 1– 10 to date • Psaltery 1– 10 to date • Harp 1– 10 to date • Clavichord 1– 10 to date • Viola 1– 10 to date • Tromba marina 1– 10 to date • All instruments 1– 10 per year • *1980: Harpsichord 10– 25 to date • Not making division viols, rebecs, psalteries, harps, violas, and tromba marinas*

Bitterroot Music
200 S. 3d St. West, Missoula, Mont. 59801 † 2/76

BKL International
Also known as: Kramer Guitar Co.

Dr. Karl Blaas
2116 Owens Ln., Lawrence, Kans. 66044
PT 1947 Active 1 emp. MTO
Historical 6/74 • Violin 1– 10 to date
† • Viola 10– 25 to date 1– 10 per year

Dude Black
Scotland, Ariz. 72141 † 4/76

David Blackburn
P.O. Box 12621, San Antonio, Tex. 78212
1971 Inactive ? emp. IA/MTO?
Historical 2/78 • Wooden flute Over 50 to date Over 50 per year • Copper flute Over 50 to date Over 50 per year • Also known as: Divine Flute Co.

Martha Blackman
3550 Park Blvd., Palo Alto, Calif. 94306 † 2/76
1980: Not making instruments

Black Mt. Instruments
Also known as: William Dahlgren

Tom Blackshear
402 Bryn Mawr, #104B, San Antonio, Tex. 78209
FT 1962 Active 1 emp. MTO
Modern ?/77 • Flamenco guitar †

M. Robert Blackwell
703 Heliotrope, Corona Del Mar, Calif. 92625
Maker of strings † • *1980: 408 Commercial, Anacortes, Wash. 98221 • FT 1966 Active 1 emp. Modern and historical 10/80 • Clay drum Over 50 to date Over 50 per year • Not making strings*

Bobby L. Blair
Mountain View, Ark. 72560
PT 1969 Active 1 emp. MTO
Historical 4/76 • Appalachian dulcimer Over 50 to date 1– 10 per year • Mouth bow Over 50 to date Over 50 per year • Also known as: Ozark Woodworking Co.

R. B. Blair
208 N. Main St., Mount Vernon, Ohio 43050
Maker of strings † 1/78

Blair Dulcimers
1704 Trenton Dr., Alexandria, Va. 22308
PT 1973 Active 1 emp. IA/MTO
Historical Brochure 8/75 • Appalachian dulcimer Over 50 to date 25– 50 per year • Primarily repairs • *1980: Appalachian dulcimer Over 50 per year • Irish folk harp 1– 10 to date* † • *Hammered dulcimer 10– 25 to date* † • *Also known as: Mark M. Blair*

Basil Blake
Rt. 2, Box 20, Exchange, W. Va. 26619
PT 1933 Active 1 emp. IA
Historical 4/76 • Appalachian dulcimer Over 50 to date 25– 50 per year

Ronald Blake
382 DeGraw St., Brooklyn, N.Y. 11231
PT Year? Active 1 emp. MTO
Modern 4/76 • Appalachian dulcimer 1– 10 to date †

William Bland
2512 N. Campbell, Tucson, Ariz. 85719
FT 1971 Active 4 emp. IA
Modern Brochure 6/74 • Steel-string guitar 10– 25 to date 1– 10 per year • Classical guitar 10– 25 to date 1– 10 per year • Electric guitar 1– 10 to date 1– 10 per year • Appalachian dulcimer

Over 50 to date   Over 50 per year • 5-string banjo   1–10 to date   †• Also known as: Mingus Guitars

Ron Blanton
5793 E. Washington, Fresno, Calif. 93727
PT   1966   Active   1 emp.   MTO
Modern   2/78 • Classical guitar   1–10 to date   †• Electric guitar   1–10 to date   †

John Blasius
87 Nevada East, Detroit, Mich. 48203
PT   1971   Active   1 emp.   MTO
Historical   5/74 • Steel-string guitar 1–10 to date   †• Hammered dulcimer 1–10 to date   †• Lute   1–10 to date †• Cittern   1–10 to date   †• Kit   1–10 to date   †

Bill Blaylock
1950 Canton Rd., Marietta, Ga. 30066
FT   1968   Active   3 emp.   IA/MTO
Modern   12/77 • 5-string banjo   25–50 to date   1–10 per year • Primarily repairs • Also known as: North Georgia Music Co.

E. K. Blessing Co., Inc.
1301 W. Beardsley, Elkhart, Ind. 46514
FT   Year?   Active   ? emp.   IA
Modern   Brochure   Date? • Cornet, trumpet, valve trombone, herald trumpet, fluegelhorn, slide trombone, rotor trombone, French horn, baritone horn, and saxophone   †

Robert Paul Block
Also known as: Aardvark Fluteworks

William Blood
R.F.D.1, Three Rivers, Mich. 49093
FT   1973   Active   1 emp.   MTO
Historical   5/74 • Harpsichord   1–10 to date   †

Tony Blozen
Newark, N.J. 07100
Maker of strings †

Blue Grass Farm
Rt. 3, Lexington, Va. 24450
Maker of strings †   2/76

The Blue Guitar
Also known as: Yaris Zeltins

Blue Guitar Workshop
3967 Arista, San Diego, Calif. 92110
Maker of steel-string guitars †   2/76

Blue Lion
Star Rt., Box 16-C, Santa Margarita, Calif. 93453
FT   1975   Active   3 emp.   IA/MTO
Modern   2/78 • Appalachian dulcimer 25–50 to date   †• 5-string banjo   1–10 to date   †• Also known as: Robert and Janita Baker • *1980: 2 emp.   Brochure • Appalachian dulcimer   Over 50 to date Over 50 per year • Steel-string guitar   1–10 to date   10–25 per year • Not making 5-string banjos*

BMC Guitars
Also known as: Donnie Wade

Olcott Boardman
2818 Country Club Rd., Olympia, Wash. 98502
Maker of strings †   2/76

Andrew Boarman
Rt. 1, Hedgesville, W. Va. 25427
Maker of 5-string banjos †   2/76

Doc Bocheneck
5455 Wilshire Blvd., Suite 1009, Los Angeles, Calif. 90036
PT   1974   Active   2 emp.   MTO
Historical   12/75 • Tenor guitar   Over 50 to date   25–50 per year

Roy Bodd and Ken Eye
150 Clinton St., Columbus, Ohio 43202
FT   1966   Active   2 emp.   IA/MTO
Modern and historical   2/75 • Appalachian dulcimer   Over 50 to date   Over 50 per year • 5-string banjo 1–10 to date   1–10 per year • Steel-string guitar   1–10 to date   1–10 per year • Autoharp   1–10 to date   1–10 per year • Also known as: Ken Eye

Janos Bodor
7114 Rising Sun Ave., Philadelphia, Pa. 19111
PT   1969   Inactive   2 emp.   MTO
Historical   5/75 • Violin   Over 50 to date   †

Thomas C. Boehm
1710 Winnebago St., Madison, Wis. 53704
PT   1975   Active   1 emp.   IA

Historical   4/78 • Baroque flute   25–50
to date   1–10 per year

Lawrence Boerner
15842 Del View, El Cajon, Calif. 92021
FT   1960   Active   1 emp.   IA
Historical   4/76 • Violin   10–25 to
date   †• Viola   1–10 to date
†• Primarily repairs

Rex Bogue
Box 45, Green Valley Station, Saugus, Calif.
91350
Maker of steel-string guitars †   2/76

Gordon Bok
Box 840, Camden, Maine 04843
PT   1975   Active   2 emp.   MTO
Modern   5/76 • Penny whistle   Over 50 to
date   †

John A. Bolander
2814 Alum Rock Ave., San Jose, Calif. 95127
FT   1930   Active   1 emp.   IA
Historical   9/75 • Bows   Over 50 to
date   †

Rick Boling
P.O. Box 6-A, Archer, Fla. 32618
Maker of steel-string guitars †   1/78 • Also
known as: Cedar Creek Dulcimer Works;
The Guitar Workshop

John Bolton
702 W. Newton St., Harrison, Ark. 72601
Maker of violins †   2/76

Dr. Fedele Bonito
1124 Waring Ave., Bronx, N.Y. 10469
PT   1956   Active   1 emp.   MTO
Modern and historical   6/74 • Violin
10–25 to date   1–10 per year • Viola
1–10 to date   1–10 per year • Viola
d'amore   1–10 to date   † • *1980: Violin
25–50 to date*

Bonnie Carol Dulcimer Co.
Wallstreet Salina Star Rt., Boulder, Colo. 80302
FT   1972   Active   1 emp.   IA/MTO
Modern   4/76 • Appalachian dulcimer
Over 50 to date   25–50 per year • Also
known as: Bonnie Carol Montgomery
• *1980: Brochure • Now known as: Bonnie
Carol*

H. E. Boomhower
Rt. 3, Box 99, Glen Allen, Va. 23060
Maker of strings †   1/78

Newton J. Booth
907 17th Ave., Honolulu, Hawaii 96816
PT   1975   Active   1 emp.   MTO
Modern   2/78 • Classical guitar   1–10 to
date   † • Ukulele   1–10 to date   †

James Borell
Also known as: Govox, Inc.

Mary Lucille Born
3115 N. 29th St., Tacoma, Wash. 98407
Maker of strings †   1/78

Andrew J. Borromey
470 N. Woodward, Birmingham, Mich. 48011
FT   1977   Active   1 emp.   IA
Modern   3/78 • Violin   1–10 to date
1–10 per year • Viola   1–10 to date
1–10 per year • Steel-string guitar   1–10
to date   1–10 per year • Mandolin   1–10
to date   1–10 per year

Roger Borys
Also known as: Wood & Sound

Kenneth Bostard
2211 Minor Ave. East, Seattle, Wash. 98102
FT   1972   Active   1 emp.   IA/MTO
Historical   7/74 • Appalachian
dulcimer   1–10 to date   † • Psaltery
1–10 to date   † • Irish harp   10–25 to
date   † • Medieval harp   1–10 to date
† • Qanun   1–10 to date   † • Harp
10–25 to date   †

Boston String Instrument Co.
295 Huntington Ave., Boston, Mass. 02115
FT   1950   Active   2 emp.   IA
Modern   7/74 • Violin   Over 50 to date
† • Steel-string guitar   Over 50 to date   †
• Primarily repairs

Bosworth and Hammer
29 Main St., Acton, Mass. 01720
FT   1975   Active   2 emp.   IA/MTO
Modern and historical   4/76 • Tabor
pipe   10–25 to date   † • Chalumeaux
1–10 to date   † • Baroque oboe   † • *1980:
Historical   Brochure • Classical oboe
10–25 to date   10–25 per year • Baroque*

oboe d'amore   10–25 to date   1–10 per year · Baroque taille oboe   1–10 to date   1–10 per year · Renaissance shawm   25–50 to date   25–50 per year · Baroque oboe   Over 50 to date   10–25 per year · Tabor pipe   1–10 per year · Chalumeaux   10–25 to date   1–10 per year · Also known as: John Bosworth; Stephen Hammer

Norman W. Botnick

543 N. Fuller Ave., Los Angeles, Calif. 90036
Maker of strings †   2/76

Parnell Boucha

3005 Andrew, Lansing, Mich. 48906
FT   1974   Active   1 emp.   IA/MTO
Modern and historical   4/78 · Violin
10–25 to date   † · Viola   1–10 to date
† · Cello   1–10 to date   † · Steel-string
guitar   1–10 to date   † · Bows   †
· *1980: Violin   1–10 per year · Viola
1–10 per year · Cello   1–10 per year
· Steel-string (and gut string) guitar   1–10
per year · Bows   1–10 to date   1–10 per year*

Boulder Junction Stringed Instruments

Also known as: Scott E. Antes

Philip Boulding

308 Melrose East, #105, Seattle, Wash. 98102
FT   1973   Active   1 emp.   MTO
Modern   9/75 · Steel-string guitar   1–10
to date   † · Hammered dulcimer   10–25
to date   1–10 per year · Appalachian
dulcimer   10–25 to date   10–25 per year

Dana W. Bourgeois

8 Page St., Brunswick, Maine 04011
PT   1975   Active   1 emp.   MTO
Modern   9/76 · Appalachian dulcimer
25–50 to date   † · Classical guitar
10–25 to date   † · Steel-string guitar
1–10 to date   † · Mandolin   1–10 to
date   †

William Bouslaugh

3719 N. 13th St., Tacoma, Wash. 98406
Maker of strings †   1/78

James C. Boyce

Box 608, North Falmouth, Mass. 02566
FT   1965   Active   2 emp.   IA/MTO

Modern   5/74 · Steel-string guitar
25–50 to date   10–25 per year

Michael Boyd

1001 Kirkwood Ave., Apt. 1, Iowa City, Iowa 52240
PT   1972   Active   1 emp.   MTO
Modern   6/74 · Steel-string guitar   1–10
to date   1–10 per year · 12-string guitar
1–10 to date   1–10 per year

Curt Boyer

Memory Town, U.S.A., Mount Pocono, Pa. 18344
†   1/78

William Boyer

3058 Myrtledale, Calistoga, Calif. 94515
PT   1974   Active   1 emp.   MTO
Modern and historical   6/75 · 5-string
banjo   1–10 to date   †

Bozeman-Gibson and Co.

68 Washington St., Lowell, Mass. 01851
FT   1971   Active   2 emp.   MTO
Modern   6/74 · Organ   † · Also known
as: David V. Gibson

Bozo Music Gallery

713 E. Valley Pkwy., Escondido, Calif. 92025
Maker of strings †   5/76 · Also known as:
Bozo Podunavac

Bradbury Piano Co., Inc.

2722 Pershing Ave., Memphis, Tenn. 38112
Also known as: Aeolian Corp.

Don Bradley

292 W. MacArthur, Sonoma, Calif. 95476
PT   1973   Active   1 emp.   MTO
Modern   1/78 · Steel-string guitar   1–10
to date   † · Electric bass guitar   1–10 to
date   † · 5-string banjo   1–10 to date   †
· Appalachian dulcimer   1–10 to date   †

Walter Bradley, Jr.

1501 Detroit, Apt. 7, Concord, Calif. 94518
PT   1977   Active   1 emp.   MTO
Modern   3/78 · Steel-string guitar   1–10
to date   1–10 per year · Electric guitar
1–10 to date   1–10 per year · Also known
as: Musique Concernz

Wesley Bradley

2209 Via Pacheco, Palos Verdes Estates, Calif. 90274

PT   1964   Active   1 emp.   MTO
Modern   4/76 • Classical guitar   1–10 to
date   1–10 per year • Flamenco guitar
1–10 to date   1–10 per year

Brady's Violin Shop
6600 Snider Plaza, Dallas, Tex. 75205
Maker of strings †   2/76

Zigfrid S. Brakmanis
P.S.C. Box 01559, Dover AFB, Del. 19901
Maker of strings †   1/78

A. W. Brandt Co.
50 Hayden Ave., Columbus, Ohio 43222
FT   1932   Active   7 emp.   MTO
Modern   4/76 • Electro-pneumatic
organ   † • Primarily repairs

Mike Branhut
4219 Frankford Ave., Philadelphia, Pa. 19124
PT   Year?   Active   1 emp.   MTO
Modern   1/77 • Steel-string guitar   1–10
to date   † • Flamenco guitar   1–10 to
date   † • 5-string banjo   1–10 to date   †

Bickford and Robert Brannon
264 Gleasondale Rd., Stow, Mass. 01775
FT   1974   Active   3 emp.   MTO
Modern and historical   Brochure   10/74
• Modern flute   1–10 to date   †

Brass City Fifecraft
43 Granite St., Waterbury, Conn. 06706
PT   1911   Active   1 emp.   IA/MTO
Modern and historical   4/75 • Fife   Over
50 to date   Over 50 per year • Also known
as: Ted Kurtz

Gray Brechin
339 63d St., Oakland, Calif. 94618
PT   1974   Active   1 emp.   MTO
Historical   3/75 • Horizontal sash harp
1–10 to date   †

Wil Bremer
104½ E. Kirkwood, #11, Bloomington, Ind.
47401 †   2/77

Larry Pohl Breslin
1263 E. Los Olas Blvd., Fort Lauderdale, Fla.
33301
FT   Year?   Active   1 emp.   IA/MTO
Modern   7/74 • Steel-string guitar

10–25 to date • Acoustic bass guitar
1–10 to date • Classical guitar   10–25 to
date • All instruments   10–25 per year
*• 1980: 1965   Brochure • Flamenco
guitar   10–25 to date • All instruments
Over 50 to date • Also known as: Lauderdale
Music Center, Inc.; Jacque Cannon*

George Brewer
300 Islington Rd., Auburndale, Mass. 02166
PT   1964   Active   1 emp.   IA/MTO
Historical   5/74 • Appalachian
dulcimer   Over 50 to date   10–25 per
year

Brian Breyre
2464 Beverly St., Santa Monica, Calif. 94015
FT   1972   Active   1 emp.   IA
Modern and historical   6/74 • Violin
Over 50 to date   † • Hammered
dulcimer   1–10 to date   † • Also known
as: Eastern, Ltd.

Jim Bridges
Princeton, W. Va. 24740 †   5/76

David Byron Briggs
963 Barclay Ln., East Lansing, Mich. 48823
PT   1977   Active   1 emp.   IA
Modern and historical   2/78 • Violin
1–10 to date   † • Cello   1–10 to date   †

John Bringe
Downs Rd., Bethany, Conn. 06525 †   5/76

Dale Briskey
404 Emery St., Longmont, Colo. 80501
Maker of strings †   1/78

Brobst Violin Shop
2760 Duke St., Alexandria, Va. 22314
Maker of violins †   5/76

Myron Brock
Rt. 2, Willow Tree Ln., Middletown, Md. 21769
PT   1950   Inactive   1 emp.   MTO
Modern   6/76 • Violin   25–50 to date
1–10 per year • Viola   10–25 to date
1–10 per year

Christopher Brodersen
4729 Walnut Lake Rd., Birmingham, Mich.
48010
Maker of harpsichords †   1/76

Daniel L. Brodrick
1610 Cass, La Crosse, Wis. 54601
PT   1974   Active   1 emp.   MTO
Modern and historical   6/75 • 5-string
banjo   10– 25 to date   1– 10 per year
• Steel-string guitar   1– 10 to date   1– 10
per year • Primarily repairs

M. Brody
412 E. 4th St., Brooklyn, N.Y. 11218
PT   1975   Active   1 emp.   IA/MTO
Historical   4/76 • Harpsichord   1– 10 to
date   1– 10 per year

Elaine Broekhuizen
404 Ellsworth, Memphis, Tenn. 38111
Maker of strings †   2/76

John Broekhuizen
Box 87, Perkinsville, Vt. 05151
PT   1974   Active   1 emp.   IA/MTO
Historical   3/75 • Appalachian
dulcimer   25– 50 to date   †

Hendrik Broekman
19 Winter St., Lebanon, N.H. 03766
FT   1972   Active   1 emp.   IA/MTO
Historical   7/74 • Harpsichord   1– 10 to
date   † • Clavichord   1– 10 to date   †
• Virginal   1– 10 to date   † • Primarily
repairs

John Brombaugh
7910 Elk Creek Rd., Middletown, Ohio 45042
FT   1968   Active   9 emp.   MTO
Modern   Brochure   5/74 • Tracker
organ   10– 25 to date   †

David R. Brooks
805 Cockletown Rd., Yorktown, Va. 23692
PT   1972   Active   1 emp.   MTO
Historical   Brochure   7/74
• Renaissance flute   25– 50 to date
10– 25 per year • Baroque flute   1– 10 to
date   1– 10 per year • Also known as:
Historical Instruments • *1980: Renaissance
flute   Over 50 to date · Renaissance harp
10–25 to date   1– 10 per year*

Donald Brosnac
99 Sanchez, San Francisco, Calif. 94114
FT   1971   Active   1 emp.   MTO
Modern and historical   12/75
• Steel-string guitar   10– 25 to date

• Appalachian dulcimer   1– 10 to date
• Clavichord   1– 10 to date • All
instruments   1– 10 per year

Don Brown
Box 789, Cloverdale, Calif. 95425
PT   1969   Inactive   1 emp.   MTO
Modern   4/76 • Reed pipe   Over 50 to
date   †

Douglas R. Brown
P.O. Box 32, Sunspot, N.M. 88349
PT   1972   Inactive   1 emp.   MTO
Historical   6/74 • Lute   1– 10 to date
1– 10 per year

Edwin A. Brown
33142 Redwood Blvd., Avon Lake, Ohio 44012
PT   1973   Inactive   1 emp.
IA/MTO   Historical   6/74 • Appalachian
dulcimer   1– 10 to date   †

Lawrence Brown
3101 Pico Blvd., Santa Monica, Calif. 90405
FT   1959   Active   3 emp.   MTO
Modern and historical   7/74 • 5-string
banjo   1– 10 to date   † • Primarily
repairs

Lawrence D. Brown
1410 Haines Ave., Columbus, Ohio 43212
FT   1972   Active   1 emp.   MTO
Historical   Brochure   9/77 • Lute
25– 50 to date   1– 10 per year • Theorbo
1– 10 to date   † • Chitarrone   1– 10 to
date   † • Orpharion   1– 10 to date   †

Robert Brown
2617 Fremont Ave. South, Minneapolis, Minn.
55408 †   2/76

Robin Brown
University of Minnesota, Minneapolis, Minn.
55414
Maker of strings †   6/74

Steve Brown
4020 Park Ave., Minneapolis, Minn. 55407
Maker of strings †   3/78

Tom Brown
568 5th Ave., San Francisco, Calif. 94118
PT   1966   Inactive   1 emp.   MTO
Historical   3/76 • Clavichord   1– 10 to

date   † • Harpsichord   1–10 to date   †
• Primarily repairs

David Brownell
2187 Yorktown, Ann Arbor, Mich. 48105
FT   1972   Active   3 emp.   MTO
Modern   3/76 • Violin   10–25 to date
1–10 per year • Viola   1–10 to date
1–10 per year • Primarily repairs • *1980: 2
emp. • Viola   10–25 to date*

Jack Brubaker
Stoney Lonesome Bazaar, Nashville, Ind. 47448
Also known as: Stoney Lonesome Bazaar

John Brueggeman
10045 Tanager Ln., Cincinnati, Ohio 45215
PT   1961   Active   1 emp.   IA/MTO
Modern and historical   5/74
• Harpsichord   1–10 to date • Virginal
1–10 to date • Clavichord   1–10 to date
• All instruments   1–10 per year • *1980:
MTO • Harpsichord   10–25 to date • All
instruments   10–25 per year*

Lawrence R. Brullo
1146 San Lori Ln., El Cajon, Calif. 92020
PT   1972   Active   1 emp.   IA
Modern   9/74 • Violin   1–10 to date   †
• *1980: IA/MTO • Viola   1–10 to date
• Cello   1–10 to date • All instruments
1–10 per year*

R. E. Brune
800 Greenwood St., Evanston, Ill. 60201
FT   1966   Active   1 emp.   MTO
Modern and historical   6/74 • Flamenco
guitar   Over 50 to date   10–25 per year •
Classical guitar   Over 50 to date   10–25
per year • Lute   1–10 to date   1–10 per
year • Harpsichord   1–10 to date   1–10
per year • Vihuela   1–10 to date   1–10
per year • *1980: Brochure • Classical
guitar   25–50 per year • Lute   Over 50 to
date • Harpsichord   10–25 to date
• Baroque guitar   1–10 to date   1–10 per
year • Not making vihuelas*

Brunetti Guitar Factory
123 S. Truesdale Ave., Youngstown, Ohio 44506
FT   1945   Active   1 emp.   IA/MTO
Modern   4/76 • Steel-string guitar   Over
50 to date   10–25 per year • Mandolin
1–10 to date   †

Bart Brush
Box 546, Cooperstown, N. Y. 13326
Maker of hurdy-gurdies †   2/76

Brushy Mt. Music Co.
Also known as: Harvey Baity

C. Alex Bryan
1461 Deerfield Rd., Deerfield, Ill. 60015
PT   1969   Active   1 emp.   IA/MTO
Modern and historical   1/78 • Hammered
dulcimer   1–10 to date • Psaltery   1–10
to date • Appalachian dulcimer   10–25 to
date • 5-string banjo   1–10 to date
• Cittern   1–10 to date • Mandolin
1–10 to date • All instruments   1–10 per
year

Clarence L. Bryan
2607 Metzgar Rd. S. W., Albuquerque, N. M.
87105
PT   1965   Active   1 emp.   IA/MTO
Modern   9/74 • Violin   1–10 to date
1–10 per year • Primarily repairs • *1980:
Steel-string guitar   1–10 per year*

Robert P. Bryan
401 Roxanne Dr., Raleigh, N. C. 27603
PT   1965   Active   1 emp.   IA/MTO
Historical   6/75 • Appalachian
dulcimer   Over 50 to date   25–50 per
year • Courting or double dulcimer   1–10
to date   1–10 per year • Also known as:
Uncle Bob's Dulcimers

Curtis Bryant
3 Trapelo Rd., Belmont, Mass. 02178
FT   1974   Active   1 emp.   MTO
Historical   5/75 • Viola da gamba   1–10
to date   1–10 per year

Joseph Bucheck, Sr., and Jr.
1529 Broadway, Riviera Beach, Fla. 33404 †
2/76

Henry L. Buck, Jr.
P. O. Box 251, Hampton, Ga. 30228
PT   1971   Active   1 emp.   MTO
Modern and historical   12/77 • 5-string
banjo   1–10 to date   1–10 per year

Buckdancer's Choice Music
Also known as: James D. Martin

Thomas R. Buckel
400 Central Ave., West View, Pa. 15229
FT 1970 Active 2 emp. MTO
Modern Brochure 5/76 • Classical
guitar 10–25 to date • Electric guitar
10–25 to date • Steel-string guitar 1–10
to date • All instruments 25–50 per year

Michael L. Buckley
Also known as: Reliable Brothers

Buck Musical Instrument Products
40 Sand Rd., New Britain, Pa. 18901
FT 1966 Active 4 emp. IA/MTO
Modern and historical Brochure 6/78
• 5-string banjo Over 50 to date †
• Appalachian dulcimer Over 50 to
date † • Also known as: Karl F. Dietrichs

Budapest String Shop
4710 Horger, Dearborn, Mich. 48126
Maker of strings † 10/76

Buecker and White
465 W. Broadway, New York, N. Y. 10012
PT 1963 Active 2 emp. IA
Modern Brochure 5/74
• Harpsichord 1–10 to date †
• Spinet 1–10 to date † • Clavichord
1–10 to date †

Buescher Band Instruments
Also known as: Selmer

Buglecraft, Inc.
43-01 39th St., Long Island City, N. Y. 11104
FT 1919 Active 32 emp. IA
Modern Brochure 6/74 • Bugle Over
50 to date Over 50 per year

Julian E. Bulley
1376 Harvard Blvd., Dayton, Ohio 45406
FT 1906 Active 6 emp. MTO
Modern 4/76 • Pipe organ Over 50 to
date 1–10 per year • Also known as:
Toledo Pipe Organ Co.

Jim Bumgardner
410 Lincoln Ave., Takoma Park, Md. 20012 †
6/74

James Bump
North Rd., Hampden, Mass. 01036

FT 1974 Active 1 emp. MTO
Historical Brochure 10/75 • Lute
1–10 to date † • Psaltery 1–10 to
date † • Gemshorn 1–10 to date †
• *1980: Renaissance lute 25–50 to date*
† • *Theorbo 1–10 to date* † • *Cittern
1–10 to date* † • *Not making psalteries
and gemshorns*

Bundy
Also known as: Selmer

Lutz Bungart
Also known as: B and G Instrument
Workshop

Jan Burda
1139 Tanglewood Trail, St. Joseph, Mich. 49085
PT 1965 Active 3 emp. MTO
Modern Brochure 11/75 • Steel-string
guitar Over 50 to date 1–10 per year
• Electric guitar 1–10 to date † • Also
known as: Dove Instruments

Lynn Burdick
537 E. Mississippi, Denver, Colo. 80210
Maker of strings † 1/78

Chris Burger
2425 6th Ave., Watervliet, N. Y. 12189 † 9/76

Burger and Shafer
Box 831, 243 Monroe, Findlay, Ohio 45840
Maker of organs † 2/76

David Burgess
627 N. Larchmont Blvd., Los Angeles, Calif.
90004
FT Year? Active 1 emp. IA/MTO?
Historical 10/74 • Violin † 1–10 per
year • Primarily repairs

Dennis Burgess
2134-D Old Middlefield Hwy., Mountain View,
Calif. 94040 † 6/75

Ralph W. Burhans
161 Grosvenor St., Athens, Ohio 45701
PT 1968 Active 1 emp. MTO
Modern 2/75 • Harpsichord 1–10 to
date † • Clavichord 1–10 to date † •
Electronic piano 1–10 to date † •
Digi-vox 1–10 to date † • *1980: Inactive*

William Burke

234 S. Elliott St., South Natick, Mass. 01760
PT   1971   Active   1 emp.   IA/MTO
Modern   8/75 • Appalachian dulcimer
Over 50 to date   † • Hammered
dulcimer   1–10 to date   † • Steel-string
guitar   1–10 to date   †

Daniel R. Burkhart

10542 Lanark St., Sun Valley, Calif. 91352
PT   1970   Active   1 emp.   MTO
Modern   6/74 • Classical guitar   1–10 to
date   †

Herbert M. Burks, Jr.

122 Kensington Rd., East Lansing, Mich. 48823
Maker of strings †   1/78

Burning Water Instruments

Also known as: Garett Alden and S.
Freegard

Brian Burns

820 Ramond St., Palo Alto, Calif. 94301
PT   1961   Inactive   1 emp.   MTO
Modern   4/76 • Flamenco guitar   1–10
to date   † • Classical guitar   1–10 to
date   †

Richard Burnside

Rt. 2, Box 957, Fredericksburg, Va. 22401
PT   1971   Active   1 emp.   IA/MTO
Historical   10/74 • Appalachian
dulcimer   10–25 to date   10–25 per year
• Also known as: East Virginia Dulcimer Co.

Walter Burr

196 Church St., Hoosick Falls, N. Y. 12090
FT   1970   Active   2 emp.   MTO
Historical   6/74 • Harpsichord   1–10 to
date   1–10 per year

Chris Burt

8042 S. E. Taylor, Portland, Ore. 97215
FT   1973   Active   1 emp.   MTO
Modern and historical   11/74 • Violin
1–10 to date   † • Viola   1–10 to date   †
• Cello   1–10 to date   † • Division viol
1–10 to date   † • Viola d'amore   1–10 to
date   †

Edwin E. Bush

2111 Edenton Dr., Fort Wayne, Ind. 46804
PT   1976   Active   1 emp.   MTO
Historical   2/78 • Appalachian
dulcimer   25–50 to date   10–25 per year
• Hammered dulcimer   1–10 to date
1–10 per year • Mandolin   1–10 to date †

Graydon Buss

4706 Duquesne, San Antonio, Tex. 78229
Maker of strings †   2/76

Butler's Music Instrument Repair

Rt. 5, Box 449, Elizabethtown, Ky. 42701
Primarily repairs †   9/75

Mark William Butler

1 W. 22d St., # 2B, Baltimore, Md. 21218
FT   1976   Active   1 emp.   IA/MTO
Historical   12/77 • Lute   10–25 to
date   † • *1980: Lute   25–50 to date
10–25 per year*

Clifton H. Butten

426 Seminole Rd., Hampton, Va. 23661 †   2/76

Robert J. Byl

P. O. Box 247, Dearborn, Mich. 48121 †   1/78

Hobart M. Cable Co.

Also known as: Story and Clark Piano Co.

Cable-Nelson Piano Co.

Also known as: Everett Piano Co.

Cable Piano Co.

Also known as: Aeolian Corp.

David Charles Calhoun

4319 Thackeray Pl. N. E., Seattle, Wash. 98105
FT   Year?   Active   1 emp.   IA/MTO
Historical   Brochure   10/74
• Harpsichord   1–10 to date   †
• Virginal   1–10 to date   †

Paul Joseph Callier

5906 Sunset Blvd., Hollywood, Calif. 90028
FT   1946   Active   2 emp.   MTO
Modern   Brochure   4/76 • Violin   1–10

to date † • Viola 1–10 to date †
• Bows Over 50 to date †

Jan E. Callister
12211 S. 1600 East, Draper, Utah 84020
PT 1973 Active 1 emp. MTO
Modern 5/78 • Classical guitar 1–10 to
date 1–10 per year • Steel-string guitar
1–10 to date 1–10 per year

Camber Cymbal
101 Horton Ave., Lynbrook, N. Y. 11563
Maker of cymbals † 12/77

Camco Drum & Accessories Co.
Also known as: Beckman Musical
Instruments

Roderick Cameron
37 Gladys St., San Francisco, Calif. 94110
FT 1974 Active 1 emp. MTO
Historical Brochure 6/78 • Baroque
flute Over 50 to date Over 50 per year
• Dulcian 1–10 to date † • Recorder
10–25 to date † • Renaissance flute
1–10 to date † • *1980: Dulcian 1–10
per year • Renaissance flute 1–10 per year
• Not making recorders*

Camille Violin Shop
7424 Beverly Blvd., Los Angeles, Calif. 90036
FT 1966 Active 3 emp. IA
Modern and historical 8/75 • Violin
Over 50 to date † • Viola 10–25 to
date † • Cello 10–25 to date † • Bass
violin 10–25 to date † • Also known as:
Camille Ayoubpour

Edward C. Campbell
R. D. #1, Lerew Rd., Boiling Springs, Pa. 17007 †
*1980: FT Year? Active 6 emp.
IA/MTO Modern 10/80 • Violin, viola,
and cello Over 50 to date † • Also known
as: The Chimneys Violin Shop*

Jon Campbell
P. O. Box 349, Charlestown, R. I. 02813
FT 1972 Active 1 emp. IA/MTO
Modern and historical Brochure 10/75
• Uilleann pipes † • Electric guitar
10–25 to date † • Also known as: Patrick
Sky

J. Ralph Campbell
Rt. 4, Box 34-A, Mannington, W. Va. 26582
PT 1970 Active 1 emp. MTO
Historical 9/74 • Hammered dulcimer
10–25 to date 1–10 per year • Psaltery
1–10 to date 1–10 per year • Also known
as: Willow Glen Crafts • *1980: Hammered
dulcimer 25–50 to date*

Richard A. Campbell
682 23d Ave., San Francisco, Calif. 94121
PT 1965 Active 1 emp. IA/MTO
Modern 9/74 • Classical guitar Over 50
to date 1–10 per year • Flamenco
guitar 1–10 to date †

Cannarsa Organs, Inc.
P.O. Box 238, Hollidaysburg, Pa. 16648
FT 1928 Active 6 emp. MTO
Modern Brochure 4/75 • Pipe organ
Over 50 to date 1–10 per year

James H. Cannon
65 Suffolk Rd., Chestnut Hill, Mass. 02167
1964 Inactive ? emp. MTO
Historical 1/76 • Harpsichord † • Also
known as: Cannon Guild, Inc.

David Cantrell
P. O. Box 713, University, Ala. 35486
Maker of strings † • *1980: FT 1971
Active 1 emp. MTO Historical
10/80 • Harpsichord, lute, viol, medieval
fiddle, and hammered dulcimer † 1–10
per year*

Denis Capadestria
Holderness, N. H. 03245 † 2/76

Capritaurus
Also known as: Rugg and Jackel Music Co.

Carey Organ Co.
335 Second St., Troy, N. Y. 12180
Maker of organs † 2/76

Richard B. Carle, Jr.
608 Pearl, Ypsilanti, Mich. 48197 †

Willis Carll
75 Johnston Rd., Gorham, Maine 04038
Maker of strings † 9/76

Fred Carlson
Also known as: Sacred Fire/Frogs Delight

David Caron
4449 Lovers Ln., Dallas, Tex. 75225
PT   1960   Active   1 emp.   MTO
Historical   Brochure   2/75 • Violin
25–50 to date   1–10 per year • Viola
10–25 to date   1–10 per year

Lane O. Carpenter
212 Lincoln Ave., Lutherville, Md. 21093
FT   1972   Active   1 emp.   MTO
Modern   6/74 • Appalachian dulcimer
10–25 to date   † • Hammered
dulcimer   1–10 to date   Steel-string
guitar   1–10 to date   †

Robert Carpenter
108 3d Ave. South, P. O., Box 517, Poulsbo,
Wash. 98370
PT   1974   Active   1 emp.   IA
Historical   2/78 • Appalachian
dulcimer   10–25 to date   10–25 per year
• Mandolin   1–10 to date   1–10 per year
• Psaltery   1–10 to date   1–10 per year
• Steel-string guitar   1–10 to date   1–10
per year • Lute   1–10 to date   †

Carpenter Co.
8236 N. Christiana Ave., Skokie, Ill. 60076 †
2/75

Sam Carrell
Rt. 1, Hwy. 73 West, Townsend, Tenn. 37782
FT   1974   Active   1 emp.   MTO
Modern and historical   Brochure   3/78
• Appalachian dulcimer   Over 50 to
date   Over 50 per year • *1980: Steel-string
guitar   25–50 to date   25–50 per year*
• *Classical guitar   25–50 to date   25–50
per year • Hammered dulcimer   25–50 to
date   25–50 per year • Hummel   25–50 to
date   25–50 per year*

Carriage House
Also known as: Robert Cooper

Ron Carriveau
4427 N. 7th Ave., Phoenix, Ariz. 85013
FT   1968   Active   2 emp.   MTO
Modern and historical   2/77 • Classical
guitar   Over 50 to date   † • Steel-string

guitar   1–10 to date   † • Appalachian
dulcimer   1–10 to date   † • Vihuela
1–10 to date   † • Primarily repairs • Also
known as: Precision Guitar Works

Randy Carroll
Box 496, Lexington, Neb. 68850
Maker of strings †   1/78

Carroll Sound
P. O. Box 88, Palisades Park, N. J. 07650
Primarily repairs †

Alan E. Carruth
91 Westland Ave., Boston, Mass. 02115
PT   1973   Active   1 emp.   IA/MTO
Modern   6/74 • Appalachian dulcimer
25–50 to date   25–50 per year • Classical
guitar   1–10 to date   †

Mikael Carstanjen
49 Minivale Rd., Stamford, Conn. 06907
PT   1971   Active   1 emp.   IA/MTO
Historical   4/76 • Appalachian
dulcimer   Over 50 to date   10–25 per
year • Hammered dulcimer   10–25 to
date   1–10 per year • Cittern   10–25 to
date   10–25 per year • Bowed psaltery
10–25 to date   1–10 per year • Lap
harp   † • 5-string banjo † • Mandolin   †
• Plucked psaltery   † • Also known as: Tree
& Anchor Musical Instrument Works

The Carvers
Also known as: Thomas B. Moore

Carvin Mfg. Co.
1155 Industrial Ave., Escondido, Calif. 92025
FT   1947   Active   25 emp.   IA
Modern   Brochure   12/77 • Electric
guitar   Over 50 to date   Over 50 per year

Casa Di Terenzio
Also known as: Terenzio Riegel

Casavent Organs
Maker of organs †

Jack Casey
Bedford Rd., Concord, Mass. 01742 †   2/76

Tom J. Caskey
Also known as: Peacewood Dulcimer

Peter Cass
Also known as: Renaissance Workshop

Stewart Cassidy
1722 Oaklawn Dr., Prescott, Ariz. 86301
PT   1970   Active   1 emp.   MTO
Modern   6/74 • Classical guitar   1– 10 to
date   †

George B. Cassis
3416 Essex Rd., Baltimore, Md. 21207
PT   1970   Active   1 emp.   MTO
Historical   4/76 • Viola da gamba   1– 10
to date   † • Rebec   1– 10 to date   †
• Spinet   1– 10 to date   † • Psaltery
1– 10 to date   † • Shawm   1– 10 to
date   † • Appalachian dulcimer   1– 10 to
date   † • Vielle   1– 10 to date   †
• Baryton   1– 10 to date   † • Bows
1– 10 to date   †

Robert M. Castellano
61 Hadley St., Bridgeport, Conn. 06610
Maker of strings †   1/78

Castiglione Accordion Co.
12644 E. 7-Mile Rd., Detroit, Mich. 48205
Maker of accordions †   2/76

Donald Caton
4510 N. W. 15th Pl., Gainesville, Fla. 32605
Maker of strings †   1/78

Michael A. Caudy
55 W. Patterson Ave., Columbus, Ohio 43202
PT   1974   Active   1 emp.   IA
Modern   12/74 • Steel-string guitar
1– 10 to date   †

CBS Musical Instruments
1300 E. Valencia, Fullerton, Calif. 92631
Also known as: Electro Music;
Fender/Rogers/Rhodes; Gemeinhardt;
Gulbransen Industries, Inc.; Lyon-Healy;
Rodgers Organ; Steinway and Sons • *1980:
100 Wilmot Rd., Deerfield, Ill. 60015*

Cedar Creek Dulcimer Works
Also known as: Rick Boling

Celestial Flute Co.
R.D. 2, Westport, N. Y. 12996
Maker of flutes †   2/78

Chuck Cellino
5746 N. 32d Dr., Phoenix, Ariz. 85017
Maker of strings †   3/78

Cembaloworks of Washington
Also known as: Mark Adler

Ron Chacey
Box 76, Rt. 1, Amesville, Ohio 45711
FT   1963   Active   1 emp.   MTO
Modern and historical   Brochure   1/76
• Appalachian dulcimer   Over 50 to
date   † • Aeolian harp   1– 10 to date   †
• Steel-string guitar   1– 10 to date   †
• 5-string banjo   10– 25 to date   †
• Mandolin   1– 10 to date   † • *1980:
Modern • 5-string banjo   25– 50 to date
10– 25 per year • Not making Appalachian
dulcimers, Aeolian harps, steel-string
guitars, and mandolins*

Chamberlin Instrument Co., Inc.
964 W. Ninth St., Upland, Calif. 91786
FT   1952   Active   6 emp.   IA
Modern   Brochure   4/76 • Electronic
piano   Over 50 to date   Over 50 per year

Chandler Instruments
Also known as: John Thierman

Garrett B. Chaney
25 Race St., Uniontown, Pa. 15401
PT   1978   Active   1 emp.   MTO
Modern   4/78 • Electric guitar   1– 10 to
date   † • Steel-string guitar   1– 10 to
date   † • Mandolin   1– 10 to date   †

Chapline Organs
624 W. Upsal St., Philadelphia, Pa. 19119
FT   1961   Active   ? emp.   MTO
Modern and historical   Brochure   10/75
• Mechanical-action organ   1– 10 to
date   †• Harpsichord   1– 10 to date   †

Alan Chapman
Montague Center, Mass. 01351
Maker of steel-string guitars †   2/76

Emmett Chapman
Also known as: Stick Enterprises, Inc.

Harold Chapman
307 W. 16th, Austin, Tex. 78701 †   2/78

Jeffrey Chapple
Box 256, Palatine Bridge, N. Y. 13428
PT 1975 Active 1 emp. IA/MTO
Modern Brochure 2/78 • Steel-string
guitar 1–10 to date † • *1980: Violin*
1–10 to date 1–10 per year

Chardavogne Folk Instruments
Also known as: Alan Albright

Charlestown Guitar Shop
Also known as: Natale Armando Strafaci

Charvel Mfg. Co.
Also known as: David Schecter; Schecter
Guitar Research

A. B. Chase
Also known as: Aeolian Corp.

Hal Chase
Box 122, Rt. 1, Peachy Canyon Rd., Paso Robles,
Calif. 93446
Maker of lutes † 2/76

Chelys
R. R. #2, Exeter, N. H. 03833
Maker of strings † 1/78

Milton Cherin
12 W. 96th St., New York, N. Y. 10025
Maker of strings † 1/78

Alan Chertok
359 North Rd., Bedford, Mass. 01730
PT 1959 Inactive 1 emp. MTO
Modern 11/74 • Appalachian dulcimer
1–10 to date † • Tamburitza 1–10 to
date †

Charles Allen Chester
3011 Lopez Rd., Jacksonville, Fla. 32216
PT 1970 Active 3 emp. MTO
Modern 2/78 • Classical guitar 1–10 to
date † • Steel-string guitar 1–10 to
date † • Electric guitar 1–10 to date
† • *1980: FT 2 emp. • Classical guitar*
1–10 per year • Steel-string guitar 1–10
per year • Electric guitar 1–10 per year

Wayland C. Chester
140 Western Ave., Glendale, Calif. 91201
PT 1969 Active 1 emp. MTO

Modern 3/75 • 5-string banjo 25–50 to
date 1–10 per year • *1980: IA/MTO*
• 5-string, tenor, and plectrum banjos
Over 50 to date 10–25 per year

Claude Chiasson
Fairfield, N. J. 07006
Maker of harpsichords † 2/76

Chicago Musical Instrument Co.
Also known as: Norlin Music, Inc.

Chickering and Sons
FT 1823 Active ? emp. IA
Modern Brochure 6/74 • † • Also
known as: Aeolian Corp.

Steve Childs
22 Graves, Northampton, Mass. 01060
PT Year? Inactive 1 emp. MTO
Modern 2/78 • Electric guitar 1–10 to
date † • 12-string guitar 1–10 to date
† • Primarily repairs

Childs Family Mt. Dulcimers
789 Maher Rd., Watsonville, Calif. 95076
PT 1969 Active 1 emp. MTO
Modern 6/74 • Appalachian dulcimer
Over 50 to date 25–50 per year

Douglas Ching, Luthier
1229-D Waimanu St., Honolulu, Hawaii 96814
FT 1970 Active 1 emp. IA/MTO
Modern and historical 4/76 • Classical
guitar 25–50 to date • Lute 10–25 to
date • Steel-string guitar 10–25 to date
• Ukulele 25–50 to date • Appalachian
dulcimer 1–10 to date • All
instruments 10–25 per year • *1980:*
Classical guitar Over 50 to date
• Steel-string guitar Over 50 to date

Jane Chouteau
4 Tuscang Park, St. Louis, Mo. 63105
PT 1970 Inactive 1 emp. MTO
Modern Brochure 4/76 • Appalachian
dulcimer 1–10 to date †

David Ludvik Chrapkiewicz
444 Margaret St., #30, Plattsburgh, N. Y. 12901
PT 1969 Active 1 emp. IA/MTO
Modern 11/75 • Balalaika 1–10 to
date †

Royce Christensen

228 Eddy, Apt. #B1, Missoula, Mont. 59801
Maker of strings † 3/78

Robert Christie

2108 Border Dr., Washington, D.C. 20022
PT 1969 Active 1 emp. MTO
Modern 7/74 • Steel-string guitar 1–10
to date 1–10 per year • Classical guitar
1–10 to date 1–10 per year • Primarily
repairs • Also known as: The Music
Workshop • *1980: 2108 Border Dr., Oxon
Hill, Md. 20022 · Classical guitar 10–25
to date*

Joe Chromey

2216 Franklin St., Bellingham, Wash. 98225
PT 1973 Active 1 emp. MTO
Modern 2/78 • Steel-string guitar 1–10
to date † • Appalachian dulcimer
10–25 to date † • 5-string banjo 1–10
to date † • Primarily repairs

John Ciano

Mechanic St., Rockport, Maine 04856
Maker of strings † 9/76

Nicholas Cichonovich

Detroit, Mich. 48200
Maker of strings †

Richard S. Cigledy

1101 Van Nuys St., San Diego, Calif. 92109
PT 1966 Active 1 emp. MTO
Modern 9/74 • Harpsichord 1–10 to
date † • Violin 10–25 to date 1–10
per year • Steel-string guitar 1–10 to
date † • *1980: Violin 25–50 to date ·
Steel-string and Spanish guitar 10–25 to
date*

Joseph Cilecek

110 High St., Hastings-on-Hudson, N. Y. 10706
PT 1950 Active 1 emp. MTO
Modern and historical 8/75 • Violin
10–25 to date 1–10 per year • Viola
1–10 to date 1–10 per year • Primarily
repairs

John Cindrich

Box 41, Cokeburg, Pa. 15324 † 4/76

Gene Clark

1327½ Solano Ave., Albany, Calif. 94706
PT 1960 Active 1 emp. IA
Modern 12/75 • Classical guitar Over
50 to date 1–10 per year

Julian Clark

8003 Lake City Way N. E., Seattle, Wash. 98115
FT 1929 Active 1 emp. IA/MTO
Modern 4/76 • Violin Over 50 to date
1–10 per year • Viola 1–10 to date
1–10 per year • *1980: Viola 10–25 to date
· Bass division gamba 1–10 to date* †

Paul S. Clark

717 Crosby South, Apt. 1, Akron, Ohio 44302
Maker of strings † 1/78

T. Clark

4970 Mt. Almagosa Dr., San Diego, Calif. 92111
Maker of strings † 2/76

Greg Clarke III

Ballston Lake, N. Y. 12019 † 2/77

Paul Clarke

888 Rancho Rd., Thousand Oaks, Calif. 91360
† 8/74

Edward Claxton

1705 Shieffer Ave., Austin, Tex. 78722
PT Year? Inactive 1 emp.
IA/MTO Modern and historical 4/78
• Oud 1–10 to date † • Appalachian
dulcimer 1–10 to date † • Steel-string
guitar Over 50 to date †

Cleveland Musical Instruments

Also known as: King Musical Instruments •
*1980: No longer affiliated with King Musical
Instruments*

Roger Clifford

Beechwood Farm, Rt. 69, Winterport, Maine
04496
PT 1971 Inactive 1 emp. MTO
Modern 10/76 • Appalachian dulcimer
10–25 to date † • Cello 1–10 to date
† • Recorder 1–10 to date † • Electric
bass 1–10 to date †

Harrold C. Clifton

4452 Raleigh, Denver, Colo. 80212
PT 1973 Active 1 emp. MTO
Modern 7/74 • Classical guitar 1–10 to
date 1–10 per year

Steve Cloutier
521 Short St., Faribault, Minn. 55021
PT   1976   Active   1 emp.   MTO
Modern   2/78 • Steel-string guitar   1–10
to date   1–10 per year

Greg Cobb
2046 Sutter Rd., McKinleyville, Calif. 95521
PT   1977   Active   1 emp.   MTO
Modern   3/78 • Steel-string guitar   1–10
to date   1–10 per year

Code Corp.
8 Hope St., Jersey City, N. J. 07307
Maker of steel-string guitars †   5/75

Don Cohen
117 Clairmont Ave., Decatur, Ga. 30030 †   1/77

Michael J. Cohen
51 Stratford Rd., Brooklyn, N. Y. 11218 †   2/76

Coin Art, Inc.
Box 249, Nogales, Ariz. 85621 †   4/76

David Colburn
20 Riverside Dr., Ashland, N.H. 03217
FT   Year?   Active   ? emp.   MTO
Modern   4/76 • Appalachian dulcimer
1–10 to date   † • Primarily repairs • *1980:*
1969   Inactive   2 emp.   Historical • Also
known as: Vintage Fret Shop

Peter Colby
74 River Rd., Andover, Mass. 01810
PT   1960   Active   1 emp.   IA/MTO
Modern and historical   12/74 • 5-string
banjo   10–25 to date   † • Autoharp
10–25 to date   †

Dr. T. E. Colby
Clinton, N.Y. 13323 †   2/76

William Colby
1900 Hess St., Saginaw, Mich. 48601
FT   1977   Active   3 emp.   MTO
Modern   4/78 • Electric guitar   1–10 to
date   † • Steel-string guitar   1–10 to
date   † • Appalachian dulcimer   1–10 to
date   † • Also known as: Saginaw Guitar
Works

Anne Cole
1317 Vassar N.E., Albuquerque, N.M. 87106
PT   1971   Active   1 emp.   MTO

Modern and historical   7/74 • Violin
1–10 to date • Alto violin   1–10 to date
• Tenor violin   1–10 to date • Viola
1–10 to date • Cello   1–10 to date • All
instruments   1–10 per year

Kenneth Reagan Cole
Box 144B, Rt. 3, Huntsville, Ark. 72742
FT   1973   Active   1 emp.   IA
Modern   4/77 • Appalachian dulcimer
Over 50 to date   † • Mando-cello   10–25
to date   † • Steel-string guitar   10–25 to
date   † • Also known as: Mountain Spring
Lutherie

Marshall Cole
Also known as: Republic Drums

Harry A. Coleman
2203 University Dr. N.W., Huntsville, Ala. 35805
PT   1975   Active   1 emp.   MTO
Modern and historical   1/78 • Steel-string
guitar   1–10 to date   1–10 per year

Coll Divine Flutes
Box 734, San Antonio, Tex. 78293
FT   1969   Active   2 emp.   IA
Modern   Brochure   4/75 • Copper
flute   Over 50 to date   Over 50 per year
• Wooden flute   Over 50 to date   † • Also
known as: David Holle; Mary Holle; Pat
Murphy

Charles Collier
Box 9442, Berkeley, Calif. 94709
FT   1973   Active   2 emp.   IA/MTO
Historical   Brochure   5/74 • Mute
cornetto   25–50 to date   † • Wooden
flute   25–50 to date   † • Shawm
10–25 to date   †

Collier's Violin Shop
5906 Sunset, Hollywood, Calif. 90028
Maker of violins †   2/76

William Collings II
1503 Wirt Rd., C-8, Houston, Tex. 77055
FT   1969   Active   1 emp.   IA/MTO
Modern   Brochure   3/78 • Steel-string
guitar   Over 50 to date   10–25 per year
• Mandolin   1–10 to date   1–10 per year

W. J. Collingsworth
2190 Country Club Rd., Woodburn, Ore. 97071
Maker of strings †   2/76

Michael Cone

R.F.D. 1, New Vineyard, Maine 04956
FT   1968   Active   1 emp.   IA/MTO
Modern and historical   7/74
• Appalachian dulcimer   25–50 to date
1–10 per year • Classical guitar   25–50 to
date   1–10 per year • Ectero   Over 50 to
date   † • Psaltery-harp   25–50 to date   †
• Clavichord   1–10 to date   †

C. G. Conn, Ltd.

616 Enterprise Dr., Oak Brook, Ill. 60521
FT   1975   Active   ? emp.   IA
Modern   Brochure   6/74 • Cornet   Over
50 to date   Over 50 per year • Trumpet
Over 50 to date   Over 50 per year • Slide
trombone   Over 50 to date   Over 50 per
year • French horn   Over 50 to date   Over
50 per year • Sousaphone   Over 50 to
date   Over 50 per year • Saxophone   Over
50 to date   Over 50 per year • Violin   †

W. H. Connelly

2201 Fairview East, Seattle, Wash. 98102
Maker of woodwinds †   2/76

David R. Conner

10601 Oak Rd., Lake Stevens, Wash. 98258
FT   1969   Active   1 emp.   MTO
Modern and historical   9/75
• Appalachian dulcimer   25–50 to date
1–10 per year • Mandolin   1–10 to date
1–10 per year • Steel-string guitar   1–10
to date   1–10 per year

Karl Conner

532 W. Berry, Fort Wayne, Ind. 46802
Maker of strings †   2/76

Conover-Cable Piano Co.

Also known as: Aeolian Corp.

A. G. Conrad

4591 Camino del Mirasol, Santa Barbara, Calif.
93110
PT   1965   Active   1 emp.   IA
Historical   7/74 • Violin   Over 50 to
date   1–10 per year • Viola   1–10 to
date   1–10 per year • Cello   1–10 to
date   1–10 per year • *1980: Bows   Over
50 to date*   †

Robert Conrad III

152 Edgewood Dr., Elkin, N.C. 28621
Maker of strings †   1/78

Contessa Guitars

Andrews Rd., Hicksville, N.Y. 11802
Maker of steel-string guitars † • *1980: Not
making guitars • Also known as: M. Hohner,
Inc.*

Richard Cook

33 Pinkney St., Boston, Mass. 02114
PT   1970   Active   2 emp.   IA
Historical   8/74 • Mute cornetto   25–50
to date   † • Also known as: Historical Brass
Workshop; Matthew Myszewski

Peter Sean Cooney

Also known as: Associated Luthiers

Gary Cooper

1641 Juliesse, Sacramento, Calif. 95815
FT   1973   Active   1 emp.   IA/MTO
Modern   10/76 • Mandolin   1–10 to
date   † • Electric bass guitar   25–50 to
date   10–25 per year • Electric guitar
25–50 to date   10–25 per year • Also
known as: Oasis Guitars

Robert Cooper

105 W. Perry St., Savannah, Ga. 31401
PT   1963   Active   1 emp.   MTO
Modern and historical   4/74 • Lute
10–25 to date   1–10 per year • Also
known as: The Carriage House

Patrick Cooperman

134 Overlook St., Mount Vernon, N.Y. 10552
FT   1961   Active   3 emp.   IA/MTO
Modern and historical   Brochure   5/74
• Fife   Over 50 to date   Over 50 per year
• Rope-tensioned drum   Over 50 to
date   †

Marten Cornelissen

10 Massasoit St., Northampton, Mass. 01060
FT   1966   Active   1 emp.   MTO
Modern   11/74 • Steel-string guitar
10–25 to date   † • Violin   Over 50 to
date   1–10 per year • Viola   Over 50 to
date   1–10 per year • Cello   10–25 to
date   1–10 per year • *1980: 1959 • Cello
25–50 to date • Classical guitar   10–25 to
date   † • Not making steel-string guitars*

Cornucopia, Ltd.

Also known as: Les Slaughter

Leonard Corsale
2874 Telegraph, Oakland, Calif. 94609
Maker of strings †   2/76

Stuart Corwin
Box 414, Monte Rio, Calif. 95462
FT   1971   Active   1 emp.   MTO
Modern and historical   6/74 • Steel-string
guitar   1– 10 to date • Classical guitar
1– 10 to date • Lute   1– 10 to date
• Appalachian dulcimer   1– 10 to date
• All instruments   1– 10 per year

Emile Cos
618 4th St., Room 20, Santa Rosa, Calif. 95404
†   2/76

Larry Cottingham
4631 Soquel Dr., Soquel, Calif. 95073
FT   1972   Active   2 emp.   IA/MTO
Modern and historical   Brochure   12/75
• Kalimba   Over 50 to date   Over 50 per
year • Appalachian dulcimer   25– 50 to
date   1– 10 per year • Wooden drum
10– 25 to date   10– 25 per year • Strings
25– 50 to date   25– 50 per year • Also
known as: Out of Your Gourd Music;
Margaret Whaley

Jenes Cottrell
Ivydale, W. Va. 25113
PT   1920   Inactive   1 emp.   MTO
Modern   4/76 • 5-string banjo   Over 50
to date   1– 10 per year

H. Couf
Also known as: W. T. Armstrong Co., Inc.

Leonard W. Coulson III
Also known as: Intermountain Guitar &
Banjo

James Cowan
1010 W. Perry, Aberdeen, Wash. 98520
PT   1966   Active   1 emp.   MTO
Modern   2/75 • Violin   1– 10 to date
†• Mandolin   1– 10 to date   †• Steel-
string guitar   1– 10 to date   †• Ukulele
1– 10 to date   †

John Cowan
Box 1307, Carbondale, Colo. 81623
Maker of strings †   1/78

Eugene A. Cox
Box 136, Byron Center, Mich. 49315
PT   1966   Active   1 emp.   MTO
Historical   Brochure   4/76 • Hammered
dulcimer   1– 10 to date   †• Primarily
repairs

Jacob Cox
1106 Stevenson Ln., Towson, Md. 21204
Maker of Appalachian dulcimers †   2/76

James Cox, Jr.
429 Fawcett St., Baltimore, Md. 21211
FT   1975   Active   4 emp.   IA/MTO
Modern and historical   Brochure   9/77
• Lute   1– 10 to date • Viol   Over 50 to
date • Vielle   1– 10 to date • Classical
guitar   1– 10 to date • Rebec   1– 10 to
date • Hurdy-gurdy   1– 10 to date • All
instruments   Over 50 per year • *1980:*
Lute   25– 50 to date   10– 25 per year
• Viol   10– 25 per year • Vielle   25-50 to
date • Rebec   10– 25 to date • Kits   Over 50
to date   Over 50 per year • Not making
classical guitars and hurdy-gurdies

Jimmy Cox
4 Garden Ln., Topsham, Maine 04086
PT   1969   Active   3 emp.   MTO
Modern and historical   Brochure   11/76
• 5-string banjo   10– 25 to date
10– 25 per year • Mandolin   1– 10 to date
1– 10 per year • Steel-string guitar   1– 10
to date   1– 10 per year

James Crabtree
47 Main St., Windsor, N.Y. 13865 †   2/76

Lee Crader
P.O. Box 327, Thornville, Ohio 43076
Maker of strings †   1/78

John Craft
Nampa, Idaho 83651 †   10/74

The Craftsman's Bench
Also known as: James Hampton

Fred Craig
Twin Falls, Idaho 83301
PT   Year?   Active   1 emp.   IA/MTO
Modern   2/75 • Violin   Over 50 to date
• Viola   Over 50 to date • All
instruments   1– 10 per year

Andrew E. Crawford
526 Elm Ave., Upper Darby, Pa. 19082
Maker of strings †   1/78

James Crawford
1375 9th Ave., San Francisco, Calif. 94122 †
1/78

C. R. Banjo Co.
4316 N. Bell Ave., Chicago, Ill. 60618
Maker of 5-string banjos †   2/76

Marcus O. Creager
19200 Portos Dr., Saratoga, Calif. 95070
PT   1973   Active   1 emp.   IA
Modern   Brochure   8/75 • 5-string
banjo   1–10 to date   †• Also known as:
Diamond Line Banjos

Anthony J. Creamer
49 S. Pleasant, Amherst, Mass. 01002
PT   1971   Inactive   3 emp.   MTO
Modern   10/74 • 5-string banjo   1–10 to
date   † • Steel-string guitar   1–10 to
date   † • Appalachian dulcimer   1–10 to
date   † • Primarily repairs • *1980: FT*
• Also known as: Fretted Instrument
Workshop

Kyle Creed
Rt. 3, Box 299, Galax, Va. 24333
PT   1964   Active   1 emp.   IA/MTO
Modern   Brochure   6/75 • 5-string
banjo   Over 50 to date   † • *1980: 5-string*
banjo   25–50 per year

Cremona Musical Instruments
Also known as: Robin Elliot

Crescent Moon Drums
Maker of African drums †

Crestline Guitars
Also known as: Grossman Music Corp.

Cripple Creek Dulcimers
P.O. Box 284, Cripple Creek, Colo. 80813
FT   1972   Active   5 emp.   IA
Modern and historical   Brochure   4/77
• Appalachian dulcimer   Over 50 to
date   Over 50 per year • Also known as:
Donna M. Ford; Gherald L. Ford, Jr.

Derwood Crocker
47 Main St., Windsor, N.Y. 13865

FT   1962   Active   1 emp.   MTO
Historical   Brochure   9/77 • Lute   Over
50 to date • Vielle   Over 50 to date
• Positive organ   Over 50 to date
• Portative organ   Over 50 to date
• Bows   Over 50 to date • All
instruments   10–25 per year

Jennifer Crocker
97 St. Mark's Pl., #7, New York, N.Y. 10009
FT   1974   Active   1 emp.   IA/MTO
Modern   Brochure   4/76 • Hammered
dulcimer   10–25 to date   1–10 per year
• Appalachian dulcimer   10–25 to date
10–25 per year • Psaltery   Over 50 to
date   25–50 per year • Lyre   1–10 to
date   1–10 per year

V. C. Crowder
955 Colton Ave., Box A, San Bernadino, Calif.
92408
Maker of strings †   10/74

Crowl and Hook
2417 Jefferson St., Berkeley, Calif. 94703
FT   Year?   Active   10 emp.   IA
Modern and historical   Brochure   6/74
• Ceramic flute   Over 50 to date   †

Crown
309 W. 4th St., Los Angeles, Calif. 90013 †
11/76

Crow Peak Music
2760 Country Club Ave., Helena, Mont. 59601
PT   1977   Active   1 emp.   MTO
Modern and historical   2/78 • Hammered
dulcimer   1–10 to date   1–10 per year
• Appalachian dulcimer   1–10 to date
1–10 per year • 5-string banjo   1–10 to
date   1–10 per year • Mandolin   1–10 to
date   1–10 per year • Primarily repairs
• Also known as: Michael S. Williams

Bill Crozier
Providence, R.I. 02900
Maker of mandolins †

Crucianelli Guitars
3625 Cahuenga Blvd., Hollywood, Calif. 90028
Maker of steel-string guitars †   5/76

P. W. Crump
187 Fickle Hill Rd., Arcata, Calif. 95521
Maker of strings †   1/78

Cucciara Harpsichord Co., Inc.

R.D. 2, Box 275, Garrettsville, Ohio 44231
FT   1970   Active   2 emp.   MTO
Historical   6/74 • Harpsichord   1−10 to
date   1−10 per year • Also known as:
David R. Pierce

William Richard Cumpiano

Also known as: Stringfellow Guitars

Cundy-Bettoney Co.

Bradlee and Madison Sts., Boston, Mass. 02136
Maker of woodwinds †   2/76

Tom Cunningham

40 E. Mt. Pleasant Rd., Port William, Ohio 45164
Maker of organs †

S. D. Curlee Mfg. Co.

21750 Main St., Matteson, Ill. 60443
FT   1976   Active   10 emp.   IA
Modern   Brochure   12/77 • Electric bass
guitar   Over 50 to date   Over 50 per year
• Steel-string guitar   Over 50 to date
Over 50 per year

Currier Piano Co.

100 S. Clay St., Marion, N.C. 28752
FT   1823   Active   70 emp.   IA
Modern   Brochure   3/75 • Piano   Over
50 to date   Over 50 per year

Donald L. Curry, Jr.

8351 S.W. 13 Terr., Miami, Fla. 33144 †   1/78

Dr. Hiram Curry

536 N. Hobcaw Dr., Mount Pleasant, S.C. 29464
PT   1959   Active   1 emp.   MTO
Modern and historical   12/74 • Violin
1−10 to date   † • Viola   1−10 to date   †
• Cello   1−10 to date   † • Also known as:
The Fiddle Shop • *1980: Violin   10−25 to
date*

Stephen H. Curtin

Box 536, Sandy Hook, Conn. 06482
Maker of strings †   1/78

Mark Cushing

P.O. Box, Andover, N.Y. 14806
FT   1975   Active   2 emp.   IA/MTO
Modern   Brochure   5/76 • Highland
pipes   10−25 to date   †

Cytha-Harp Co.

535 Adella Ln., Coronado, Calif. 92118
PT   1971   Active   1 emp.   IA
Modern   Brochure   8/75 • Cytha harp
Over 50 to date   Over 50 per year • Also
known as: John R. Rohrbough

Ole Dahl

409 E. Kirkwood, Bloomington, Ind. 47401 †
6/74

William Dahlgren

Box 589, Boonville, Calif. 95415
FT   1970   Active   2 emp.   IA
Modern   Brochure   9/74 • Appalachian
dulcimer   Over 50 to date   Over 50 per
year • Also known as: Black Mt. Instruments

Tom Dailey

Box 271, Elizabeth, W. Va. 26143
PT   1971   Active   1 emp.   IA/MTO
Modern   4/76 • Appalachian dulcimer
25−50 to date   † • 5-string banjo   1−10
to date   1−10 per year

Daimaru New York Corp.

212 Fifth Ave., New York, N.Y. 10010 †

Malcolm Dalglish

1127 Goshen Pike, Milford, Ohio 45150
FT   1974   Active   1 emp.   MTO
Modern   Brochure   5/74 • Hammered
dulcimer   1−10 to date   †

Tom Daly, Jr.

R.D. #2, Canajoharie, N.Y. 13317
PT   Year?   Active   1 emp.   MTO
Modern   2/78 • Steel-string guitar   1−10
to date   †

Rik Damin

1612-14 J St., Modesto, Calif. 95354
FT   1971   Active   1 emp.   MTO
Modern and historical   9/74 • Violin
1−10 to date   † • Viola   1−10 to date   †
• Cello   1−10 to date   † • Viola da
gamba   1−10 to date   † • Lute   1−10 to
date   † • Appalachian dulcimer,
hurdy-gurdy, viola d'amore, herald
trumpet, Baroque oboe, and recorder   †
• Primarily repairs

Fritz Damler

Box 8, Sandia Park, N.M. 87047

FT 1970 Active 1 emp. IA/MTO
Modern 12/75 • Classical guitar 25–50
to date 1–10 per year • Flamenco
guitar 10–25 to date 1–10 per year
• Steel-string guitar 10–25 to date
1–10 per year • Also known as: Leitch
Guitars

Edward A. Damm and Anne Damm
118 Ledgelawn, Bar Harbor, Maine 04609
FT 1974 Active 1 emp. IA/MTO
Modern Brochure 12/77 • Appalachian
dulcimer Over 50 to date Over 50 per
year • Hammered dulcimer 1–10 to
date 1–10 per year • Limber Jim Over
50 to date Over 50 per year • Kantele
10–25 to date 10–25 per year • Harp
10–25 to date 10–25 per year • Also
known as: Great Lakes Dulcimers • *1980:*
Hammered dulcimer Over 50 to date
Over 50 per year • Kantele Over 50 to
date 25–50 per year • Children's harp
Over 50 to date 25–50 per year
• Bodhran 25–50 to date 10–25 per
year

Danelectro Corp.
207 W. Sylvania Ave., Neptune City, N.J. 07753
† 2/75

Jim Daniellson
1965 Broadview, Eugene, Ore. 97405 † 10/76

Arthur Daniels
12 Kent Ave., Hastings-on-Hudson, N.Y. 10706
Maker of strings † 1/78

Sam W. Daniels
808 N. Fillmore, Jerome, Idaho 83338
FT 1936 Active 2 emp. IA/MTO
Modern and historical 9/74 • Viola
1–10 to date 1–10 per year • Violin
Over 50 to date 10–25 per year
• Steel-string guitar 10–25 to date †

Karen J. Danko
P.O. Box 686, Ligonier, Pa. 15658
Maker of strings † 1/78

John Danner
R.R. 2, Linton, Ind. 47441 † 1/78
1980: Maker of dulcimers (inactive)

James D'Aquisto
523 Jericho Tpke., Huntington Station, N.Y.
11746
FT 1952 Active 1 emp. MTO
Modern Brochure 5/74 • Steel-string
guitar Over 50 to date †

David F. Darby
W. Highway 76, Branson, Mo. 65616
FT 1973 Active 2 emp. IA/MTO
Modern and historical Brochure 2/78
• Appalachian dulcimer Over 50 to
date Over 50 per year • Hammered
dulcimer 1–10 to date 1–10 per year
• Psaltery 1–10 to date 1–10 per year
• Also known as: Shady Grove Dulcimer
Works

John Darnell
Rt. 1, Fort Blackmore, Va. 24250 † 4/76

Dario D'Attili
16 W. 61 St., New York, N.Y. 10023
PT Year? Active 1 emp. MTO
Modern and historical 6/74 • Violin
25–50 to date † • Viola 1–10 to date
† • Cello 1–10 to date †

William Daum
Also known as: Renaissance Gilde

George Dauphinais
2021 Willemoore, Springfield, Ill. 62704
Maker of strings † 1/78

Ken J. Davenport
2536 S. Lafayette, Denver, Colo. 80210
Maker of flutes † 10/76

Roy Davenport
939 Vernal Ave., Mill Valley, Calif. 94941
FT 1971 Active 1 emp. IA
Modern and historical 7/74 • Classical
guitar 10–25 to date 1–10 per year
• Violin 10–25 to date 1–10 per year

Herbert David
302 E. Liberty, Ann Arbor, Mich. 48104
FT 1962 Active 4 emp. IA/MTO
Modern and historical 4/74 • Lute Over
50 to date 10–25 per year • Steel-string
guitar Over 50 to date 10–25 per year
• Harp Over 50 to date 10–25 per year

• Appalachian dulcimer   Over 50 to date   Over 50 per year • 5-string banjo   Over 50 to date   10–25 per year • Mandolin   † • *1980: Mandolin   25–50 to date   1–10 per year • Psaltery   Over 50 to date   10–25 per year • Racket   1–10 to date   † • Hammered dulcimer   10–25 to date   1–10 per year • Electric instruments   Over 50 to date   10–25 per year • Classical guitar   †*

David's Dulcimers

Also known as: Mr. and Mrs. David S. Pizzini

F. R. Davidson

630 Broadway St., Leipsic, Ohio 45856
FT   1956   Active   1 emp.   IA
Modern   6/75 • Violin   25–50 to date   †
• Viola   1–10 to date   † • Appalachian dulcimer   1–10 to date   †

Keith S. Davidson

2716 N. 19th St., Tacoma, Wash. 98406
Maker of strings †   1/78

Al H. Davis

1506 Sunset, Albert Lea, Minn. 56007
PT   1966   Active   1 emp.   MTO
Historical   5/74 • Violin   Over 50 to date   10–25 per year • Viola   1–10 to date   1–10 per year • *1980: Viola   25–50 to date*

Bill Davis

P.O. Box 515, Gatlinburg, Tenn. 37738
Maker of Appalachian dulcimers †   2/76

Carroll Davis

729 N. Ocala Ave., La Puente, Calif. 91744
Maker of strings †   10/74

E. David Davis

5602 Holiday Dr., Stockton, Calif. 95207
Maker of strings †   1/78

Keith Davis

715 4th, David City, Neb. 68632
Maker of strings †   1/78

Roy Davis

Also known as: Robert L. Wendt

Tom Davis

4435 Collingdale Rd., Columbus, Ohio 43229
PT   Year?   Active   1 emp.   MTO
Modern   6/74 • Classical guitar   †

William Davis

Also known as: Santa Cruz Guitar Co.

Harley A. Day, Jr., and Michael Batell

4550 37th St. North, St. Petersburg, Fla. 33714
FT   1965   Active   2 emp.   IA/MTO
Modern and historical   4/76 • Steel-string guitar   25–50 to date • Harpsichord   1–10 to date • Viola da gamba   1–10 to date • Vihuela   1–10 to date • Lute   1–10 to date • Vielle   1–10 to date • Psaltery   10–25 to date • Gothic harp   1–10 to date • All instruments   25–50 per year • Also known as: Michael Batell

Stanley Dayan

1021 E. Ferry St., Buffalo, N.Y. 14211
Maker of recorders †   2/76

J. C. Deagan, Inc.

1770 W. Berteau Ave., Chicago, Ill. 60613
FT   1880   Active   5 emp.   IA
Modern   Brochure   5/74 • Xylophone   Over 50 to date   Over 50 per year • Marimba   Over 50 to date   Over 50 per year • Vibraharp   Over 50 to date   Over 50 per year • Orchestra bells   Over 50 to date   Over 50 per year • Orchestra chimes   Over 50 to date   Over 50 per year • Bell lyra   Over 50 to date   Over 50 per year • *1980: Marching bells, vibes, and electronic vibraharps   Over 50 to date   Over 50 per year • Not making bell lyras • Also known as: J. C. Deagan Division of Slingerland Drum Co.*

Maurice De Angeli

Box 190, Upper Ridge Rd., R.D. 1, Pennsburg, Pa. 18073
FT   1967   Active   1 emp.   MTO
Modern   Brochure   4/74 • Clavichord   1–10 to date   † • Spinet   1–10 to date   † • Harpsichord   10–25 to date   † • *1980: PT   Historical • Harpsichord   25–50 to date*

Decatur Instruments, Inc.

1014 E. Olive St., Decatur, Ill. 62526

Maker of vibraharps, marimbas, xylophones, orchestra bells, and orchestra chimes † 12/77 • Also known as: Jenco Musical Products

John DeCavage
Lennoxville, Pa. 18441
PT 1959 Active 1 emp. IA Historical 4/76 • Violin 10–25 to date 1–10 per year • Steel-string guitar 1–10 to date † • Primarily repairs

Deering Banjo Co.
3615 Costabella St., Lemon Grove, Calif. 92045
FT 1975 Active 2 emp. IA Modern 2/78 • Appalachian dulcimer Over 50 to date † • 5-string banjo 1–10 to date † • *1980: 10 emp. Brochure • Appalachian dulcimer Over 50 per year • 5-string banjo Over 50 per year • Also known as: Greg and Janet Deering*

DeFord Flutes
57760 Holiday Pl., P.O. Box 971, Elkhart, Ind. 64514
FT 1971 Active 40 emp. IA Modern Brochure 6/74 • Modern flute Over 50 to date Over 50 per year • *1980: Also known as: King Musical Instruments*

DEG Music Products, Inc.
Highway H North, Lake Geneva, Wis. 53147
FT 1965 Active 25 emp. IA Modern Brochure 4/76 • Cornet, trumpet, slide trombone, fluegelhorn, French horn, alto horn, baritone horn, clarinet, flute, piccolo, saxophone, sousaphone, and euphonium †

Douglas Deihl
65 South St., Northampton, Mass. 01060
FT 1972 Active 1 emp. IA Modern Brochure 2/76 • Wooden flute Over 50 to date Over 50 per year • Bamboo flute Over 50 to date Over 50 per year

Dekley Corp.
6 E. Newberry Rd., Bloomfield, Conn. 06002
FT 1976 Active 11 emp. IA Modern Brochure 1/78 • Pedal steel guitar Over 50 to date Over 50 per year

Delaware Organ Co., Inc.
Tonawanda, N.Y. 14150
FT 1956 Active 10 emp. MTO Modern Brochure 4/75 • Pipe organ Over 50 to date 1–10 per year

Candelario Delgado
1066 Sunset Blvd., Los Angeles, Calif. 90012
Maker of strings † 4/76

Albert Hampson Dell
301 Grady Ave., Tryon, N.C. 28782
PT 1965 Active 1 emp. IA Historical 5/74 • Baroque oboe 1–10 to date † • Rebec 1–10 to date † • Harpsichord 1–10 to date † • Baroque flute 10–25 to date † • Recorder 10–25 to date † • Viola d'amore 1–10 to date 1–10 per year • Viola da gamba 1–10 to date 1–10 per year

John Delmarto
1675 Clay Ct., Melrose Park, Ill. 60160
Maker of strings † 1/78

William DelPilar
220 Atlantic Ave., Brooklyn, N.Y. 11201 † 11/76

Del's Guitar Gallery
Also known as: Delwyn J. Langejans

Gennara DeLuccia
520 S. Miami Ave., Miami, Fla. 33130
FT 1916 Active 1 emp. MTO Historical 4/76 • Violin Over 50 to date 1–10 per year

DeLuccia and Son
1230 S. 13th St., Philadelphia, Pa. 19147
Maker of strings † 2/76

De Mano Guitars
2318 Wisconsin N.E., Albuquerque, N.M. 87110
Maker of strings †• Also known as: Lorenzo Pimentel and Son

Trish Dempsey
322 Tulane N.E., Albuquerque, N.M. 87106
PT 1972 Active 1 emp. MTO

Modern   3/75 • Steel-string guitar   1– 10
to date   1– 10 per year

Richard J. DeNeve
Oneida River Rd., Pennellville, N.Y. 13132
PT   1969   Active   1 emp.   IA
Modern   12/74 • Steel-string guitar
10– 25 to date   1– 10 per year • 12-string
guitar   1– 10 to date   †

R. H. Denzer
176 Millborn Ave., Millborn, N.J. 07041
Maker of woodwinds †   2/76

Clive Andy Vincent DePaul
481 Della Ave., P.O. Box 1068, Willits, Calif.
95490
FT   1969   Active   1 emp.   IA/MTO
Modern and historical   10/75
• Steel-string guitar   25– 50 to date
1– 10 per year • Classical guitar   10– 25 to
date   1– 10 per year • Appalachian
dulcimer   25– 50 to date   10– 25 per year
• Mandolin   1– 10 to date   1– 10 per year
• Violin   1– 10 to date   1– 10 per year
• Bass violin   1– 10 to date   1– 10 per
year • Irish harp   1– 10 to date   1– 10 per
year

Lynn Derderian
343 Walnut St., #6, San Francisco, Calif. 94118
†   2/76

Stephen Derek
895 Serenidad Pl., Goleta, Calif. 93017
FT   1970   Active   1 emp.   IA
Historical   6/74 • Violin   10– 25 to
date   1– 10 per year

DeRose and Co.
3190 W. 32d St., Cleveland, Ohio 44109
Maker of strings †   1/78

Bob Desmond
578 Hatherly Rd., North Scituate, Mass. 02060
Maker of strings †   1/78

Charles DeVeto
1087 Irene, Lyndhurst, Ohio 44124
FT   1968   Active   1 emp.   IA
Modern   Brochure   5/75 • Classical
guitar   10– 25 to date   1– 10 per year

D'Georgio Guitars
442 N. La Brea, Los Angeles, Calif. 90036
Maker of steel-string guitars †   5/76

Morton S. and Louise Diamond
2317 Briggs Rd., Silver Spring, Md. 20906
FT   1972   Active   2 emp.   IA/MTO
Modern and historical   Brochure   10/74
• Appalachian dulcimer   Over 50 to
date   Over 50 per year • *1980: Rt. 1, Bristol,
Vt. 05443 (1981)*

Diamond Designs
Also known as: Denise and Richard Wilson

Diamond Line Banjos
Also known as: Marcus O. Creager

David Demetrius Diaz
2329 Madrid St., New Orleans, La. 70122
Maker of strings †   2/76

Fred T. Dickens
7 High St., Randolph, N. J. 07801
PT   1967   Active   1 emp.   MTO
Modern   10/74 • Classical guitar   Over
50 to date   10– 25 per year

Arthur S. Dickinson
218 S. Ardmore Ave., Los Angeles, Calif. 90004
Maker of strings †   1/78

L. Eugene Dickinson
Rt. 2, Box 236, Fairmont, W.Va. 26554
PT   1971   2 emp.   IA/MTO
Historical   10/74 • Appalachian
dulcimer   Over 50 to date   25– 50 per
year • 5-string banjo   10– 25 to date
10– 25 per year • Hammered dulcimer
1– 10 to date   1– 10 per year • Also known
as: Bill Kennedy

Rev. Gordon Dickson
Presbyterian Manse, Montauk Hwy., East
Moriches, N. Y. 11940
PT   1969   Active   1 emp.   MTO
Modern   8/75 • Appalachian dulcimer
10– 25 to date   1– 10 per year

T. Pieter Diehl
Box 447, Stony Brook, N. Y. 11790
FT   1972   Active   1 emp.   MTO
Historical   6/75 • Harpsichord   1– 10 to
date   1– 10 per year

Karl F. Dietrichs
Also known as: Buck Musical Instrument
Products

Warren Dillman
28 Grove St., Norfolk, Mass. 02056
PT   1975   Active   1 emp.   IA
Modern   9/75 • Tenor banjo   1– 10 to
date   † • 5-string banjo   1– 10 to date   †
• Appalachian dulcimer   1– 10 to date   †

Otto B. Dingus
Dungannon, Va. 24245 †   4/76

Timothy W. Dippold
2515 French, Erie, Pa. 16503
PT   1975   Active   1 emp.   MTO
Historical   6/75 • Classical guitar   1– 10
to date   † • Steel-string guitar   1– 10 to
date   † • Psaltery   1– 10 to date   †

Frank Di Salvo
1705 E. Los Altos, Fresno, Calif. 93710
PT   1968   Active   1 emp.   IA/MTO
Modern   4/78 • Electric guitar   25– 50 to
date   1– 10 per year • Electric bass
guitar   1– 10 to date   1– 10 per year
• Steel-string guitar   1– 10 to date   1– 10
per year

Nadya Disend
927 Cayuga Heights Rd., Ithaca, N. Y. 14850
Maker of strings †   2/76

Daniel Dishaw
4900 Bear Rd., Liverpool, N. Y. 13088 †   1/78

Divine Flute Co.
Also known as: David Blackburn

Arthur Dixon
402 Tennessee Ave., Whitesburg, Ky. 41858
FT   1960   Active   1 emp.   MTO
Historical   6/74 • Appalachian
dulcimer   Over 50 to date   1– 10 per year

Robert T. Dixon
Rt. 1, Box 239A, Lynnville, Tenn. 38472
PT   1975   Inactive   1 emp.
IA/MTO   Modern   Brochure   1/78
• Appalachian dulcimer   1– 10 to date   †
• Hammered dulcimer   1– 10 to date   †
• Bodhran   1– 10 to date   † • 5-string

banjo   1– 10 to date   † • Irish harp
1– 10 to date   † • 1980: Inactive
(1977– 1980) • Appalachian dulcimer
10– 25 to date

D'Merle Guitars
535 Broadhollow Rd., Melville, N. Y. 11746
PT   1964   Inactive   5 emp.   MTO
Modern   5/75 • Steel-string guitar
25– 50 to date   † • Primarily repairs

L. C. Doan
Santa Cruz, Calif. 95000 †

Dobro, Inc.
Also known as: Original Musical
Instrument Co., Inc.

Ivan Dodson
212 Dellview Ave., Santa Cruz, Calif. 95062
PT   1969   Active   1 emp.   MTO
Modern and historical   9/74 • Violin
1– 10 to date   † • Viola   1– 10 to date   †
• Electronic violin   1– 10 to date   †
• Banjolin   1– 10 to date   †

Mark Donnan
1503 Beachfront, Point Pleasant Beach, N. J.
07842 †
1980: PT   1970   Active   1 emp.
MTO   Modern   10/80 • Electric guitar   †

Don's Guitar Shop
2319 S. Stiles, Oklahoma City, Okla. 73129
FT   1961   Inactive   1 emp.   MTO
Modern   4/76 • Classical guitar   1– 10 to
date   † • Flamenco guitar   1– 10 to
date   † • Steel-string guitar   1– 10 to
date   † • 12-string guitar   1– 10 to date
† • Appalachian dulcimer   10– 25 to
date   † • Primarily repairs • 1980:
Brochure • Requinte   1– 10 to date   †
• Also known as: Don E. Teeter

Dr. Herman Dorenvaes
8115 S. W. 17 Terr., Miami, Fla. 33134 †   2/76

David Dorenz
5417 Junction Blvd., Elmhurst, N. Y. 11373
PT   Year?   Active   1 emp.   MTO
Modern   12/75 • Mandolin   1– 10 to
date   † • 1980: 1963   Inactive

Solomon Dornhelm
236 E. 4th St., Brooklyn, N. Y. 11218
FT   1924   Active   1 emp.   IA
Modern   6/74 • Violin   Over 50 to date
† • Viola   1– 10 to date   † • Cello   1– 10
to date   †

Dennis Dorogi
Ellicott Rd., Brocton, N. Y. 14716
FT   1969   Active   1 emp.   IA/MTO
Modern and historical   Brochure   4/74 •
Appalachian dulcimer   Over 50 to date
Over 50 per year • Hammered dulcimer
25– 50 to date   10– 25 per year
• Psaltery   Over 50 to date   Over 50 per
year • Rebec   1– 10 to date   1– 10 per
year • *1980: Hammered dulcimer   Over 50
to date   25–50 per year*

Brian N. Dorris
313 118th St., Tacoma, Wash. 98444 †   10/76

Al D'Ossche
2000 22d St., Bellingham, Wash. 98225
PT   1972   Active   1 emp.   MTO
Modern   4/75 • Appalachian dulcimer
10– 25 to date   10– 25 per year

Dan Doty's Dulcimers
3773 Wychemere, Memphis, Tenn. 38128
PT   1973   Active   1 emp.   IA
Historical   6/75 • Appalachian
dulcimer   Over 50 to date   † • *1980:
IA/MTO   Historical   Brochure*

Dove Instruments
Also known as: Jan Burda

Daniel Dover
R. F. D. 1, North Stratford, N. H. 03590
FT   1976   Active   1 emp.   IA
Historical   4/76 • Appalachian
dulcimer   10– 25 to date   10– 25 per year
• Classical guitar   1– 10 to date   †

William Dowd
25 Thorndike St., Cambridge, Mass. 02141
FT   1949   Active   8 emp.   MTO
Historical   Brochure   6/74
• Harpsichord   Over 50 to date   Over 50
per year • *1980: Harpsichord   10–25 per
year*

William F. Dowling & Co.
Southwest Harbor, Maine 04679
FT   1970   Active   1 emp.   IA/MTO
Historical   Brochure   10/74
• Harpsichord   1– 10 to date   † • *1980:
Forte-piano, keyboard, and kit   †*

Downeast Dulcimer Shop
Rivers Bend, Turner, Maine 04282
Maker of Appalachian dulcimers †   10/74

Peter Sargent Draves
223 Franklin Ct., Dousman, Wis. 53118
PT   1973   Active   1 emp.   MTO
Modern   9/74 • Flamenco guitar   1– 10
to date   † • Harpsichord   1– 10 to
date   †

Drews Custom Guitars
308 Norfolk Ave., Norfolk, Neb. 68701
FT   1968   Active   2 emp.   MTO
Modern   Brochure   10/75 • Steel-string
guitar   Over 50 to date   10– 25 per year
• *1980: IA/MTO · Electric guitar   1–10 to
date   1–10 per year · Repairs · Also known
as: Don L. Drews*

Dromedary Musical Instruments
Also known as: Ritch Kelly

Drum City—Guitar Town
15255 Sherman Way, Van Nuys, Calif. 91405
†   2/75

Drumland
2216 N. Dixie Hwy., Lake Worth, Fla. 33460
Maker of drums †   12/77 • Also known as:
Ralph Kester

Charles Dudley
120 E. 11th St., New York, N. Y. 10003
PT   1973   Active   1 emp.   MTO
Modern   6/75 • Appalachian dulcimer
1– 10 to date   †

The Dulcimer Den
Also known as: Robert Wilson Harmon IV

Dulcimer Seed
Also known as: Dennis Murphy

Dulcimer Shop
Box 653, Central City, Colo. 80427
Maker of Appalachian dulcimers †   2/76

Dulcimer Shoppe
Also known as: Lynn McSpadden

Dulcimer Works
Also known as: Carmie Simon

Harold Dunham
South St., Cato, N. Y. 13033 †   2/76

Robert E. Dunkle
113 Brookfield Rd., Avon Lake, Ohio 44012
PT   Year?   Active   1 emp.   MTO
Historical   1/75 • Appalachian
dulcimer   1– 10 to date   †

James Dunning
R. R. 1, Cooperstown, N. Y. 13326
Maker of strings † • *1980: 1335 Washington
St., San Francisco, Calif. 94109 • Not making
instruments*

Jay Dunovan
Hillsville, Va. 24343 †   4/76

Duo-Art Player-Piano
FT   1920   Active   ? emp.   IA
Modern   Brochure   4/76 • † • Also
known as: Aeolian Corp.

Brad DuPont
3801 Soquel Dr., #8, Soquel, Calif. 95073 †

David Dushkin
Winnetka, Ill. 60093
PT   1939   Inactive   1 emp.   MTO
Historical   4/76 • Recorder   †

Dynastar
1425 S. Salina St., Syracuse, N. Y. 13025 †   2/76

Eagle Banjos
Athens, Ohio 45701
Also known as: Stewart-MacDonald Mfg.
Co.

Eames Drum Co.
229 Hamilton St., Saugus, Mass. 01880
FT   1950   Active   2 emp.   IA/MTO
Historical   Brochure   1/75
• Rope-tensioned drum   Over 50 to date
Over 50 per year • *1980: Modern and
historical • Snare drum   Over 50 to date
Over 50 per year • Bass drum   Over 50 to
date   Over 50 per year • Tom tom   Over 50*

*to date   Over 50 per year • Also known as:
Joseph F. MacSweeney*

Early Internal
Also known as: David Kortier

Early Keyboards and Strings
Also known as: Leo McLaughlin

Early Strings
Also known as: Neil Hendricks

Earnest Instrument Co.
Also known as: Joel Eckhaus

Earthwood, Inc.
Box 2117, Newport Beach, Calif. 92663
Maker of steel-string guitars †   12/77
• Also known as: Ernie Ball; George
Fullerton

Earthworks
Also known as: Charles Fox

East Virginia Dulcimer Co.
Also known as: Richard Burnside

Eastern, Ltd.
Also known as: Brian Breyre

Eastern Musical Instrument Co.
Box 455, Peekskill, N. Y. 10566 †   2/75

Eastman Violin Shop
2375 Roxboro Rd., Cleveland, Ohio 44106
Maker of violins †   2/76

Bill Eaton
5445 E. Washington, Phoenix, Ariz. 85034 †
1/77

L. Allen Ebert
1074 Senseny Rd., Winchester, Va. 22601
Maker of strings †   1/78

Ebert Organ Co.
210 Natchez St., Pittsburgh, Pa. 15211
FT   1967   Active   1 emp.   MTO
Modern   10/75 • Portative organ   1– 10
to date   †

Eckerworks
Box 731, Brookline, Mass. 02147
PT   1972   Active   1 emp.   MTO

Modern   Brochure   2/76 • Appalachian dulcimer   1–10 to date   † • Hammered dulcimer   1–10 to date   † • Irish harp 1–10 to date   † • *1980: Modern and historical • Hammered dulcimer   25–50 to date   10–25 per year • Irish harp   10–25 to date   1–10 per year • Not making Appalachian dulcimers • Also known as: Douglas Stuart Ecker*

Martin Eckhardt

3511 Burlingame Rd., Topeka, Kans. 66611
PT   1973   Active   1 emp.   MTO
Modern   4/75 • Classical guitar   1–10 to date   † • Steel-string guitar   1–10 to date   †

Joel Eckhaus

11 Commerce St., Williston, Vt. 05495
PT   1976   Active   1 emp.   MTO
Modern   1/77 • 5-string banjo   1–10 to date   † • Mandolin   1–10 to date   †
• Primarily repairs • Also known as: Earnest Instrument Co.

Larry G. Eckstein

333 Lawn Ave., West Lafayette, Ind. 47906
FT   1971   Active   1 emp.   MTO
Historical   5/74 • Harpsichord   10–25 to date   †

E. B. Edkford

3605 Vista del Valle, San Jose, Calif. 95132
Maker of strings †   2/76

Emul P. Edmon

4371 Francis Rd., Cazenovia, N. Y. 13035 †
11/76

Ed's Musical Instruments

Also known as: L. Edward McGlincy

Harold Edson

15300 Brand Blvd., Space 33, Katy Ln., Mission Hills, Calif. 91345
PT   Year?   Active   1 emp.   IA
Modern   4/76 • Violin   25–50 to date 1–10 per year • *1980: 1916 • Violin and viola   25–50 to date   1–10 per year*

Samuel Eisenstein

140 W. 57th St., New York, N. Y. 10019
Maker of violins †   2/76

Donald Ekland

3350 Mary St., Coconut Grove, Fla. 33133
Maker of strings †   2/76

Karl Eklund

66 Cliff Ave., Hempstead, N. Y. 11550
PT   1974   Active   1 emp.   IA/MTO
Modern   Brochure   4/76 • Appalachian dulcimer   10–25 to date   10–25 per year
• 5-string banjo   1–10 to date   1–10 per year

John R. Ekstedt

15201 40th Ave. West, Lynnwood, Wash. 98036
PT   1971   Active   1 emp.   MTO
Modern   4/76 • Steel-string guitar   1–10 to date   † • Harp   1–10 to date   †

Art Elcombe

Snow Rt., Box 7U, Finley, Okla. 74543
FT   1977   Active   1 emp.   IA/MTO
Modern   1/77 • Steel-string guitar   1–10 to date   1–10 per year

El Degas Guitars

5 Canal Rd., Pelham Manor, N. Y. 10803
Maker of steel-string guitars †   5/76

Lyn Elder

Dominican College, San Rafael, Calif. 94901
FT   1968   Active   1 emp.   MTO
Historical   Brochure   9/77 • Lute   Over 50 to date   10–25 per year
• Hurdy-gurdy   25–50 to date   1–10 per year • Psaltery   10–25 to date   1–10 per year • Rebec   Over 50 to date   10–25 per year • Strings   † • *1980: Viol   10–25 to date   1–10 per year • Baroque violin and viola   10–25 to date   1–10 per year • Early guitar   10–25 to date   1–10 per year • Medieval fiddle   Over 50 to date 1–10 per year • Medieval and Renaissance strings   Over 50 to date   1–10 per year*

Elderly Instruments

Also known as: Bart Reiter

Electro Music

Also known as: CBS Musical Instruments

Electro String Instrument Corp.

Box 1321, Santa Ana, Calif. 92702
Maker of strings †   2/76

Electro-Voice, Inc.
626 Cecil St., Buchanin, Mich. 49107 † 2/76

Pico Elgin
1308 Rosemary, Apt. #1, Columbia, Mo. 65201
PT 1971 Active 1 emp. MTO
Modern 6/74 • 5-string banjo 1– 10 to
date 1– 10 per year • Steel-string guitar
1– 10 to date 1– 10 per year • Primarily
repairs

Ernest Lee Elliott
5653 Johnson St., Hollywood, Fla. 33021
PT 1972 Active 1 emp. MTO
Historical 12/75 • 5-string banjo 1– 10
to date 1– 10 per year • Also known as:
Lee's Banjo Shop • *1980: Inactive • Now
known as: The Banjo Shop (Dave and Paul
Stype)*

J. C. Elliott
1515 Seagate Ln., Houston, Tex. 77058
PT 1969 Active 1 emp. IA/MTO
Modern 8/75 • Classical guitar 25– 50
to date 1– 10 per year • Electric guitar
1– 10 to date 1– 10 per year
• Appalachian dulcimer 10– 25 to date
10– 25 per year • Kalimba 1– 10 to date
1– 10 per year

Jeffrey R. Elliott
3748 S. E. Taylor, Portland, Ore. 97214
FT 1966 Active 4 emp. MTO
Modern 5/75 • Classical guitar Over 50
to date 10– 25 per year • Flamenco
guitar 1– 10 to date 1– 10 per year
• Steel-string guitar 1– 10 to date †
• Electric guitar 10– 25 to date †
• 5-string banjo 1– 10 to date † • *1980:
Baroque, classical, and steel-string
guitars Over 50 to date 10– 25 per year*

Ellis Mandolins
7208 Cooper Ln., Austin, Tex. 78745
FT 1977 Active 1 emp. IA/MTO
Modern and historical 2/78 • Mandolin
1– 10 to date † • Electric mandolin
1– 10 to date † • Electric guitar 1– 10 to
date † • 5-string banjo 1– 10 to date †
• *1980: MTO • Mandolin 25– 50 to date
10– 25 per year • Electric mandolin 1– 10
per year • Electric guitar 1– 10 per year
• 5-string banjo 1– 10 per year • Also
known as: Tom H. Ellis*

Arpad Elo, Jr.
5720 S. Harper Ave., Chicago, Ill. 60637
PT 1967 Active 1 emp. MTO
Historical 5/74 • Baroque flute 1– 10 to
date • Baroque oboe 1– 10 to date •
Baroque clarinet 1– 10 to date • Basset
horn 1– 10 to date • All instruments
1– 10 per year • *1980: Inactive*

Fred Elton
Evart, Mich. 49631
Maker of hammered dulcimers † 2/76

Michael Elwell
P. O. Box 81, Santa, Idaho 83866
Maker of strings † 1/78

Emerson Piano Co.
Also known as: Aeolian Corp.

The Emmanuel Violin Shop
Also known as: Claude H. Watson

Emmons Guitar Co.
1771 E. Webb Ave., Box 1336, Burlington, N. C.
27215
FT 1964 Active 20 emp. IA
Modern Brochure 3/75 • Pedal steel
guitar Over 50 to date Over 50 per year

Albert Emola
504 Oak Hill Ave., Endicott, N. Y. 13760
Maker of pipe organs † 2/76

Emperador Guitars
56 W. 103d St., Chicago, Ill. 60628
Maker of steel-string guitars † 5/76

Empire Accordion Corp.
337 6th Ave., New York, N. Y. 10014
Maker of accordions † 2/75

Engelhardt-Link
185 King St., Elk Grove, Ill. 60007
FT 1970 Active 7 emp. IA
Modern Brochure 2/75 • Bass violin
Over 50 to date Over 50 per year • Cello
Over 50 to date Over 50 per year

John Engels
229 Wood St., Woodville, Mass. 01784 † 2/76

Larry English
P. O. Box 615, Arnold, Calif. 95223

FT 1971 Active 1 emp. IA
Modern and historical Brochure 8/75
• Appalachian dulcimer Over 50 to
date Over 50 per year • Steel-string
guitar 1–10 to date 1–10 per year
• Harp 1–10 to date 1–10 per year
• Also known as: Songbird

English Sales, Inc.
1131 E. Michigan Ave., Lansing, Mich. 48912
† 2/76

Bryan Enright
Box 288, Southwick, Mass. 01077
PT 1976 Active 1 emp. IA/MTO
Modern 2/78 • Electric guitar 1–10 to
date † • Jazz guitar 1–10 to date †
• Steel-string guitar 1–10 to date †
• Primarily repairs • Also known as: BFE
Guitars • *1980: FT • Steel-string and electric
guitars 1–10 per year*

Ensenada Guitars
177 W. Hintz Rd., Wheeling, Ill. 60090
Maker of steel-string guitars † 5/76

Persis Ensor
Also known as: Renaissance Workshop

Epcor, Inc.
Box 422, Beverly Hills, Calif. 90213 † 2/76

Epiphone Guitars
Also known as: Norlin Music, Inc.

Raymond Epler
4508 Country Club Blvd., South Charleston,
W. Va., 25309
PT 1972 Active 1 emp. IA
Historical Brochure 10/74
• Appalachian dulcimer Over 50 to
date 25–50 per year

Alexander Illitch Eppler
2245 Yale Ave. East, #1M, Seattle, Wash. 98102
FT 1970 Active 1 emp. IA/MTO
Modern and historical 9/74 • Kaval
Over 50 to date • Gaida Over 50 to date
• Wooden flute 10–25 to date
• Balalaika Over 50 to date • Dombra
Over 50 to date • Violin, viola, cello, viola
d'amore, and lute † • All instruments
25–50 per year

Art Erbel
300 N. Dean St., Bay City, Mich. 48706
PT 1935 Active 1 emp. MTO
Modern 6/75 • Violin 25–50 to date
1–10 per year

John P. Erdman
709 Ashford Rd., Wilmington, Del. 19803
PT Year? Active 1 emp. MTO
Modern 2/78 • Classical guitar 1–10 to
date 1–10 per year • *1980: 1970
• Hobbyist*

Charles W. Erickson
14731 Lull St., Van Nuys, Calif. 97213
FT 1963 Active 4 emp. MTO
Modern and historical 11/74 • 5-string
banjo 25–50 to date † • Also known as:
Erika Banjos

Lyle J. Erickson
7631 212 St., Edmonds, Wash. 98020 † 1/77

Erika Banjos
Also known as: Charles W. Erickson

Dave Erler
Also known as: Here, Inc.

Erlewine Guitars
3004 Guadalupe, Austin, Tex. 78705
FT 1969 Active 1 emp. MTO
Modern 10/75 • Electric guitar 10–25
to date † • *1980: 3 emp. IA/MTO
Brochure • Electric guitar Over 50 to
date Over 50 per year • Also known as:
Mark Erlewine*

John Bruce Erwin
4509 Cole Ave., Dallas, Tex. 75205
PT 1956 Active 1 emp. IA
Modern 4/76 • Violin 25–50 to
date 1–10 per year • *1980: Violin Over
50 to date*

Essex Banjo Co.
Ferry St., Essex, Conn. 06426
Maker of 5-string banjos † • *1980: Only
repairs*

Paul S. Estenson
220 Broadway, Fargo, N. Dak. 58102
FT 1974 Active 1 emp. MTO
Modern and historical 12/77

• Mandolin † • Lute † • Primarily repairs

Peter Estes
52 Fahnestock Rd., Malvern, Pa. 19355
PT 1974 Active 1 emp. IA/MTO
Modern 1/75 • Steel-string guitar 1–10
to date 1–10 per year • *1980: Hammered and Appalachian dulcimers 25–50 to date 1–10 per year • Not making steel-string guitars*

Estey (Division of Miner Industries, Inc.)
200 Fifth Ave., New York, N. Y. 10010
Maker of organs † 5/74

Estey Musical Instrument Corp.
Harmony, Pa. 16037 † 10/76

Estey Piano Corp.
2810 Morris Ave., Union, N. J. 07083
Maker of pianos † 2/76

Euturpe Instruments
Also known as: Clyde Tyndale

Linda Evans
South Fork Farm, Rt. 3, Clinton, Ark. 72031
Maker of wooden drums † 4/74

Ruth Esther Evans
2176 Sycamore Canyon Rd., Santa Barbara, Calif. 93108
PT 1962 Active 1 emp. IA
Modern and historical 6/74 • Violin 1–10 to date • Viola 1–10 to date • Cello 1–10 to date • Viola d'amore 1–10 to date • All instruments 1–10 per year

Everett Piano Co.
900 Indiana Ave., South Haven, Mich. 49090
FT 1883 Active 350 emp. IA
Modern Brochure 5/74 • Piano Over 50 to date Over 50 per year • Also known as: Cable-Nelson Piano Co.; Yamaha International Corp.

Evergreen Mt.
Bear, Idaho 83603 † 2/76

Howard Everngam
210 E. 96th St., New York, N. Y. 10028

FT 1954 Active 1 emp. MTO
Historical Brochure 7/74
• Harpsichord 25–50 to date 1–10 per year

Ron and Nancy Eversole
1124 E. 3d St., Mishawaka, Ind. 46544 †
*1980: 1958 Active 2 emp. IA/MTO
Historical 10/80 • Appalachian dulcimer † • Also known as: Shanan Carvings*

Exinde Corp.
23 Winter St., Franklin, Mass. 02038 † 2/76

Ken Eye
PT 1966 Active 1 emp. IA/MTO
Modern and historical 2/75 • † • Also known as: Roy Bodd and Ken Eye

Kevin M. Fahey
Halibut Point, Rockport, Mass. 01966
Maker of strings † 1/78

Harvey Fairbanks
19 Schubert St., Binghamton, N. Y. 13901
PT 1942 Active 1 emp. IA
Modern 4/74 • Violin 25–50 to date • Viola 10–25 to date • Cello 1–10 to date • All instruments 1–10 per year

Joe Fallon
47 James St., Arlington, Mass. 02174
Maker of strings † 3/78

Family Piano Service
Also known as: Sam Schliff

Paul Farrar
Spring St., Bethel, Maine 04217
FT 1978 Active 1 emp. MTO
Modern 2/78 • Classical guitar 1–10 to date 1–10 per year • Electric guitar 1–10 to date 1–10 per year • Electric mandolin 1–10 to date 1–10 per year • 12-string guitar 1–10 to date 1–10 per year

Eugene Farrell
287 Waltham St., Lexington, Mass. 02173
PT 1970 Active 1 emp. MTO
Historical 6/74 • Steel-string guitar 1–10 to date 1–10 per year • Lute

1– 10 to date   1– 10 per year • Vihuela
1– 10 to date   1– 10 per year
• Harpsichord   1– 10 to date   1– 10 per
year

Susan Caust Farrell

R. F. D. 1, Searsport, Maine 04974
FT   1964   Active   1 emp.   MTO
Modern   2/79 • Appalachian dulcimer
1– 10 to date   1– 10 per year • Wooden
drum   1– 10 to date   1– 10 per year
• Primarily repairs

Favilla Guitars

P. O. Box 308, Deer Park, N. Y. 11729
FT   1890   Active   ? emp.   IA
Modern   Brochure   6/75 • Steel-string
guitar   Over 50 to date   Over 50 per year
• Ukulele   Over 50 to date   Over 50 per
year

Matthew Fawcett

534 West St., Vacaville, Calif. 95688
Maker of strings †   2/76

Cabell J. Fearn

Rec. Svcs. Crafts, APO, N. Y. 09154
PT   1976   Active   1 emp.   MTO
Modern and historical   2/78 • 5-string
banjo   1– 10 to date   † • Zither   1– 10 to
date   † • Steel-string guitar   1– 10 to
date   † • Electric guitar   1– 10 to
date   †

Yves Albert Feder

N. Chestnut Hill Rd., Killingworth, Conn. 06417
FT   1973   Active   1 emp.   IA/MTO
Historical   11/78 • Clavichord   1– 10 to
date   1– 10 per year • Harpsichord
1– 10 to date   1– 10 per year • *1980: 2
emp.*   *Brochure · Harpsichord*   *10– 25 to
date*

Roy Feidelberg

P. O. Box, Monte Rio, Calif. 95462 †   6/74

Ronald Feinman

90 Madison Ave., Island Park, N. Y. 11558
Maker of strings †   1/78

Mark Felder

Whitefield, Maine 04362
PT   1975   Active   1 emp.   IA/MTO

Modern   12/77 • Appalachian dulcimer
10– 25 to date   †

Fender Musical Instruments

Also known as: Fender/Rogers/Rhodes

Fender/Rogers/Rhodes

1300 E. Valencia, Fullerton, Calif. 92631
Maker of electric guitars, electric bass
guitars, drums, and electric pianos † • Also
known as: CBS Musical Instruments; Fender
Musical Instruments

Ren Ferguson

1809 Lincoln Blvd., Venice, Calif. 90291
FT   1970   Active   1 emp.   MTO
Modern and historical   4/76 • Steel-string
guitar   Over 50 to date   † • 5-string
banjo   25– 50 to date   † • Mandolin
10– 25 to date   †

Jose A. Fernandez

3990 S. W. 2 Terr., Miami, Fla. 33134 †   2/76

Henry E. Ferrary

126 Dennison Rd., Essex, Conn. 06426
PT   Year?   Active   1 emp.   IA
Modern and historical   3/76 • Fife   1– 10
to date   †

Ferretta Music Service

Also known as: George Becker

Frank Ferry

Lake St., Lexington, Mass. 02173 †   2/76

Fiber Age Products

444 S. Broadway, Yonkers, N. Y. 10705 †   2/76

The Fibes Drum

Also known as: C. F. Martin Organisation

The Fiddle Barn

Also known as: Owen E. Griffith

Fiddle Factory, Inc.

1503 S. 9th St., P. O. Box 817, Sheboygan, Wis.
53081
FT   1975   Active   5 emp.   IA
Modern   Brochure   1/78 • Stumpf
fiddle   Over 50 to date   Over 50 per year
• Also known as: Stumpf Fiddle

The Fiddle Shop
Also known as: Dr. Hiram Curry

David Field
424 W. High St., Glassboro, N.J. 08028
PT   1964   Active   1 emp.   MTO
Historical   5/74 • Appalachian
dulcimer   Over 50 to date   25–50 per
year • Hammered dulcimer   1–10 to
date   1–10 per year

Henry Finck
612 S. Dallas Ave., Pittsburgh, Pa. 15217
PT   Year?   Active   1 emp.   IA
Historical   6/74 • Classical guitar   1–10
to date   †

The Fingerboard
Also known as: Danny R. Jones

Scott Finlayson
66 Hillview Rd., Gorham, Maine 04038 †   9/76
1980: Inactive • Appalachian dulcimer
1–10 to date • Hobbyist

Emit Finn
Box 168, Umpqua Star Rt., Umpqua, Ore. 97486
Maker of strings †   3/78

Albert W. Fischer
2443 Calle del Oro, La Jolla, Calif. 92037
PT   1967   Active   1 emp.   MTO
Modern   9/74 • Violin   1–10 to date   †

J. and C. Fischer
FT   1940   Active   ? emp.   IA
Modern   Brochure   6/74 • † • Also
known as: Aeolian Corp.

Troy Fish
15216 2d S. W., Seattle, Wash. 98166
FT   1971   Active   1 emp.   MTO
Modern   9/74 • Classical guitar   10–25
to date   † • Electric guitar   1–10 to
date   † • Steel-string guitar   1–10 to
date   † • Primarily repairs • Also known
as: Joe Farmer's Music

Alfred L. Fisher
1000 Jersey St., Bellingham, Wash. 98225
FT   1923   Active   1 emp.   IA/MTO
Modern and historical   4/76 • Violin
Over 50 to date   † • Steel-string guitar

10–25 to date   † • 5-string banjo   10–25
to date   †

David B. Fisher
114 Frederick St., #15, San Francisco, Calif.
94117
Maker of strings †   1/78

Zachariah Fisher
10221 Tyburn Terr., Bethesda, Md. 20014
PT   1972   Active   1 emp.   IA
Modern   Brochure   4/77 • Fife   Over 50
to date   25–50 per year • Copper flute
1–10 to date   † • Also known as: Zack
Fifes

C. B. Fisk, Inc.
P. O. Box 28, Gloucester, Mass. 01930
FT   1956   Active   11 emp.   MTO
Modern   4/74 • Pipe organ   25–50 to
date   1–10 per year • *1980: 20 emp.*
• Mechanical-action tracker organ   Over
50 to date   1–10 per year • Not making
pipe organs • Also known as: Charles Fisk

Bill Fitzsimons
196 Main St., Annapolis, Md. 21401
Maker of Appalachian dulcimers †   2/76

Russell Flagg
Rutland, Vt. 05701 †

Flashy Banjo Works
Also known as: Sam Jones

Stuart H. Flavell
120 Pleasant St., Rumford, R. I. 02916
PT   1969   Active   1 emp.   IA/MTO
Modern   Brochure   12/74 • Steel-string
guitar   25–50 to date   10–25 per year
• 5-string banjo   10–25 to date   1–10
per year • Also known as: Green Mt. Guitar
& Banjo Workshop

H. Fleisher
45 Dudley Ave., Staten Island, N. Y. 10301 †
5/75

C. H. Fleming
744 88th Ave., St. Petersburg, Fla. 33702
Maker of strings † • *1980: Inactive*

H. A. Fleming
Rt. 2, Gatlinburg, Tenn. 37738

PT   1967   Active   1 emp.   MTO
Historical   Brochure   12/74
• Appalachian dulcimer   Over 50 to
date   † • Steel-string guitar   1–10 to
date   † • Mandolin   1–10 to date   †

Richard Fletcher
R. D. 1, Box 83, Roaring Branch, Pa. 17765
FT   1969   Active   1 emp.   IA/MTO
Modern and historical   5/76 • Psaltery
25–50 to date   † • Appalachian
dulcimer   25–50 to date   † • Classical
guitar   25–50 to date   † • Lute   10–25
to date   † • *1980: Brochure (1981) • Lute
25–50 to date   10–25 per year • Theorbo
† • Archlute   †*

J. Robert Flexer
595 Matedero Ave., Palo Alto, Calif. 94306
PT   1972   Active   1 emp.   MTO
Modern   9/74 • Violin   1–10 to date
1–10 per year • Gadulka   1–10 to date   †

Ed Florence
P. O. Box 82, Idaho City, Idaho 83631
PT   Year?   Inactive   1 emp.   MTO
Modern and historical   12/77
• Appalachian dulcimer   10–25 to date
† • Lyre   1–10 to date   † • 5-string
banjo   1–10 to date   †

James Flowers
305 Burlwood Ct., Santa Rosa, Calif. 95401
PT   1967   Active   2 emp.   IA/MTO
Historical   10/75 • Harpsichord   1–10 to
date   1–10 per year

Clifford J. Flynn
8316 E. Roma, Scottsdale, Ariz. 85251
FT   1964   Active   1 emp.   MTO
Historical   9/74 • Violin   10–25 to
date   † • Primarily repairs

Ovie Flynn
301 W. North St., Boswell, Ind. 47921
Maker of strings †   1/77

Linda Foley
1217 Bemis S. E., Grand Rapids, Mich. 49506
FT   1975   Active   2 emp.   IA
Modern   2/78 • Appalachian dulcimer
25–50 to date   10–25 per year • Also
known as: Curt Sanders and Linda Foley

Folkcraft Instruments
Also known as: David Marks

Catherine E. Folkers
P. O. Box 284, Ypsilanti, Mich. 48197
Maker of Baroque flutes †

Jack and Shirley Folkertsma
Also known as: J-Folks Dulcimers

The Folkstore
5238 University Way N.E., Seattle, Wash. 98105
FT   1972   Active   1 emp.   MTO
Modern   9/74 • 5-string banjo   1–10 to
date   † • Appalachian dulcimer   1–10 to
date   † • Steel-string guitar   1–10 to
date   † • Mandolin   1–10 to date   †
• Primarily repairs • Also known as: Darrel
McMichaels • *1980: Now known as: Stuart
E. Herrid*

Lee Follmer
Also known as: American Dream
Instruments Mfg.

Sandy Fontwit
General Delivery, Big Sur, Calif. 93920
FT   1969   Active   1 emp.   MTO
Historical   10/74 • Harpsichord   1–10 to
date   1–10 per year

Robert Lewis Force, Jr.
P. O. Box 5, Royal City, Wash. 99357
PT   1971   Active   1 emp.   MTO
Modern and historical   7/74
• Appalachian dulcimer   25–50 to date
10–25 per year • Zither   10–25 to date
1–10 per year • Langaleik   1–10 to date
1–10 per year • Lanspil   1–10 to date
1–10 per year

Donna M. Ford
Also known as: Cripple Creek Dulcimers

Franklin Ford
Also known as: Gryphon Stringed
Instruments

Gherald L. Ford, Jr.
Also known as: Cripple Creek Dulcimers

Ford Platz Oboe Co.
1700 Silver, Elkhart, Ind. 46514
Maker of oboes †   2/76

Jerry G. Forestiere
281 The Arcade, Cleveland, Ohio 44114
Maker of violins † 2/76

Kent Forrester
806 Sha Wa Circle, Murray, Ky. 42071
PT 1976 Active 1 emp. IA
Historical 6/78 • Krumhorn 1–10 to
date 1–10 per year • Recorder Over 50
to date 25–50 per year • Flute 1–10 to
date 1–10 per year

Abel Fortune
406½ E. John, Seattle, Wash. 98102
Maker of strings † 1/78

Charles C. Foster
824 Mystic Ave., Gretna, La. 70053
PT 1969 Active 1 emp. IA/MTO
Historical 2/76 • Minstrel harp 1–10 to
date † • Medieval fiddle 1–10 to date
† • Crwth 1–10 to date †
• Rauschpfeifer 1–10 to date † • *1980:*
Bass viola da gamba 1–10 to date
1–10 per year

Daniel Foster
Rt. 6, Decorah, Iowa 52101
FT 1976 Active 1 emp. MTO
Modern Brochure 9/77 • Viol 1–10
to date †

Douglas Foster
907 Pine, Dewitt, Mich. 48820
FT 1976 Active 1 emp. IA
Modern and historical 4/78 • Steel-string
guitar 1–10 to date • Violin 1–10 to
date • Viola 1–10 to date • All
instruments 1–10 per year

Charles Fox
South Strafford, Vt. 05070
FT 1973 Active 1 emp. MTO
Modern Brochure 5/70 • Classical
guitar 10–25 to date • Flamenco guitar
1–10 to date • Steel-string guitar 10–25
to date • Acoustic bass guitar 1–10 to
date • All instruments 1–10 per year
• Also known as: Earthworks • *1980:*
1967 3 emp. IA/MTO • Steel-string
guitar Over 50 to date • Electric guitar
Over 50 to date Over 50 per year • All
instruments Over 50 per year • Now
known as: GRD Instruments

Fox Products Corp.
South Whitley, Ind. 46787
FT 1949 Active 18 emp. IA/MTO
Modern Brochure 5/74 • Bassoon
Over 50 to date Over 50 per year
• Contrabassoon 10–25 to date 10–25
per year • Oboe Over 50 to date Over 50
per year • *1980: 35 emp.*

Manuel Fraguela
4027 Bender Rd., Jacksonville, Fla. 33207
PT 1966 Active 1 emp. MTO
Modern 6/74 • Classical guitar 10–25
to date 1–10 per year

Framus of Nashville
2596 Bransford Ave., Box 40412, Nashville,
Tenn. 37204
Maker of steel-string guitars † 5/76

Framus-Phila Music Co., Inc.
Limerick, Pa. 19468 † 2/75

Ray Frank
Schoolhouse Rd., West Lebanon, N. Y. 12195
Maker of strings † 2/76

Dr. Emanuel Frankel
Floral Park, N. Y. 11000
Maker of mandolins †

William Frankel
75 Grove St., Montclair, N. J. 07302 † 2/76

Franklin County Workshop
Also known as: Nicholas Kukick

Franklin Guitars
Rt. 1, Box 541, Sandpoint, Idaho 87834
FT 1975 Active 3 emp. IA
Modern and historical Brochure 2/78
• Steel-string guitar 10–25 to date †
• Primarily repairs • Also known as: Guitar's
Friend

Frank's Drum Shop
226 S. Wabash Ave., Chicago, Ill. 60604 † 2/75

Rod Fraser
Rt. 5, Sparta, Tenn. 38583 † 4/77

Franz Frederick
2221 Miami Trails, West Lafayette, Ind. 47906
† 2/76

Peach Frederick
Rt. 69, Mystic Hills, Winterport, Maine 04496
Maker of Appalachian dulcimers †   9/76

Stephen Freegard
P. O. Box 377, Cambria, Calif. 93428 †   1/75

David Freeman
26 Stony Brook Rd., Sherborn, Mass. 01770 †
2/76

Morris Freeman
P. O. Box 393, Paradise, Calif. 95969 †   2/76

S. D. Freeman, Jr.
R. D. 7, Box 28, Carlisle, Pa. 17013
FT   1970   Active   1 emp.   IA/MTO
Modern   9/76 • Violin   10– 25 to date   †
• Viola   1– 10 to date   † • Cello   1– 10 to
date   †

Rubin S. Frels Co.
210 E. Constitution, Victorio, Tex. 77901
FT   1950   Active   5 emp.   MTO
Modern   10/75 • Pipe organ   25– 50 to
date   1– 10 per year

Fret Shop
5210 S. Harper St., Chicago, Ill. 60615
Maker of strings †   2/76 • *1980: Inactive*

Fretted Industries, Inc.
1234 Sherman Ave., Evanston, Ill. 60202
Maker of steel-string guitars, 5-string
banjos, and mandolins †   1/77 • Also
known as: Washburn Guitars

Fret Works
Also known as: Steven Millhouse

John N. Fricker
52 Turtle Cove Ln., Huntington, N. Y. 11743
Maker of strings †   1/78

Stephen Frieg
1793 W. 31, Cleveland, Ohio 44113
Maker of tabors, tambourines, and
xylophones †

Max Frirsz
130 W. 57th St., New York, N. Y. 10019
Maker of violins †   2/76

Froggy Bottom Guitars
Also known as: Michael Millard

Mario Frosali
1229 S. Ridgeley Dr., Los Angeles, Calif. 90019
FT   1925   Active   1 emp.   IA
Modern and historical   9/75 • Violin
Over 50 to date   † • Cello   1– 10 to date
† • Bows   1– 10 to date   † • Viola   1– 10
to date   † • *1980: Inactive*

William Fry
5612 Lake Mendota Dr., Madison, Wis. 53705
FT   1965   Active   1 emp.   IA/MTO
Modern and historical   10/74 • Violin
25– 50 to date   1– 10 per year • Viola
10– 25 to date   1– 10 per year • Cello
10– 25 to date   1– 10 per year

Ed Fuchs
R. R. 1, Arnold, Mo. 63010 †   4/76

Carl Fudge
208 Ridge St., Winchester, Mass. 01890
FT   1963   Active   3 emp.   MTO
Historical   Brochure   9/74
• Harpsichord   10– 25 to date   †
• Virginal   1– 10 to date   †
• Clavichord   1– 10 to date   † • *1980:
Harpsichord   25– 50 to date • Virginal
10– 25 to date • Clavichord   25– 50 to date
• Clavichord kit   Over 50 to date   †*

John Fullenwider and Sons
822 S. W. 152 St., Seattle, Wash. 98166
FT   1964   Active   4 emp.   MTO
Modern   Brochure   4/76 • Violin   1– 10
to date   1– 10 per year • Primarily repairs

George Fullerton
Also known as: Earthwood, Inc.

William Fulton
3121 Dumas St., San Diego, Calif. 92106
PT   1965   Active   1 emp.   IA
Modern and historical   9/74 • Violin
25– 50 to date   1– 10 per year

James Furey
140 Geary St., San Francisco, Calif. 94108 †
2/76

Rodney J. Furgason
1901 W. 34th, Topeka, Kans. 66611
PT   1974   Active   1 emp.   MTO
Modern   3/75 • Classical guitar   1– 10 to
date   1– 10 per year • Steel-string guitar

1– 10 to date   1– 10 per year • 5-string banjo   1– 10 to date   1– 10 per year

John Gabbanelli
9402 Bevlyn, Houston, Tex. 77025
Maker of strings †   2/76

Charles W. Gadd
3773 Indian Trail, Orchard Lake, Mich. 48033
PT   Year?   Inactive   1 emp.   MTO
Historical   9/74 • Violin   1– 10 to
date   †

Norman Gadoury
106 Columbia St., Wakefield, R. I. 02879 †
2/78

Clark Gaiennie
81 Conwell Ave., Somerville, Mass. 02144
FT   1969   Active   1 emp.   MTO
Historical   9/77 • Psaltery   Over 50 to
date   † • Appalachian dulcimer   Over 50
to date   † • Steel-string guitar   1– 10 to
date   † • Viol   25– 50 to date   1– 10 per
year

Galanti Brothers, Inc.
581 Bergen Blvd., Ridgefield, N. J. 07657 †
2/75

Galaxie Guitars
138 N. W. Greeley, Bend, Ore. 97701
Maker of steel-string guitars †   11/77

Galizi and Sordoni
975 2d Ave., New York, N. Y. 10013 †   9/76

J. W. Gallagher and Son
P. O. Box 182, Wartrace, Tenn. 37183
FT   1966   Active   2 emp.   MTO
Modern   Brochure   6/74 • Steel-string
guitar   Over 50 to date   Over 50 per year

Russell Galloway
Box 252, Morganton, Ga. 30560
Maker of strings †   3/78

Larry Gamble
740 Manitou Blvd., Manitou Springs, Colo.
80829
Also known as: Cornucopia, Ltd.; Les
Slaughter

T. G. Gandy
2818 W. Lakeshore Dr., Tallahassee, Fla. 32313
FT   1962   Active   1 emp.   IA
Modern   1/77 • Violin   10– 25 to date   †
• Viola   1– 10 to date   † • Primarily
repairs

Don Gannuck
4216 Tarton Dr., Metairie, La. 70003
Maker of strings †   1/78

Ignacio Garabieta
25 Hayward Ave., Lexington, Mass. 02173
PT   1953   Active   1 emp.   MTO
Modern and historical   Brochure   6/74
• Steel-string guitar   10– 25 to date   †
• Cuartro   Over 50 to date   † • Ukulele
1– 10 to date   †

Asel Gardner
213 Sanders Ave., Kingwood, W. Va. 26537
PT   1966   Active   1 emp.   MTO
Historical   Brochure   9/74 • Hammered
dulcimer   Over 50 to date   1– 10 per year
• Also known as: The Gardner Brothers
(Asel, Worley M., and Willis Gardner)

Worley M. Gardner
1332 Cain St., Morgantown, W. Va. 26505
Also known as: Asel Gardner (The Gardner
Brothers)

Harry Garfield II
3511 Rittenhouse St. N. W., Washington, D. C.
20015
PT   1974   Active   1 emp.   MTO
Modern   4/75 • Appalachian dulcimer
1– 10 to date   1– 10 per year

Ralph Garhardt
Also known as: Unicorn Musical
Instruments

Joseph H. Gariepy
6708 Long Beach Blvd., Long Beach, Calif. 90805
†   4/75

Becky Garland
6410 Cornell, Indianapolis, Ind. 46220 †   2/76

Craig Garrison
5533 Mystic Ct., Columbia, Md. 21043
Maker of strings †   1/78

David William Garrison
938 Central Ave., Harrisonburg, Va. 22801
PT   1967   Inactive   1 emp.   MTO
Modern   6/74 • Veena   1–10 to date   †

Gar-Zim
762 Park Pl., Brooklyn, N. Y. 11216
Maker of strings †   5/76

Gordon A. Gasser
Box 819, Azusa, Calif. 91702
Maker of strings †   1/78

Arthur Gaudette
Wells Ave., Georgetown, Mass. 01833
PT   1972   Active   1 emp.   MTO
Historical   11/74 • 5-string banjo   1–10
to date   1–10 per year • Also known as:
American Banjo Co.

Gault's Violin Shop
5502 Kenilworth Ave., Riverdale, Md. 20840
FT   1932   Active   1 emp.   MTO
Modern   5/74 • Violin   Over 50 to date
1–10 per year • Viola   Over 50 to date
1–10 per year • Viola d'amore   Over 50 to
date   1–10 per year • Cello   1–10 to
date   1–10 per year • Viol   1–10 to
date   † • Viola da gamba   25–50 to
date   † • Troubador harp   1–10 to
date   † • Primarily repairs • *1980: 1916*
• Bass viol   1–10 to date   † • Classical
guitar   25–50 to date   † • Irish harp
1–10 to date   † • Not making troubador
harps • Also known as: Willis M. Gault

William A. Gautz
1972 El Dorado, Berkeley, Calif. 94707 †   2/76

Bob Gawley
2112 Elba St., Durham, N. C. 27705
PT   1973   Active   1 emp.   MTO
Modern and historical   1/76 • 5-string
banjo   1–10 to date   1–10 per year

Paul Geiger
4019 Edgeford Pl., Las Vegas, Nev. 89102
FT   1978   Active   1 emp.   IA/MTO
Modern   3/78 • Appalachian dulcimer
1–10 to date   † • Steel-string guitar
1–10 to date   † • Electric guitar   1–10 to
date   †

K. G. Gemeinhardt Co.
Box 788, Elkhart, Ind. 46514
FT   1956   Active   152 emp.
IA   Modern   Brochure   2/75 • Modern
flute   Over 50 to date   Over 50 per year
• Piccolo   Over 50 to date   Over 50 per
year

Bela Gemza
1282 Summit Dr., Mayfield Heights, Ohio 44124
FT   1925   Active   1 emp.   IA/MTO
Modern and historical   4/76 • Classical
guitar   Over 50 to date • Flamenco
guitar   10–25 to date • Steel-string
guitar   10–25 to date • 12-string guitar
10–25 to date • Lute   10–25 to date
• Violin   1–10 to date • Mandolin   1–10
to date • Appalachian dulcimer   1–10 to
date • All instruments   25–50 per year
• *1980: Not making violins, mandolins, and*
Appalachian dulcimers

Mark Steven Gendron
1119 W. McGee St., Greensboro, N. C. 27403
Maker of strings †   12/74

General Electro Music
Box 196, Northvale Industrial Pk., Northvale,
N. J. 07647
Maker of electronic pianos and electronic
organs †   2/76

Gentle Winds Flute Co.
4503 N. W. 6th St., Gainesville, Fla. 32601
FT   1974   Active   1 emp.   IA
Modern and historical   Brochure   11/75
• Flute   Over 50 to date   † • Fife   Over
50 to date   † • Baroque clarinet   1–10 to
date   † • Also known as: Fred G. Miller

Randy Gerke
5515 Cresthill Dr., Fort Wayne, Ind. 46804
PT   Year?   Inactive   1 emp.   MTO
Modern and historical   6/74 • 5-string
banjo   † • Steel-string guitar   †
• Primarily repairs

Fred Gerlach
2229 Glyndon Ave., Venice, Calif. 90291
Maker of strings †   8/74

Sheridan Germann
32 Chestnut St., Boston, Mass. 02108

FT 1972 Active 1 emp. IA
Historical Brochure 4/76
• Harpsichord † • Clavichord †
• Virginal † • *1980: No brochure*
• *Painting only*

John Germer
1791 Mt. Vernon Dr., San Jose, Calif. 95125
PT 1960 Active 1 emp. IA/MTO
Historical 4/76 • Harpsichord 1–10 to
date 1–10 per year • Clavichord 1–10
to date 1–10 per year • Viola da gamba
1–10 to date †

John Gertner
16 Harden Ave., Camden, Maine 04843
Maker of strings † 1/78

Getzen Co.
211 W. Centralia, Elkhorn, Wis. 53121
FT 1939 Active 90 emp. IA
Modern Brochure 2/75 • Cornet Over
50 to date Over 50 per year • Trumpet
Over 50 to date Over 50 per year • Slide
trombone Over 50 to date Over 50 per
year • Fluegelhorn Over 50 to date Over
50 per year • Valve trombone Over 50 to
date Over 50 per year • Baritone horn
Over 50 to date Over 50 per year • *1980:
Marching trumpet Over 50 to date Over
50 per year • Piccolo trumpet Over 50 to
date Over 50 per year*

Giardinelli Band Instrument Co.
1725 Broadway, New York, N. Y. 10019 † 2/75

Vittore E. Giardinieri
2444 Gardener Rd., Eagle Point, Ore. 97524
FT 1928 Active 1 emp. MTO
Modern 6/74 • Cello 25–50 to date
1–10 per year • Viola 25–50 to date
1–10 per year • Violin 10–25 to date
1–10 per year

David Gibson
Also known as: Bozeman-Gibson Co.

Gibson, Inc.
225 Parson St., Kalamazoo, Mich. 49007
FT 1894 Active 700 emp. IA
Modern Brochure 2/75 • Electric
guitar Over 50 to date Over 50 per year
• Mandolin Over 50 to date Over 50 per

year • 5-string banjo Over 50 to date
Over 50 per year • Steel-string guitar Over
50 to date Over 50 per year • Classical
guitar Over 50 to date Over 50 per year
• *1980: Not making steel-string guitars*

Julius Gido
6053 Springvale Dr., Los Angeles, Calif. 90042
FT 1957 Active 1 emp. MTO
Modern and historical 5/76 • Classical
guitar Over 50 to date 1–10 per year
• Lute 10–25 to date 1–10 per year
• Bandurria 1–10 to date †
• Tamburitza 1–10 to date †
• Vihuela 1–10 to date †

Paul Gifford
1046 Withington, Ferndale, Mich. 48220
FT 1973 Active 1 emp. MTO
Modern 9/74 • Hammered dulcimer
1–10 to date 1–10 per year

James H. Gilbert
39388 Monterey Way, Fremont, Calif. 94538
PT 1975 Active 1 emp. IA/MTO
Modern 1/78 • Steel-string guitar 1–10
to date 1–10 per year • Classical guitar
1–10 to date 1–10 per year • 5-string
banjo 1–10 to date 1–10 per year
• Mandolin 1–10 to date 1–10 per year
• Primarily repairs

John M. Gilbert
1485 La Honda Rd., Woodside, Calif. 94062
FT 1966 Active 1 emp. MTO
Modern 9/74 • Classical guitar 10–25
to date 1–10 per year • Primarily repairs
• *1980: Classical guitar Over 50 to date
10–25 per year • No repairs*

Thomas Gillespie
R. F. D. #2, West Branch, Iowa 52358
FT 1974 Active 1 emp. MTO
Modern and historical 4/76 • 5-string
banjo 1–10 to date † • Appalachian
dulcimer 1–10 to date † • Steel-string
guitar 1–10 to date † • Primarily
repairs

George Gilmore
1229 Waimanu St., Honolulu, Hawaii 96814
PT 1960 Active 1 emp. MTO
Modern and historical Brochure 4/76

• Steel-string guitar † 1–10 per year
• Lute † 1–10 per year • Viola da
gamba † 1–10 per year • Appalachian
dulcimer † 1–10 per year • Vihuela
† 1–10 per year • Cittern † 1–10 per
year • Pandora † 1–10 per year
• Orpharion † 1–10 per year • Also
known as: Guitar and Lute Workshop

John Tunnoch Gilmour III
6116 Dixie Hwy., Bridgeport, Mich. 48722
FT 1974 Active 1 emp. IA
Historical 6/75 • 5-string banjo †
• Appalachian dulcimer † • Also known
as: Old World Instruments

Neal K. Girard
53 Elm St., Apt. 3, Milford, N. H. 03055
Maker of strings † 1/78

Giulietti Accordion Corp.
Park Ave. South, New York, N. Y. 10003
Maker of accordions † 2/75

Glenn Giuttari
9 Chestnut St., Rehoboth, Mass. 02769
PT 1972 Active 1 emp. MTO
Historical 6/74 • Harpsichord 1–10 to
date 1–10 per year • Appalachian
dulcimer 1–10 to date 1–10 per year
• Psaltery 1–10 to date 1–10 per year
• *1980: Harpsichord 10–25 to date*
• *Psaltery 10–25 to date • Not making
Appalachian dulcimers*

Bob Givens
375 Pine Ave., Goleta, Calif. 93017
Maker of strings † 10/75

Givens-Gourley, Inc.
Wexford, Pa. 15090 † 2/76

H. G. Glaubitz
212 McCosh Rd., Clifton, N. J. 07000 † 2/76

William Russell Gleaves
738 N. Brandywine Ave., Schenectady, N. Y.
12308
FT 1971 Active MTO Modern and
historical 9/74 • Lute 1–10 to date †
• Classical guitar 1–10 to date †
• Bouzoukee 1–10 to date † •
Primarily repairs

Walter C. Glemann
26 Holly St., Cranford, N. J. 07016
Maker of strings † 1/78

Charlie Monroe Glenn
Rt. 2, Box 567, Beech Creek Rd., Banner Elk,
N. C. 28604
PT 1969 Active 1 emp. IA/MTO
Modern and historical 11/74
• Appalachian dulcimer † • 5-string
banjo Over 50 to date †

Clifford Glenn
Rt. 1, Sugar Grove, N. C. 28679
FT 1955 Active 1 emp. MTO
Modern and historical 4/76
• Appalachian dulcimer Over 50 to
date † • 5-string banjo Over 50 to
date †

Leonard Glenn
Rt. 1, Box 197, Sugar Grove, N. C. 28679
PT 1955 Active 1 emp. MTO
Modern and historical 4/76
• Appalachian dulcimer Over 50 to
date † • 5-string banjo Over 50 to
date †

George A. Gluck, Jr.
Also known as: Total Technology

Robert Godfried
3451 Giles Pl., #M-32, Bronx, N. Y. 10463
PT 1974 Active 1 emp. IA/MTO
Modern and historical 6/76
• Appalachian dulcimer 1–10 to date
1–10 per year • Psaltery 1–10 to date
1–10 per year

Golden Bells Music Co.
418 W. Evergreen Ave., Monrovia, Calif. 91016
FT 1949 Active 1 emp. IA/MTO
Modern Brochure 5/75 • Marimba
1–10 to date • Xylophone 1–10 to date
• Boomagong 1–10 to date • All
instruments 1–10 per year • Primarily
repairs • Also known as: Del Roper

Alan Goldstein
Also known as: B and G Instrument
Workshop

Robert Goldzweig
3052 Telegraph Ave., Berkeley, Calif. 94705

FT 1976 Active 1 emp. IA
Modern 4/76 • Steel-string guitar 1– 10
to date 1– 10 per year • Also known as:
Little Wing Guitars

Tom Golze
Stockton Springs, Maine 04981 † 9/76

Gon-Bops
2302 E. 38th St., Los Angeles, Calif. 90058
FT 1954 Active ? emp. IA
Modern Brochure 4/76 • Conga Over
50 to date Over 50 per year • Bongo
Over 50 to date Over 50 per year • Cow
bell Over 50 to date Over 50 per year

Joseph Gonzales
529 Indian Hill Blvd., Claremont, Calif. 91711
† 2/76

Jimmy L. Good
223 John St., Weston, W. Va. 26452
PT Year? Active 1 emp. MTO
Historical 10/74 • Appalachian
dulcimer Over 50 to date †

Ted Goodfellow
3455 Santa Rosa Ave., #73, Santa Rosa, Calif.
95401
Maker of penny whistles † 2/76

Goodman Drum Co.
141 Kneeland Ave., Yonkers, N. Y. 10705
FT 1940 Active 2 emp. IA
Modern Brochure 3/75 • Pedal
tympani 25– 50 to date † • Chain
tympani Over 50 to date †

David C. Goodrich
1045 Pearl St., Boulder, Colo. 80302
Maker of strings † 1/78

Theodore O. Goodrich
203 Robbins Ln., Newtown Square, Pa. 19073
PT 1977 Active 1 emp. MTO
Modern 3/78 • Steel-string guitar 1– 10
to date † • Electric guitar 1– 10 to
date † • Appalachian dulcimer 1– 10 to
date †

Goose Acres Thumbpiano Factory & Dulcimer Works
Also known as: Peter Smakula

Goose Nest Prairie Banjos
R. R. 1, Lerna, Ill. 62440
FT 1974 Active 1 emp. MTO
Modern and historical Brochure 2/77
• 5-string banjo † • Steel-string guitar
10– 25 to date † • Classical guitar 1– 10
to date † • Also known as: Thomas
William Phipps • *1980: 5-string banjo
10– 25 per year • Not making steel-string
and classical guitars*

David Gootnick
3 Trapello Rd., Belmont, Mass. 02178
PT 1976 Active 1 emp. MTO
Modern and historical 11/76 • Viola da
gamba 1– 10 to date 1– 10 per year
• Violin 1– 10 to date 1– 10 per year

Tom Gooze
R.F.D. 1, Box 113C, Franklin, Maine 04634
PT 1975 Inactive 1 emp. MTO
Historical 10/76 • 5-string banjo 1– 10
to date †

Russell Gordon
5437 La Jolla, Garland, Tex. 75043
Maker of strings † 1/78

William B. Gordon, Jr.
2879 N. W. Thurman, Portland, Ore. 97210
PT 1963 Inactive 1 emp. MTO
Modern 3/78 • Classical guitar Over 50
to date † • Appalachian dulcimer
10– 25 to date †

Herb Gorey
77 Causeway St., Hudson, Mass. 01749 † 2/76

Gorish Violin Shop
3821 S. Shepherd, Houston, Tex. 77006
Maker of violins † 2/76

J. T. Gotjen
7 Lyndon St., Warren, R. I. 02885 † 4/78
1980: Not making instruments

Carl Gotzmer
Rt. 2, Box 2286A, La Plata, Md. 20646
FT 1967 Active 1 emp. IA
Modern and historical 7/74 • Autoharp
1– 10 to date 1– 10 per year
• Appalachian dulcimer Over 50 to
date Over 50 per year • Clavichord

1–10 to date   1–10 per year
• Harpsichord   1–10 to date   1–10 per
year • 5-string banjo   1–10 to date   †
• Steel-string guitar   1–10 to date   †

Hugh Gough, Inc.
80 Fifth Ave., New York, N. Y. 10011
Maker of harpsichords †   2/76 • *1980:*
Clavichord   †

Roger D. Gough
Rt. 3, Box 198, Charlottesville, Va. 22901
FT   1975   Active   1 emp.   MTO
Historical   Brochure   2/76
• Harpsichord   1–10 to date   †
• Forte-piano   1–10 to date   †
• Clavichord   1–10 to date   †

Jan Gould
Box 111, Gila, N. M. 88038
Maker of strings †   9/76

Govox, Inc.
1318 W. Oak St., Kissimmee, Fla. 32741
PT   1962   Active   3 emp.   IA
Modern   Brochure   1/78
• Guitar-organ   1–10 to date   † • Also
known as: James Borell

John T. Graber
Rt. 2, Box 2660, Bonita Springs, Fla. 33923
FT   1918   Active   1 emp.   IA
Modern and historical   6/74 • Violin
Over 50 to date   25–50 per year

Dennis Grace
3052 Telegraph Ave., Berkeley, Calif. 93305
Maker of steel-string guitars †   1/77
• *1980: Inactive*

John S. Graham, Jr.
315 Bear Creek Rd., Sarver, Pa. 16055
Maker of strings †   3/78

Roy Graham
Also known as: Lark in the Morning

Dr. Louis L. Grand
Box 198 G, R. D. 1, New Paltz Rd., Highland,
N. Y. 12528
PT   1964   Active   1 emp.   IA/MTO
Historical   9/74 • Violin   10–25 to
date   1–10 per year • Viola   1–10 to

date   † • *1980: FT • Viola   25–50 to*
date   1–10 per year

Grand Piano Co., Inc.
P. O. Box 1238, Morganton, N. C. 28655
Also known as: Kincaid Pianos

Robert S. Grant, Jr.
1806 W. Plain, San Antonio, Tex. 78227
PT   1977   Active   1 emp.   MTO
Modern and historical   2/78 • Steel-string
guitar   1–10 to date   † • Electric
guitar   †

Grassroots Music Shop
Also known as: Charles G. Whitcomb

Grassroots Productions
Box 22, Hartwick, N. Y. 13348
PT   1962   Inactive   1 emp.   MTO
Modern and historical   5/76 • 5-string
banjo   10–25 to date   † • Steel-string
guitar   1–10 to date   † • Mandolin
1–10 to date   † • *1980: Active*
• *Autoharp   1–10 to date   † • Also known*
as: Andrew Wallace

Tom Gravelin
Box 72, Nerstrand, Minn. 55053
PT   1974   Active   1 emp.   MTO
Modern and historical   5/78 • Steel-string
guitar   1–10 to date   1–10 per year
• Appalachian dulcimer   1–10 to date
1–10 per year • Hurdy-gurdy   1–10 to
date   † • Autoharp   1–10 to date   †
• 5-string banjo   1–10 to date   1–10 per
year

Chester Gray
Box 465, Plainfield, Ohio 43836
Maker of strings †   2/76

Gary Gray
110½ 1st Ave., Coralville, Iowa 52241
PT   1971   Active   1 emp.   IA/MTO
Modern   Brochure   6/74 • Kalimba   †

John Gray
813 N. Neil St., Champaign, Ill. 61820
FT   1967   Active   1 emp.   MTO
Modern and historical   12/74 • Strings   †
• Primarily repairs • *1980: IA/MTO*
• *Steel-string and electric guitars   †*
10–25 per year

GRD Instruments
Also known as: Charles Fox

Great Lakes Banjo Co.
1342 N. Main, Ann Arbor, Mich. 48104
FT   1974   Active   4 emp.   IA/MTO
Modern and historical   Brochure   12/74
• 5-string banjo   Over 50 to date   † • Also
known as: Dennis Lake; Michael Smith;
Mark Zimmerman

Great Lakes Dulcimers
Also known as: Edward A. Damm and Anne
Damm

David H. Green
Also known as: Aeolian Workshop

Gerald Green, Jr.
1643 Wurts Ave., Ashland, Ky. 41101 †   11/76

Robert Greenberg
340 Moore St., Santa Cruz, Calif. 95060
FT   1974   Active   1 emp.   IA/MTO
Historical   10/75 • Harpsichord   1–10 to
date   1–10 per year

Blaine Greene
Rt. 1, Box 175A, Johnson City, Tenn. 37601
PT   1963   Active   1 emp.   MTO
Historical   4/76 • Appalachian
dulcimer   10–25 to date   † • Steel-string
guitar   1–10 to date   † • Violin   10–25
to date   †

Edward R. Greene
3 Emerson St., Sanford, Maine 04073
PT   1969   Active   1 emp.   MTO
Historical   10/75 • Clavichord   1–10 to
date   † • Harpsichord   1–10 to date   †
• Virginal   1–10 to date   † • Lute   1–10
to date   †

Green Mt. Guitar & Banjo Workshop
Also known as: Stuart Flavell

Green River Dulcimers
Also known as: William P. Walker

Sidney Greenstein
6307 Acorn St., San Diego, Calif. 92115 †   2/76

Greenwood Organ Co.
P. O. Box 12254, Charlotte, N. C. 28205
FT   1964   Active   3 emp.   MTO
Modern   4/75 • Pipe organ   Over 50 to
date   1–10 per year

Gregoire Harpsichord
Charlemont, Mass. 01339
FT   1946   Active   5 emp.   IA
Modern and historical   Brochure   5/74
• Harpsichord   Over 50 to date   †
• Spinet   Over 50 to date   † • Also known
as: Sassman Harpsichords

Gregory Musical Instrument Corp.
3650 Dyre Ave., Bronx, N. Y. 10466 †   2/75

Gress-Miles Organ Co., Inc.
Washington Rd., Princeton, N. J. 08540
Maker of organs †   2/76 • *1980: FT
1959   Active   12 emp.   MTO   10/80 •
Pipe organ   1–10 to date   †*

The Fred Gretsch Co.
1801 Gilbert Ave., Cincinnati, Ohio 45202
FT   1883   Active   250 emp.   IA
Modern   Brochure   12/77 • Drum   Over
50 to date   Over 50 per year • Steel-string
guitar   Over 50 to date   Over 50 per year
• 5-string banjo   Over 50 to date   Over 50
per year • Also known as: Baldwin Piano
Co.; Ode Banjos

John Greven
111 4th Ave. North, Nashville, Tenn. 37219
FT   1971   Active   2 emp.   IA/MTO
Modern   1/77 • 5-string banjo   Over 50 to
date • Harpsichord   1–10 to date
• Mandolin   1–10 to date • Steel-string
guitar   25–50 to date • All instruments
10–25 per year

W. T. Griffin
401 St. Helens, Apt. 3B, Tacoma, Wash. 98402
Maker of strings †   1/78 • *1980: Inactive*

Owen E. Griffith
Rt. 2, Box 204, Greenup, Ill. 62428
FT   1965   Active   1 emp.   MTO
Historical   4/77 • Steel-string guitar
1–10 to date   † • 5-string banjo   10–25
to date   † • Violin   1–10 to date   †
• Mandolin   1–10 to date   † • Primarily
repairs • Also known as: The Fiddle Barn;
Odot Instruments

Griffith Piano Co.
605 Broad St., Newark, N. J. 07102
Maker of pianos †   2/76

Stephen Grimes
3413 Fremont Ave., Seattle, Wash. 98103
FT   1971   Active   1 emp.   IA/MTO
Modern   9/74 • Mandolin   10–25 to
date   1–10 per year

Russell Groethe
[?], Vt. 00000
Maker of keyboards †

Richard Gronning
2026 Flint Ln., Eagan, Minn. 55122
FT   1974   Active   1 emp.   MTO
Historical   2/78 • Steel-string guitar
1–10 to date   † • Lute   10–25 to date
10–25 per year

James Grossman
315 Columbia St., Brooklyn, N. Y. 11231
FT   1964   Active   1 emp.   MTO
Historical   5/74 • Cornet   Over 50 to
date   † • Primarily repairs

Grossman Music Corp.
1278 W. 9th St., Cleveland, Ohio 44113
Also known as: Crestline Guitars

Gary Grout
Rt. 4, Box 14, Poulsbo, Wash. 98370 †   2/78

George Gruhn
410 Broadway, Nashville, Tenn. 37203
FT   1970   Active   8 emp.
MTO   Modern and historical   Brochure
4/76 • Steel-string guitar   10–25 to date
† • Electric guitar   1–10 to date   †
• Primarily repairs • Also known as: GTR,
Inc. • 1980: 17 emp. • Also known as: Gruhn
Guitars, Inc.

Gryphon Stringed Instruments
4041 El Camino Way, Palo Alto, Calif. 94306
FT   1970   Active   2 emp.   MTO
Modern and historical   6/74 • Steel-string
guitar   25–50 to date   † • Mandolin
10–25 to date   † • Appalachian
dulcimer   1–10 to date   † • 5-string
banjo   † • Primarily repairs • Also known
as: Franklin Ford; Richard Johnston

GTR, Inc.
Also known as: George Gruhn

GTR Products, Inc.
42 Jackson Dr., Cranford, N. J. 07016
FT   1969   Active   200 emp.   IA
Modern   Brochure   4/76 • Chord
organ   Over 50 to date   Over 50 per year

Dennis Guglielmo
259 Bleecker St., New York, N. Y. 10014 †   2/76

Guild Musical Instruments
225 W. Grand St., Elizabeth, N. J. 07202
FT   1952   Active   ? emp.   IA
Modern   Brochure   4/75 • Steel-string
guitar   †

Guitar and Banjo Workshop
70 Turner Hill Rd., New Canaan, Conn. 06840
Maker of strings †   2/76

Guitar and Lute Workshop
Also known as: George Gilmore; Donald C.
Marienthal; Ervin Somogyi

The Guitar Farm
Also known as: Raymond Miller

Guitar Hospital
310 Eversham Rd., Glendora, N. J. 08029
PT   1968   Active   3 emp.   MTO
Modern   3/75 • Classical guitar   1–10 to
date   † • Steel-string guitar   10–25 to
date   † • Electric guitar   25–50 to date
† • 1980: 1230 S. 13th St., Philadelphia, Pa.
19147 • Modern and historical • Classical
guitar   25–50 to date • Steel-string
guitar   Over 50 to date • Electric guitar
Over 50 to date • Violin and viola   10–25
to date   † • Bass bows   10–25 to date †

The Guitar Lab
Also known as: Charles Lo Bue

Guitar's Friend
Also known as: Franklin Guitars

Guitar Shop
Also known as: Carl Barney

The Guitar Shop
Also known as: R. E. Brune

The Guitar Works
809 Pacific Ave., Santa Cruz, Calif. 95051
Maker of steel-string guitars †   1/77
• *1980: FT   1975   Active   2 emp.*
IA/MTO   Modern   10/80 · Electric guitar
and electric bass guitar   25–50 to date
10–25 per year · Not making steel-string
guitars

Guitar Workshop
233 N. Pleasant, Amherst, Mass. 01002
Maker of strings †   2/76

The Guitar Workshop
Also known as: Rick Boling

Guitorgan
Also known as: MCI, Inc.

Gulbransen Industries, Inc.
8501 W. Higgins Rd., Chicago, Ill. 60631
FT   1904   Active   400 emp.   IA
Modern   Brochure   6/74 • Electronic
organ   Over 50 to date   Over 50 per year
• Also known as: CBS Musical Instruments

Jackson Guldan
1439 Olentangy River Rd., Columbus, Ohio
43212 †   2/76

Shannon Gunn
2060 Gorton St., Beloit, Wis. 53511 †   4/76

Michael Gurian
Canal St., Hinsdale, N. H. 03451
FT   1964   Active   1 emp.   IA/MTO
Modern and historical   Brochure   5/74
• Classical guitar   Over 50 to date   †
• Lute   Over 50 to date   †

Steven K. Gustafson
Also known as: D. Ross Vaughan and Steven
K. Gustafson

Marvin L. Guthrie
Rt. 1, Box 407, Bonners Ferry, Idaho 83805
PT   1942   Active   1 emp.   IA/MTO
Modern   4/78 • Violin   25–50 to date
1–10 per year

John Guttenberg
2092 Massachusetts Ave., Cambridge, Mass.
02139
Maker of violins †   12/77

The Gyld
R. F. D. 2, Box 200, West Branch, Iowa 52358
FT   1975   Active   2 emp.   IA/MTO
Modern   Brochure   10/75 • Modern
flute   1–10 to date   1–10 per year • Also
known as: Paul Krumm

Ron Haas
6797 Soquel Dr., Aptos, Calif. 95003
FT   1968   Active   1 emp.   MTO
Historical   11/74 • Harpsichord   1–10 to
date   1–10 per year • Clavichord   25–50
to date   1–10 per year

Stephan Habekoss
430 Judah St., San Francisco, Calif. 94122 †
2/76

Daniel Hachez
10351 4th St. N. W., Alameda, N. M. 87114
FT   1971   Active   1 emp.   MTO
Historical   10/75 • Lute   Over 50 to
date   10–25 per year • Chitarrone   1–10
to date   † • Flamenco guitar   1–10 to
date   †

Ronald J. Hachez
Box 3171, Newport Beach, Calif. 92663
FT   1973   Active   1 emp.   IA/MTO
Modern and historical   10/75 • Classical
guitar   10–25 to date • Flamenco guitar
1–10 to date • Baroque guitar   1–10 to
date • Vihuela   1–10 to date • Lute   †
• All instruments   1–10 per year • *1980:*
Brochure · Classical guitar   Over 50 to
date   10–25 per year · Flamenco guitar
10–25 to date   1–10 per year · Vihuela
10–25 to date   1–10 per year · Lute
1–10 to date   1–10 per year · All
instruments   10–25 per year

Richard Hacker
14036 S. E. 38th, Bellevue, Wash. 98006 †   2/76

Haddorff Pianos
Also known as: Krakauer Brothers

Frederick Haenel
Merryall, New Milford, Conn. 06776
PT   1917   Inactive   1 emp.   MTO
Modern and historical   5/76 • Violin
25–50 to date   †

Frank Haensel
116-08 95th Ave., Richmond Hill, N. Y. 11419
Maker of strings † 1/78

Hagler Banjo Craftsmen
51 S. E. Ronald, P. O. Box 738, Winston, Ore.
97496
FT 1970 Active 2 emp. IA/MTO
Modern and historical Brochure 5/76
• 5-string banjo 10– 25 to date †
• Mandolin 1– 10 to date † • Violin
1– 10 to date † • Also known as: Cleve and
Tim Hagler • *1980: 5-string banjo Over 50
to date • Mandolin Over 50 to date
• Violin Over 50 to date 10–25 per year
• Steel-string guitar † • Repairs*

Hagstrom Guitars
33 Frost St., Westbury, N. Y. 11590
Maker of steel-string guitars, classical
guitars, electric guitars, and electric bass
guitars † 2/75

Thomas Vose Haile
3238 Beals Branch Rd., Louisville, Ky. 40206
PT 1946 Active 1 emp. MTO
Historical 12/74 • 5-string banjo 1– 10
to date 1– 10 per year • Steel-string
guitar 1– 10 to date 1– 10 per year
• Appalachian dulcimer 10– 25 to date
1– 10 per year • Violin 1– 10 to date †

Haile Guitars
605 4th St. Blvd., Tomkinsville, Ky. 42167
FT 1969 Active 2 emp. MTO
Historical 11/74 • Classical guitar Over
50 to date 10– 25 per year • Steel-string
guitar Over 50 to date 1– 10 per year

Bill Halback
Rt. 2, Box 255 A, Gainesville, Fla. 32601 † 2/76

Halcyon Studios
Also known as: Q. J. Bailey

Charles Haldon
Box 47, Overlook Dr., Bolinas, Calif. 94924
Maker of strings † 2/76

Mike Hales
P. O. Box 159, Paducah, Tex. 79248
Maker of strings † 1/78

Halifax Musical Instruments, Ltd.
1425 S. Salina St., Syracuse, N. Y. 13205
Electronic organs Over 50 to date Over
50 per year

Don E. Hall, Jr.
102 W. Lincoln, Searcy, Ariz. 72143
Maker of strings † 1/78

Jack Reed Hall
Rt. 3, Box 170, Whitesburg, Ky. 41858
Maker of Appalachian dulcimers † 2/76

James Newell Hall
3825 25th Ave. South, Minneapolis, Minn.
55406
PT 1975 Active 1 emp. MTO
Modern 2/78 • 5-string banjo 1– 10 to
date • Appalachian dulcimer 1– 10 to
date • Electric guitar 1– 10 to date
• Steel-string guitar 1– 10 to date • All
instruments 1– 10 per year • Primarily
repairs • Also known as: Big Horn Guitars

Merle Hall
5975 N. W. Oakwood Pl., Des Moines, Iowa
50324
PT 1974 Active 1 emp. MTO
Modern 4/76 • 5-string banjo 1– 10 to
date †

Wesley Hall
11845 E. 86th St., Indianapolis, Ind. 46236
PT 1973 Active 1 emp. MTO
Modern 4/76 • Appalachian dulcimer
25– 50 to date †

Hallet & Davis Piano Co.
Also known as: Aeolian Corp.

Oscar Halvorsen
1824 Granger Ave., Wilmington, Calif. 90747
Maker of strings † 10/74

Roy Ham
1219 N. Frye Ave., Newton, N. C. 28658
PT 1940 Active 1 emp. IA/MTO
Modern and historical 3/78
• Appalachian dulcimer Over 50 to
date † • Violin 10– 25 to date †
• Steel-string guitar Over 50 to date †

Ken Hamblin
P. O. Box 894, Salem, Va. 24153

PT 1974 Active 1 emp. IA/MTO
Modern Brochure 1/76 • Appalachian
dulcimer Over 50 to date 25–50 per
year • 5-string banjo 1–10 to date 1–10
per year

Leo Hamel
25 Queens Byway, Falmouth, Mass. 02540 †
2/76

Hammond Organ Co.
4200 Diversey, Chicago, Ill. 60639
FT Year? Active ? emp. IA
Modern Brochure 6/74 • Piano Over
50 to date Over 50 per year

James Hampton
170 W. 1st St., P. O. Box 243, Sherwood, Ore.
97223
FT 1976 Active 1 emp. IA
Modern and historical 2/78 • Steel-string
guitar 1–10 to date † • Cittern 1–10
to date † • Appalachian dulcimer 1–10
to date † • Also known as: The
Craftsman's Bench

Larry Hanks
3101 Pico Blvd., Santa Monica, Calif. 90405
Maker of strings † 2/76

Lynn Hannings and George Rubino
Hollowell Rd., Pownal, Maine 04069
FT 1972 Active 2 emp. IA/MTO
Modern and historical Brochure 10/76
• Bows Over 50 to date †

Hanover Stringed Instrument Co.
68 S. Main St., Hanover, N. H. 03755
Maker of strings † 1/77

Jack Hanson
1000 Harris, Bellingham, Wash. 98225
Also known as: Telegraph Music Works
• *1980: Inactive*

Hardman Peck & Co.
Also known as: Aeolian Corp.

Jay Hardy
13 E. Maple Ave., Bellmawr, N. J. 08031
PT 1975 Active 1 emp. MTO
Modern and historical 4/78
• Appalachian dulcimer 1–10 to date
1–10 per year • Hammered dulcimer

1–10 to date 1–10 per year • Steel-string
guitar 1–10 to date 1–10 per year
• Also known as: Armadillo Instruments

P. J. Hardy Musical Instruments
30462 County Rd., 12 West, Elkhart, Ind. 46514
FT 1949 Active ? emp. MTO
Modern Brochure 7/78 • Modern
flute Over 50 to date Over 50 per year
• Piccolo Over 50 to date Over 50 per
year

Harlin Brothers
359 N. Illinois St., Indianapolis, Ind. 46204 †
2/76

Leonard Harlos
5 Carolina Trail, Marshfield, Mass. 02050
Maker of strings † 2/76

Harmolin, Inc.
Box 244, La Jolla, Calif. 92037 † 2/75

Robert Wilson Harmon IV
P. O. Box 727, Blowing Rock, N. C. 28605
PT 1966 Active 2 emp. IA
Historical Brochure 4/76
• Appalachian dulcimer 25–50 to date
† • Also known as: The Dulcimer Den

Ted Harmon
Sugar Grove, N. C. 28679
Maker of strings † 2/76

Harps Unlimited
Also known as: Jay Witcher

Alan Harris
3 Clark St., Eastport, Maine 04631
Maker of strings † 2/76

Rodger Harris
9607 Stratford, Oklahoma City, Okla. 73120
PT 1973 Active 1 emp. MTO
Modern and historical 8/75
• Appalachian dulcimer 10–25 to date
1–10 per year

William Reed Harris
4285½ Olive Ave., La Mesa, Calif. 92041
FT 1975 Active 1 emp. MTO
Modern 1/77 • Steel-string guitar 1–10
to date † • Appalachian dulcimer 1–10
to date † • Electric guitar 1–10 to
date †

Benjamin F. Harrison, Jr.
2689 Coolidge, Berkley, Mich. 48072
FT 1960 Active 3 emp. IA
Modern and historical 9/74 • Violin
Over 50 to date 1–10 per year • Viola
1–10 to date †

Paul Hart
1167 Windsor, Salt Lake City, Utah 84105
FT 1967 Active 1 emp. MTO
Modern and historical 5/76 • Viol
25–50 to date 1–10 per year • Violin
1–10 to date 1–10 per year • Viola
10–25 to date 1–10 per year • Cello
10–25 to date 1–10 per year • Cittern
1–10 to date 1–10 per year • Lute
1–10 to date 1–10 per year • Viola
d'amore 1–10 to date 1–10 per year

Richard Hart
P. O. Box F, Arlington, Mass. 02174
FT 1967 Active 1 emp. IA/MTO
Historical Brochure 5/74 • Viola da
gamba Over 50 to date † • Viola
d'amore 1–10 to date † • Vielle
10–25 to date † • Strings Over 50 to
date †

Dr. William Hart
5237 Hewlett Dr., San Diego, Calif. 92115
Maker of strings † 2/76

John Hartley III
1532 N. W. 74 Terr., Hollywood, Fla. 33024
Maker of strings † 1/78

Steven H. Hartley
Orlando, Fla. 32800
Maker of steel-string guitars †

Jim Hartsell
Rt. 1, Box 438, Walland, Tenn. 37886
FT 1974 Active 1 emp. MTO
Modern 2/78 • Appalachian dulcimer
25–50 to date 10–25 per year

Albert Hash
Rt. 2, Mouth of Wilson, Va. 24363
PT 1927 Active 1 emp. MTO
Modern 6/74 • Violin 25–50 to date †
• Mandolin 10–25 to date † • 5-string
banjo 10–25 to date † • Appalachian
dulcimer 1–10 to date † • *1980: FT*
• *Violin Over 50 to date 1–10 per year*

• *Not making mandolins, 5-string banjos,
and Appalachian dulcimers*

Dale C. Hathaway
1814 Ridgeway, Colorado Springs, Colo. 80906
Maker of strings † 1/78

Eric Hathaway
Crouseville, Maine 04738 † 9/76

Scott Hauser
40065 Little Fall Creek Rd., Fall Creek, Ore.
97438
PT 1965 Active 5 emp. MTO
Modern 12/74 • Appalachian dulcimer
Over 50 to date 25–50 per year
• Autoharp 1–10 to date †
• Steel-string guitar 1–10 to date †
• Mandolin 1–10 to date † • 5-string
banjo 10–25 to date † • Also known as:
Livewood

Lt. Frank J. Hawkins
206 Union St., Occoquan, Va. 22125
PT 1971 Active 1 emp. MTO
Historical 6/74 • 5-string banjo 1–10 to
date 1–10 per year

Nick Hayden
1558 Jackson St., Aliquippa, Pa. 15001
PT 1966 Active 1 emp. IA
Historical 2/75 • Tamburitza †

Stephen Hayes
91 Jordan Rd., Colonia, N. J. 07067
FT 1974 Active 1 emp. MTO
Modern 1/77 • Octave guitar 1–10 to
date • Electric guitar 1–10 to date
• Electric bass guitar 1–10 to date
• Steel-string guitar 1–10 to date • All
instruments 1–10 per year • Primarily
repairs

Robert Haynes
4965 Rockwood Pkwy. N. W., Washington, D. C.
20016 † 2/76

William S. Haynes Flute Co., Inc.
12 Piedmont St., Boston, Mass. 02116
FT 1888 Active 47 emp. MTO
Modern Brochure 8/75 • Modern
flute Over 50 to date Over 50 per year
• Piccolo Over 50 to date Over 50 per
year

Dan Hebert
56 Little Falls Trailer Pk., Wappingers Falls,
N. Y. 12590
Maker of strings †   1/78

Louis V. Hegedus
15599 Peachwalker Dr., Bowie, Md. 20716
FT   1965   Active   1 emp.   MTO
Modern and historical   12/74 • Violin
10–25 to date   † • Primarily repairs

Chris Heineman
6 Church St., Burlington, Vt. 05401 †   2/78

David Heitzman
Box 147C, Cohasset Stage, Chico, Calif. 95926
PT   1970   Active   1 emp.   MTO
Modern and historical   9/74 • Electric
guitar   10–25 to date   1–10 per year
• Steel-string guitar   25–50 to date
1–10 per year • Harpsichord   1–10 to
date   † • Clavichord   1–10 to date   †
• Mandolin   †   1–10 per year

Frank V. Henderson
18445 16th Ave. N. W., Seattle, Wash. 98177
PT   1954   Active   1 emp.   IA
Modern   9/74 • Violin   25–50 to date
• Viola   1–10 to date • Cello   1–10 to
date • Bows   10–25 to date • All
instruments   1–10 per year • *1980: FT
IA/MTO • Violin   Over 50 to date • Bows
Over 50 to date   10–25 per year • All
instruments   10–25 per year*

Guy Fred Henderson
199 Amity St., Brooklyn, N. Y. 11201 †   2/76

Wayne Henderson
Rt. 2, Mouth of Wilson, Va. 24363
FT   1960   Active   1 emp.   MTO
Modern and historical   4/76 • Steel-string
guitar   25–50 to date   1–10 per year
• Mandolin   10–25 to date   1–10 per
year • 5-string banjo   1–10 to date   1–10
per year • *1980: PT • Steel-string guitar
Over 50 to date • Mandolin   25–50 to date*

Daniel Hendricks
Rt. 1, Box 193, Blue River, Wis. 53518
PT   1975   Active   1 emp.   MTO
Modern   3/78 • Steel-string guitar   1–10
to date   † • Appalachian dulcimer   1–10
to date   † • *1980: Steel-string guitar*

*1–10 per year • Appalachian dulcimer
1–10 per year • Hammered dulcimer
1–10 to date   1–10 per year • Classical
guitar   1–10 to date   1–10 per year*

Neil Hendricks
1920 Wilder, Reno. Nev. 89512
FT   1973   Active   1 emp.   MTO
Modern   Brochure   9/77 • Viola da
gamba   25–50 to date   † • Appalachian
dulcimer   25–50 to date   † • Bows
Over 50 to date   † • *1980: Viola da
gamba   Over 50 to date   10–25 per year
• Gamba bows   25–50 per year • Not
making Appalachian dulcimers • Also
known as: Early Strings*

Floyd Hendrickson
Lot 100, Stadium Mobile Homes, Key West, Fla.
33040
PT   1953   Active   1 emp.   IA/MTO
Historical   10/74 • Violin   25–50 to
date   1–10 per year

George Hendrickson
440 Maryland Ave., Norfolk, Va. 23508 †   8/74

S. J. Hendrickson
3104 Wintergreen Ave., District Heights, Md.
20028
FT   1960   Active   1 emp.   IA
Modern   4/76 • Steel-string guitar
25–50 to date   †• 5-string banjo   10–25
to date   †• Violin   1–10 to date   †
• Mandolin   1–10 to date   †•
Appalachian dulcimer   1–10 to date
†• Primarily repairs

Patrick Henly
10159 Prospect Ave., Chicago, Ill. 60643
Maker of Uilleann pipes †

Eugene E. Henn
1316 Berwin Ave., Kettering, Ohio 45429
PT   1950   Active   1 emp.   MTO
Historical   4/76 • Violin   1–10 to date
†• Primarily repairs

Arnold Henning
1302 Washington Ave., Kalamazoo, Mich. 49001
PT   1973   Active   1 emp.   MTO
Modern and historical   1/76 • Classical
guitar   10–25 to date • Steel-string
guitar   1–10 to date • Lute   1–10 to date

• Bajo sexto   1– 10 to date • All
instruments   1– 10 per year

H.E. Products, Inc.
920 S. Logan St., Mishawaka, Ind. 26544 †
2/76

Here, Inc.
410 Cedar Ave., Minneapolis, Minn. 55404
FT   1968   Active   3 emp.   IA/MTO
Modern and historical   Brochure   5/74
• Appalachian dulcimer   Over 50 to
date   Over 50 per year • 5-string banjo
Over 50 to date   10– 25 per year
• Psaltery   Over 50 to date   10– 25 per
year • Kalimba   Over 50 to date   25– 50
per year • Also known as: Dave Erler; Len
MacEachron; Craig Peterson

Heritage Dulcimers
Main St., Phoenicia, N.Y. 12464
Maker of Appalachian dulcimers †   4/76

Bruce Herman
7240 Glengary Pl., Takoma Park, Md. 20012
PT   1973   Active   1 emp.   IA/MTO
Modern and historical   4/75 • Classical
guitar   1– 10 to date   †• Steel-string
guitar   1– 10 to date   †• Appalachian
dulcimer   1– 10 to date   †

Erwin Hertel
Carnegie Hall, 56 St. and 7 Ave., New York, N.Y.
10019
FT   1951   Active   2 emp.   IA/MTO?
Historical   6/74 • Violin   †• Primarily
repairs

Eric Herz Harpsichords, Inc.
12 Howard St., Cambridge, Mass. 02139
FT   1955   Active   ? emp.   MTO
Modern and historical   Brochure   6/74
• Harpsichord   Over 50 to date   25– 50
per year • Clavichord   1– 10 to date
1– 10 per year • *1980: 7 emp.   IA/MTO
Historical · Clavichord   10– 25 to date*

Stanley Hess
1631 32d, Des Moines, Iowa 50312
PT   1976   Active   1 emp.   IA
Modern and historical   1/77 • Mandora
1– 10 to date • Cittern   1– 10 to date
• Kit   1– 10 to date • Appalachian
dulcimer   1– 10 to date • Recorder

10– 25 to date • All instruments   1– 10 per
year • *1980: IA/MTO   Brochure
· Appalachian dulcimer   10– 25 per year ·
All instruments   10– 25 per year*

Hettinger Guitars, Ltd.
Plain Rd., R.F.D. I, Berlin, N. H. 03570
PT   1975   Active   1 emp.   MTO
Modern   12/77 • Steel-string guitar
1– 10 to date   1– 10 per year • Classical
guitar   1– 10 to date   1– 10 per year

Al Hewitt
1528 Elizabeth Rd., Vacaville, Calif. 95688
Maker of strings †   1/78

Vern Hickerson
715 Scott Ave., Bemidgi, Minn. 56601
FT   1918   Active   1 emp.   IA/MTO
Historical   5/74 • Violin   Over 50 to
date   10– 25 per year • Viola   1– 10 to
date   †

Floyd Hicks
Rt. 3, Box 658, Banner Elk, N.C. 28604
PT   1924   Active   1 emp.   IA
Historical   5/74 • 5-string banjo   Over 50
to date   †• Appalachian dulcimer   Over
50 to date   †

Jim D. Hicks
4129 Vicksburg, North Highlands, Calif. 95660
Maker of strings   †   3/78

Stanley Hicks
Rt. 2, Vilas, N.C. 28692
PT   1932   Active   1 emp.   MTO
Historical   5/74 • Appalachian
dulcimer   †• 5-string banjo   †

Hidden Valley Harps
Also known as: Lee Yoder

Larry Higgins
484 Frederick St., San Francisco, Calif. 94114
PT   1970   Active   1 emp.   MTO
Modern and historical   7/74 • Steel-string
guitar   1– 10 to date • Classical guitar
1– 10 to date • Baroque guitar   1– 10 to
date • Vihuela   1– 10 to date • Lute
1– 10 to date • All instruments   1– 10 per
year

David G. Hild
1356 Lake Rd., New Carlisle, Ohio 45344
Maker of strings † 1/78

Barney Hill
4413 Primrose Ln., Kettering, Ohio 45429
Maker of strings † 1/78

Keith Hill
2037 S. Division Ave., Grand Rapids, Mich.
49507
FT 1973 Active 1 emp. IA/MTO
Historical 5/74 • Harpsichord 10–25 to
date †

Kenny Hill
208 San Jose Ave., Capitola, Calif. 95010
FT 1972 Active 2 emp. IA
Modern 2/78 • Appalachian dulcimer
25–50 to date †• Harpsichord 1–10 to
date †• Clavichord 1–10 to date
†• Classical guitar 1–10 to date 1–10
per year

Richard Hill
38693 Logan Dr., Fremont, Calif. 94536
PT 1965 Active 1 emp. IA/MTO
Historical 9/74 • Classical guitar
25–50 to date 1–10 per year • Flamenco
guitar 10–25 to date 1–10 per year
• Steel-string guitar 1–10 to date
†• Baroque guitar 1–10 to date †

Norman L. Hills
247 56th, Des Moines, Iowa 50312
PT 1968 Active 1 emp. IA
Modern 2/78 • Classical guitar 1–10 to
date †• *1980: Inactive*

Chet Hines
9760 E. Hasket Ln., Dayton, Ohio 95424
Maker of Appalachian dulcimers † 2/76

Hinger Touch-Tone Corp.
Box 232, Leonia, N.J. 07605
FT 1973 Active 4 emp. MTO
Modern Brochure 2/78 • Tympani
Over 50 to date 25–50 per year • Snare
drum Over 50 to date Over 50 per year
• *1980: Tympani Over 50 per year*

J. Steele Hinton III
P.O. Box 207, Flemington, Ky. 41041
Maker of strings † 1/78

Martin Hird
180 Riverside Dr., New York, N.Y. 10024
PT 1972 Active 1 emp. IA
Historical 6/74 • Viola 1–10 to date
1–10 per year

Harold Hirsch
756 Amalfi Dr., Pacific Palisades, Calif. 90272
PT 1967 Active 1 emp. IA
Modern 5/76 • Violin 10–25 to date
1–10 per year • Viola 1–10 to date
1–10 per year • *1980: IA/MTO Modern
and historical*

Historical Brass Workshop
Also known as: Richard Cook

Historical Instruments
Also known as: David R. Brooks

Historical Stringed Instruments
Also known as: Robert Smith

John Hitter
Dearborn, Mich. 48100 †

William N. Hockenberry
408 Westinghouse Ave., North Versailles, Pa.
15137
FT 1966 Active 1 emp. IA/MTO
Historical Brochure 12/77 • Violin
Over 50 to date 1–10 per year • Viola
1–10 to date †• Bass violin 1–10 to
date †• Also known as: Matchmaker
Violin • *1980: Bows Over 50 to date Over
50 per year • Not making violins, violas, and
bass violins*

Tony Hoeber
8695 S.W. Firland Terr., Portland, Ore. 97223
Maker of strings † 1/78 • *1980: Inactive*

Thomas E. Hoeffgen
Rt. 3, Winfield, Kans. 67156
FT 1972 Active 1 emp. IA
Modern 1/76 • Classical guitar 1–10 to
date †• Dobro 1–10 to date
†• Electric guitar 1–10 to date
†• Appalachian dulcimer 1–10 to date †

John Henry Hoerster
522 Pleasant Creek Rd., Rogue River, Ore. 97537
PT 1920 Active 1 emp. MTO
Historical 10/74 • Violin 1–10 to
date †

Charles A. Hoffman
Also known as: Bellville and Hoffman

David Hoffman
P.O. Box 20, Independence, Va. 24348
PT 1975 Active 2 emp. IA/MTO
Modern Brochure 4/78 • Appalachian
dulcimer 25–50 to date 10–25 per year
• Also known as: Razor Ridge Workshop

Mark Hoffman
Box 201, Moretown, Vt. 05660
PT 1975 Active 1 emp. MTO
Modern 6/78 • Appalachian dulcimer
1–10 to date †• Electric guitar 1–10 to
date †• Classical guitar 1–10 to date
†• Steel-string guitar 1–10 to date
†• Dobro 1–10 to date †• Primarily
repairs

Hoffman Guitars
Also known as: Bellville and Hoffman

Virgil Hoffses
33 Harbor View Ave., South Portland, Maine
04106
PT 1972 Active 1 emp. MTO
Modern Brochure 1/77 • Steel-string
guitar 1–10 to date 1–10 per year

Willy Hofmann
306 E. 12th St., Kansas City, Mo. 64106
Maker of strings † 6/75

Kirk Hogan
459 Bacon Ave., Webster Groves, Mo. 63119
FT 1976 Active 1 emp. MTO
Modern and historical 2/78
• Appalachian dulcimer 1–10 to date †
• Primarily repairs • Also known as:
Rosewood Lutherie

Hog Fiddle Music Co.
27 W. Main, Lexington, Ohio 44904
Maker of strings † 11/77

Ben Hogue
307 W. 16th, Austin, Tex. 78701
FT 1975 Active 1 emp. IA
Modern 2/78 • Mandolin 1–10 to
date 1–10 per year • Steel-string guitar
1–10 to date 1–10 per year
• Appalachian dulcimer 1–10 to date
1–10 per year • 1980: MTO Brochure

• Mandolin 10–25 to date • Steel-string
guitar 10–25 to date • Classical guitar
1–10 to date 1–10 per year

Paul Hohman
3700 Taft Ave., Alexandria, Va. 22304 † 2/76

Ed Holick
c/o Mossman, Rt. 3, Strothersfield, Winfield,
Kans. 67156
Maker of strings † 3/78

Holland Organ Co., Inc.
2317B Plainfield Ave., Plainfield, N. J. 07036
FT 1968 Active 2 emp. MTO
Modern Brochure 6/75 • Electronic
organ †

David Holle
Also known as: Coll Divine Flutes

Mary Holle
Also known as: Coll Divine Flutes

Clyde Hollifield
Rt. 1, Box 221, Old Fort, N. C. 28762
FT 1971 Active 1 emp. MTO
Modern and historical 4/74
• Gourdamer 1–10 to date • Epinette
1–10 to date • Appalachian dulcimer
25–50 to date • Mandolin 1–10 to date
• Autoharp 1–10 to date • Zither 1–10
to date • All instruments 10–25 per year

Holloway Pipe Organs
823 Massachusetts Ave., Indianapolis, Ind.
46204
FT 1888 Active 15 emp. MTO
Modern Brochure 10/75 • Pipe organ
Over 50 to date 10–25 per year

Henry Hollwedel, Jr.
Bushy Hill Rd., Ivoryton, Conn. 06442
PT 1965 Active 2 emp. MTO
Historical Brochure 4/75
• Rope-tensioned drum Over 50 to date
10–25 per year

Dan Holm
Fargo, N. Dak. 58102
Maker of violins † 6/78

Raymond Holsclaw
188 King St., Charleston, S. C. 29401

PT 1970 Active 1 emp. MTO
Modern 5/74 • Classical guitar 10–25
to date 1–10 per year

Holsman Instruments
4736 17th St., San Francisco, Calif. 94117 †
4/76
1980: FT 1972 Active 1 emp.
IA/MTO Modern and historical 10/80
• Steel-string guitar 25–50 to date †
• Classical guitar 1–10 to date †
• Electric guitar 1–10 to date †
• Appalachian dulcimer 25–50 to date
† • Hammered dulcimer 1–10 to date †
• Psaltery 25–50 to date †

Alan Holt
General Delivery, Searsmont, Maine 04973
Maker of strings † 1/78

Stan Holt
R.R. #3 Newton, Ill. 62448
Maker of strings † 1/78 • *1980: Deceased*
(8/78)

Holtkamp Organ Co.
2909 Meyer Ave., Cleveland, Ohio 44109
FT 1855 Active 24 emp. MTO
Modern 6/75 • Pipe organ Over 50 to
date 1–10 per year • *1980: Pipe organ*
10–25 per year

Frank Holton & Co.
Also known as: G. LeBlanc Corp.

Carl C. Holzapfel
222 W. Fayette St., Baltimore, Md. 21201 †
2/76

Tom Hom
37A Bedford St., New York, N. Y. 10014
PT 1969 Active 1 emp. MTO
Modern 5/74 • Classical guitar 10–25
to date • Lute 1–10 to date • All
instruments 1–10 per year

Home Spun Song Shop
Also known as: J. P. Jenks

Honahlee Dulcimer
Also known as: William Louis Masasso

Hondo Guitar Co.
P. O. Box 2344, Fort Worth, Tex. 76101
Maker of steel-string guitars † 1/77

John T. Honeycutt
408 Hermosa Dr. S. E., Albuquerque, N. M.
87108
PT 1967 Active 1 emp. MTO
Historical 6/74 • Violin 1–10 to date †

Robert T. Hood
Rt. 3, Box 90, Brighton, Tenn. 38011
PT 1967 Active 1 emp. MTO
Historical 1/78 • Classical guitar
25–50 to date 1–10 per year • Flamenco
guitar 1–10 to date 1–10 per year
• Violin 1–10 to date 1–10 per year
• Strings 1–10 to date 1–10 per year
• *1980: Temporarily inactive*

W. G. Hood
3932 W. Maricopa, Phoenix, Ariz. 85009 †
4/78
1980: PT 1959 Inactive 1 emp.
Historical 10/80 • Violin Over 50 to
date †

Basil J. Hooker
129 E. Garvey, Monterey Park, Calif. 91754
FT 1967 Active 1 emp. MTO
Modern and historical 9/75 • Violin
10–25 to date † • Viola 1–10 to date
† • Cello 25–50 to date † • Harp
1–10 to date †

Edgar Hoover
15331 Bohlman Rd., Saratoga, Calif. 95070
PT 1952 Active 1 emp. MTO
Historical 9/77 • Psaltery 1–10 to date
• Viola d'amore 1–10 to date • Tromba
marina 1–10 to date • Rebec 1–10 to
date • Viola da gamba 1–10 to date
• Baroque violin 1–10 to date • All
instruments 1–10 per year • *1980: Viola*
da gamba 10–25 to date

Richard Hoover
Also known as: Otis B. Rodeo; Santa Cruz
Guitar Co.

John Hoppe
1712 N. High St., Columbus, Ohio 43201
Maker of strings † 2/76

Dave Horine
1400 Elm St., Cincinnati, Ohio 45210
Maker of strings † 2/76

Guy Horn
P. O. Box 977, Carmel, Calif. 93921
Maker of strings †   1/78

Michael Hornpipe
201 Church Rd., Ardmore, Pa. 19003
FT   1975   Active   1 emp.   IA
Modern and historical   10/75 • Chanter
10–25 to date   † • Shawm   10–25 to
date   † • Irish war pipe   1–10 to date   †
• Bagpipe   1–10 to date   † • Fife
25–50 to date   † • Also known as: Michael
Jig

William Horowitz
2849 W. Jerome Ave., Chicago, Ill. 60645
PT   Year?   Active   1 emp.   IA
Modern   1/78 • Classical guitar   10–25
to date   1–10 per year

Joe Horvath
Cleveland, Ohio 44100 †

Marian Horvath
320 156 Pl., Calumet City, Ill. 60409
Maker of classical guitars †   12/77

Tom Hosmer
726 Euclid Ave., Syracuse, N. Y. 13210
FT   1970   Active   1 emp.   MTO
Modern   7/74 • 5-string banjo   1–10 to
date   † • Primarily repairs

House of Musical Traditions
Also known as: Henry Levin

Adrianus J. M. Houtsma
3 Ames St., Cambridge, Mass. 02139 †   6/74
*1980: PT   1973   Inactive   1 emp.
Modern   10/80 • Classical guitar   1–10
to date   † • Steel-string guitar   1–10 to
date   †*

Ben Huang
5710 S. Woodlawn, Chicago, Ill. 60637
Maker of strings †   1/78

Frank Hubbard
185A Lyman St., Waltham, Mass. 02154
FT   1949   Active   10 emp.   IA/MTO
Historical   Brochure   10/74
• Harpsichord   Over 50 to date   †

John R. Huber
P. O. Box 23, Nazareth, Pa. 18064 †   2/76

Carl W. Hubert
3303 E. 44th St., Minneapolis, Minn. 55406
Maker of strings †   12/74

Peter Hudd
1205 W. Groverner St., Springfield, Ill. 62704
Maker of strings †   2/76

A. D. Hudgens
P. O. Box 236, White Oak, Tex. 75693
FT   1970   Active   1 emp.   MTO
Modern   12/77 • Classical guitar   †
• Appalachian dulcimer   † • Primarily
repairs

Richard P. Hughes, Jr.
Hotchkiss School, Lakeville, Conn. 06039
PT   1968   Active   1 emp.   MTO
Historical   5/74 • Aeolian harp   1–10 to
date   †

Hughes Dulcimer Co., Inc.
4419 W. Colfax, Denver, Colo. 80204
FT   1962   Active   8 emp.   IA/MTO
Modern and historical   Brochure   5/74
• Appalachian dulcimer   Over 50 to
date   Over 50 per year • 5-string banjo
Over 50 to date   Over 50 per year • Folk
harp   Over 50 to date   Over 50 per year
• Hammered dulcimer   Over 50 to date
Over 50 per year

David Hummer and Karl D. Wienand
Pine Brook Hills, Boulder, Colo. 80302
PT   1974   Active   1 emp.   MTO
Historical   4/75 • Portative organ   1–10
to date   † • Also known as: Karl D.
Wienand

Scott Humphrey
5588 Brave Chief Ln., Ravenna, Ohio 44266
FT   1971   Active   1 emp.   MTO
Modern   11/74 • Steel-string guitar
1–10 to date   † • Appalachian dulcimer
1–10 to date   † • Hammered dulcimer
1–10 to date   † • Hurdy-gurdy   1/10 to
date   †

Thomas Humphrey
54 Spring St., New York, N. Y. 10012
FT   1970   Active   1 emp.   IA
Historical   5/74 • Classical guitar
10–25 to date   10–25 per year
• Steel-string guitar   1–10 to date   †

David Hunt
3723 E. 11th, Spokane, Wash. 99202
Maker of strings †   1/78

Clyde Hunter
Charles St., Lyndonville, Vt. 05851 †   9/76

Fred Hunter
652 California, #B, Mountain View, Calif. 94040
Maker of strings †   1/78

F. Jack Hurley
Memphis State University, Memphis, Tenn.
38152 †   2/76

Carleen Hutchins
112 Essex Ave., Montclair, N. J. 07042
FT   1947   Active   1 emp.   IA/MTO
Modern   Brochure   7/75 • Viola   Over
50 to date • Cello   1–10 to date • Violin
10–25 to date • Bass violin   25–50 to date
• New (catgut) violin   25–50 to date • All
instruments   10–25 per year • *1980: 3
emp. • Viola   1–10 per year • Cello   1–10
per year • Violin   1–10 per year • Bass
violin   1–10 to date   1–10 per year • New
(catgut) violin   1–10 per year*

Frank Hutchinson
Hollywood, Fla. 33000 †

Robert D. Hutchinson
Also known as: North Country Music Store

H. E. Huttig
P. O. Box 603, Kendall Branch, Miami, Fla.
33156
PT   1956   Active   1 emp.   MTO
Modern and historical   6/74 • Steel-string
guitar   1–10 to date • Balalaika   1–10 to
date • Cuatro   1–10 to date
• Medialuna   1–10 to date • All
instruments   1–10 per year • Primarily
repairs • Also known as: Allied Traders of
Miami

Anthony J. Huvard
Box 30698, Seattle, Wash. 98103
Maker of strings †   3/78 • Also known as:
Northwest School of Instrument Design

Andrew Huzela
75 Place Plan, Donara, Pa. 15033
PT   1966   Active   1 emp.   IA/MTO

Modern   4/76 • Flamenco guitar   1–10
to date   1–10 per year • Steel-string
guitar   1–10 to date   1–10 per year
• Bouzoukee   1–10 to date   1–10 per
year • Balalaika   1–10 to date   1–10 per
year • Mandolin   1–10 to date   †

Max Hyndman
5631 S. Lawrence, Tacoma, Wash. 98409
Maker of strings †   1/78

Imperial Accordion Mfg. Co.
38504 Riverside Dr., Mount Clemens, Mich.
48043
Maker of accordions †   2/76

Imperial Banjo Co.
2527 S. W. 59th, Oklahoma City, Okla. 73119
Maker of 5-string banjos †   4/76 • *1980:
FT   1970   Active   2 emp.   MTO
Modern   Brochure   10/80 • 5-string
banjo   Over 50 to date   Over 50 per year
• Also known as: Ty and Mona Piper*

Indian Jim
208 Carlester Dr., Los Gatos, Calif. 95030
PT   1956   Active   1 emp.   MTO
Historical   1/76 • American Indian
drums, rattles, flutes, whistles, clappers,
and Apache violins   † • Also known as:
American Indian Arts

John T. Ingalls
378 Somerville Ave., Somerville, Mass. 02143
FT   1974   Active   1 emp.   IA/MTO
Modern and historical   4/76 • Baroque
flute   10–25 to date   † • Renaissance
flute   Over 50 to date   † • Bamboo
flute   25–50 to date   † • Ceramic flute
Over 50 to date   † • North and South
Indian flute   10–25 to date   † • Also
known as: Karsen & Ingalls

Kermit Ingraham
Box 361, Lima, N. Y. 11485
PT   1974   Active   1 emp.   MTO
Modern   2/78 • Steel-string guitar   1–10
to date   † • Electric guitar   1–10 to
date   † • Appalachian dulcimer   1–10 to
date   †

The Instrument Guild, Inc.
Box 254, Lexington, Mass. 02173
Maker of harpsichords †   2/76 • Also

known as: Caleb Warner • *1980: FT
1956   Active   IA/MTO   Modern
Brochure   10/80 • Virginal, spinet,
dulcimers, and chamber pipe organ
25–50 to date*   †

Instruments for Meditation and Celebration
Also known as: Natraj

Intermountain Guitar and Banjo
370 W. 1st South, Salt Lake City, Utah 84101
FT   1965   Active   2 emp.   IA/MTO
Historical   Brochure   10/75 • 5-string
banjo   Over 50 to date   10–25 per year
• Also known as: Leonard W. Coulson III
• *1980: 5-string banjo   25–50 per year*

International Musical Instruments, Inc.
Marion, N. C. 28752 †   2/75

Iorio Accordion Corp.
42-71 Steinway St., Long Island City, N. Y. 11103
Maker of accordions †   2/75

Howard Irving
P. O. Box 164, Cobden, Ill. 62920
PT   1973   Active   1 emp.   MTO
Modern and historical   1/77 • Steel-string
guitar   1–10 to date   † • Electric
guitar   1–10 to date   †

Douglas Irwin
3625 Sebastopol Rd., Santa Rosa, Calif. 95401
FT   1973   Active   2 emp.   IA/MTO
Modern and historical   3/75 • Electric
guitar   25–50 to date   † • Electric bass
guitar   25–50 to date   † • Steel-string
guitar   1–10 to date   †

Lew Irwin
1284 Florence, Galesburg, Ill. 61401
PT   1963   Active   1 emp.   MTO
Modern and historical   4/76 • 5-string
banjo   1–10 to date   † • Mandolin
1–10 to date   † • Steel-string guitar
1–10 to date   †

Irwin and Son Piano Co.
6 Greenvale Dr., Rochester, N. Y. 14618
Maker of pianos †   2/76

Norman E. Isaac
11210 Sprague Rd., Parma, Ohio 44130 †   5/76

Robert Isenbanger
P. O. Box 36, Dola, Ohio 45835 †   2/78

Italo-American Accordion Mfg. Co.
3137 W. 51st St., Chicago, Ill. 60632
Maker of accordions †   2/75

Ivers & Pond Piano Co.
Also known as: Aeolian Corp.

Capt. Derek Iverson
812 Chestnut St., Cheny, Wash. 99004
PT   1971   Active   1 emp.   MTO
Modern   5/74 • 5-string banjo   1–10 to
date   1–10 per year • Classical guitar
1–10 to date   1–10 per year • Steel-string
guitar   1–10 to date   1–10 per year
• Appalachian dulcimer   1–10 to date
1–10 per year

Richard Izzo
1520 Longleaf Dr., P. O. Box 1204, Thomasville,
Ga. 31792
Maker of strings †   1/78

Richard L. Jacks
601 34th Pl., Fort Madison, Iowa 52627
Maker of strings †   2/76

M. Eli Jackson
R. R. #1, Parker City, Ind. 47368
PT   1974   Active   1 emp.   MTO
Historical   4/77 • Appalachian
dulcimer   10–25 to date   † • Hammered
dulcimer   1–10 to date   †

Chester James
701 W. Rancho, Phoenix, Ariz. 85013 †   2/76
*1980: PT   1962   Active   1 emp.
IA/MTO   Modern   10/80 • Guitars,
Appalachian dulcimer, Irish harp, and
zither*   †

Clarence R. James
1352 Castelton Rd. North, Columbus, Ohio
43220
PT   1974   Active   1 emp.   IA
Modern and historical   4/76 • Recorder
1–10 to date   † • *1980: Recorder   Over 50
to date   10–25 per year*

Lester L. James
3719 E. Wyoming Ave., Las Vegas, Nev. 89104

FT 1964 Active 1 emp. IA/MTO
Modern 4/75 • Violin 10–25 to date
1–10 per year • *1980: 1974 • Violin 25–50
to date • Viola 1–10 to date 1–10 per
year*

Cliff Jamison

7276 S. Dexter St., Littleton, Colo. 80122
Maker of strings † 1/78

J and D Resonator Co.

P. O. Box 112, Paramount, Calif. 90723 † 2/76

John Janke

3132 Sandalwood Ct., Lafayette, Calif. 94549
PT 1948 Active 1 emp. MTO
Modern and historical 9/74 • Violin
1–10 to date † • Steel-string guitar
1–10 to date † • Lute 1–10 to date †
• Viola da gamba 1–10 to date †
• *1980: Classical guitar 1–10 to date †
• Rebec 1–10 to date † • Dulcimer
1–10 to date † • Not making steel-string
guitars*

John Jannotti

1111 S. Hull, Westchester, Ill. 60153
Maker of strings † 3/78

Stephen Janofsky

519 E. 86th St., New York, N. Y. 10028
Maker of strings † 1/78

Timothy Jansma

3055 Ramshorn Dr., Freemont, Mich. 49412
FT 1976 Active 1 emp. IA/MTO
Modern and historical 11/76 • Violin
1–10 to date 1–10 per year • Viola
1–10 to date 1–10 per year • Cello
10–25 to date 10–25 per year • Bass
violin 1–10 to date 1–10 per year

John Janzegers

6906 Parkwood St., Landover Hills, Md. 20784
PT 1971 Active 1 emp. MTO
Historical Brochure 4/76 • 5-string
banjo 10–25 to date 1–10 per year

Jasper Corp.

Jasper, Ind. 47546 † 2/76

Jean's Dulcimer Shop

Also known as: Jean and Lee Schilling

A. W. Jeffreys, Inc.

232 W. Frederick St., Staunton, Va. 24401
PT 1956 Active 4 emp. IA/MTO
Modern and historical Brochure 5/74
• Appalachian dulcimer Over 50 to
date Over 50 per year • Kit 1–10 to
date † • Harpsichord 1–10 to date †
• Mandolin 1–10 to date †

Jenco Musical Products

Also known as: Decatur Instruments

J. P. Jenks

131 E. Kalamazoo Ave., Kalamazoo, Mich.
49006
PT 1971 Active 2 emp. MTO
Modern 11/74 • Appalachian dulcimer
25–50 to date † • Also known as: Home
Spun Song Shop

Dane Jensen

2700 S. 30th, Bellingham, Wash. 98225
PT 1971 Active 1 emp. MTO
Modern and historical 10/74
• Appalachian dulcimer 1–10 to date †
• Steel-string guitar 1–10 to date †
• Primarily repairs

J-Folks Dulcimers

5477 McCords, Alto, Mich. 49302
PT 1972 Active 2 emp. IA/MTO
Historical 2/78 • Appalachian
dulcimer Over 50 to date † • *1980:
Brochure • Appalachian dulcimer Over 50
per year • Also known as: Jack and Shirley
Folkertsma*

Michael Jig

Also known as: Michael Hornpipe

Charles Jirousek

4424 Regent St., Duluth, Minn. 55804
FT 1972 Active 2 emp. MTO
Modern 5/74 • 12-string guitar 1–10 to
date 1–10 per year • Steel-string guitar
1–10 to date 1–10 per year • Also known
as: Arrowhead Music; Brian Morgan

Joe Farmer's Music

Also known as: Troy Fish

Brian and Mary Lou Johnson

2745 5th Ave., Sacramento, Calif. 95818
Maker of strings † 1/78

Carl Albanus Johnson
1909 Wilson Ave., Chicago, Ill. 60640 † 10/76

Charles V. Johnson
3689 University, San Diego, Calif. 92104
PT 1924 Active 1 emp. IA
Modern 10/74 • Violin Over 50 to
date 10– 25 per year • *1980: 1919
• Violin 1– 10 per year*

D. Ray Johnson
126 S. Wilson Ave., Dunn, N. C. 28334
PT 1930 Active 1 emp. IA
Modern Brochure 1/78 • Steel-string
guitar †

Erik A. Johnson II
6925 Pasadena, Cheyenne, Wyo. 82001
Maker of steel-string guitars and lutes
(primarily repairs) † 2/77 • *1980: FT
Active 1 emp. IA/MTO Modern and
historical 10/80 • Flamenco guitar,
classical guitar, and lute † • Not making
steel-string guitars*

Frank A. Johnson
917 Hawthorne Ln., Aberdeen, Wash. 98520
PT 1973 Inactive 1 emp. MTO
Modern and historical 2/75 • 5-string
banjo 1– 10 to date † • Mandola
1– 10 to date †

Louis Johnson
Rt. 1, Box 64, Elk, Wash. 99009
PT Year? Active 1 emp. MTO
Modern 12/74 • Classical guitar 1– 10
to date † • *1980: Hobbyist*

Mary Lou Johnson
Also known as: Brian and Mary Lou Johnson

Paul Johnson
P. O. Box 417, Austin, Tex. 78767
FT 1973 Active 1 emp. IA
Modern Brochure 3/78 • Occarina
Over 50 to date Over 50 per year • Also
known as: Little Flutes

Thomas F. Johnson
2409 S. Lake Michigan Dr., Rt. 5, Sturgeon Bay,
Wis. 54235
FT 1967 Active 1 emp. MTO
Modern and historical 4/76 • Classical
guitar 25– 50 to date 10– 25 per year

• Flamenco guitar 10– 25 to date 1– 10
per year • Steel-string guitar 1– 10 to
date † • Appalachian dulcimer †

Johnson Organ Co., Inc.
806 NP Ave., Box 1228, Fargo, N. Dak. 58107
FT 1954 Active 10 emp. MTO
Modern and historical Brochure 10/75
• Pipe organ Over 50 to date 1– 10 per
year • Band organ 10– 25 to date 1– 10
per year

David Johnston
125 19th Ave., San Francisco, Calif. 94121
PT 1973 Active 1 emp. MTO
Modern 7/74 • Steel-string guitar 1– 10
to date 1– 10 per year • Appalachian
dulcimer 1– 10 to date 1– 10 per year
• Mandolin 1– 10 to date 1– 10 per year
• Electric guitar 1– 10 to date 1– 10 per
year

Neil M. Johnston
Box 225, Tenino, Wash. 98589
PT 1970 Active 1 emp. MTO
Modern 4/76 • Violin 1– 10 to date
1– 10 per year • Bows 1– 10 to date †
• Primarily repairs • *1980: Deceased*

Richard Johnston
Also known as: Gryphon Stringed
Instruments

Woodie Johnston
132 E. Fulton, Grand Rapids, Mich. 49502 †
2/76

Danny F. Jones
405 N. Washington, Livingston, Tex. 77351
PT 1971 Active 2 emp. MTO
Historical 4/76 • Steel-string guitar
1– 10 to date † • Appalachian dulcimer
1– 10 to date † • 5-string banjo 1– 10 to
date † • Also known as: The Fingerboard

Freeman Jones
2002 E. 13th St., Tucson, Ariz. 85719
FT 1973 Active 1 emp. MTO
Modern and historical 5/74
• Appalachian dulcimer 25– 50 to date
25– 50 per year

Glenn L. Jones
P. O. Box 521, San Marcus, Calif. 92069
Maker of strings † 1/78

Sam Jones
1705 Shieffer, Austin, Tex. 78722
FT   1973   Active   2 emp.   IA/MTO
Modern   4/78 • 5-string banjo   10–25 to
date   1–10 per year • Steel-string guitar
1–10 to date   1–10 per year • Also known
as: Flashy Banjo Works; Scott Hauser • *1980:*
PT   1 emp.

William Jones
Also known as: Alpine Dulcimer Co.

Jones-Clayton Harpsichords, Inc.
3421 Glendale Blvd., Pasadena, Calif. 90039
Maker of harpsichords †   3/76

Bob Jordan
Also known as: Takoma Banjo Works

David Jorgenson
2065 Leif St., Muskegon, Mich. 49441
Maker of strings †   1/78

Eugene Joseph
Anawan St., Rehoboth, Mass. 02769
Maker of Appalachian dulcimers and
hurdy-gurdies †   2/76

Joyful Noise Dulcimers
Also known as: Dave Murray

The Joynery
Also known as: Donald K. Polifka, Jr., and
Judy Polifka

Bruce R. Kahn
704 Towne House Village, Hauppauge, N. Y.
11787
Maker of strings †   1/78

McWilliam Kaiserling
273 Ellington Ave., San Francisco, Calif. 94112
†   2/76

Stephen Kakos
1412 18th Ave. North, Minneapolis, Minn. 55411
Maker of strings †   1/78 • *1980: FT*
1972   Active   1 emp.   MTO   Modern
10/80 • Classical guitar   Over 50 to date
10–25 per year

Steve Kalb
Box 24, Bearsville, N. Y. 12409
Maker of strings †   2/76

Hideo Kamimoto
330 14th St., Oakland, Calif. 94612
Maker of strings †   2/76

Wayne Kamp
6410 Cornell, Indianapolis, Ind. 46220 †   2/76

Jeff Kamps
R. R. 3, Rochelle, Ill. 61068
Maker of strings †   1/78

Michael Barry Kanner
2205 Felt St., P. O. Box 2586, Santa Cruz, Calif.
95062
FT   1971   Active   3 emp.   IA
Historical   6/75 • Bamboo flute   Over 50
to date   Over 50 per year

Kantele Guitars
Sunset Blvd., Los Angeles, Calif. 90000
Maker of steel-string guitars †

Jay Kantor
532 Fifth St., Brooklyn, N. Y. 11215
Maker of keyboards †   11/77 • *1980: FT*
1975   Active   1 emp.   MTO
Historical   Brochure   10/80 • Baroque
and Renaissance woodwinds   25–50 to
date   † • Not making keyboards

Kapa Guitars
7221 Wisconsin Ave., Bethesda, Md. 20014
Maker of steel-string guitars †   2/76

Wilhelm Kapfhammer
1265 Bryan Ave., Salt Lake City, Utah 84105
FT   1956   Active   1 emp.   MTO
Modern and historical   6/76 • Violin
25–50 to date   1–10 per year • Viola
10–25 to date   1–10 per year • Cello
1–10 to date   1–10 per year

Andy Kardos
Box 34, Harpers Ferry, W. Va. 25425
PT   1970   Active   1 emp.   IA
Modern and historical   12/74
• Appalachian dulcimer   10–25 to date
1–10 per year • 5-string banjo   10–25 to
date   10–25 per year

Karpek Accordion Mfg. Co.
820 S. 16th St., Milwaukee, Wis. 53204
Maker of accordions †   2/75 • *1980: FT*
1915   Inactive   2 emp.   IA   Modern

*Brochure   10/80 · Accordion and
concertina   † · Importing only*

Karsen & Ingalls
Also known as: John T. Ingalls

Joseph and Nancy Kasik
Star Rt., Vida, Ore. 97488
FT   1970   Active   2 emp.   IA
Modern   10/74 · Bamboo flute   Over 50
to date   Over 50 per year · Shakuhachi
Over 50 to date   Over 50 per year
· Duoinitza   10–25 to date   10–25 per
year

Kasino
908 W. Chestnut, Chanute, Kans. 66720
Maker of strings †   2/76 · *1980: Now
known as: Kustom Gretsch/A Division of
Baldwin Piano and Organ*

Thomas J. Kaster
Box 1711, Aspen, Colo. 81611
Maker of strings †   1/78

Henryk Kaston
10 Woodland Ave., White Plains North, N. Y.
10603
Maker of violins †   2/76

Don Katz
Box J, Marlboro, Vt. 05344
FT   1966   Active   1 emp.   MTO
Historical   4/75 · Harpsichord   25–50 to
date   1–10 per year

Robert Katz
7571 Caminito de Oivay, San Diego, Calif. 92111
PT   1962   Active   1 emp.   MTO
Modern   9/74 · Violin   1–10 to date   †
· Appalachian dulcimer   1–10 to date   †

C. O. Kauffman
1238 S. Parton, Santa Ana, Calif. 92707
PT   1928   Active   1 emp.   MTO
Modern   3/75 · Electric guitar   Over 50
to date   † · Steel-string guitar   Over 50 to
date   †

Kay Musical Instrument Co.
3057 N. Rockwell Ave., Chicago, Ill. 60618
Maker of steel-string guitars †   1/78

KCS Enterprises
Also known as: K. C. Schmidt

Robert Keans
318 E. McArthur, Appleton, Wis. 54911 †   2/76

J. B. Keith
108 Billy Byrd Dr., Clinton, Miss. 39056
PT   1972   Active   1 emp.   IA/MTO
Modern and historical   2/78
· Appalachian dulcimer   Over 50 to
date   10–25 per year · Hammered
dulcimer   1–10 to date   † · *1980: FT ·
Appalachian dulcimer   Over 50 per year
· Not making hammered dulcimers*

George Kelishek
Brasstown, N. C. 28901
FT   1955   Active   2 emp.   IA
Modern and historical   Brochure   4/76
· Viola da gamba   Over 50 to date   1–10
per year · Lute   Over 50 to date   1–10
per year · Hurdy-gurdy   Over 50 to date
1–10 per year · Appalachian dulcimer
Over 50 to date   25–50 per year
· Krumhorn   Over 50 to date   25–50 per
year · Cornett   Over 50 to date   25–50
per year · Also known as: Workshop of
Historical Instruments

Helmuth A. Keller
1701 Pine St., Philadelphia, Pa. 19103
FT   1948   Active   2 emp.   IA/MTO
Modern and historical   6/74 · Viola
Over 50 to date   1–10 per year · Violin   †
· Cello   † · *1980: 4 emp. · Violin   25–50
to date   1–10 per year · Cello   1–10 to
date   1–10 per year*

James Kelly
Moravia, N. Y. 13118 †   2/76

Ritch Kelly
Box 23, Jefferson, Md. 21755
FT   1969   Active   1 emp.   IA
Modern and historical   Brochure   4/75
· Steel-string guitar   25–50 to date   †
· Appalachian dulcimer   Over 50 to
date   † · Drum   Over 50 to date   †
· Strings   Over 50 to date   † · Also known
as: Dromedary Musical Instruments

Michael Kemnitzer
P. O. Box 712, Nederland, Colo. 80466
FT   1976   Active   1 emp.   IA/MTO
Modern and historical   2/78
· Appalachian dulcimer   10–25 to date

10–25 per year • Mandolin   10–25 to
date   10–25 per year • 5-string banjo
10–25 to date   1–10 per year

Bob Kemper
627 S. Flood, Norman, Okla. 73069 †   2/76

Wayman A. Kendall and Son
505 S. Fir Ave., Roswell, N. M. 88201
PT   1965   Active   3 emp.   MTO
Modern   10/74 • Mandolin   1–10 to
date   † • 5-string banjo   1–10 to date   †
• Violin   1–10 to date   • Steel-string
guitar   25–50 to date   †

Jim Kendrick
Crouseville, Maine 04738 †   9/76

Bill Kennedy
Rt. 2, Box 233, Fairmont, W. Va. 26554
PT   1973   Active   2 emp.   IA/MTO
Historical   10/74 • Appalachian
dulcimer   25–50 to date   25–50 per year
• Also known as: L. Eugene Dickinson

Davis E. Kennedy
Drawer F, Athens, W. Va. 24712 †   2/76

Maurice Kent
336 W. Wellington, Chicago, Ill. 60657
Maker of strings †   3/76

Kentucky Hill Stringed Instrument Shop
Also known as: Ronald Lee Reuter

Richard Lee Kenyon
32 Almond Tree Ln., Irvine, Calif. 92664
Maker of strings †   2/76

John C. Kepley
14501 Hubbell, Detroit, Mich. 48227
Maker of strings †   2/76

Gil Kepner
27 Meacham Rd., #2, Somerville, Mass. 02144
PT   1968   Active   3 emp.   IA/MTO
Modern and historical   Brochure   6/75
• Steel-string guitar   25–50 to date
10–25 per year • Appalachian dulcimer
Over 50 to date   25–50 per year
• Hurdy-gurdy   1–10 to date   1–10 per
year • Harp   1–10 to date   1–10 per year
• 5-string banjo   10–25 to date   †
• Mandolin   1–10 to date   †
• Banjo-guitar   1–10 to date   †

Dr. Evan Kern
434 W. Main St., Kutztown, Pa. 19530
PT   1958   Active   1 emp.   IA/MTO
Modern   5/78 • Harpsichord   1–10 to
date   † • Clavichord   1–10 to date   †
• Lute   1–10 to date   † • Appalachian
dulcimer   10–25 to date   † • Steel-string
guitar   1–10 to date   † • *1980:
Harpsichord   1–10 per year
• Clavichord   1–10 per year • Appalachian
dulcimer   1–10 per year • Classical
guitar   1–10 to date   1–10 per year
• Upright harpsichord   1–10 to date
1–10 per year • Not making steel-string
guitars*

Michael C. O. Kerson
38 Lagoon Rd., Belvedere-Tiburon, Calif. 94920
†   2/76

Ralph Kester
Also known as: Drumland

Rupert Kettle
56 Wallinwood N. E., Grand Rapids, Mich.
49503
Maker of strings †   1/78 • *1980: FT
1976   Active   1 emp.   IA/MTO
Modern   10/80 • Classical guitar, vihuela,
Appalachian dulcimer, strings,
percussion   Over 50 to date   †*

Kharma Bodies
P. O. Box 82, West Hempstead, N. Y. 11552
Maker of electric guitars †   11/77 • *1980:
FT   1973   Active   1 emp.   IA/MTO
Modern   Brochure   10/80 • Electric
guitar   Over 50 to date   Over 50 per year*

John Kiersten
16 Spruce St., Pompton Lakes, N. J. 07442
Maker of strings †   1/78

J. R. Kilpatrick
P. O. Box 5092, North Texas State University,
Denton, Tex. 76203
PT   1956   Active   1 emp.   MTO
Historical   5/74 • Flute   25–50 to date
1–10 per year • Piccolo   25–50 to date
1–10 per year

Dean Kimball
2420 State Rt., #343, Yellow Springs, Ohio 45387
PT   1969   Active   1 emp.   IA/MTO

Modern and historical 2/75
• Appalachian dulcimer 1–10 to date †
• Classical guitar 1–10 to date †
• Violin 1–10 to date †

Kimball Piano and Organ Co.
1037 E. 15th St., Jasper, Ind. 47546
FT 1857 Active 4,000 emp. IA
Modern Brochure 4/76 • Piano Over
50 to date Over 50 per year • Electronic
organ Over 50 to date Over 50 per year

James Kimbel
125 Park Pl., Brooklyn, N. Y. 11212 † 11/76

Kincaid Pianos
Also known as: Grand Piano Co.

Don Kinch
5249 N. E. Sandy Blvd., Portland, Ore. 97213 †
2/76

Paul D. Kinderman
W. 607 First Ave., Spokane, Wash. 99204
Maker of strings † 1/78

Eric King
Box 4297, Berkeley, Calif. 94704
PT 1967 Active 1 emp. MTO
Modern and historical 6/74 • Bansuri
Over 50 to date 1–10 per year
• Shakuhachi Over 50 to date 1–10 per
year • Flute Over 50 to date 10–25 per
year • *1980: Peruvian flute Over 50 to
date 1–10 per year • Indian flute Over
50 to date 1–10 per year*

Geoffrey King
122 Maple St., West Orange, N. J. 07052
FT 1970 Active 1 emp. IA/MTO
Modern 5/74 • Classical guitar 1–10 to
date 1–10 per year • Steel-string guitar
1–10 to date 1–10 per year

King Banjos
Box 45A, Rt. 1, Tunnelton, W. Va. 26444
FT 1974 Active 1 emp. IA
Modern 10/74 • 5-string banjo 10–25
to date † • Steel-string guitar 1–10 to
date † • Appalachian dulcimer 1–10 to
date † • *1980: Box 313, Cotopaxi, Colo.
81223 • PT MTO Modern and
historical 10/80 • 5-string banjo Over 50
to date • Not making steel-string guitars
• Also known as: Paul King*

King Musical Instruments
33999 Curtis Blvd., Eastlake, Ohio 44094
FT 1893 Active 350 emp. IA
Modern Brochure 4/76 • French horn
Over 50 to date Over 50 per year
• Baritone horn Over 50 to date Over 50
per year • Euphonium Over 50 to date
Over 50 per year • Trombonium Over 50
to date Over 50 per year • Trombone
Over 50 to date Over 50 per year
• Trumpet Over 50 to date Over 50 per
year • Altonium Over 50 to date Over
50 per year • Sousaphone Over 50 to
date Over 50 per year • Bass horn Over
50 to date Over 50 per year • Cornet
Over 50 to date Over 50 per year •
Fluegelhorn Over 50 to date Over 50 per
year • Flute Over 50 to date Over 50 per
year • Piccolo Over 50 to date Over 50
per year • Clarinet Over 50 to date Over
50 per year • Saxophone Over 50 to
date Over 50 per year • Oboe Over 50 to
date Over 50 per year • Bassoon Over
50 to date Over 50 per year • Also known
as: Benge Trumpet Co.; Cleveland Musical
Instruments; Tempo Band Instruments
• *1980: Now known as: Benge Trumpet Co.;
DeFord Flutes; The H. N. White Co.*

John Kingan
3925 W. Osborn Rd., Phoenix, Ariz. 85019
FT 1965 Active 1 emp. MTO
Modern 8/74 • Classical guitar 10–25
to date 1–10 per year • Steel-string
guitar 1–10 to date 1–10 per year
• 5-string banjo 1–10 to date 1–10 per
year • Primarily repairs • *1980: PT*

Kingsbury Pianos
Also known as: Story and Clark Piano Co.

Craig Kingsley
R. F. D. 1, Box 224, West Baldwin, Maine 04091
PT 1975 Active 1 emp. IA
Modern and historical 10/76
• Appalachian dulcimer 10–25 to date
10–25 per year • *1980: Inactive*

J. William Kingsley
1738 Sotogrande, #208, Hurst, Tex. 76053
PT 1969 Active 1 emp. IA/MTO
Modern 3/75 • Classical guitar 10–25
to date 1–10 per year

Richard Kingston
212 S. Walton St., Dallas, Tex. 75226
FT   1970   Active   2 emp.   MTO
Historical   Brochure   5/74
• Harpsichord   25–50 to date   1–10 per
year

Kinhaven
545 W. 11th St., New York, N. Y. 10025 †   11/76

Pitt Kinsolving
7 Silk St., Norwalk, Conn. 06850 †   2/76

Russell P. Kirby
244 Boston Post Rd., Sudbury, Mass. 01776
PT   1959   Active   1 emp.   MTO
Historical   4/76 • Fife   Over 50 to date
25–50 per year • *1980: 1969*

Kirk's Musical Instruments
408 Winchester Rd., Huntsville, Ala. 35811
FT   1955   Active   4 emp.   MTO
Modern   6/75 • 5-string banjo   Over 50 to
date   25–50 per year • Steel-string
guitar   25–50 to date   † • Mandolin
25–50 to date   1–10 per year • Primarily
repairs • *1980: Mandolin   Over 50 to
date   10-25 per year • Not making
steel-string guitars • Also known as: Marion
Kenneth Kirk*

Charles N. Kish
2-A Kirby Rd., Saratoga Springs, N. Y. 12866
PT   Year?   Active   1 emp.   MTO
Modern   2/78 • Appalachian dulcimer
1–10 to date   †

B. F. Kitching and Co.
505 E. Shawmut Ave., La Grange, Ill. 60325 †
2/76

John O. Klein
Pleasantville, N. J. 08232 †

Richard Klein
8009 94th St., Milwaukee, Wis. 53224
Maker of strings †   1/78

Klein Custom Guitars
22522 Burndale Rd., Sonoma, Calif. 95476
FT   1969   Inactive   1 emp.
IA/MTO   Modern   1/75 • Steel-string
guitar   1–10 to date   † • 12-string
guitar   1–10 to date   † • *1980: Active*

*MTO   Brochure • Steel-string guitar and
12-string guitar   1–10 per year • Electric
guitar   1–10 to date   1–10 per year
• Also known as: Steve Klein*

Gene Klemmedson
Eureka Springs, Ark. 72632 †   4/76

Howard Klepper
2214 Grove, Berkeley, Calif. 93305
Maker of steel-string guitars †   2/76

John Kleske
23 Bennett Ave., Binghamton, N. Y. 13905
PT   1969   Active   1 emp.   IA/MTO
Modern and historical   5/74
• Appalachian dulcimer   Over 50 to
date   † • *1980: Hammered dulcimer
1–10 to date   † • 5-string banjo   1–10 to
date   † • Lap harp   1–10 to date   †*

Horst L. Kloss
609 Teetshorn St., Houston, Tex. 77009
Maker of violins †   6/74

William Knabe and Co.
Also known as: Aeolian Corp.

Eugene Knapik
551 Graham Dr., Chesterton, Ind. 46304
FT   1935   Active   1 emp.   MTO
Modern   Brochure   8/75 • Viola   †
• Violin   † • Cello   † • All instruments
1–10 per year • Primarily repairs

Richard V. Knapp
7212 Waite Dr., Lemon Grove, Calif. 92045
FT   1973   Active   1 emp.   MTO
Historical   9/74 • Violin   1–10 to date
† • Primarily repairs

Thomas Knatt
83 Riverside Ave., Concord, Mass. 01742
FT   1964   Active   3 emp.   IA/MTO
Modern   Brochure   6/74 • Classical
guitar   Over 50 to date   10–25 per year
• Flamenco guitar   Over 50 to date
10–25 per year • Lute   1–10 to date
1–10 per year • Viol   1–10 to date   1–10
per year • Appalachian dulcimer   1–10 to
date   1–10 per year • Also known as: La
Gitana Instruments • *1980: Flamenco
guitar   10-25 to date   1–10 per year
• Appalachian dulcimer   10–25 to date*

· *Violin   1–10 to date   1–10 per year*
· *Lap harp   1–10 to date   1–10 per year*
· *Steel-string guitar   10–25 to date   1–10*
per year · Hurdy-gurdy   10–25 to date
1–10 per year · Hammered dulcimer
1–10 to date   1–10 per year · Not making
viols

Tom Knight

8 Bromley Pl., Green Lawn, N. Y. 11740
PT   1972   Active   1 emp.   MTO
Modern and historical   4/78 · Classical
guitar   1–10 to date   † · Steel-string
guitar   1–10 to date   † · Virginal   1–10
to date   † · Lute   1–10 to date   †

Knight Royale Pianos

737 Washington St., Royersford, Pa. 19468
FT   1976   Active   50 emp.   IA
Modern   Brochure   2/78 · Piano   Over
50 to date   Over 50 per year

Martin Kob

2501 28th St., Santa Monica, Calif. 90405
PT   1969   Active   1 emp.   IA
Historical   10/74 · Viola   1–10 to
date   †

Koch Recorders

Haverhill, N. H. 03765
PT   1934   Active   1 emp.   IA
Modern   Brochure   5/74 · Recorder
Over 50 to date   Over 50 per year

Al Koenig

Colrain, Mass. 01340
Maker of strings †

Kohler and Campbell, Inc.

Granite Falls, N. C. 28630
Maker of pianos †   2/76

Samuel Kolstein and Son, Ltd.

2801 Shore Dr., 1, Merrick, N. Y. 11566
FT   1941   Active   6 emp.   MTO
Historical   6/75 · Bass violin   10–25 to
date   † · Primarily repairs · *1980: IA/MTO*
Brochure · Cello   10–25 to date   †
· *Viola   1–10 to date   † · Bows   Over 50*
to date   †

Mitchell Komisar

Also known as: Westminster Dulcimers

Ron Konzak

12248 Peterson Hill Rd., Bainbridge Island,
Wash. 98110
PT   1976   Active   1 emp.   MTO
Modern   Brochure   1/77 · Uilleann
pipes   10–25 to date   1–10 per year

Sam Koontz

19 E. Elizabeth Ave., Linden, N. J. 07036
Maker of strings †   2/76

David E. Kopp

1033 8th St. South, Naples, Fla. 33940
PT   Year?   Inactive   1 emp.   MTO
Modern   4/78 · Jazz guitar   1–10 to
date   † · Steel-string guitar   1–10 to
date   †

J. D. Korechoff

125 Prospect Park West, Brooklyn, N. Y. 11215
Maker of strings †   1/78

Herman Korenvaes

8115 S. W. 17th Terr., Miami, Fla. 33155
PT   1960   Active   1 emp.   IA
Modern and historical   4/76 · Flamenco
guitar   1–10 to date   † · Classical
guitar   Over 50 to date   †

M. L. Korpal

P. O. Box 6061, Arlington, Va. 22206 †   2/76

David Kortier

2620 N. High, Box 02263, Columbus, Ohio 43202
Maker of strings †   1/78 · Also known as:
Early Interval

John Koscak

2180 Pilgrim Pkwy. East, Milwaukee, Wis.
53200
Maker of violins †   1/77

John Koster

8 Choate Rd., Belmont, Mass. 02178
FT   1974   Active   1 emp.   MTO
Historical   Brochure   9/74 · Violin   †
· *1980: No brochure · Harpsichord and*
forte-piano   † · Not making violins

Edward L. Kottick

2001 Muscatine, Iowa City, Iowa 52240
PT   1971   Active   1 emp.   MTO
Historical   5/74 · Appalachian
dulcimer   1–10 to date   † · Cittern

1–10 to date † • Harpsichord 1–10 to date † • Clavichord 1–10 to date † • Lute 1–10 to date † • Steel-string guitar 1–10 to date † • *1980: Harpsichord 10–25 to date · Classical guitar 1–10 to date † · Bass viola da gamba 1–10 to date † · Forte-piano 1–10 to date † · Medieval fiddle 1–10 to date † · Vihuela 1–10 to date † · Psaltery 1–10 to date † · Not making steel-string guitars*

William Koucky
14 Center Woods, Saginaw, Mich. 48603
PT 1977 Active 1 emp. MTO
Modern 1/78 • Appalachian dulcimer 10–25 to date 10–25 per year
• Steel-string guitar 1–10 to date 1–10 per year

Frank Kovanda
4170 Bakman Ave., North Hollywood, Calif. 91602 † 2/76

Roger Kraft
712 W. 6th St., Bloomington, Ind. 47401
PT 1977 Active 1 emp. MTO
Modern 4/78 • Steel-string guitar 1–10 to date † • Electric guitar 1–10 to date † • Appalachian dulcimer 1–10 to date †

Krakauer Brothers
115 E. 138th St., Bronx, N. Y. 10451
PT 1869 Active 40 emp. IA
Modern Brochure 5/74 • Piano Over 50 to date Over 50 per year • Also known as: Haddorff Pianos

Ira B. Kramer
626 Central Ave., East Orange, N. J. 07018
Maker of strings † 6/75

Kramer Guitar Co.
1111 Green Grove Rd., Neptune, N. J. 07753
FT 1976 Active 28 emp. IA
Modern Brochure 10/77 • Electric guitar Over 50 to date Over 50 per year • Electric bass guitar Over 50 to date Over 50 per year • Also known as: BKL International Distributing • *1980: 47 emp.*

William Kramer-Harrison
2188 Stoll Rd., Saugerties, N. Y. 12477

FT 1969 Active 1 emp. MTO
Modern and historical 2/78 • Classical guitar 1–10 to date • Steel-string guitar 1–10 to date • Psaltery Over 50 to date • Hammered dulcimer 1–10 to date • Appalachian dulcimer 1–10 to date • Tromba marina 1–10 to date • Kalimba 1–10 to date • All instruments 10–25 per year

Kranich and Bach
Also known as: Aeolian Corp.

Walter Krasicki
2868 W. Grand, Chicago, Ill. 60612 † 4/76

William Kratt Co.
988 Johnson Pl., Union, N. J. 07083
FT 1936 Active 45 emp. IA
Modern Brochure 4/76 • Harmonica Over 50 to date Over 50 per year

John W. Kreutziger, Jr.
1535 8th Ave., Belvedere, Ill. 61008
Maker of strings † 1/78

Russell Krieg
106 E. High St., Jefferson City, Mo. 65101
PT 1975 Active 1 emp. MTO
Modern 2/78 • Appalachian dulcimer 1–10 to date † • Steel-string guitar 1–10 to date 1–10 per year • *1980: Appalachian dulcimer 1–10 per year · Mandolin 1–10 to date 1–10 per year · Primarily repairs*

Max Krimmel
Salina Star Rt.—Wallstreet, Boulder, Colo. 80302
FT 1965 Active 1 emp. IA/MTO
Modern 6/74 • Steel-string guitar Over 50 to date 10–25 per year • Appalachian dulcimer 10–25 to date † • 5-string banjo 1–10 to date † • *1980: Brochure · Not making Appalachian dulcimers and 5-string banjos*

Charles J. Kriskey
36 Ellsworth Ave., Harrison, N. Y. 10528 † 2/76

Lambert Kroon
3731 Greenleaf Circle—306, Kalamazoo, Mich. 49008
Maker of strings † 2/76

Richard Krueger
Also known as: B and G Instrument Workshop

Paul Krumm
Also known as: The Gyld

Krupp Music Co.
1621 N. Kedzie Ave., Chicago, Ill. 60647 † 2/76

T. A. Kuehnert
1901 S. Dewey, Bartlesville, Okla. 74003
Maker of strings † 1/78

Garry Kuistad
219 Hosea, Cincinnati, Ohio 45215
PT Year? Active 1 emp. IA/MTO
Modern 5/78 • Wooden blocks 25–50
to date † • Log drum 10–25 to date †

Nicholas Kukick
32722 Franklin Rd., Franklin, Mich. 48025
FT 1975 Active 1 emp. MTO
Modern and historical 5/76 • Steel-string
guitar 1–10 to date † • Classical
guitar 1–10 to date † • Primarily
repairs • Also known as: Franklin County
Workshop

George F. Kuniche
719 Carlton Ave., Plainfield, N. J. 07060
Maker of strings † 1/77

Samuel Kuntz
Main St., Red Bank, N. J. 07701 † 8/74

Ulrich Kunz
86 Rogerine Way, P. O. Box 442, Landing, N. J.
07850
Maker of violins † 12/77

Arthur Kuriloff
2701 Barrymore Dr., Malibu, Calif. 90265
PT Year? Active 1 emp. MTO
Historical 10/74 • Violin 1–10 to
date †

Ted Kurtz
Also known as: Brass City Fifecraft

James Kuspa
930 Brookview Circle, Pensacola, Fla. 32503
Maker of strings † 1/78

Kustom Gretsch/A Division of Baldwin
Piano and Organ
908 W. Chestnut, Chanute, Kans. 66720
*1980: FT Year? Active ?emp. IA
Modern Brochure 10/80 • Electronic
piano, drums, electric guitar, steel guitar,
5-string banjo, and cymbals † • Also
known as: Kasino; Ode Banjos*

Peter Kyvelos
165 Belmont St., Belmont, Mass. 02178
FT 1964 Active 1 emp. MTO
Historical 5/74 • Classical guitar
10–25 to date 1–10 per year • Flamenco
guitar 1–10 to date † • Lute 1–10 to
date 1–10 per year • Oud 25–50 to
date 10–25 per year • Bouzoukee 1–10
to date † • Qanun 10–25 to date
1–10 per year • Santouri 1–10 to date
1–10 per year • Appalachian dulcimer
Over 50 to date Over 50 per year
• Violin 10–25 to date 1–10 per year
• Cello 1–10 to date 1–10 per year
• Also known as: Unique Strings • *1980:
Only making santouris*

John B. Lafoy
14 Glenwood Rd., Apt. 108, Greenville, S. C.
29607
PT 1974 Active 1 emp. MTO
Modern 5/75 • 5-string banjo 1–10 to
date 1–10 per year • Mandolin 1–10 to
date †

La Gitana Instruments
Also known as: Thomas Knatt

LaGrandeur Music
2939 De la Vina, Santa Barbara, Calif. 93105
Maker of strings † 2/76

Dennis Lake
Also known as: Great Lakes Banjo Co.

Lakefront Dulcimore Shoppe
Also known as: Paul Adams

L. LaMay
1507 Versailles Rd., Lexington, Ky. 40504
Maker of strings † 2/76

Neil Lamb
Box 206, Wardtown Rd., Freeport, Maine 04032
† 9/76

N. D. Lamberson
1208 S. 11th St., Oskaloosa, Iowa 52577
FT   1968   Active   3 emp.   MTO
Modern   Brochure   5/74 • Modern
flute   Over 50 to date   Over 50 per year

Peter Lamont
1831 Riverside Dr., #14, Glendale, Calif. 91201
Maker of strings †   1/78

Lamont Band Instruments
5 Canal Rd., Pelham Manor, N. Y. 10583
Maker of woodwinds and brass †   2/76

Cal Lamoreaux
R. R. 1, Shelbyville, Mich. 49334
FT   1973   Active   1 emp.   IA
Modern and historical   Brochure   11/74
• Appalachian dulcimer   1–10 to date   †
• Hammered dulcimer   1–10 to date   †
• Mouth bow   1–10 to date   † • *1980:
IA/MTO   No brochure • Appalachian
dulcimer   25–50 to date • Lyre   1–10 to
date   † • Zither   1–10 to date   †*

Don Lancaster
Artesia, N. M. 88210 †   2/76

Jonathon Landell
180 Walnut St., Watertown, Mass. 02172
FT   1970   Active   2 emp.   IA/MTO
Modern and historical   Brochure   11/74
• Modern flute   1–10 to date   1–10 per
year • Fife   Over 50 to date   †
• Renaissance flute   10–25 to date   †

Felix Landis
2237 Euclid, El Cajon, Calif. 92020
Maker of strings †   2/76

Robert F. Landry
8195 Lincoln St., Lemon Grove, Calif. 92045
Maker of strings †   1/78

Harris Lane
327 Jefferson St., Savannah, Ga. 31401
Maker of 5-string banjos †   2/76

Peter Laney
190 Jerusalem Rd., Cohasset, Mass. 02025
PT   1977   Active   1 emp.   MTO
Modern   3/78 • Steel-string guitar   1–10
to date   †

Delwyn J. Langejans
28 E. Eighth St., Holland, Mich. 49423
FT   1970   Active   1 emp.   MTO
Modern   Brochure   11/74 • Steel-string
guitar   25–50 to date • 12-string guitar
10–25 to date • All instruments   10–25
per year • Also known as: Del's Guitar
Gallery • *1980: Steel-string guitar   Over 50
to date • 12-string guitar   Over 50 to date
• Classical guitar   Over 50 to date   1–10
per year*

Henry Lanini
2814 Alum Rock Ave., San Jose, Calif. 95127 †
2/76

Joellen Lapidus
907 4th St., Santa Monica, Calif. 90403
PT   1967   Active   1 emp.   IA/MTO
Modern   9/75 • Appalachian dulcimer
10–25 to date • Zither   10–25 to date • All
instruments   1–10 per year • Also known
as: Shimmering Musical Instrument Co.

Lloyd G. LaPlant
Rt. 1, Box 386, Grand Rapids, Minn. 55744
PT   1959   Active   1 emp.   IA
Modern   5/74 • Steel-string guitar
10–25 to date • Classical guitar   1–10 to
date • All instruments   1–10 per year

LaPrima Accordions, Inc.
3267 Steinway St., Astoria, N. Y. 11102
Maker of accordions †   2/75

William Largen
1934 Avon Rd. S. W., Roanoke, Va. 24015 †
4/76

Larilee Oboe Co.
1700 Edwardsburg Rd., Elkhart, Ind. 46514
FT   1945   Active   5 emp.   IA/MTO
Modern   Brochure   5/74 • Oboe   Over
50 to date   Over 50 per year

Lark in the Morning
Box 1176, Mendocino, Calif. 95460
FT   1975   Active   2 emp.   IA/MTO
Historical   Brochure   4/78 • Early
percussion   10–25 to date   †
• Bodhran   Over 50 to date   † • Also
known as: Roy Graham; Mickie Zekley
• *1980: Bagpipes   1–10 to date   †*

· Hurdy-gurdy   1–10 to date   † · Also known as: Roy Graham; Stan Kelley; Mickie Zekley

John M. Larsen
315 O'Farrell, Boise, Idaho 82702
Maker of strings †   5/74

William Larsen
Leaning Pine Dr., Miami, Fla. 33100 †   2/76

Howard Lasky
1418 Haight St., San Francisco, Calif. 94117
PT   1972   Active   2 emp.   MTO
Modern   11/74 · Steel-string guitar
1–10 to date   † · Appalachian dulcimer
10–25 to date   †

Joe Latham
2754 Chain Bridge Rd., Vienna, Va. 22180
FT   1965   Active   1 emp.   MTO
Modern   4/76 · Electric guitar   1–10 to date   † · Appalachian dulcimer   1–10 to date   † · Primarily repairs

Latin Percussion
454 Commercial Ave., Palisades Park, N. J. 07650
FT   Year?   Active   ? emp.   IA
Modern   Brochure   2/75 · Conga   Over 50 to date   Over 50 per year · Bongo Over 50 to date   Over 50 per year · Cow bell   Over 50 to date   Over 50 per year · Vibra-slap   Over 50 to date   Over 50 per year · Cabasa/a fuche   Over 50 to date Over 50 per year · Timbales   Over 50 to date   Over 50 per year

Carl Latray
R. F. D. 2, Box 355, Frankfort, N. Y. 13340
FT   1969   Active   1 emp.   IA/MTO
Modern and historical   9/74
· Appalachian dulcimer   25–50 to date
1–10 per year · Irish harp   1–10 to date
† · Hammered dulcimer   1–10 to date   †
· Tromba marina   1–10 to date   †
· Steel-string guitar   1–10 to date   †
· *1980: Portative organ   1–10 to date   †*
· Clavichord   1–10 to date   † · Not making steel-string guitars

A. Laubin, Inc.
37 N. Central Ave., Elmsford, N. Y. 10523

FT   1930   Active   4 emp.   MTO
Modern   5/74 · Oboe   Over 50 to date
Over 50 per year · English horn   Over 50 to date   25–50 per year · *1980: English horn   10–25 per year*

Laughead Co.
Box 274, Grand Haven, Mich. 49417
Maker of pianos †   2/76

Bill Lawrence
Nashville, Tenn. 37200
Maker of strings †

Raymond Layne
123 Adams St., Berea, Ky. 40403
PT   1965   Active   1 emp.   MTO
Historical   5/74 · Appalachian dulcimer   Over 50 to date   †

Tom Layton
513 C Ave., Lawton, Okla. 73501 †   3/78

G. LeBlanc Corp.
7019 Thirtieth Ave., Kenosha, Wis. 53140
FT   1946   Active   ? emp.   IA
Modern   Brochure   4/75 · Clarinet
Over 50 to date   † · Flute   Over 50 to date   † · Saxophone   Over 50 to date   †
· Alto horn   Over 50 to date   † · Baritone horn   Over 50 to date   † · Cornet
Over 50 to date   † · Fluegelhorn   Over 50 to date   † · French horn   Over 50 to date   † · Mellophone   Over 50 to date   †
· Sousaphone   Over 50 to date   † · Slide trombone   Over 50 to date   †
· Trumpet   Over 50 to date   † · Tuba
Over 50 to date   † · Also known as: Frank Holton & Co.; Noblet Woodwinds; Vito Woodwinds

Harry Lebovit
Also known as: Stradi-Varni Co.

Rose LeCler
125 19th Ave., San Francisco, Calif. 94121
Maker of strings †   2/76

Lee's Banjo Shop
Also known as: Ernest Lee Elliott

Joseph Ledbetter
77 Lakeview Dr., Centerville, Ohio 45459

PT 1967 Inactive 1 emp. IA
Historical 4/76 • Classical guitar 1–10
to date †

Homer Ledford
125 Sunset Heights, Winchester, Ky. 40391
FT 1946 Active 2 emp. MTO
Historical Brochure 7/74
• Appalachian dulcimer Over 50 to
date † • 5-string banjo Over 50 to
date † • Dulcitar 1–10 to date † •
Courting or double dulcimer 1–10 to
date † • Ukulele 10–25 to date †
• Steel-string guitar 10–25 to date †
• Mandolin 1–10 to date † • 1980:
Dulcitar 25–50 to date • Courting or
double dulcimer 10–25 to date

Billy Lee
86 Kerland Dr., Wright City, Mo. 63390
FT 1959 Active 1 emp. MTO
Modern 10/75 • Mandolin 1–10 to
date 1–10 per year • Steel-string guitar
1–10 to date † • Violin 1–10 to date
† • Primarily repairs • 1980: Steel-string
guitar 1–10 per year • Violin 1–10 per
year

Lorraine Lee
234 Eliot St., South Natick, Mass. 01760 † 2/76
1980: Inactive

Melvin D. Lee
Rt. 1, Box 109A, McGaheysville, Va. 22840
PT 1973 Active 1 emp. MTO
Historical 12/74 • Appalachian
dulcimer 10–25 to date †

Richard J. Lee
75 Homer Ave., P. O. Box 277, Palo Alto, Calif.
94302
FT 1971 Active 1 emp. MTO
Historical 10/74 • Harpsichord 1–10 to
date 1–10 per year

Steven D. Lee
639 Colusa Ave., Oroville, Calif. 95965
Maker of strings † 1/78

Lee Music Mfg. Co.
525 Venezia Ave., Venice, Calif. 90291 † 2/76

Leedy Drum Co.
6633 N. Milwaukee Ave., Chicago, Ill. 60648
Maker of drums † 2/76

Lehigh Organ Co.
24 Pine St., P. O. Box 474, Macungie, Pa. 18062
FT 1963 Active 4 emp. MTO
Modern 4/76 • Pipe organ 10–25 to
date 1–10 per year • Harpsichord
1–10 to date † • 1980: Pipe organ
25–50 to date

Bernard E. Lehmann
30A Mill Ln., Arlington, Mass. 02174
PT 1973 Active 1 emp. IA/MTO
Modern and historical Brochure 9/75
• Steel-string guitar 10–25 to date
1–10 per year • Appalachian dulcimer
25–50 to date 10–25 per year
• Mandolin 1–10 to date 1–10 per year
• Lute 1–10 to date 1–10 per year
• Also known as: Arlington Stringed
Instruments

Jeff Lehmann
P. O. Box 2235, Minot, N. Dak. 58701
Maker of strings † 1/78

John A. Lehrer
16 E. Summit St., Chagrin Falls, Ohio 44022
Maker of strings † 2/76

Leigh Artisans
Also known as: Irvin Reis

Alfred C. Leis
82 Spring St., Newport, R. I. 02840 † 3/78
1980: FT 1974 Active 1 emp. MTO
Modern 10/80 • Classical and steel-string
guitars 10–25 to date † • Violin
1–10 to date † • Primarily repairs

Leitch Guitars
Also known as: Fritz Damler

Manuel Leiva
10627 Dunmoor Dr., Silver Spring, Md. 20901
† 2/76

Sandy Lemberg
Rt. 1, Livermore, Colo. 80536
Maker of woodwinds † 2/76

Arthur Lennard
6943 Linda Vista Rd., La Jolla, Calif. 92037
Maker of strings † 3/76

Michael Lennon
Also known as: The Apprentice Shop

Richard L. Lenz, Jr.
1729 E. Charleston Blvd., Las Vegas, Nev. 89104
FT   1977   Active   1 emp.   IA
Modern   Brochure   2/78 • Steel-string
guitar   1–10 to date   † • Electric
guitar   1–10 to date   † • Classical
guitar   1–10 to date   † • Electric bass
guitar   1–10 to date   † • Primarily
repairs

Joseph Lenzi
SR #10737, Fairbanks, Alaska 99701
Maker of strings †   1/78

D. A. Leonard
39 North St., B-2, Columbus, Ohio 43202 †
2/76

Rose-Ellen Leonard
Box 46, Cohasset Stage, Chico, Calif. 95926
FT   1971   Active   1 emp.   IA
Modern   7/74 • Classical guitar   1–10 to
date   1–10 per year • *1980: IA/MTO*

Lesher Woodwind Co.
Also known as: Selmer

Michael D. Leslie
7531 S. W. 31 Ave., Portland, Ore. 97219
Maker of strings †   2/76

Lauren A. Lesmeister
1109 5th Ave. South, Apt. 11, Fargo, N. Dak.
58102
Maker of strings †   1/78

Lester Piano Mfg. Co.
1 Belmont Ave., Bala Cynwyd, Pa. 19004
Maker of pianos †   2/76

W. Robert Levelle
Rt. 1, Box 150, Cosmic Farms, Fairfield, Wash.
99012
FT   1970   Active   1 emp.   IA/MTO
Modern and historical   1/77 • Classical
guitar 1–10 to date   † • Flamenco
guitar   1–10 to date   † • Appalachian
dulcimer   25–50 to date   †

Monty Levenson
Rt. 1, P. O. Box 294, Hilltop Dr., Willits, Calif.
95490
FT   1970   Active   1 emp.   MTO
Historical   Brochure   6/74

• Shakuhachi   Over 50 to date   Over 50
per year

Henry Levin
80 St. Mark's Pl., New York, N. Y. 10003
Maker of strings †   2/76 • Also known as:
House of Musical Traditions; Musical
Traditions Co.

Jeff Levin
25-36 Jackson Ave., Long Island City, N. Y.
11101
FT   1968   Active   1 emp.   MTO
Modern and historical   6/74 • Steel-string
guitar   10–25 to date   † • Primarily
repairs

Phillip Levin
437 E. 6th St., New York, N. Y. 10009
FT   1973   Active   2 emp.   MTO
Historical   Brochure   3/76 • Baroque
bassoon   †

Lynne Lewandowski
253 E. 10th St., New York, N. Y. 10009
FT   1975   Active   1 emp.   IA/MTO
Historical   4/76 • Psaltery   10–25 to
date   † • Memling harp   10–25 to
date   † • *1980: 67 Main St., Brattleboro, Vt.
05301 • Modern and historical   Brochure
• Psaltery   Over 50 to date   • Gothic
harp   Over 50 to date   † • Celtic harp
1–10 to date   †*

Juno Lewis
1906 W. 23d St., Apt. 1, Los Angeles, Calif. 90018
Maker of wooden drums †   5/74

Larry L'Heureux
Crown St. Extension, #133, Meriden, Conn.
06450
PT   1952   Active   1 emp.   IA/MTO
Historical   4/76 • Rope-tensioned drum
Over 50 to date   †

Liberty Banjo Co.
2367 Main St., Bridgeport, Conn. 06606
FT   1968   Active   5 emp.   IA/MTO
Modern and historical   Brochure   4/76
• 5-string banjo   Over 50 to date   Over 50
per year

Lifton Mfg. Co.
84-40 101st St., Richmond Hill, N. Y. 11418 †
2/75

Anton Lignell
R. D. 2, Box 201, Lubec, Maine 04652
PT   1966   Active   1 emp.   MTO
Historical   10/75 • Harpsichord   10–25
to date   †

Lima Pipe Organ Co.
P. O. Box 3023, Elida, Ohio 45807
Maker of pipe organs †   2/76

Richard Limbursky
6330 N. Lakewood Ave., Chicago, Ill. 60626
PT   1971   Active   1 emp.   MTO
Modern   12/75 • Appalachian dulcimer
10–25 to date   1–10 per year • 5-string
banjo   1–10 to date   1–10 per year
• Hammered dulcimer   1–10 to date
1–10 per year

Dick Lindberg
5852 Glendora Ave., Dallas, Tex. 75230
Maker of strings †   1/78

Thomas Lindenwood
Also known as: Thomas Lipiczky

Robert Lindner
Rt. 1, Box 143 B, Chelan, Wash. 98816
FT   1972   Active   2 emp.   IA/MTO
Modern and historical   Brochure   4/75
• Flute   Over 50 to date   1–10 per year
• Fife   Over 50 to date   1–10 per year
• Oboe   1–10 to date   1–10 per year
• Harp   1–10 to date   1–10 per year
• Lyre   1–10 to date   1–10 per year
• Also known as: Wild Flower Musical
Instrument Co.

Lindner Pianos
31 Union Square West, #907, New York, N. Y.
10003
Maker of pianos †   2/75

Linrud Harp Co.
Also known as: Earl Thompson

Linton Mfg. Co.
711 Middleton Run Rd., Elkhart, Ind. 46514
FT   1935   Active   40 emp.   IA
Modern   Brochure   4/76 • Oboe   Over
50 to date   Over 50 per year • English
horn   Over 50 to date   Over 50 per year
• Bassoon   Over 50 to date   Over 50 per
year • Clarinet   Over 50 to date   Over 50

per year • Modern flute   Over 50 to date
Over 50 per year • Saxophone   Over 50 to
date   Over 50 per year • Also known as:
W. T. Armstrong Co., Inc.

Thomas Lipiczky
Box 121, R. F. D. 1, West Stockbridge, Mass.
01266
PT   1975   Active   1 emp.   IA/MTO
Modern   4/76 • Appalachian dulcimer
1–10 to date   † • Cane flute   1–10 to
date   † • Wooden flute   1–10 to date   †
• Also known as: Thomas Lindenwood

William Lipnick
5470 Mary Lane Dr., San Diego, Calif. 92115
Maker of strings †   2/76

Walter Lipton
Orford, N. H. 03777
FT   1960   Active   1 emp.   IA/MTO
Modern   5/74 • Steel-string guitar   1–10
to date   10–25 per year • 5-string banjo
1–10 to date   1–10 per year • *1980:
Brochure • Steel-string and classical
guitars   Over 50 to date • Not making
5-string banjos*

Kenneth J. Lissant
12804 Westledge Ln., St. Louis, Mo. 63131
PT   1968   Active   1 emp.   IA
Historical   1/78 • Door harp   1–10 to
date   † • Appalachian dulcimer   10–25
to date   † • 5-string banjo   1–10 to
date   † • Steel-string guitar   1–10 to
date   † • *1980: IA/MTO • Door harp
10–25 to date   1–10 per year
• Appalachian dulcimer   1–10 per year
• 5-string banjo   1–10 per year
• Steel-string guitar   1–10 per year
• Thumbpiano   1–10 to date   1–10 per
year • Ganbos   1–10 to date   1–10 per
year*

Kurt R. Listug
7936 Lester Ave., Lemon Grove, Calif. 92045
FT   1974   Active   8 emp.   IA
Modern   3/78 • Steel-string guitar   Over
50 to date   Over 50 per year • 5-string
banjo   10–25 to date   † • Mandolin
1–10 to date   † • Appalachian dulcimer
10–25 to date   † • Also known as: Taylor
Guitars; Westland Music Co. • *1980: 3
emp.   IA/MTO   Brochure • Not making
5-string banjos and Appalachian dulcimers*

Homer Little
Shelbyville, Ill. 62565 † 2/77

Henry Littleboy and Son
7 Sentry Hill Pl., Boston, Mass. 02114
Maker of strings † 2/76

Little Flutes
Also known as: Paul Johnson

Little Wing Guitars
Also known as: Robert Goldzweig

Litwin Luthiers
Box 1057, Brattleboro, Vt. 05301
Maker of strings † 11/77

Lloyd Liu
11 Monument Ave., Old Bennington, Vt. 05201
FT 1953 Active 1 emp. MTO
Modern and historical Brochure 6/74
• Violin 10–25 to date • Viola 10–25 to date • Cello 1–10 to date • Bows Over 50 to date • All instruments 1–10 per year • Primarily repairs

Livewood
Also known as: Scott Hauser

Jerry Lobdill
5706 B Gloucester, Austin, Tex. 78723
Maker of strings † 6/74

Charles Lo Bue
169 W. 48th St., New York, N. Y. 10036
FT 1969 Active 1 emp. MTO
Modern 4/76 • Electric guitar Over 50 to date Over 50 per year • Also known as: The Guitar Lab

Barry Lockard
P. O. Box 297, Harris, N. Y. 12742
PT 1967 Active 1 emp. IA
Modern and historical 11/74
• Harpsichord 1–10 to date †

LoDuca Brothers Musical Instruments, Inc.
400 N. Broadway, Milwaukee, Wis. 53202
FT 1941 Active 45 emp. IA
Modern Brochure 2/75 • Reed organ Over 50 to date Over 50 per year
• Electronic organ Over 50 to date Over

50 per year • Electronic piano Over 50 to date Over 50 per year

Kitty Logan
Rt. 1, Del Rio, Tenn. 37727
PT 1973 Active 1 emp. IA/MTO
Modern and historical 5/74
• Appalachian dulcimer 1–10 to date †

Logi-Rhythm, Inc.
420 Jericho Tpke., Jericho, N. Y. 11753
Maker of percussion † 2/76

Ernst Lohberg
5105 Morella Ave., North Hollywood, Calif. 91607 † 2/76

Craig F. Lohman
Rt. 3, Box 22, Hedgesville, W. Va. 25427
Maker of strings † 1/78

John A. Lomax
410 E. Jefferson St., Media, Pa. 19063
Maker of strings † 1/78

Joseph Lomonaco
Box 239, Gilsum Village, N. H. 03448
FT 1973 Active 1 emp. IA
Modern 1/75 • Steel-string guitar 1–10 to date 1–10 per year

London Stringed Instrument Repairs
2639½ N. 48th, Lincoln, Neb. 68504
Maker of strings † 1/75 • Also known as: Dale London

Robbie Long
Box 19, Laguanitas, Calif. 94438
FT 1968 Active 1 emp. MTO
Modern and historical 9/75
• Appalachian dulcimer Over 50 to date † • Steel-string guitar 1–10 to date † • Strings 10–25 to date †

A. LoPrinzi Guitars, Inc.
P. O. Box 247, Plainsboro, N. J. 08536
FT 1958 Active 5 emp. IA
Modern Brochure 5/78 • Steel-string guitar Over 50 to date Over 50 per year • 12-string guitar Over 50 to date Over 50 per year

Augustine LoPrinzi
P. O. Box 137, Baptistown, N. J. 08803
FT 1976 Active 4 emp. IA

Modern   Brochure   3/78 • Steel-string guitar   Over 50 to date   Over 50 per year • Also known as: Augustine Co.

Eugene E. Lorello
138 5th Ave., Kings Park, N. Y. 11754
PT   1949   Active   1 emp.   MTO
Modern   Brochure   5/75 • Modern flute   †

Larry Lostumo
408 S. 5th Ave., Maywood, Ill. 60153
Maker of strings †   1/78

Robert A. Loughton
1851 Oleander Ave., Merced, Calif. 95340 † 4/78

E. Lourdley
1810 S. Woodward, Birmingham, Mich. 48011 †   2/76

Douglas A. Low
40 E. Main St., Marcellus, N. Y. 13108
PT   Year?   Active   1 emp.   MTO
Modern   2/78 • Steel-string guitar   1–10 to date   † • Lute   1–10 to date   † • Appalachian dulcimer   25–50 to date † • 5-string banjo   1–10 to date   †

Wade W. Lowe
2102 N. Decatur Rd., Decatur, Ga. 30033
FT   1966   Active   1 emp.   IA/MTO
Modern   Brochure   6/74 • Tenor banjo 1–10 to date   † • Balalaika   1–10 to date   † • Classical guitar   1–10 to date † • Primarily repairs • *1980: No brochure • Classical guitar   10–25 to date   1–10 per year • Not making tenor banjos and balalaikas • Also known as: Diapason Guitar Shop*

Lowrey Pianos
Also known as: Norlin Music, Inc.

Frank E. Lucchesi
Also known as: Sound Guitar Co.

James Ludden
Box 411, Enfield, N. H. 03748
Maker of pipe organs †   5/74

Otto Luderer
1514 Prospect Ave., Cleveland, Ohio 44100
Maker of violins †   2/76

Ludwig Industries
1728 N. Damen Ave., Chicago, Ill. 60647
FT   1909   Active   500 emp.   IA
Modern   Brochure   3/75 • Drum   Over 50 to date   Over 50 per year • Tympani Over 50 to date   Over 50 per year • Orchestra chimes   Over 50 to date Over 50 per year • Also known as: Musser Marimbas, Inc.

Tim Luedeke
P. O. Box 27, Wapakoneta, Ohio 45895
Maker of strings †   1/78

B. E. Luffman
Rt. 1, Box 373-D, Warrenville, S. C. 29851
Maker of strings †   1/78

Luke Dulcimers
22 Crandol Dr., Tabb, Va. 23602
FT   1973   Active   2 emp.   IA/MTO
Modern   Brochure   5/75 • Appalachian dulcimer   Over 50 to date   † • Steel-string guitar   1–10 to date   †

Robert Lundberg
6532 S. E. 71st Ave., Portland, Ore. 97206
FT   1973   Active   5 emp.   IA/MTO
Historical   Brochure   4/77 • Lute   Over 50 to date • Theorbo   1–10 to date • Chitarrone   1–10 to date • All instruments   25–50 per year • *1980: 1969   2 emp. • Lute   10–25 per year • Theorbo   25–50 to date • Chitarrone 10–25 to date*

Lawrence Lundy
5003 Terminal Rd., McFarland, Wis. 53558
FT   1977   Active   1 emp.   MTO
Historical   2/78 • Lute   1–10 to date   †

James D. Luther
111 Stanley Ave., Maryville, Tenn. 37801
PT   1966   Active   1 emp.   IA
Modern   4/76 • Appalachian dulcimer Over 50 to date   1–10 per year • *1980: Inactive*

Fred Lyman, Jr.
P. O. Box 28, Port Murray, N. J. 07865
FT   1969   Active   1 emp.   MTO
Modern   7/74 • Steel-string guitar 10–25 to date   † • Bass violin   10–25 to date   † • Violin   1–10 to date   †

• Viola   1–10 to date   † • *1980: Cello*
1–10 to date   †

Steve Lynch

141 Towne Terr., Santa Cruz, Calif. 95060
PT   1977   Active   1 emp.   MTO
Modern   1/77 • Appalachian dulcimer
1–10 to date   † • 5-string banjo   1–10 to
date   †

Lyon-Healy

243 S. Wabash Ave., Chicago, Ill. 60614
FT   1864   Active   641 emp.
IA/MTO?   Modern/historical?
Brochure   2/76 • Harp   † • Also known
as: CBS Musical Instruments

Jim Lyons

Rt. 8, Box 8733A, Bainbridge Island, Wash.
98110 †   2/76

Maas-Rowe Carillons, Inc.

2255 Meyers Ave., Escondido, Calif. 92025
Maker of carillons †   3/76 • *1980: FT
1922   Active   35 emp.   IA/MTO
Modern   Brochure   10/80 • Electronic
carillon, amplified carillon, chimes, bell
systems*   †

Mr. and Mrs. Eppes Mabry

P. O. Box 84, Mountain View, Ark. 72560
PT   1962   Active   2 emp.   IA
Historical   4/76 • Pickin' bow   Over 50 to
date   Over 50 per year • Steel-string
guitar   1–10 to date   †

Jeff Mabry

P. O. Box 591, Norman, Okla. 73069
Maker of strings †   3/78

John R. McCann

P. O. Box 4543, Arlington, Va. 22204
PT   1974   Active   1 emp.   IA/MTO
Historical   10/75 • Cornett   10–25 to
date   10–25 per year

R. J. McCarthy

1551 10th Ave. East, Seattle, Wash. 98102 †
2/76

Cecil A. McConnell, Sr.

Rt. 1, Box 431A, Coeburn, Va. 24230
PT   Year?   Active   1 emp.   MTO
Modern   4/76 • 5-string banjo   1–10 to
date   †

Robin James McConnell

535 S. 28th, Lincoln, Neb. 68510
PT   1976   Active   1 emp.   MTO
Modern   2/78 • Steel-string guitar   1–10
to date   † • Appalachian dulcimer   1–10
to date   † • Also known as: Robin's Song

McCormick Strings

5615 S. 77th, Ralston, Neb. 68127
FT   1962   Active   1 emp.   MTO
Modern and historical   2/75 • Steel-string
guitar   Over 50 to date   † • 12-string
guitar   1–10 to date   † • 5-string banjo
25–50 to date   † • Appalachian
dulcimer   10–25 to date   † • Primarily
repairs

Dan McCrimmon

204 Rob Roy Rd., Southern Pines, N. C. 28387
Maker of strings †   1/78

Mr. and Mrs. John McDevitt

Rt. 7, Box 850, Tallahassee, Fla. 32303
PT   1962   Active   2 emp.   MTO
Modern and historical   2/78
• Appalachian dulcimer   Over 50 to
date   10–25 per year • Irish harp   10–25
to date   1–10 per year • Hammered
dulcimer   1–10 to date   1–10 per year
• 5-string banjo   1–10 to date   1–10 per
year

Zeke McDonald

Grassy Fork, Hartford, Tenn. 37753
FT   1973   Active   2 emp.   IA/MTO
Modern   6/74 • Appalachian dulcimer
10–25 to date   † • Steel-string guitar
1–10 to date   † • 5-string banjo   1–10 to
date   † • *1980: PT   Modern and historical
• Appalachian dulcimer   Over 50 to date*

Len MacEachron

Also known as: Here, Inc.

Jeremiah T. McElroy

125 Wagon Trail, San Antonio, Tex. 78231
PT   1967   Active   1 emp.   MTO
Historical   6/74 • Appalachian
dulcimer   25–50 to date   1–10 per year
• Steel-string guitar   10–25 to date
1–10 per year

R. W. MacGibbon

3109 W. National Ave., Milwaukee, Wis. 53215

PT 1931 Inactive 1 emp. MTO
Modern 5/74 • Bassoon 1–10 to date
1–10 per year • Oboe 1–10 to date
1–10 per year

L. Edward McGlincy
470 Rt. 9, Bayville, N. J. 08721
PT 1968 Active 1 emp. MTO
Modern 10/75 • Steel-string guitar
1–10 to date † • Appalachian dulcimer
1–10 to date † • Primarily repairs • Also
known as: Ed's Musical Instruments

Don McGreevy
Box 215, White Thorn, Calif. 95489
Maker of strings † 1/78

Bruce McGuire
327 Market St., Santa Cruz, Calif. 95050
PT 1969 Active 1 emp. IA/MTO
Modern 3/78 • Classical guitar 1–10 to
date 1–10 per year • Steel-string guitar
1–10 to date † • Appalachian dulcimer
1–10 to date †

Terry McInturff
123 Warrior Woods, Carthage, N. C. 28327
Maker of strings † 3/78

McIntyre Clarinet Co.
105 Mill St., Naugatuck, Conn. 06770
Maker of clarinets † 6/78

Leo McLaughlin
35 Knollwood Dr., Tinton Falls, N. J. 07724
Maker of clarinets † 1/78 • Also known as:
Early Keyboards and Strings

Michael McLellan
2913 S. Spruce St., Santa Ana, Calif. 92704
Maker of woodwinds † 2/76 • *1980: FT
1974 Inactive 1 emp. MTO
Historical 10/80 · Renaissance and
Baroque woodwinds 10–25 to date* †

Frank L. MacLerran
P. O. Box 516, Mackay, Idaho 83251
PT 1969 Active 1 emp. MTO
Historical 1/78 • Classical guitar 1–10
to date 1–10 per year

McManis Organs, Inc.
1903 N. 10th St., Kansas City, Kans. 66104
FT 1938 Active 6 emp. IA

Modern Brochure 10/75
• Electro-pneumatic organ Over 50 to
date • Tracker organ 1–10 to date
• Portative organ 1–10 to date • All
instruments 1–10 per year

Darrel McMichaels
Also known as: The Folkstore • *1980:
Inactive*

Andrew Macnak
1712 Stanton Ave., Whiting, Ind. 46394
Maker of strings † 1/78

Lee McNeese
Rt. 1, Box 1029, Roseburg, Ore. 97470
Maker of strings † 10/74

Macoy and Masonic
3011 Dunbarton Rd., Richmond, Va. 23228 †
6/76

Dennis McQuen
120 Kansas St., Geneva, Ill. 60134
Maker of strings † 1/78

Charles McRuggles
Cleveland, Ohio 44100
Maker of organs †

Lynn McSpadden
Drawer E, Hwy. 14N, Mountain View, Ark.
72560
FT 1962 Active 9 emp. MTO
Modern and historical Brochure 10/74
• 5-string banjo 25–50 to date
• Appalachian dulcimer Over 50 to date
• Steel-string guitar 1–10 to date
• Mandolin 1–10 to date • All
instruments Over 50 per year • Also
known as: Dulcimer Shoppe • *1980: 6
emp. IA/MTO · Appalachian dulcimer
Over 50 per year · Not making steel-string
guitars*

McWillis and Strauss
Box 775, Seaside, Calif. 93955 † 5/76

Erling Madsen
Rt. 1, Box 7, Laurel Hill, Fla. 32567
Maker of strings † 1/78

Christopher Madison
106 Erlington Dr., Cinnaminson, N. J. 08077

PT 1976 Active 1 emp. IA/MTO
Modern and historical 2/78 • Steel-string
guitar 10—25 to date 1—10 per year

Edward Maestro
Goose Hill Rd., Jefferson, Maine 04348
FT 1970 Active 1 emp. MTO
Historical Brochure 4/76 • Bass
violin 1—10 to date 1—10 per year
• Primarily repairs

Martin Mager
St. Anselm's College, Manchester, N. H. 03102
PT 1972 Active 1 emp. MTO
Modern 11/74 • Appalachian dulcimer
10—25 to date 1—10 per year

Andreas Mages
627 N. Larchmont Blvd., Los Angeles, Calif.
90004 † 2/76

The Magic Flute
Also known as: Steven Allerton

Magic Mountain Instruments
P. O. Box 3531, San Rafael, Calif. 94902
FT 1972 Active 3 emp. IA
Modern Brochure 5/74 • Appalachian
dulcimer Over 50 to date Over 50 per
year • Also known as: J. C. Shellnutt and Co.

Magiworks
Also known as: Dennis Ackley

Magnus Organ Corp.
1600 W. Edgar Rd., Linden, N. J. 07036
Maker of organs † 2/76

Kalman Magyar, Sr.
P. O. Box 262, Bogota, N. J. 07603
PT 1974 Active 1 emp. MTO
Historical 2/76 • Citera 10—25 to
date 1—10 per year • *1980: Brochure
• Citera Over 50 to date 25—50 per year*

Richard Maheu
6275 Montezuma Rd., San Diego, Calif. 92115
Maker of woodwinds † 2/76

Howard A. Maier
200 Cæsar Blvd., Williamsville, N. Y. 14221
Maker of strings † 2/76

Lewis Main
1205 Walnut, Long Beach, Calif. 90813 † 2/76

Meeme Malgi
8-05 119th St., College Point, N. Y. 10056
PT 1959 Active 1 emp. IA/MTO
Modern 5/74 • Violin Over 50 to date
† • Viola 10—25 to date † • Cello
10—25 to date † • Lute 1—10 to date †

Ernest J. Maliha
69 Atlantic Ave., Brooklyn, N. Y. 11201
Maker of strings † 5/74

Malmark, Inc.
100 Doyle St., Doylestown, Pa. 18901
FT 1974 Active 8 emp. MTO
Brochure 6/75 • English handbell Over
50 to date Over 50 per year

Milton G. Malmquist
1800 Wilson Ave., St. Paul, Minn. 55119
Maker of lyres † 5/78

John Maluda
1901 Ashmoor Ln., Anchorage, Ky. 40223 †
2/76

Michael Manderen
24 Lakeview Ave., North Tarrytown, N. Y. 10591
PT 1971 Active 1 emp. MTO
Historical 6/74 • Lute 1—10 to date
• Mandolin 1—10 to date • Vihuela
1—10 to date • All instruments 1—10 per
year

Michael Mandile
337 Pine St., Amherst, Mass. 01002
PT 1975 Active 1 emp. IA
Modern Brochure 10/76 • Drum Over
50 to date Over 50 per year

Otto W. Mandl
546 Oxford Ave., Palo Alto, Calif. 94306
Maker of strings † 1/78 • *1980: Not
making instruments*

Mandrake Music
Colrain, Mass. 01340 † 5/76

Dick Manley
Also known as: Sugar Loaf Folk Instruments

Ivie W. Mann
R. D. 2, Box 27A, Orrington, Maine 04474

PT 1927 Active 1 emp. MTO
Modern 10/76 • Violin Over 50 to date
• Viola 10–25 to date • All instruments
1–10 per year

Diane Manne
2002 E. 13th St., Tucson, Ariz. 85719 † 2/76

Michael Marcantonio
30 Cimmorelli Dr., Newburgh, N. Y. 12550 †
1/78

E. and O. Mari
38-01 23d Ave., Long Island City, N. Y. 11105
Maker of strings † 2/76

Donald C. Marienthal
1229 Waimanu St., Honolulu, Hawaii 96814
Also known as: Guitar and Lute Workshop

Ralph Markert
Also known as: North Country Music Store

Cecil Markle
102 W. Burlington Ave., La Grange, Ill. 60525
Maker of oboes † 2/76

David Marks
Box 488, Lyndonville, Vt. 05851
FT 1974 Active 1 emp. IA
Historical Brochure 9/76
• Appalachian dulcimer Over 50 to
date † • Kalimba Over 50 to date †
• Hammered dulcimer 1–10 to date †
• 5-string banjo 1–10 to date †
• Mandolin 1–10 to date † • Psaltery
1–10 to date † • Also known as: Folkcraft
Instruments

Frank Markusic
Box 358, R.D. 1, Lemont Furnace, Pa. 15456
FT 1926 Inactive 1 emp.
IA/MTO Modern 10/74 • Violin Over
50 to date † • Tamburitza Over 50 to
date †

Marlen Guitar Co.
924 S. Scales St., Reidsville, N.C. 27320
FT 1960 Active 2 emp. IA
Modern Brochure 2/75 • Pedal steel
guitar Over 50 to date † • Also known
as: Stadler Music Co.

Sean Maroney
Also known as: Charles Bardin and Sean
Maroney

Bill Marquardt, Jr.
4408 Summercrest Ct., Fort Worth, Tex. 76109
Maker of strings † 1/78

John Marshall
Henry Apts., H314, Frazer/King Rd., Malvern,
Pa. 19355
Maker of strings † 1/78

Marshall Music Co.
235 Ann St., East Lansing, Mich. 48823
Maker of Strings † 2/76

Walter Marston
W. Main St., Conway, N. H. 03818
FT 1970 Active 1 emp. MTO
Modern and historical 12/77
• Steel-string guitar 25–50 to date
1–10 per year

Eugene R. Marteney
Tahanto Trail, Harvard, Mass. 01451
PT 1964 Active 1 emp. MTO
Historical Brochure 4/76 • Baroque
oboe 10–25 to date † • Oboe d'amore
1–10 to date †

C. F. Martin Organisation
510 Sycamore St., Nazareth, Pa. 18064
FT 1833 Active 165 emp. IA
Modern Brochure 6/74 • Steel-string
guitar Over 50 to date Over 50 per year
• Classical guitar Over 50 to date Over
50 per year • 12-string guitar Over 50 to
date Over 50 per year • Tenor guitar
Over 50 to date Over 50 per year • 5-string
banjo Over 50 to date Over 50 per year
• Ukulele Over 50 to date Over 50 per
year • Drum Over 50 to date Over 50
per year • Also known as: The Fibes Drum;
Sigma Guitars; Vega Instrument Co. • *1980:
425 emp. IA/MTO • Electric guitar Over
50 to date Over 50 per year • Not making
drums; not affiliated with The Fibes Drum
• Also known as: Christian F. Martin IV*

Charles T. Martin
65 French St., Berea, Ohio 44017
Maker of strings † 1/78

Christian F. Martin IV

510 Sycamore St., Nazareth, Pa. 18064
Maker of strings †   1/78 • Also known as:
C. F. Martin Organisation

Edsel Martin

Box 367, Swannanoa, N. C. 28778
Maker of Appalachian dulcimers †   2/76

Henry Martin

12309 W. 8th, Helena Dr., Los Angeles, Calif.
90049
PT   Year?   Active   1 emp.   IA
Modern   4/76 • Viola   1–10 to date   †
• Violin   1–10 to date   †

James D. Martin

5½ Moulton St., Portland, Maine 04111
FT   1976   Active   1 emp.   IA
Modern and historical   11/76
• Hammered dulcimer   10–25 to date   †
• Appalachian dulcimer   10–25 to date
† • Psaltery   10–25 to date   † • Spinet
1–10 to date   † • Primarily repairs • Also
known as: Buckdancer's Choice Music

Walter P. Martin

R. D. 1, Box 74, Roaring Springs, Pa. 16673
FT   1970   Active   3 emp.   IA
Historical   Brochure   4/76
• Appalachian dulcimer   Over 50 to
date   Over 50 per year • Hammered
dulcimer   10–25 to date   10–25 per year
• 5-string banjo   Over 50 to date   25–50
per year • Also known as: Sunhearth
Musical Instruments

Howard Martindale

R. D. 1, Box 163, Dean Rd., Hudson Falls, N. Y.
12839
PT   1960   Active   1 emp.   MTO
Historical   4/76 • Appalachian
dulcimer   † • Zither-harp   10–25 to
date   †

Leo J. Martone

5045 Maderia Rd., Virginia Beach, Va. 23455
PT   1976   Active   1 emp.   MTO
Modern   2/78 • Classical guitar   1–10 to
date   †

Lawrence E. Marum

Also known as: Reliable Brothers

William Louis Masasso

711 W. 17th St., Merced, Calif. 95340
PT   1976   Active   1 emp.   MTO
Historical   4/78 • Appalachian
dulcimer   1–10 to date   1–10 per year
• Also known as: Honahlee Dulcimer

Robert M. Mason

Rt. 1, Box 16, Norwick, Ohio 43767
PT   1969   Active   1 emp.   MTO
Modern and historical   6/74 • Steel-string
guitar   1–10 to date   1–10 per year
• Violin   1–10 to date   † • 5-string
banjo   1–10 to date   †

Steve Mason

737 New Hampshire, Lawrence, Kans. 66044
PT   1975   Active   1 emp.   MTO
Modern   3/78 • Steel-string guitar   1–10
to date   † • Appalachian dulcimer   1–10
to date   † • *1980: 1968*

Mason & Hamlin Co.

Also known as: Aeolian Corp.

Richard Massey

P. O. Box 335, Eureka Springs, Ark. 72632
FT   1975   Active   1 emp.   MTO
Modern   3/78 • 5-string banjo   10–25 to
date   1–10 per year • Appalachian
dulcimer   10–25 to date   1–10 per year
• Mandolin   1–10 to date   1–10 per year
• Also known as: Ozark Mt. Banjo Co.

John Masters

230 Fallis Rd., Columbus, Ohio 43214
FT   1971   Active   1 emp.   IA/MTO
Modern   12/77 • Violin   25–50 to date
• Viola   10–25 to date • Cello   1–10 to
date • All instruments   1–10 per year •
*1980: 1961 · Viola   25–50 to date · All
instruments   10–25 per year · Also known
as: Masters Violin Shop*

Matchmaker Violin

Also known as: William Hockenberry

Herman Edmond Matheny

13550 Hill Ave. N. W., Uniontown, Ohio 44685
FT   1924   Active   1 emp.   MTO
Historical   5/74 •   †

Rod Matheson

3415 280th N. W., Stanwood, Wash. 98292
Maker of strings   1/78

Ron D. Matheson

Rt. 1, Box 245, Jerome, Idaho 83338
PT   1977   Active   1 emp.   MTO
Modern   1/77 • Steel-string guitar
10–25 to date   1–10 per year

C. Weldon Mathews

721 Highland Dr., Columbus, Ohio 43214 †
1/78

R. L. Mattingly

1738 E. 7th St., Long Beach, Calif. 90813
FT   1967   Active   3 emp.   IA/MTO
Historical   10/74 • Classical guitar   Over
50 to date   10–25 per year • Also known
as: World of Strings

Boris Matusewitch

853 7th Ave., New York, N. Y. 10019 †   9/76

Charles Maxson

Volga, W. Va. 26238
FT   1954   Active   1 emp.   IA
Modern and historical   9/74
• Appalachian dulcimer   Over 50 to
date   † • Hammered dulcimer   10–25 to
date   † • 5-string banjo   1–10 to date   †
• Guitar-lute   1–10 to date   †

John Maxwell

545 E. 20th St., Cookeville, Tenn. 38501
Maker of Appalachian dulcimers †   2/76

Mayland Co.

P. O. Box 368, Lakeville, Conn. 06039
FT   1866   Active   ? emp.   IA/MTO
Modern   4/75 • Amphion chimes   Over
50 to date   Over 50 per year • Xylophone
Over 50 to date   Over 50 per year •
Orchestra bells   Over 50 to date   Over 50
per year • 1980: Electric chimes and
percussion † • Also known as: The Mayland
Chime Co. (Cincinnati, Ohio)

Judson Maynard

4925 49th, Lubbock, Tex. 79414
PT   Year?   Active   1 emp.   IA/MTO?
Historical   2/76 • Harpsichord   1–10 to
date   † • Viola da gamba   1–10 to date
† • Lute   1–10 to date   † • Rebec   1–10

to date   † • Primarily repairs • 1980:
Vielle   1–10 to date   † • Hurdy-gurdy
1–10 to date   † • Mandolin   1–10 to
date   † • Baroque guitar   1–10 to date
† • Hobbyist

Salvador Mayo

3520 S. W. 100 Ave., Miami, Fla. 33165 †   2/76

Mazza Guitar Shop

460 S. Main St., Mansfield, Ohio 44907
Maker of strings †   1/76 • 1980: 1977
• Primarily repairs • Also known as: Guy
Mazza

Rosario Mazzeo

Rt. 1, Box 213, Carmel, Calif. 93921
PT   1940   Active   1 emp.   IA
Modern   Brochure   10/75 • Clarinet   †

MCI, Inc.

7400 Imperial Dr., Box 8053, Waco, Tex. 76710
Maker of guitar-organs † • Also known as:
Guitorgan • 1980: FT   1968   Active   68
emp.   IA/MTO   Modern   10/80
• Guitar-organ   Over 50 to date   Over 50
per year

John Meador

P. O. Box 567, Bellflower, Calif. 90706
Maker of strings †   1/78

Robert Meadow

60 Harvard Ave., Rockville Center, N. Y. 11570
FT   1976   Active   1 emp.   MTO
Historical   Brochure   4/78 • Lute
10–25 to date   †

James H. Meads II

Ripley Rd., Spencer, W. Va. 25276
PT   1970   Active   1 emp.   MTO
Historical   Brochure   10/74
• Appalachian dulcimer   Over 50 to
date   †

Douglas W. Medearis

Box 273, Winnebago, Ill. 61088
PT   1968   Active   1 emp.   IA
Historical   Brochure   5/74
• Appalachian dulcimer   Over 50 to
date   †

Jimmie Meek

506 S. Belleview St., Amarillo, Tex. 79106

FT 1938 Active 1 emp. MTO Modern and historical 1/76 • Violin 10–25 to date 1–10 per year • Steel-string guitar 1–10 to date 1–10 per year

Paul G. Mehlin and Sons, Inc.
Also known as: Aeolian Corp.

K. Lothar Meisel
1450 E. Main St., Owatonna, Minn. 55060 FT 1957 Active 2 emp. IA/MTO Historical 4/76 • Violin Over 50 to date † • Viola 10–25 to date † • Bass violin 1–10 to date †

Maribel Meisel
Also known as: Philip Belt and Maribel Meisel

Henry Meissner and Son
4585 El Carro Ln., Carpinteria, Calif. 93013 FT 1941 Active 2 emp. IA/MTO Modern and historical 9/75 • Violin Over 50 to date 10–25 per year • Viola 10–25 to date 1–10 per year • *1980: Violin 1–10 per year • Viola 25–50 to date • Repairs*

Fredrico Mejia
1750 Sir Francis Drake Blvd., Fairfax, Calif. 94930 Maker of strings † 8/74

John F. Mello
2277 Shattuck Ave., Berkeley, Calif. 94704 FT 1972 Active 1 emp. MTO Modern 11/74 • Classical guitar 1–10 to date • Steel-string guitar 1–10 to date • All instruments 1–10 per year • Primarily repairs

Mellobar
P. O. Drawer A, Payette, Idaho 83661 Maker of strings † 5/76

Melodiana Accordion Co.
6501 Bergenline Ave., West New York, N. J. 07093 Maker of accordions † 2/75

Melodigrand Corp.
Also known as: Aeolian Corp.

Melody Flute Co.
P. O. Box 276, Laurel, Md. 20810 FT 1938 Active 1 emp. IA Modern Brochure 5/74 • Flute Over 50 to date Over 50 per year • *1980: 3 emp. • Penny whistle Over 50 to date Over 50 per year*

Raymond W. Melton
Rt. 1, Box 211, Woodlawn, Va. 24381 PT Year? Active 1 emp. MTO Historical 10/75 • Appalachian dulcimer 1–10 to date †

Michael Menkevich
5725 N. 7th St., Philadelphia, Pa. 19120 FT 1969 Active 1 emp. IA Modern 10/76 • Classical guitar 25–50 to date 1–10 per year

Meramec Handcrafts
P. O. Box 3845, Kirkwood, Mo. 63122 Maker of strings † 2/76

Thomas Mercer
418-F Locust St., Columbia, Pa. 17512 PT 1972 Active 1 emp. MTO Historical Brochure 2/76 • Harpsichord 1–10 to date 1–10 per year • Virginal 1–10 to date 1–10 per year

Merlin Mfg. Corp.
3545 N. Clark St., Chicago, Ill. 60657 † 2/76

Edward Merrifield
Sprague River, Ore. 97639 PT 1968 Active 1 emp. IA Modern Brochure 6/74 • Lyre 10–25 to date • Gourd harp 1–10 to date • Minstrel harp 1–10 to date • Spinet 1–10 to date • All instruments 1–10 per year

Deborah Merwin
199 Main St., Northampton, Mass. 01060 † 2/76

Richard Merz
2473 Jackson St., San Francisco, Calif. 94115 Maker of harpsichords † 2/76

Casimer Messer
5825 Mildred St., San Diego, Calif. 92110 Maker of strings † 2/76

Kenton Meyer

2934 N. Stowell, Milwaukee, Wis. 53211
PT   1969   Active   1 emp.   MTO
Historical   5/76 • Clavichord   1−10 to
date   †

Meyer Brothers

Box 367, Northport, N. Y. 11768 †   2/75

Jan D. Michael

R. F. D. 1, Box 64, Solon, Iowa 52333
PT   1968   Active   1 emp.   MTO
Modern   4/76 • Steel-string guitar
25−50 to date   † • 12-string guitar   1−10
to date   † • Classical guitar   1−10 to
date   † • 5-string banjo   1−10 to date   †

Micoa, Inc.

346 N. Justine, Chicago, Ill. 60609
Maker of tambourines †

Micro-Frets

100 Grove Rd., Frederick, Md. 21701
Maker of electric guitars and electric bass
guitars †   2/76

Art Middleton

R. R. 1, Springville, Iowa 52336
FT   1970   Active   1 emp.   IA/MTO
Historical   10/74 • Clavichord   1−10 to
date   † • Harpsichord   1−10 to date   †
• Lute   1−10 to date   †

Mignon-Loew Mfg. Co.

Also known as: Ed Taylor

Jeffrey Milian

1532 Crain, Evanston, Ill. 60202
Maker of strings †   1/78

Michael Millard

Box 69, Winchester, N. H. 03470
FT   1971   Active   2 emp.   MTO
Modern   Brochure   10/74 • Steel-string
guitar   Over 50 to date • 12-string guitar
25−50 to date • Autoharp   1−10 to date
• Appalachian dulcimer   1−10 to date
• All instruments   10−25 per year • Also
known as: Froggy Bottom Guitars

A. A. Miller

4214 Devon Dr., Corpus Christi, Tex. 78415
PT   1967   Active   1 emp.   IA

Historical   4/76 • Violin   10−25 to
date   †

Audrey Hash Miller

Rt. 2, Box 119, Mouth of Wilson, Va. 24363
FT   1967   Active   1 emp.   IA
Historical   7/74 • Appalachian
dulcimer   10−25 to date   1−10 per year
• 1980: Appalachian dulcimer   Over 50 to
date • Violin   1−10 to date   1−10 per year

Don R. Miller

1326 S. Church St., Burlington, N. C. 28215
Maker of steel-string guitars †   1/78

Exmar Miller

2610 Hugh St., Parkersburg, W. Va. 26101
PT   1971   Active   1 emp.   IA/MTO
Modern   1/76 • Steel-string guitar
10−25 to date   1−10 per year

Fred G. Miller

Also known as: Gentle Winds Flute Co.

H. Burritt Miller

3602 Hamilton St., Philadelphia, Pa. 19104
FT   1969   Active   1 emp.   IA/MTO
Historical   3/76 • Violin   1−10 to date
• Viola   1−10 to date • Cello   1−10 to
date • Viola da gamba   1−10 to date
• Lute   1−10 to date • Strings   1−10 to
date • All instruments   1−10 per year

Henry F. Miller Piano Co.

Also known as: Aeolian Corp.

James Miller

5017 Sherwood Rd., Bethel Park, Pa. 15102
Maker of strings †   1/78

Janet Miller

12 Donlon St., Rochester, N. Y. 14607
PT   1974   Active   1 emp.   IA
Historical   5/74 • Cornett   1−10 to
date   1−10 per year

Joseph Bernard Miller

300 Stratford Dr., Lexington, Ky. 40503
PT   1929   Active   1 emp.   IA
Historical   5/74 • Violin   25−50 to
date   † • Primarily repairs • 1980: FT
• Classical guitar   10−25 to date • Viola
1−10 to date • Mandolin   1−10 to date

*· Bows   10–25 to date · All instruments
1–10 per year · No repairs*

Kenneth Miller

Rt. 1, Box 83, Cambridge, Maine 04923
FT   1962   Active   1 emp.   MTO
Modern and historical   10/76
· Appalachian dulcimer   1–10 to date   †
· 5-string banjo   1–10 to date   †
· Steel-string guitar   1–10 to date   †
· Mandolin   1–10 to date   † · Ukulele
1–10 to date   † · Rebec   1–10 to date   †
· Primarily repairs · *1980: IA/MTO*
*· Mandolin   25–50 to date · Ukulele
1–10 per year · Also known as: String
Instrument Workshop*

Raymond Miller

P. O. Box 6, Singers Glen, Va. 22850
FT   1976   Active   1 emp.   IA/MTO
Modern   1/77 · Steel-string guitar   1–10
to date   † · Electric guitar   1–10 to
date   † · Also known as: The Guitar Farm

Russ Miller

2234 Durfee Ave., El Monte, Calif. 91732 †
2/76

Stanley P. Miller

Also known as: Nevada City Dulcimers

Miller Guitars

806 N. 2d St., Chillocothe, Ill. 61523
Maker of steel-string guitars †   5/76

Steven Millhouse

913 Virginia Beach Blvd., #207, Virginia Beach,
Va. 23451
Maker of strings †   1/78 · Also known as:
Fret Works · *1980: 4307 Minnesota Dr.,
Anchorage, Alaska 99503*

Weldon Eugene Milligan

1040 Cedar, Broomfield, Colo. 80020
PT   1971   Active   1 emp.   MTO
Modern   6/75 · Steel-string guitar   1–10
to date   1–10 per year · Mandolin   1–10
to date   1–10 per year · 5-string banjo
1–10 to date   1–10 per year · *1980:
Steel-string guitar   10–25 to date*

Scott Mills

Blue Lick Rd., Greenville, W. Va. 24945

PT   1975   Active   1 emp.   IA
Modern   4/76 · Classical guitar   1–10 to
date   † · Steel-string guitar   1–10 to
date   †

Bernie Millstein

1124 Douglas Dr., Pomona, Calif. 91768
Maker of strings †   2/76

Mind Dust Music

P. O. Box 3177, Elida, Ohio 45807
Maker of strings †   2/76

Mingus Guitars

Also known as: William Bland

Donald Minnerly

419 Fremont Ave., Los Altos, Calif. 94022
FT   1970   Active   1 emp.   MTO
Historical   9/77 · Harpsichord   1–10 to
date   1–10 per year · Virginal   1–10 to
date   1–10 per year · Early bows   Over
50 to date   10–25 per year · Rebec   1–10
to date   1–10 per year · Baroque bows
1–10 to date   1–10 per year · Lyra da
braccia   1–10 to date   1–10 per year
· Steel-string guitar   1–10 to date   1–10
per year

Percy Minnerly

P. O. Box 984, Tarpon Springs, Fla. 33589 †
11/76

Larry Minnich

Box 9712, Hollins College, Va. 24020 †   2/76

Minstrel Guitars

1995 E. Oak, Kankakee, Ill. 60901
Maker of steel-string guitars †   1/78 · Also
known as: Richard Muniz

Harry P. Misuriello

Rt. 2, Box 149, Greenville, N. Y. 12083
Maker of strings †   2/76

Danlee Mitchael

Box 640, San Diego State University, San Diego,
Calif. 92115 †   4/78

Henry Mitchell

928 Pleasant Ave., Bremerton, Wash. 98310 †

Howard Mitchell

6027 Ridge Dr., Washington, D.C. 20016
PT   1958   Inactive   1 emp.   MTO
Modern   Brochure   5/76 • Appalachian
dulcimer   Over 50 to date   †
• Hammered dulcimer   10–25 to date   †
• Mouth bow   1–10 to date   †

William J. Mitchell

17500 Mayall St., Northridge, Calif. 91324
FT   1964   Active   1 emp.   IA/MTO
Historical   9/75 • Psaltery   Over 50 to
date   10–25 per year • Rebec   10–25 to
date   1–10 per year • Lyre   1–10 to
date   1–10 per year • Tromba marina
1–10 to date   1–10 per year • Epinette
1–10 to date   1–10 per year • Mouth
bow   10–25 to date   † • Also known as:
Rural Delights • *1980: MTO • Crwth   1–10
to date   † • Talharpa   1–10 to date   †
• Highland harp   1–10 to date   † • Gothic
harp   1–10 to date   † • Rhythm bones
10–25 to date   † • Oud   1–10 to date   †
• Sistrum   1–10 to date   † • No longer
known as Rural Delights*

Mixoldian Musical Woodworks

Also known as: Brian Mumford

Bill Mixon

278 Harvard St., Apt. 9, Cambridge, Mass.
02139
PT   1975   Active   1 emp.   IA/MTO
Modern and historical   1/76
• Appalachian dulcimer   1–10 to date   †

Robert R. Mize

Rt. 2, Blountville, Tenn. 37617
PT   1957   Active   3 emp.   MTO
Historical   Brochure   5/74
• Appalachian dulcimer   Over 50 to
date   †

Douglas Moats

22511 Main St., Doylesburg, Pa. 17219
FT   1976   Active   1 emp.   IA/MTO
Modern and historical   Brochure   2/78
• 5-string banjo   10–25 to date   1–10
per year • Primarily repairs • Also known
as: Stringed Instrument Repair

Edwin Moe

13921 Country Ln., Orange, Calif. 92668
Maker of strings †   2/76

Albert Moglie

1329 F St. N. W., Washington, D. C. 20004
Maker of violins †   2/76

M. P. Moller, Inc.

Hagerstown, Md. 21740
FT   1875   Active   250 emp.   MTO
Modern   Brochure   4/76 • Pipe organ
Over 50 to date   † • *1980: 220 emp. • Pipe
organ   Over 50 per year*

Manocher Molvai

P. O. Box 146, Warwick, N. Y. 10990
Maker of flutes †   2/76 • Also known as:
Mountain Top Flutes

Jay H. Monari

141 Cuthbert Rd., Oaklyn, N. J. 08107
PT   1960   Active   1 emp.   IA
Modern   2/78 • Steel-string guitar   1–10
to date   † • Jazz guitar   1–10 to date   †

I. Mondragon

320 Hayes St., San Francisco, Calif. 94102
Maker of violins †   2/76

Louis Gayle Monette

421 Madison St., Sauk City, Wis. 53583
PT   1974   Active   3 emp.   MTO
Modern and historical   4/76
• Harpsichord   1–10 to date   †
• Primarily repairs

Fred Montague

16 Patriot Rd., Tewksbury, Mass. 01876
PT   1974   Active   1 emp.   IA/MTO
Modern   6/75 • Appalachian dulcimer
25–50 to date   25–50 per year
• Hammered dulcimer   1–10 to date   †

Marc Montefuso

427 E. Main St., Chester, N. J. 07930
FT   Year?   Active   1 emp.   MTO
Modern   10/75 • Appalachian dulcimer
10–25 to date   1–10 per year • 5-string
banjo   1–10 to date   1–10 per year
• Mandolin   1–10 to date   1–10 per year
• Steel-string guitar   1–10 to date   1–10
per year

John Monteleone

41 Degnon Blvd., Bay Shore, N. Y. 11706
FT   1974   Active   1 emp.   MTO
Modern   6/78 • Mandolin   10–25 to

date   10–25 per year • 5-string banjo
10–25 to date   1–10 per year
• Steel-string guitar   1–10 to date   1–10
per year • *1980: 1963 • Mandolin   Over 50
to date • Steel-string guitar   10–25 to date*

Bonnie Carol Montgomery
Also known as: Bonnie Carol Dulcimers

John Montgomery
287 W. 4th St., New York, N. Y. 10014
Maker of hurdy-gurdies †

Lowell Montz
125 E. Alvarado St., Pomona, Calif. 91767 †
5/75

Moog Music, Inc.
Academy St., Williamsville, N. Y. 14221
Maker of synthesizers †   12/77

A. David Moore
North Pomfret, Vt. 05053
FT   1972   Active   4 emp.   IA/MTO
Modern and historical   Brochure   4/76
• Tracker organ   1–10 to date   †

Dave Moore
5445 E. Washington, Phoenix, Ariz. 85034 †
1/77

Grant Moore
109 North St., Ypsilanti, Mich. 48197
PT   1978   Active   1 emp.   MTO
Historical   11/78 • Baroque oboe   1–10
to date   1–10 per year • Oboe da caccia
1–10 to date   1–10 per year • Classical
oboe   1–10 to date   1–10 per year

Howard Moore
1702 N. Island Ave., Wilmington, Calif. 90744
Maker of strings †   2/76

S. Brook Moore
16700 Norwood Rd., Sandy Spring, Md. 20860
PT   1973   Active   1 emp.   IA/MTO
Historical   9/77 • Appalachian
dulcimer   10–25 to date • Harp   10–25
to date • Viola da gamba   1–10 to date
• Violin   1–10 to date • All instruments
1–10 per year

Thomas B. Moore
20912 2d South, Seattle, Wash. 98148

PT   1972   Active   1 emp.   IA
Modern and historical   6/75
• Appalachian dulcimer   Over 50 to
date   Over 50 per year • Also known as:
The Carvers

Thomas L. Moore
100 E. Irving, Normal, Ill. 61761
Maker of strings †   1/78

Timothy Moore
1201 Jackson St., Albion, Mich. 49224
PT   1970   Active   1 emp.   IA/MTO
Modern   9/74 • Appalachian dulcimer
1–10 to date   1–10 per year • Hammered
dulcimer   1–10 to date   1–10 per year

Arlie Moran
10551 Moorpark St., North Hollywood, Calif.
91602 †   2/76

Rene Morel
87 Belmohr St., Belleville, N. J. 07109
PT   1964   Inactive   5 emp.   MTO
Historical   6/74 • Violin   Over 50 to
date   † • Viola   Over 50 to date   †
• Cello   10–25 to date   † • Primarily
repairs • *1980: 1944   7 emp.*

Brian Morgan
Also known as: Charles Jirousek

Tom and Mary Morgan
Rt. 3, Box 147-1, Morgan Springs, Dayton, Tenn.
37321
FT   1954   Active   2 emp.   MTO
Historical   12/74 • 5-string banjo   25–50
to date   1–10 per year • Mandolin   1–10
per year • Autoharp   10–25 to date
1–10 per year

John Moroz
695 Webster Ave., New Rochelle, N. Y. 10801
PT   1973   Active   1 emp.   MTO
Modern   6/76 • Steel-string guitar   1–10
to date   † • Appalachian dulcimer   1–10
to date   †

Bob Morris
Also known as: American Dream
Instruments Mfg.

George Morris
South Stratford, Vt. 05070
Maker of steel-string guitars †   2/78

William V. Morris
HHB 2/4 FA, Fort Lewis, Wash. 98433
Maker of strings †   1/78

Chuck Morrison
4950 E. Pearl St., Boulder, Colo. 80301
Maker of strings †   1/78

Mark Mortenson
1607 Pole Line Rd., Davis, Calif. 95616
Maker of strings †   1/78

Wayne Moskow
2126 Fifth Ave., San Rafael, Calif. 94901
FT   1941   Active   1 emp.   IA/MTO
Historical   Brochure   4/76 • Strings   †

Mosrite of California
1215 N. Highland Ave., Hollywood, Calif. 90038
†   2/76

Edward B. Moss
4001 Lester, Bartlesville, Okla. 74003
PT   1958   Active   1 emp.   IA/MTO
Modern   9/74 • Violin   25–50 to date
1–10 per year • Viola   1–10 to date   †
• Steel-string guitar   1–10 to date   †
• Electric guitar   1–10 to date   † • *1980:*
FT • Violin   Over 50 to date • Viola
10–25 to date   1–10 per year • Cello
1–10 to date   † • Not making steel-string
and electric guitars • Repairs

Bob Mossay
Also known as: Moze Guitars

S. L. Mossman Co., Inc.
Rt. 3, Strothers Field, Winfield, Kans. 67156
FT   1969   Active   16 emp.   IA/MTO
Modern and historical   Brochure   6/74
• Steel-string guitar   Over 50 to date
Over 50 per year

L. W. Moudy
5903 El Mio Dr., Los Angeles, Calif. 90042
PT   1960   Active   1 emp.   MTO
Modern and historical   12/75
• Appalachian dulcimer   Over 50 to
date   † • 5-string banjo   1–10 to date   †

Peter Moulton
R. D. 2, Canton, N. Y. 13617
Maker of strings †   1/78

Mountain Spring Lutherie
Also known as: Kenneth Reagan Cole

Mountain Top Flutes
Also known as: Manocher Molvai

Mt. Lebanon Banjo Co.
Box 249, Sturbridge, Mass. 01262
FT   1973   Active   3 emp.   IA/MTO
Modern   Brochure   2/75 • 5-string
banjo   10–25 to date   †

Moze Guitars
4701 College Ave., San Diego, Calif. 92115
FT   1975   Active   2 emp.   MTO
Modern and historical   4/78 • Steel-string
guitar   25–50 to date   † • Electric
guitar   10–25 to date   † • Classical
guitar   1–10 to date   † • Also known as:
Bob Mossay • *1980: IA/MTO • Steel-string*
guitar   Over 50 to date   10–25 per year
• Electric guitar   1–10 per year • Classical
guitar   1–10 per year

Mr. Jew's Harp
Also known as: Thomas P. Bilyeu

Mudler-Hunter Co.
2638 W. Gordon, Philadelphia, Pa. 19144
Maker of organs †   2/76

Philip Muehl
1432 Park Ave., Baltimore, Md. 21217
Maker of strings †   1/78

Albert Mueller
5249 Walnut Ave., Sacramento, Calif. 95841
FT   1961   Active   1 emp.   IA/MTO
Modern   7/74 • Violin   25–50 to date
1–10 per year • Viola   1–10 to date
1–10 per year • Cello   1–10 to date
1–10 per year

Dave Muelrath
General Delivery, Forest Glen, Calif. 96030
PT   1966   Active   1 emp.   MTO
Modern and historical   10/76
• Appalachian dulcimer   10–25 to date
† • Steel-string guitar   1–10 to date   †

Multi-Kord Factory
359-A Illinois St., Indianapolis, Ind. 46204
Maker of pedal steel guitars †   12/77

Multivox
370 Vanderbilt Motor Pkwy., Hauppauge, N. Y.
11787
Maker of synthesizers and electronic pianos
† 12/77 • *1980: FT 1952 Active*
? emp. IA Modern Brochure 10/80
• Electronic keyboards † • Also known as:
Sorkin Music Co., Inc.

Brian Mumford
2526 Modoc Rd., Santa Barbara, Calif. 93105
FT 1970 Active 1 emp. MTO
Modern and historical Brochure 9/74
• Appalachian dulcimer Over 50 to
date Over 50 per year • Hummel 10–25
to date 1–10 per year • Hammered
dulcimer 10–25 to date 10–25 per year
• Bowed psaltery Over 50 to date 25–50
per year • Santouri 1–10 to date †
• Salterio 1–10 to date † • Epinette
25–50 to date † • Also known as:
Mixoldian Musical Woodworks

Richard Muniz
Also known as: Minstrel Guitars

Robert L. Murdock
1601 Ulster St., Denver, Colo. 80220
FT 1972 Active 1 emp. MTO
Modern 1/78 • Appalachian dulcimer
10–25 to date 1–10 per year • Electric
guitar 1–10 to date 1–10 per year
• Primarily repairs

Tom Murdock
121 35th St., Manhattan Beach, Calif. 90266
Maker of Appalachian dulcimers and
psalteries † 12/77

Barry Murphy
2219 Pennington Bend Rd., Nashville, Tenn.
37214
PT 1958 Active 1 emp. IA/MTO
Historical 6/74 • Appalachian
dulcimer 10–25 to date † • Classical
guitar 1–10 to date † • Lute 1–10 to
date †

Dennis Murphy
P. O. Box 7473, Carmel, Calif. 93921
PT 1970 Active 1 emp. IA/MTO
Modern and historical Brochure 4/76
• Appalachian dulcimer Over 50 to

date 10–25 per year • Bowed psaltery
10–25 to date 10–25 per year •
Hammered dulcimer 1–10 to date †
• Violin 1–10 to date † • Also known as:
Dulcimer Seed

Michael Murphy
R. R. 3, Mills Rd., St. Clairsville, Ohio 43950
FT 1972 Active 1 emp. IA
Historical Brochure 12/74
• Appalachian dulcimer Over 50 to
date Over 50 per year • Hammered
dulcimer 10–25 to date 1–10 per year
• 5-string banjo Over 50 to date 10–25
per year

Pat Murphy
Also known as: Coll Divine Flutes; Sunrise

Anthony Murray
1408 A Allyson Ct., Virginia Beach, Va. 23454
FT 1964 Active 1 emp. MTO
Modern and historical 7/74 • Classical
guitar Over 50 to date 10–25 per year
• Lute 10–25 to date 1–10 per year
• Renquinto 1–10 to date † • *1980:*
Classical guitar 1–10 per year • Lute
25–50 to date • Not making renquintos

Dave Murray
Rt. 1, Box 132, Ellenboro, N. C. 28040
FT 1975 Active 1 emp. IA/MTO
Modern and historical 4/78
• Appalachian dulcimer 25–50 to date
10–25 per year • Also known as: Joyful
Noise Dulcimers

Jeff Murza
1204 Sylvan Ave., Haddon Heights, N. J. 08035
† 4/78

Thomas Guy Musco
27 Dartmouth St., Watertown, Mass. 02172
PT 1972 Active 1 emp. MTO
Historical 5/74 • Lute 1–10 to date
1–10 per year • Appalachian dulcimer
1–10 to date 1–10 per year • Hammered
dulcimer 1–10 to date 1–10 per year

Musette Player-Piano
Also known as: Aeolian Corp.

Musical Arts Academy
Also known as: Marjorie Tayloe

Musical Instrument Workshop
Also known as: Frederick Battershell

Musical Traditions Co.
Also known as: Henry Levin

Musical Woodcraft
Also known as: Charles Bardin and Sean Maroney

Music Factory
1264 Monterey St., San Luis Obispo, Calif. 94123
Maker of strings † 2/76

Music Man, Inc.
1338 State College Pkwy., Anaheim, Calif. 92806
Maker of electric guitars † 1/78 • Also known as: Leo Fender

Musiconics International, Inc.
7400 Imperial Dr., Box 8053, Waco, Tex. 76710
FT 1967 Active 52 emp. IA
Modern Brochure 4/75
• Guitar-organ Over 50 to date Over 50 per year • Electric bass guitar Over 50 to date Over 50 per year

Musicraft, Inc.
Box 173, Astoria, Ore. 97103 † 2/75

Music Technology, Inc.
105 Fifth Ave., Garden City, N. Y. 11040
Maker of electric pianos † 12/77

Music Workshop
Also known as: Roger Thurman

The Music Workshop
Also known as: Robert Christie

Musique Concernz
Also known as: Walter Bradley, Jr.

Mussehl and Westphal
31 Elm St., Fort Atkinson, Wis. 53538
FT 1921 Active 1 emp. IA
Modern Brochure 5/75 • Musical saw Over 50 to date Over 50 per year

Musser Marimbas, Inc.
Also known as: Ludwig Industries

Mussi Accordions
144 Nassau Ave., Brooklyn, N. Y. 11222
Maker of accordions † 2/75

Herb Myers
2180 Monterey, Menlo Park, Calif. 94025
FT 1969 Active 1 emp. MTO
Historical 5/75 • Cittern 1–10 to date † • Vielle 1–10 to date †
• Primarily repairs • 1980: PT • Gothic harp 1–10 to date 1–10 per year

McAllen C. Myers
Box 6, Young Harris, Ga. 30582
PT 1960 Active 1 emp. MTO
Historical 5/74 • Appalachian dulcimer 25–50 to date 1–10 per year

Rodney Myrvaagnes
780 Boylston St., 17E, Boston, Mass. 02199
FT 1973 Active 1 emp. MTO
Historical Brochure 4/74
• Harpsichord 1–10 to date 1–10 per year

Matthew Myszewski
Also known as: Richard Cook

Sando Alex Nagy
292 W. 92 St., New York, N. Y. 10025
FT 1970 Active 1 emp. IA/MTO
Historical 7/74 • Viola 25–50 to date †

John Nargesian
63 Otis St., Newtonville, Mass. 02160
FT 1966 Active 1 emp. MTO
Historical 5/74 • Harpsichord 10–25 to date 1–10 per year

National Guitars
177 W. Hintz Rd., Wheeling, Ill. 60090
Maker of steel-string guitars † 5/76

Natraj
Box 307, Lucerne Valley, Calif. 92356
FT 1973 Active 2 emp. IA/MTO
Historical Brochure 5/76 • Tabor 10–25 to date † • Hand drum Over 50 to date Over 50 per year • Tambourine Over 50 to date Over 50 per year • Jingle rings Over 50 to date Over 50 per year
• Also known as: Instruments for Meditation and Celebration

John Nattelson
Goshen, Mass. 01032
Maker of steel-string guitars † 5/74

NBN Guitars
7823 County Line Rd., Longmont, Colo. 80501
FT 1967 Active 4 emp. IA
Modern Brochure 11/74 • Steel-string
guitar Over 50 to date Over 50 per year

William A. Nealon
3263 W. 153, Cleveland, Ohio 44111
Maker of strings † 2/76

Neato Productions
Also known as: Laura Rachel Allen

Hans Nebel
101 Garfield St., Dumont, N. J. 07628
FT 1957 Active 1 emp. MTO
Modern and historical 6/74 • Violin
10– 25 to date † • Viola 1– 10 to date
† • Cello 1– 10 to date † • Viola da
gamba 1– 10 to date † • Steel-string
guitar 1– 10 to date † • *1980: Classical
guitar 1–10 to date † • Not making
steel-string guitars • Primarily repairs*

Otto Neecker and Sons
9607 Dallas Ave., Silver Spring, Md. 20901 †
2/76

Howard Needham
28 S. 4th Ave., Ilion, N. Y. 13357
FT 1974 Active 2 emp. MTO
Modern 2/78 • 5-string banjo 1– 10 to
date 1– 10 per year • Steel-string guitar
10– 25 to date 1– 10 per year

Rusty Neff
317 Pleasant St., Yellow Springs, Ohio 45387
PT 1969 Active 1 emp. MTO
Modern and historical 1/75
• Appalachian dulcimer 10– 25 to date
† • 12-string guitar 1– 10 to date †
• Classical guitar 1– 10 to date †
• Mandolin 1– 10 to date †

Tom Nehil
2167 Stone Dr., Ann Arbor, Mich. 48105
PT 1975 Active 1 emp. IA
Modern 4/76 • Hammered dulcimer
10– 25 to date 10– 25 per year

Robert L. Nelson
Rt. 1, Box 218, Ceres, Va. 24318
Maker of strings † 2/76 • *1980: Not
making instruments*

Phil and Gayle Neuman
687 Leonard, Ashland, Ore. 95720
PT 1976 Active 2 emp. MTO
Historical Brochure 12/76 • Rackett
10– 25 to date † • Sordonne 1– 10 to
date † per year • Bladder pipe 1– 10 to
date †

Nevada City Dulcimers
Also known as: M. W. Vance and Stanley P.
Miller

Larry Newcomb
243 State St., Apt. 3, Portland, Maine 04101
Maker of strings † 1/78

The New Expression
Also known as: Robert Zink

B. E. Newman
3121 Veteran Ave., Los Angeles, Calif. 90034
Maker of strings † 2/76

Brett Newman
3470 Cannon Pl., G-42, Bronx, N. Y. 10463 †
6/76
*1980: FT 1975 Active 1 emp. MTO
Modern 10/80 • Appalachian dulcimer,
psaltery, and limberjack †*

Richard Scott Newman
66 Frost Ave., Rochester, N. Y. 14608
PT 1965 Active 2 emp. IA/MTO
Modern 10/75 • 5-string banjo 1– 10 to
date † • *1980: 5-string banjo 25– 50 to
date 1–10 per year • Also known as: Ruff
Alley Banjo Works*

William Newman
2159 10th Ave. West, Seattle, Wash. 98119
FT 1964 Active 2 emp. MTO
Modern Brochure 11/74
• Harpsichord 25– 50 to date 1– 10 per
year • Virginal 1– 10 to date 1– 10 per
year

New Orleans Banjo Sales
8424 S. Claiborne Ave., #A, New Orleans, La.

70118
Maker of strings † 2/76

David A. Newton
4022 Fonville, Beaumont, Tex. 77705
PT 1975 Active 1 emp. IA/MTO
Historical 2/78 • Steel-string guitar
1– 10 to date † • Mandolin 1– 10 to
date † • Ukulele 1– 10 to date †

New Traditions Banjo Co.
4688 Ridgeview Rd., Dunwoody, Ga. 30338
Maker of 5-string banjos † 1/77

New World Harp Co.
Also known as: Parker Adams

NHF Musical Merchandise Corp.
231 N. Third St., Philadelphia, Pa. 19106 †
2/76

General Custer Nicholas and Sons
2271 Autumn Rd. S. E., Carrollton, Ohio 44615
PT 1938 Active 4 emp. IA
Historical Brochure 6/74
• Appalachian dulcimer Over 50 to
date †

David R. Nichols
P.O. Box 338, 1 Nell Manor Dr., Waddington,
N. Y. 13694
FT 1964 Active 2 emp. IA/MTO
Historical Brochure 2/78 • 5-string
banjo Over 50 to date Over 50 per year
• Mandolin 25– 50 to date 10– 25 per
year • Steel-string guitar 10– 25 to date
1– 10 per year • *1980: 5-string banjo
25–50 per year • Also known as: Nichols
Custom Pearl Inlay*

Milan S. Nicksic
303 E. Harmon, #87, Las Vegas, Nev. 89109
Maker of strings † 1/78

Nick's Music Store
1055 Market St. Plaza, Wheeling, W. Va. 26003
Maker of strings † 1/78

Paul Niebell
Potomac, Md. 20854 †

Nielsen Violin Shop
1905 Harney St., #233, Omaha, Neb. 68102
FT 1912 Inactive 2 emp. MTO
Historical 4/76 • Violin † • Primarily
repairs • Also known as: Norvald C. Nielsen
• *1980: Deceased • Now known as: N. Chris
Nielsen*

Vahakn Nigogosian
111 W. 57th St., New York, N. Y. 10019
FT 1933 Inactive 3 emp. MTO
Modern and historical Brochure 4/76
• Violin 1– 10 to date † • Steel-string
guitar 1– 10 to date † • Cello 1– 10 to
date † • Primarily repairs • Also known
as: Stradivarius Studios

The Noack Organ Co., Inc.
Main/School Sts., Georgetown, Mass. 01833
FT 1960 Active 7 emp. MTO
Modern Brochure 5/74 • Organ
10– 25 to date † • Pipe organ Over 50 to
date † • *1980: 12 emp. Modern and
historical • Tracker organ Over 50 to
date 1–10 per year • Not making pipe
organs • Also known as: Fritz Noack*

Mr. and Mrs. Roy Noble
14829 LeMay St., Van Nuys, Calif. 91405
FT 1963 Active 2 emp. MTO
Modern and historical Brochure 12/75
• Lute 1– 10 to date † • Steel-string
guitar Over 50 to date †

Tim Noble
425 Ridge St., Emmaus, Pa. 18049
Maker of strings † 1/77

Noble and Cooley Co.
Water St., Granville, Mass. 01034
Maker of drums † 2/76

Noblet Woodwinds
Also known as: G. LeBlanc Corp.

Robert Noehren †

Mr. and Mrs. Jerome Nolte
Evergreen Mtn., Bear, Idaho 83612
FT 1972 Active 2 emp. MTO
Historical Brochure 4/76
• Appalachian dulcimer Over 50 to
date 10– 25 per year • Mandolin 1– 10
to date †

Brian Nonamaker
2600 Greenfield Ave., Los Angeles, Calif 90064

FT 1973 Active 1 emp. IA/MTO Historical 6/74 • Gothic harp 1– 10 to date † • Bardic harp 1– 10 to date † • Celtic harp 1– 10 to date †

Nordenholz
West Hempstead, N. Y. 11552 †

Norlin Music, Inc.
7373 N. Cicero, Lincolnwood, Ill. 60646
Also known as: Chicago Musical Instrument Co.; Epiphone Guitars; Lowrey Pianos; F. E. Olds and Sons; Pearl Drums; F. A. Reynolds Co.

Norman's Rare Guitars
6753 Tampa Ave., Reseda, Calif. 91335
Maker of strings † 2/76

Joseph Norris
9 N. Preston St., Philadelphia, Pa. 19104
Maker of harpsichords † 2/76

Paul E. Norris
2309 Bonnie Brae, Santa Ana, Calif. 92706 † 2/76

North Country Music Store
P. O. Box 311, Chapel Dr. North, Wexford, Pa. 15090
FT 1976 Active 1 emp. IA/MTO Modern and historical Brochure 2/78 • Appalachian dulcimer Over 50 to date † • Hammered dulcimer 1– 10 to date † • Also known as: Robert D. Hutchinson; Ralph Markert

North Georgia Music Co.
Also known as: Bill Blaylock

Northwest School of Instrument Design
Also known as: Anthony J. Huvard

Jesse Norton
General Delivery, Etowah, N. C. 28729
PT 1973 Active 1 emp. MTO Modern 5/74 • Appalachian dulcimer 1– 10 to date †

William F. Norton
313 Norris Ct., Madison, Wis. 53703
Maker of strings † 1/78

Tom Norwood
921 Primrose, Monrovia, Calif. 91016
Maker of strings † 2/76

Will Norwood
402 Occidental Ave. South, Seattle, Wash. 98104
PT 1971 Active 1 emp. IA/MTO Modern 9/74 • Appalachian dulcimer 25– 50 to date 10– 25 per year • Classical guitar 1– 10 to date 1– 10 per year • 5-string banjo 1– 10 to date 1– 10 per year • Also known as: The Wood Shop

Nota Bene: A Harpsichord Workshop
Also known as: Donald Bell

Peter Nothnagle
Also known as: Aardvark Fluteworks

Novaline, Inc.
P. O. Box 574, Norwood, Mass. 02062
Maker of electronic pianos† 12/77

Oasis Guitars
Also known as: Gary Cooper

Oberheim Electronics, Inc.
1549 Ninth St., Santa Monica, Calif. 90401
FT 1969 Active 32 emp. IA Modern Brochure 2/78 • Synthesizer Over 50 to date Over 50 per year

Frank S. O'Brian
27 Maple Hill Dr., Larchmont, N. Y. 10538
PT Year? Active 1 emp. IA Modern 2/75 • Tenor banjo 25– 50 to date • 5-string banjo 25– 50 to date • All instruments 1– 10 per year

Vincent O'Brien
216 New Hyde Park Rd., Garden City, N. Y. 11530
PT 1938 Active 1 emp. IA Modern and historical 4/75 • Viola da gamba 1– 10 to date † • Viola d'amore 1– 10 to date † • Violin 1– 10 to date † • Viola 1– 10 to date † • Cello 1– 10 to date † • Irish harp Over 50 to date † • *1980: Bows 1– 10 to date † • Not making Irish harps • Primarily repairs*

Walter O'Brien
8116 S. Park, Garretsville, Ohio 44231

PT 1960 Active 1 emp. MTO
Historical 4/76 • Virginal 1–10 to
date † • Harpsichord 1–10 to date †
• *1980: 1959 • Pedal harpsichord 1–10
to date*

Octave Electronics, Inc.
32-73 Steinway St., Long Island City, N. Y. 11103
Maker of synthesizers and electric pianos
† 12/77 • Also known as: Syn-cordion
Musical Instrument Corp.

Ode Banjos
1801 Gilbert Ave., Cincinnati, Ohio 45202
FT Year? Active ? emp. IA
Modern Brochure 12/77 • 5-string
banjo Over 50 to date Over 50 per year
• Also known as: The Fred Gretsch Co.
• *1980: Now known as: Kustom Gretsch*

Roger O'Donnell
16635 Gazeley, Saugus, Calif. 91350
Maker of strings † 2/76

Odot Instruments
Also known as: Owen E. Griffith

Albert Ogawa
2671 Tantalus Dr., Honolulu, Hawaii 96813
PT 1974 Active 1 emp. MTO
Modern 2/78 • Classical guitar 1–10 to
date 1–10 per year

David Ohannesian
87 E. 12th St., Arcata, Calif. 95521
FT 1974 Active 1 emp. MTO
Historical Brochure 1/75 • Recorder
10–25 to date † • Voice flute 1–10 to
date †

Thomas Ohrstrom
7801 Rochester, Pittsburgh, Pa. 15206
Maker of flutes and drums †

F. E. Olds and Son
Also known as: Norlin Music, Inc.

Dr. John Olds
4040 Sunset Rd., San Diego, Calif. 92103
PT Year? Active 1 emp. MTO
Modern 12/74 • Appalachian dulcimer
1–10 to date †

Old Time Pickin' Parlor
Also known as: Randy Wood

Old World Guitars
Also known as: James Ariail

Old World Instruments
Also known as: John Tunnoch Gilmour III

Cheston Olsen
2512 Winfred St., Metairie, La. 70003
Maker of strings † 2/76

Richard S. Olsen
732 S. Broadalbin, Albany, Ore. 97321
Maker of strings † 1/78

Rudolf Olsen
292 Cherry Ln., Teaneck, N. J. 07666
Maker of violins † 2/76

Timothy Olsen
8222 S. Park Ave., Tacoma, Wash. 98408
FT 1971 Active 3 emp. MTO
Modern Brochure 5/74 • Electric
guitar 10–25 to date 1–10 per year
• Steel-string guitar 10–25 to date
1–10 per year • Appalachian dulcimer
10–25 to date † • Jazz guitar 1–10 to
date 1–10 per year • Primarily repairs
• Also known as: Leo Bidne; Bob Petrulis
• *1980: 1 emp. • Classical guitar 1–10 to
date 1–10 per year • Bass guitar 1–10
to date 1–10 per year • Not making
Appalachian dulcimers • No repairs • Now
known as: Olsen Lutherie*

Daniel R. Olson
2009 Hopkins, Berkeley, Calif. 94707 † 2/76

Olympic Organ Builders
Also known as: Glenn White

Robert Olyslager
35 Mayfield St., Rochester, N. Y. 14607 † 1/78

Omar Mfg. Co.
Also known as: John Sloan

Ome Banjo Co., Inc.
5595 Arapahoe, Boulder, Colo. 80303
FT 1971 Active 7 emp. IA/MTO
Modern Brochure 10/74 • 5-string
banjo Over 50 to date Over 50 per year

Jan Oosting
Old Stump Rd., Brookhaven, N. Y. 11719
PT   1967   Active   1 emp.   MTO
Historical   9/74 • Appalachian
dulcimer   10–25 to date   † • Hammered
dulcimer   1–10 to date   † • 5-string
banjo   1–10 to date   †

Marilije Oosting
Box 36, FPO Naval Station, Seattle, Wash. 98791
†   10/74

G. K. Oppedal
2215 Walnut Ave., Tucson, Ariz. 85706 †   4/78

George Opperman Woodwinds
1117 Clover St., South Bend, Ind. 46615
FT   1947   Active   2 emp.   MTO
Modern   Brochure   6/74 • Modern
flute   †

Opsonar Organ Co.
New Kensington, Pa. 15068
Maker of organs †   2/76

Jose Oribe
1120 N. La Brea Ave., Inglewood, Calif. 90302
FT   1962   Active   1 emp.   MTO
Modern   Brochure   9/74 • Classical
guitar   Over 50 to date • Flamenco
guitar   Over 50 to date • All instruments
25–50 per year

Original Musical Instrument Co., Inc.
1404 Gaylore St., Long Beach, Calif. 90813
FT   1928   Active   14 emp.   IA/MTO
Modern and historical   Brochure   10/74
• Dobro   Over 50 to date   Over 50 per
year • Mandolin   Over 50 to date   Over
50 per year • Porta-bass   † • 5-string
banjo   Over 50 to date   Over 50 per year
• Also known as: Dobro, Inc.

Patrick O'Riordan
7516 Avalon Dr., Fort Wayne, Ind. 46819
PT   1970   Active   1 emp.   MTO
Historical   1/77 • Appalachian
dulcimer   25–50 to date   10–25 per year
• Flute   1–10 to date   1–10 per year
• Fife   1–10 to date   1–10 per year
• Hammered dulcimer   1–10 to date   †
• Steel-string guitar   1–10 to date   † •
Irish harp   1–10 to date   1–10 per year
• *1980: Appalachian dulcimer   Over 50 to*
date   1–10 per year • Fife   10–25 to date
• Not making hammered dulcimers and
guitars • Also known as: A Music Workshop

Juan Orozco
156 W. 56th St., New York, N. Y. 10019
PT   Year?   Active   3 emp.   MTO
Modern   6/74 • Steel-string guitar   Over
50 to date   25–50 per year

Orphic Endeavors
Also known as: Tony Pizzo and Laura
Fontana Pizzo

R. S. Orren, Jr.
3828 Ryan, Fort Worth, Tex. 76110
Maker of strings †   1/78

Orthey Dulcimers
R.D. 1, Box 34A, Newport, Pa. 17074
PT   1965   Active   3 emp.   IA
Modern   Brochure   5/74 • Appalachian
dulcimer   Over 50 to date   † • Psaltery
Over 50 to date   † • Hammered
dulcimer   1–10 to date   †
• Harpsichord   1–10 to date   † • 5-string
banjo   1–10 to date   † • Steel-string
guitar   1–10 to date   † • Primarily
repairs • *1980: 1 emp.   Historical*
• Hammered dulcimer   10–25 to date • No
repairs • Also known as: George F. Orthey

Oscar Ortiz
731 Girard St., San Francisco, Calif. 94134
Maker of strings †   2/76

Foy D. Osborne
822 Spring Garden St., Greensboro, N. C. 17403
PT   1975   Active   1 emp.   IA/MTO
Modern   1/77 • Steel-string guitar
10–25 to date   †

Joseph Osborne
505 Hamilton St., Carlisle, Pa. 17013
FT   1970   Active   1 emp.   MTO
Historical   Brochure   10/74
• Harpsichord   1–10 to date   †
• Clavichord   1–10 to date   †

Osco Mfg. Corp.
27 Bleecker St., New York, N. Y. 10003 †   3/76

Neil Ostberg
W. 15130 N., 84 Knoll Terr., Menomenee Falls,

Wis. 53051
Maker of lutes † 2/76

Doran Oster
311 N. Main St., Gainesville, Fla. 32601
Maker of Appalachian dulcimers,
hammered dulcimers, and flutes † 2/76

Thaddeus Outerbridge III
11 Bayview Ave., Beverly, Mass. 01915
FT 1968 Active 1 emp. MTO
Modern 4/76 • Pipe organ 1–10 to
date †

Out of Your Gourd Music
Also known as: Larry Cottingham

Ovation Instruments, Inc.
Greenwoods Rd., New Hartford, Conn. 06057
Maker of steel-string guitars, electric
guitars, and electric bass guitars † 2/76

A. E. Overholtzer
618 Orient St., Chico, Calif. 95926
FT 1926 Active 1 emp. MTO
Modern Brochure 5/74 • Steel-string
guitar 10–25 to date 1–10 per year

Barbara Owen
P. O. Box 28, Gloucester, Mass. 01930 † 4/75

Ozark Mt. Banjo Co.
Also known as: Richard Massey

Ozark Woodworking Co.
Also known as: Bobby L. Blair

John A. Paganoni and Sons
167 White Birch Dr., Pease AFB, N. H. 03801
PT 1970 Active 1 emp. MTO
Historical Brochure 1/75 • Mandolin
10–25 to date 1–10 per year

Gilbert Owen Page
R.F.D. 1, Dutch Village, Apt. 3, North
Stonington, Conn. 06359
Maker of strings † 1/78

Palco Products Corp.
15 W. 20th St., New York, N. Y. 10011 † 2/75

Charles A. Palis
1307 Delwin, Cape Girardeau, Mo. 63701
Maker of strings † 1/78

Richard Palm
Space Q11, 2547 8th St., Berkeley, Calif. 94710
FT 1974 Active 1 emp. MTO
Historical Brochure 6/75 • Recorder
1–10 to date †

Victor Palmason
935 Electric S. E., Salem, Ore. 97302
Maker of strings † 2/76

Pancordion, Inc.
111 Park Ave. South, New York, N. Y. 10017 †
2/75

Manouk Papazian
24 W. 30th St., New York, N. Y. 10001
FT 1934 Active 1 emp. IA
Modern and historical 5/74 • Classical
guitar Over 50 to date 1–10 per year
• Lute 25–50 to date 1–10 per year
• Violin 10–25 to date 1–10 per year
• Viola 10–25 to date 1–10 per year
• Cello 10–25 to date 1–10 per year
• Vihuela 10–25 to date †

Joe Park
3504 Taft Hwy., Signal Mountain, Tenn. 37377
PT 1960 Active 1 emp. IA
Modern and historical 6/74
• Appalachian dulcimer 25–50 to date
• Steel-string guitar 1–10 to date
• Mandolin 1–10 to date • 5-string
banjo 1–10 to date • Strings 1–10 to
date • All instruments 25–50 per year
• *1980: Appalachian dulcimer Over 50 to
date 25–50 per year • All instruments
Over 50 per year*

Kenneth Parker
60 Harvard Ave., Rockville Center, N. Y. 11570
FT 1975 Active 1 emp. MTO
Modern 3/78 • Jazz guitar 1–10 to
date † • Electric bass guitar 1–10 to
date † • Electric guitar 1–10 to date
†

Gary C. Parks
1810 Laurel Dr., Columbus, Ind. 47201
PT 1974 Inactive 1 emp. MTO
Modern 6/74 • Appalachian dulcimer
1–10 to date 1–10 per year • Sitar
1–10 to date †

Clyde H. Parmelee, Jr.
151 Willow Rd., Menlo Park, Calif. 94025

FT 1971 Active 1 emp. MTO
Historical 10/74 • Harpsichord 1– 10 to
date • Virginal 10– 25 to date • All
instruments 1– 10 per year

Charles Parson
509 Laurel St., Greenup, Ky. 41144
Maker of strings † 2/76

David Partridge
P.O. Box 1322, Myrtle Creek, Ore. 97457
Maker of strings † 1/78

Bob Pascoe and Doug Perry
3253 N. Bartlet Ave., Milwaukee, Wis. 53211 †
2/78

Theodore Patashne
24 Glenwood Ave., Minneapolis, Minn. 55403
Maker of violins † 2/76

Josef Patchen
699 Broad St., Augusta, Ga. 30914
FT 1968 Active 1 emp. MTO
Modern 6/74 • Classical guitar 25– 50
to date 10– 25 per year • Primarily repairs
• *1980: Classical guitar 1– 10 per year*
• *Also known as: Patchen, Mingledorff &*
Associates, Inc.

Etoyse Patterson
411 Dora Dr., Newport News, Va. 23602
PT 1966 Active 2 emp. IA
Modern 10/74 • Violin 1– 10 to date †
• Mandolin 1– 10 to date †
• Steel-string guitar 1– 10 to date †
• Primarily repairs

James E. Patterson
715 Gharkey St., Santa Cruz, Calif. 95060
PT 1964 Active 1 emp. MTO
Modern 3/78 • Steel-string guitar Over
50 to date 1– 10 per year • Classical
guitar 1– 10 to date 1– 10 per year
• Appalachian dulcimer Over 50 to
date 10– 25 per year • Hammered
dulcimer 1– 10 to date †

Frank Pausic
11346 Coriender Ave., Fountain Valley, Calif.
92708
Maker of strings † 8/74

G. L. Payne
Box 118, Garrett Park, Md. 20766 † 2/76
1980: Inactive

Dr. Richard W. Payne
1211 N. Shartel St., Oklahoma City, Okla. 73103
PT 1965 Active 1 emp. MTO
Historical 12/75 • Flute Over 50 to
date †

Thomas Payne
3923 Fetlock Circle, Colorado Springs, Colo.
80917
PT 1972 Active 1 emp. IA
Modern 9/77 • Appalachian dulcimer
Over 50 to date † • *1980: Inactive MTO*

Peacewood Dulcimer
Box 188, Rt. 1, Lawton, Mich. 49065
FT 1968 Active 1 emp. MTO
Historical Brochure 6/74
• Appalachian dulcimer Over 50 to
date 25– 50 per year • Also known as:
Tom J. Caskey

George Peacock
2200 15th St., San Francisco, Calif. 94114
FT 1967 Active 2 emp. IA
Modern and historical 5/74 • Classical
guitar 10– 25 to date • Steel-string
guitar 10– 25 to date • Appalachian
dulcimer 1– 10 to date • All
instruments 1– 10 per year

Pearl Drums
Also known as: Norlin Music, Inc.

Don Pease
64 Russell Rd., Marion, N. Y. 14505
Maker of strings † 1/78

Elizabeth Peck
932 Hilltop Mobile Home Ct., Asheville, N. C.
28800 † 6/75

Byrne Pedit
P. O. Box 681, Healdsburg, Calif. 95448 † 4/76

Sid Pedler
Box 38, Bristol, Ind. 46507
Maker of oboes † 2/76

Pedulla/Orsini Guitars
183 Washington St., Whitman, Mass. 02140
FT 1975 Active 2 emp. IA/MTO
Modern Brochure 4/76 • Steel-string
guitar 10– 25 to date 10– 25 per year

Clifford Pelton
8 Lindbergh Dr., Latham, N. Y. 12110
PT 1970 Active 1 emp. IA/MTO
Modern 5/74 • Appalachian dulcimer
1–10 to date † • Steel-string guitar
1–10 to date † • 5-string banjo 1–10 to
date †

Ralph Pennington
Rockwell, N.C. 28138 † 2/76

Mueller Penzel, Inc.
36-11 33d St., Long Island City, N. Y. 11106
Maker of accordions † 2/75

Richard Douglas Peoples
2019 Haste St., Apt. 1, Berkeley, Calif. 94704
Maker of strings † 2/76

Sergio Peresson
430 W. Kings Hwy., Haddonfield, N. J. 08033
FT 1945 Active ? emp. IA/MTO?
Historical 11/78 • Violin Over 50 to
date † • *1980: 1 emp. MTO • Violin,
viola, and cello Over 50 to date 10–25
per year*

Allen Perez
1051 Newport Ave., Long Beach, Calif. 90805
FT 1973 Active 1 emp. MTO
Modern and historical 11/75
• Mandolin 1–10 to date †
• Steel-string guitar 1–10 to date †
• Flamenco guitar 1–10 to date †
• Violin 1–10 to date †

John Perfect
Rt. 1, Box 205, Jerome, Idaho 83338
PT 1968 Active 1 emp. IA
Modern 4/76 • Violin 25–50 to date
1–10 per year • Steel-string guitar 1–10
to date 1–10 per year • Mandolin 1–10
to date 1–10 per year • Ukulele 1–10 to
date 1–10 per year

Wallace Pergram
9986 Arch St., Germantown, Ohio 45327
PT 1967 Active 1 emp. MTO
Historical 9/75 • Appalachian
dulcimer Over 50 to date 10–25 per
year • *1980: Hobbyist*

Peripole, Inc.
51-17 Rockaway Beach Blvd., Far Rockaway,
N. Y. 11691 † 2/75

C. B. Perkins
1600 Cherry Ave., San Jose, Calif. 95125 † 4/78

Latham Perkins
3535 Shanley St., Fairbanks, Alaska 99701
PT 1964 Active 1 emp. IA/MTO
Historical 6/74 • Appalachian
dulcimer 25–50 to date • 5-string
banjo 10–25 to date • Steel-string
guitar 1–10 to date • 12-string guitar
1–10 to date • All instruments 10–25 per
year • *1980: PT MTO • Psaltery 1–10 to
date • Hammered dulcimer 1–10 to date
• All instruments 1–10 per year • Not
making guitars • Primarily repairs*

Alan Perlman
Windham R.F.D., West Townshend, Vt. 05359
FT 1972 Active 1 emp. MTO
Modern 6/75 • Classical guitar 1–10 to
date 1–10 per year • Steel-string guitar
1–10 to date 1–10 per year
• Appalachian dulcimer 25–50 to date
10–25 per year

Cliff Perry
Also known as: Telegraph Music Works

Darell Perry
Clincho, Va. 24226 † 4/76

Douglas M. Perry
3253 N. Bartlett Ave., Milwaukee, Wis. 53211
FT 1975 Active 1 emp. MTO
Modern and historical 4/78 • Classical
guitar 1–10 to date † • Steel-string
guitar 1–10 to date † • Primarily
repairs

William Perry
90 Haverhill Rd., Salem, N. H. 03079
PT 1970 Active 1 emp. MTO
Modern and historical 7/74
• Appalachian dulcimer 25–50 to date
10–25 per year

Daniel B. Perryman
33147 Lake Superior Pl., Fremont, Calif. 94536
Maker of strings † 1/78

Jack Peters
2610 24th Ave. East, Seattle, Wash. 98112
PT 1971 Active 1 emp. MTO
Historical 9/74 • Clavichord 1–10 to

date † • Harpsichord 10–25 to date †
• *1980: 2 emp. Brochure • Harpsichord*
25–50 to date 1–10 per year
• *Clavichord 1–10 per year*

Craig Peterson
Also known as: Here, Inc.

Jesper Peterson
R.F.D. 1, Box 101A, Hartford, Tenn. 37753
FT 1964 Active 2 emp. IA/MTO
Modern and historical 7/74 • Classical
guitar Over 50 to date 1–10 per year
• Flamenco guitar 1–10 to date 1–10
per year • Mandolin 1–10 to date 1–10
per year • Lute 1–10 to date 1–10 per
year • Violin 1–10 to date 1–10 per
year

Jon Peterson
415 S. 118th, Tacoma, Wash. 98444
Maker of strings † 1/78 • *1980: FT*
1977 Active 1 emp. 10/80 • Strings
(repairs)

Thomas Peterson
P. O. Box 143, Calistoga, Calif. 94515
PT 1976 Active 1 emp. MTO
Modern 2/78 • Steel-string guitar 1–10
to date 1–10 per year

Zenon W. Petesh
4617 N. Anthony Ave., Chicago, Ill. 60656
FT 1937 Active 1 emp. MTO
Modern 6/74 • Violin 25–50 to date †
• Viola 1–10 to date † • Cello 1–10 to
date † • Primarily repairs • *1980: Cello*
Over 50 to date

Philip Joseph Petillo
Also known as: Phil-Lu Inc.

Petosa Accordions
313 45th St., Seattle, Wash. 98105
FT 1922 Active 3 emp. IA
Modern Brochure 2/75 • Accordion
Over 50 to date 10–25 per year • *1980: 5*
emp.

Bruce Petros
Rt. 7, Box 123, Appleton, Wis. 54911
FT 1972 Active 1 emp. MTO
Modern 1/78 • Steel-string guitar 1–10
to date † • Classical guitar 1–10 to

date † • Appalachian dulcimer 10–25
to date †

Stephen J. Petrula
931 E. Providencia Ave., Burbank, Calif. 91501
PT 1970 Active 1 emp. IA
Historical 9/74 • Violin 1–10 to date
† • Viola 1–10 to date †

Bob Petrulis
Also known as: Leo Bidne; Timothy Olsen
• *1980: Inactive*

Lou Petrulis
Also known as: Stanly and Lou Petrulis

Stanly and Lou Petrulis
2000 S. 6th St., Terre Haute, Ind. 47802
Maker of strings † 2/76

Denver L. Pettitt
2108 Johnson, Big Spring, Tex. 79720 † 2/76

Lawrence Phelps and Associates
Box 1421, Erie, Pa. 16512
FT 1973 Active 50 emp. MTO
Modern Brochure 4/75 • Pipe organ
10–25 to date 10–25 per year • *1980: 18*
emp. • Pipe organ 25–50 to date 1–10
per year

Bill Phillips
911 Burch Ave., Durham, N. C. 27705
PT 1972 Active 1 emp. IA/MTO
Historical 1/76 • Appalachian
dulcimer 10–25 to date † • 5-string
banjo 10–25 to date †

John M. Phillips
609 B Talbot St., Albany, Calif. 94706
PT 1972 Active 1 emp. MTO
Historical 10/74 • Harpsichord 1–10 to
date 1–10 per year • Lute 1–10 to
date †

Todd Phillips
210 Mission, Suite B, San Rafael, Calif. 94902 †
4/78

Phil-Lu Inc.
1206 Herbert Ave., Ocean, N. J. 07712
FT 1962 Active 1 emp. MTO
Modern and historical 10/74 • Classical
guitar Over 50 to date • Steel-string

guitar   Over 50 to date • Electric guitar
Over 50 to date • 5-string banjo   1– 10 to
date • Mandolin   10– 25 to date • All
instruments   10– 25 per year • *1980:*
Brochure • Repairs • Also known as: Philip
Joseph Petillo; Petillo Guitars

Thomas William Phipps

Also known as: Goose Nest Prairie Banjos

Pianola Player-Piano

Also known as: Aeolian Corp.

Michael Piasecki

2720 23d St., San Francisco, Calif. 94110
PT   1969   Active   1 emp.   MTO
Modern   9/74 • Classical guitar   25– 50
to date   1– 10 per year

The Pickin' Post

1434 E. 3d, Winfield, Kans. 67156
Maker of strings †   1/78 • Also known as:
Bob Westbrook • *1980: FT   1975   Active*
2 emp.   MTO   Modern   10/80 • 5-string
banjo   1– 10 to date   1– 10 per year

David R. Pierce

Also known as: Cucciara Harpsichord
Co., Inc.

R. Brent Pierce

323½ N. Main, Hutchinson, Kans. 67501
FT   1970   Active   3 emp.   MTO
Modern   2/78 • Classical guitar   1– 10 to
date   1– 10 per year • Steel-string guitar
1– 10 to date   1– 10 per year
• Appalachian dulcimer   1– 10 to date
1– 10 per year • 5-string banjo   1– 10 to
date   1– 10 per year • Primarily repairs
• Also known as: Acoustic Stringed
Instruments

Otto Pietz

Box 143, Tuttletown, Tenn. 37391
PT   1960   Active   1 emp.   MTO
Modern and historical   7/74 • Harp
1– 10 to date   † • Paraguayan harp
1– 10 to date   † • Lap harp   1– 10 to
date   1– 10 per year • Appalachian
dulcimer   1– 10 to date   1– 10 per year
• *1980: 1970 • Paraguayan harp   10– 25 to*
date   1– 10 per year • Lap harp   10– 25 to
date • Also known as: Weehutty Industries

John Pigman

220 Broad St., Berlin, Md. 21811
Maker of strings †   3/78

Lorenzo Pimentel and Son

3316 Lafayette Dr. N. E., Albuquerque,
N. M. 87107
FT   1951   Active   5 emp.   IA/MTO
Historical   Brochure   4/76 • Classical
guitar   Over 50 to date   Over 50 per year
• Steel-string guitar   Over 50 to date
Over 50 per year • Lute   1– 10 to date
1– 10 per year • Vihuela   10– 25 to date
1– 10 per year • Also known as: De Mano
Guitars

William S. Pinches

3464 M St., Eureka, Calif. 95501
FT   1967   Active   1 emp.   MTO
Modern   6/74 • Violin   1– 10 to date   †
• Primarily repairs • Also known as:
Sequoia Violin Shop

Pinelands Dulcimer Shop

2 Allen Ave., Medford, N. J. 08055
PT   1976   Active   1 emp.   IA
Modern   12/77 • Appalachian dulcimer
25– 50 to date   10– 25 per year • 5-string
banjo   1– 10 to date   1– 10 per year
• Hammered dulcimer   1– 10 to date   †
• Also known as: Ed Smith; Larry Smith

Ron Pinkham

Youngstown Rd., Lincolnville, Maine 04849
Maker of strings †   9/76

Lazlo Pinter

3804 N. Clarke St., Chicago, Ill. 60613
Maker of strings †   2/76

Ty Piper

2404 S. W. 54, Oklahoma City, Okla. 73119
FT   1973   Active   1 emp.   IA/MTO
Historical   Brochure   10/74 • 5-string
banjo   10– 25 to date   10– 25 per year
• Steel-string guitar   1– 10 to date   1– 10
per year

Ty and Mona Piper

Also known as: Imperial Banjo Co.

Sylvia Pippin

630 31st St., Richmond, Calif. 94804

PT   1974   Active   1 emp.   MTO
Historical   10/75 • Hammered
dulcimer   1–10 to date   1–10 per year

R. Alva Pirtle
204 E. Pere Marquette St., Ludington,
Mich. 49431
PT   1958   Active   1 emp.   IA
Modern   11/74 • Violin   25–50 to date
1–10 per year • Viola   1–10 to date   †
• *1980: IA/MTO • Violin   Over 50 to date
• Viola   1–10 per year • Cello   1–10 to
date   1–10 per year*

Enzo Pizzi
68-05 43d St., Woodside, N. Y. 11377 †   2/76

Mr. and Mrs. David S. Pizzini
5231 Broadway, Indianapolis, Ind. 46220
PT   1974   Active   2 emp.   IA/MTO
Historical   11/74 • Appalachian
dulcimer   10–25 to date   10–25 per year
• Psaltery   1–10 to date   † • Also known
as: David's Dulcimers

Laura Fontana Pizzo
Also known as: Tony Pizzo and Laura
Fontana Pizzo

Tony Pizzo and Laura Fontana Pizzo
Box 70A, Whitefield, N. H. 03598
PT   1976   Active   2 emp.   MTO
Modern   Brochure   10/76 • Appalachian
dulcimer, psaltery, Aeolian harp,
hammered dulcimer, glockenspiel, log
drum, rebec, and ektar   † • Also known as:
Orphic Endeavors

Stanley Plant
5145 N. 7th St., #330, Phoenix, Ariz. 85014
Maker of strings †   1/78

Mark Platin
Also known as: Wildwood Music

Joseph Platz
Metacomet St., Belchertown, Mass. 01007
FT   Year?   Active   1 emp.   IA
Modern   7/74 • Bamboo flute   Over 50 to
date   Over 50 per year • Recorder   1–10
to date   † • Wooden flute   1–10 to date
† • Aulos   1–10 to date   †

Plektron Corp.
8981 Complex Dr., San Diego, Calif. 92123
FT   1970   Active   8 emp.   IA
Modern   Brochure   4/76
• Tambourine   Over 50 to date   Over 50
per year • Hand drum   Over 50 to date
Over 50 per year • Caluba drum   Over 50
to date   Over 50 per year • Temple
blocks   Over 50 to date   Over 50 per year

D. B. Plesnicar
279 E. 214 St., Euclid, Ohio 44123 †   2/76

Robert F. Plott
6342 Castejon Dr., La Jolla, Calif. 92037
Maker of strings †   2/76

Phillip S. Plumbo
1750 Selby Ave., St. Paul, Minn. 55104
FT   1973   Active   1 emp.   MTO
Modern and historical   6/74 • Classical
guitar   †

Bozo Podunavac
Also known as: Bozo's Guitar Gallery

Donald K. Polifka, Jr., and Judy Polifka
P. O. Box 104, Rapidan, Va. 22733
FT   1977   Active   2 emp.   IA/MTO
Modern   1/77 • Mandolin   1–10 to
date   1–10 per year • 5-string banjo
1–10 to date   1–10 per year
• Appalachian dulcimer   1–10 to date
1–10 per year • Steel-string guitar   1–10
to date   1–10 per year • *1980: Mandolin
10–25 to date • 5-string banjo   10–25 to
date • Appalachian dulcimer   Over 50 to
date • Steel-string guitar   10–25 to date
• Autoharp   1–10 to date   † • Ukulele
1–10 to date   † • Also known as: The
Joynery*

Polisi Bassoon Corp.
244 W. 49th St., New York, N. Y. 10019
Maker of bassoons †   1/78

David Polla
17127 Chandler Park Dr., Detroit, Mich. 48224
Maker of strings †   1/78

Gary Pollard
849 Cambon Circle, Ojai, Calif. 93023
Maker of strings †   2/76

Pollard Industries, Inc.
9014 Lindblade, Culver City, Calif. 90230
FT   1977   Active   ? emp.   IA
Modern   Brochure   12/77 • Drum   Over
50 to date   Over 50 per year • Also known
as: Syndrum

Pollina Accordion Mfg. Co.
6921 Gratiot Ave., Detroit, Mich. 48207
Maker of accordions †   2/75

P. Gio. Polsinelli
1785 S.O.M. Center Rd., Cleveland, Ohio 44124
PT   1927   Active   1 emp.   IA
Modern   Brochure   6/75 • Violin
10–25 to date   † • *1980: FT • Violin   1–10
per year*

Allan Polts
3000 Braydon, Billings, Mont. 59101
Maker of strings †   2/76

Ponziani Violin
2063 E. 4th St., Cleveland, Ohio 44115
Maker of violins †   2/76

Poole Piano Co.
Also known as: Aeolian Corp.

Martin A. Pope
62 Granville Rd., Southwick, Mass. 01077
PT   1966   Active   1 emp.   MTO
Historical   2/75 • Fife   Over 50 to date
10–25 per year

Ray E. Popelka
P. O. Box 1598, Santa Cruz, Calif. 95060
PT   1971   Active   1 emp.   MTO
Historical   3/78 • Appalachian
dulcimer   Over 50 to date   10–25 per
year

Bill Porter
404 White Store Rd., Wadesboro, N. C. 28170
†   2/76

Leonard V. Porter
4908 W. 83d St., Kansas City, Mo. 64114
Maker of violins †

Steve Porter
1450 13th Ave., Oakland, Calif. 94606
FT   1969   Active   1 emp.   IA
Modern   4/76 • Classical guitar   25–50

to date   † • Steel-string guitar   1–10 to
date   1–10 per year • Primarily repairs

Elliott Postol
101 W. 78th St., New York, N. Y. 10024
FT   1966   Active   2 emp.   MTO
Historical   6/75 • Harpsichord   Over 50
to date   1–10 per year

Boyd Poulsen
33 North B, San Mateo, Calif. 94401 †

Curt A. Poulton
1637 Dieter St., St. Paul, Minn. 55106
Maker of harpsichords and clavichords †
5/74

Verne Q. Powell
70 Bow St., Arlington Heights, Mass. 02174
FT   1972   Active   24 emp.   MTO
Modern   Brochure   4/76 • Modern
flute   Over 50 to date   Over 50 per year

George V. Poynor
4006 Delancy Dr., Silver Spring, Md. 20906 †
2/76

Jerome Prager
2611 Woodstock Rd., Los Angeles, Calif. 90046
†   2/76

Rusty Prall
532 S. 45th St., Philadelphia, Pa. 19104   4/77

Larry Prang
1921 5th Ave., Seattle, Wash. 98101 †   1/77

Samuel O. Pratt Co.
407 Park St., Upper Montclair, N. J. 07043 †
11/76

Precision Guitar Works
Also known as: Ron Carriveau

Thomas M. Prescott Workshop
99 Washington St., Melrose, Mass. 02176
FT   1974   Active   1 emp.   MTO
Historical   Brochure   3/75 • Baroque
flute   25–50 to date   † • Baroque
recorder   10–25 to date   † • Baroque
clarinet   1–10 to date   † • *1980: 3 emp.
• Baroque flute   Over 50 to date   25–50
per year • Baroque recorder   Over 50 to
date   Over 50 per year • Not making
Baroque clarinets*

Edd Presnell
P. O. Box 235, Banner Elk, N. C. 28604
FT   1935   Active   1 emp.   MTO
Modern   Brochure   5/74 • Appalachian
dulcimer   Over 50 to date   Over 50 per
year • 5-string banjo   10–25 to date
1–10 per year • Mandolin-banjo   1–10 to
date   1–10 per year

B. W. Prevo
11924 Leisure Dr., Dallas, Tex. 75238
Maker of strings †   3/78

Rodney Price
300 Radcliffe Ave., Hagerstown, Md. 21740
PT   1976   Active   1 emp.   MTO
Modern   2/78 • Steel-string guitar   1–10
to date • Electric guitar   1–10 to date
• Appalachian dulcimer   1–10 to date
• All instruments   1–10 per year
• Primarily repairs • Also known as: Red
Bird Guitars

Peter Prier
308 E. Second South, Salt Lake City, Utah 84111
FT   1965   Active   5 emp.   MTO
Modern and historical   6/74 • Violin
Over 50 to date   † • Viola   Over 50 to
date   † • Cello   10–25 to date   † • Bass
violin   1–10 to date   †

Cheryl Prihoda
2550 Cowper, Evanston, Ill. 60201
Maker of hurdy-gurdies †   2/76

Ralph Prince
6116 Orchard St., El Cerrito, Calif. 94530 †
9/75

Jim Prior
3602 N. E. Wasco, Portland, Ore. 97232
PT   1960   Active   1 emp.   MTO
Modern and historical   6/76 • 5-string
banjo   25–50 to date   † • Mandolin
1–10 to date   † • *1980: FT • 5-string,
plectrum, and tenor banjos   Over 50 to
date • Mandolin   10–25 to date
• Hammered dulcimer   25–50 to date   †
• Repairs*

Bruce Privratsky
Three Bells United Methodist Church, Duffield,
Va. 24219
FT   1973   Active   1 emp.   IA/MTO

Modern   Brochure   1/78 • Hammered
dulcimer   25–50 to date   1–10 per year
• Appalachian dulcimer   25–50 to date
1–10 per year • 5-string banjo   1–10 to
date   1–10 per year • Steel-string guitar
1–10 to date   1–10 per year • Also known
as: Redeemed Earth Associates • *1980: PT
MTO • Appalachian dulcimer   Over 50 to
date • No longer known as Redeemed Earth
Associates*

Frank Proffitt, Jr.
Rt. 2, Todd, N. C. 28684
FT   1965   Active   1 emp.   IA
Historical   5/74 • Appalachian
dulcimer   Over 50 to date   10–25 per
year • 5-string banjo   Over 50 to date
10–25 per year

Brad Prokopow
76845 North Ave., Armada, Mich. 48005 †
5/76

Protexorgan Co.
36 First St. N. W., Massillon, Ohio 46646 †   2/75

Proto-Fab & Mfg. Co.
Also known as: Jack Samhat

Providence Guitar and Banjo
Also known as: Michael Allison

Joseph Puskas
631 N. Larchmont Blvd., Los Angeles, Calif.
90004
PT   1947   Active   1 emp.   IA/MTO
Modern   9/74 • Violin   Over 50 to date
† • Viola   25–50 to date   † • Cello
1–10 to date   † • *1980: FT   1938
Brochure*

John F. Putnam
1905 Hopefield Rd., Silver Spring, Md. 20904
Maker of Appalachian dulcimers †   1/77

Harry Pyle
P. O. Box 775, Los Gatos, Calif. 95030
Maker of strings †   10/74

Mr. and Mrs. Paul Pyle
414 Campbell Ave., Tullahoma, Tenn. 37388
FT   1970   Active   2 emp.   IA/MTO
Historical   Brochure   6/74
• Appalachian dulcimer   Over 50 to
date   †

Russell Quagliata
Also known as: Ziedler and Quagliata
Harpsichords

Quality Banjo Co.
6906 Parkwood St., Landover, Md. 20784
Maker of 5-string banjos † 2/76

Sam Radding
Also known as: American Dream
Instruments Mfg.

Richard Raimi
4028 Woodland Park North, Seattle, Wash.
98103
FT 1974 Active 1 emp. IA/MTO
Modern 9/75 • 5-string banjo 1−10 to
date 1−10 per year • Steel-string guitar
1−10 to date 1−10 per year

Rainbow Electric Glitars
1917 E. Grant Rd., Tucson, Ariz. 85719
Maker of electric guitars † 1/77

Ramblin' Conrad's Guitar Shop
4318 Hampton Blvd., Norfolk, Va. 23508
Maker of strings † 2/76

Harry Ramey
Rt. 5, Box 272, Berea, Ky. 40403
PT 1950 Active 1 emp. MTO
Historical 4/76 • Violin 10−25 to
date 1−10 per year • Viola 1−10 to
date † • Viola d'amore 1−10 to date †
• Viola da gamba 1−10 to date † • *1980:
Violin 25−50 to date*

Agustin Ramos, Jr.
555 Chili Ave., Rochester, N. Y. 14611
FT 1973 Active 1 emp. IA/MTO
Modern/Historical? Brochure? 5/74
• Steel-string guitar 10−25 to date †

Jim Rampulla
17 Penn St., Nazareth, Pa. 18064
FT 1967 Active 1 emp. MTO
Modern and historical 4/76 • Electric
guitar 1−10 to date † • Steel-string
guitar 1−10 to date † • Primarily
repairs

Henry Ramsey
Michigan Ave., Boise, Idaho 83706 † 2/76

John Ramsey
Rt. 1, Box 59, Banner Elk, N. C. 28604
PT 1960 Active 2 emp. IA
Modern and historical 4/76
• Appalachian dulcimer 1−10 to date †
• 5-string banjo 1−10 to date †

Thomas R. Randall, Jr.
R. D. 10, Box 153, Clifton Park, N. Y. 12065
PT 1977 Active 1 emp. MTO
Modern 2/78 • Steel-string guitar 1−10
to date 1−10 per year

Allan J. Rapp
1344 N. Yale, Tulsa, Okla. 74115
FT 1951 Active 1 emp. IA/MTO
Modern and historical 11/74 • Violin
10−25 to date 1−10 per year • Primarily
repairs • Also known as: Tulsa Music Center

Joseph G. Rashid
27620 Eldena Dr., San Pedro, Calif. 90732
FT 1933 Active 1 emp. IA
Modern 9/74 • Violin 25−50 to date
1−10 per year • Viola 1−10 to date
1−10 per year • Cello 1−10 to date
1−10 per year

Aage Rasmussen Violin Shop
5710 N. Ridge, Chicago, Ill. 60626
Maker of violins † 2/76

Paul J. Rasmussen
1625 N. 31 Pl., Phoenix, Ariz. 85008
PT 1977 Active 1 emp. MTO
Modern 3/78 • Steel-string guitar 1−10
to date † • Electric guitar 1−10 to
date † • Acoustic bass guitar 1−10 to
date † • Appalachian dulcimer 1−10 to
date † • Also known as: Spirit of Jubal
• *1980: Now known as: Sound Guitar Co.*

W. P. Ratajak
1636 Brook Ln., Corvallis, Ore. 97330
FT 1969 Active 1 emp. MTO
Modern and historical Brochure 7/74
• Clavichord 10−25 to date †
• Virginal 1−10 to date †
• Harpsichord 1−10 to date †

Raybern's Music Co.
Also known as: Raymond Clifton Aydlett

Ray Rayburn
S. 4th Ave., Tucson, Ariz. 85700 †

Kent Rayman
7409 146th St. N. W., Tacoma, Wash. 98439
Maker of strings †   5/78

Razor Ridge Workshop
Also known as: David Hoffman

Robert Read
2021 Park Blvd., Palo Alto, Calif. 94306 †   2/76

Red Bird Guitars
Also known as: Rodney Price

Redeemed Earth Associates
Also known as: Bruce Privratsky

Robert F. Redfern
Box 322, Water St., Searsport, Maine 04974
PT   1976   Active   1 emp.   MTO
Modern   1/79 • Hammered dulcimer
1 – 10 to date   1 – 10 per year

Redman Organ Co.
816 E. Vickery, Fort Worth, Tex. 76104
FT   1966   Active   3 emp.   MTO
Modern   Brochure   10/75 • Pipe organ
† • *1980: 8 emp.* • *Pipe organ   25 – 50 to
date   1 – 10 per year*

Peter and Kathryn Redstone
Box 75, Claremont, Va. 23899
FT   1965   Active   2 emp.   MTO
Modern and historical   6/74
• Harpsichord   10 – 25 to date   †
• Clavichord   1 – 10 to date   †
• Forte-piano   1 – 10 to date   †

Rick Reeck
P. O. Box 22725, Robinsdale, Minn. 55422
Maker of strings †   1/78

Abijah Reed
225 Thoreau St., Concord, Mass. 01742
PT   1963   Active   1 emp.   MTO
Historical   2/78 • Harpsichord   1 – 10 to
date   † • Clavichord   1 – 10 to date   †
• Classical guitar   1 – 10 to date   †

David Reed
Box 155, 171 N. Main St., East Granby, Conn.

06026
PT   1973   Active   1 emp.   IA/MTO
Modern and historical   9/75
• Appalachian dulcimer   10 – 25 to date
1 – 10 per year • 5-string banjo   1 – 10 to
date   1 – 10 per year

Dennis Reed
P. O. Box 19, Greenbank, Whidbey Island, Wash.
98253
PT   1974   Active   4 emp.   IA
Modern   12/74 • 5-string banjo   1 – 10 to
date   † • Also known as: Space Banjo Co.

John M. Reed
30 Saddle Club Rd., Lexington, Mass. 02173
Maker of harpsichords †   5/74

Duane Reeder
5409 W. Sanna, Glendale, Ariz. 85302
PT   1970   Active   1 emp.   IA/MTO
Modern and historical   7/74 • Classical
guitar   1 – 10 to date   1 – 10 per year
• Steel-string guitar   1 – 10 to date   1 – 10
per year

Harold S. Rees
22631 Barton Rd., Colton, Calif. 92324
PT   1948   Active   1 emp.   IA/MTO
Modern and historical   9/74 • Violin
1 – 10 to date   † • Mandolin   1 – 10 to
date   † • 5-string banjo   1 – 10 to date   †
• *1980: Ukulele 1 – 10 to date*   †

Harry J. Reeve
P. O. Box 2797, Batesville, Ark. 72501
Maker of strings †   2/76 • *1980: FT
1960   Active   1 emp.   IA/MTO
Modern   10/80 • Violin, viola, cello, bass
violin, and bows   Over 50 to date   †
• Repairs*

Bill Reeves
10 Village Square, Galesburg, Ill. 61401
Maker of strings †   1/78

Thomas G. Rein
Box 1097, Lexington, Ky., 40501
FT   1976   Active   1 emp.   MTO
Modern   4/76 • Steel-string guitar   1 – 10
to date   † • Appalachian dulcimer
10 – 25 to date   †

John Reints
Stony Brook Rd., Hopewell, N. J. 08525
FT 1968 Active 1 emp. IA/MTO
Modern and historical 6/74 • Classical
guitar 10–25 to date 1–10 per year
• Lute 1–10 to date 1–10 per year
• Mandolin 1–10 to date 1–10 per year

Irvin Reis
Rt. 1, Box 109A, Beaumont, Tex. 77706
PT 1976 Active 1 emp. MTO
Modern 1/77 • Appalachian dulcimer
25–50 to date 10–25 per year • Also
known as: Leigh Artisans

Paul Reisler
Canaan Valley, Davis, W. Va. 26260
FT 1968 Active 1 emp. MTO
Modern 9/74 • Appalachian dulcimer
Over 50 to date † • Steel-string guitar
1–10 to date † • Hammered dulcimer
1–10 to date † • Mandolin 1–10 to
date † • Courting or double dulcimer
1–10 to date †

Bart Reiter
6058 Gibson Ave., East Lansing, Mich. 48823
FT 1975 Active 1 emp. MTO
Modern 2/78 • Steel-string guitar 1–10
to date 1–10 per year • Electric guitar
1–10 to date † • Appalachian dulcimer
10–25 to date 1–10 per year • Primarily
repairs • Also known as: Elderly
Instruments • *1980: IA/MTO • Steel-string
guitar 10–25 to date • Electric guitar
1–10 per year • Now known as: B. Reiter,
Guitar Maker*

Albert Reitz
6925 Emilie Rd., Levittown, Pa. 19057
Maker of strings † 1/78

Reliable Brothers
1224 Ceres St., Crockett, Calif. 94525
FT 1972 Active 15 emp. IA
Modern Brochure 5/74 • Ceramic
flute Over 50 to date Over 50 per year
• Also known as: Michael L. Buckley;
Lawrence E. Marum

Remarkable Flutes
Also known as: Alan Aldridge; Steve Rowles

Rembrand Co.
R.R. #3, Newton, Iowa 50208

FT 1972 Active 2 emp. IA
Modern and historical Brochure 4/76
• Appalachian dulcimer Over 50 to
date † • Hammered dulcimer 10–25 to
date † • Classical guitar 1–10 to date
† • Strings 10–25 to date † • Also
known as: Jerry Rempp

Remo, Inc./Pro-Mark
12804 Raymer St., North Hollywood, Calif.
91605
FT 1957 Active ? emp. IA
Modern Brochure 4/76 • † • *1980:
Drum † • Also known as: Remo Belli; Herb
Brockstein; Lloyd McCausland*

Jerry Rempp
Also known as: Rembrand Co.

Renaissance Gilde
Box 5, Cambridge, Wis. 53523
FT 1967 Active 1 emp. MTO
Historical Brochure 6/74 • Lute Over
50 to date † • Viola da gamba † • Also
known as: William Daum

Renaissance Workshop
165B Putnam Ave., Cambridge, Mass. 02139
FT 1975 Active 1 emp. MTO
Modern and historical 6/76 • Psaltery
10–25 to date 10–25 per pear • Vielle
10–25 to date 10–25 per year • Also
known as: Peter Cass; Persis Ensor

Robert Reppert
2006 Greenview Dr., Beloit, Wis. 53511 † 2/76

Republic Drums
5 Hemlock Dr., Shelton, Conn. 06484
Maker of drums † 2/76 • Also known as:
Marshall Cole

Thomas Lee Resek
P. O. Box 51, Carnation, Wash. 98014
FT 1972 Active 1 emp. IA/MTO
Modern 9/74 • Appalachian dulcimer
25–50 to date 10–25 per year • 5-string
banjo 1–10 to date † • Steel-string
guitar 1–10 to date †

Dr. Andrew Philip Restivo
112 Oxford Ln., Aberdeen Township, N. J. 07747
PT 1969 Active 1 emp. MTO
Modern 10/74 • Classical guitar 1–10
to date † • *1980: Inactive*

Fritz Reuter and Sons
1565 W. Howard St., Chicago, Ill. 60625
Maker of violins † 2/76

Ronald Lee Reuter
Rt. 7, Porter Pike, Bowling Green, Ky. 42101
FT 1973 Active 1 emp. IA
Modern and historical 10/75
• Appalachian dulcimer 10–25 to date
1–10 per year • Zither 1–10 to date †
• 5-string banjo 1–10 to date †
• Steel-string guitar 1–10 to date †
• Also known as: Kentucky Hill Stringed
Instrument Shop

Reuter Organ Co.
612 New Hampshire St., Box 486, Lawrence,
Kans. 66044
FT 1917 Active 50 emp. IA/MTO
Modern Brochure 4/75 • Organ Over
50 to date † • *1980: 70 emp. • Pipe organ
Over 50 to date 25–50 per year*

F. A. Reynolds Co.
Also known as: Norlin Music, Inc.

Nicholas Reynoso
306 Garden St., Hoboken, N. J. 07030 † 2/76

Rheem Mfg. Co.
5922 Bowcraft St., Los Angeles, Calif. 90016 †
2/76

Rhodes Keyboard Instruments
1300 E. Valencia, Fullerton, Calif. 92631
Maker of electric pianos † 5/75 • Also
known as: Fender/Rogers/Rhodes

B. C. Rich
Also known as: Bernardo C. Rico

C. C. Richelieu
Also known as: Banjos by Richelieu

Rickenbacker, Inc.
201 E. Stevens St., Santa Ana, Calif. 92707
Maker of electric guitars † 5/76

Bradford Rickert
351 Salmon Brook St., Granby, Conn. 06035
FT 1975 Active 1 emp. MTO
Modern 9/75 • Steel-string guitar 1–10
to date † • Appalachian dulcimer 1–10
to date †

Bernardo C. Rico
4770 Valley Blvd., Suite 120, Los Angeles, Calif.
90036
FT 1948 Active ? emp. IA/MTO
Modern Brochure 4/76 • Electric
guitar Over 50 to date † • Steel-string
guitar Over 50 to date † • Also known
as: B. C. Rich

Ridge Runner Music
3035 Townsend Dr., Fort Worth, Tex. 76110
Maker of strings † 2/76

Terenzio Riegel
407 W. King St., Lancaster, Pa. 17603
FT 1972 Active 1 emp. MTO
Modern and historical 6/74 • Violin
1–10 to date † • Primarily repairs • Also
known as: Casa Di Terenzio • *1980:
Brochure • Violin Over 50 to date • Now
known as: Terenzio Violins*

James A. Riesenberger
1301 Bishop, Grosse Point Park, Mich. 48230
FT Active 1 emp. MTO Modern
6/74 • Steel-string guitar 25–50 to date
1–10 per year • Appalachian dulcimer
10–25 to date 1–10 per year

Ken Riportella
East Calais, Vt. 05650
FT 1970 Active 1 emp. IA/MTO
Modern 2/78 • Appalachian dulcimer
10–25 to date • Mandolin 1–10 to date
• Steel-string guitar 1–10 to date
• 5-string banjo 1–10 to date • Harp
1–10 to date • All instruments 1–10 per
year • *1980: Brochure • Elastic sound
synthesizer 10–25 to date † • Makes
sculptures*

Jean Ritchie
7A Locust Ave., Port Washington, N. Y. 11050
PT 1948 Active ? emp. IA
Historical 6/74 • Appalachian
dulcimer Over 50 to date Over 50 per
year • *1980: Also known as: Folklife
Productions; George Pickow; John Rourke*

Raymond Ritchie
1404 Melvin St., Ypsilanti, Mich. 48197 † 2/76
*1980: Maker of dulcimers † • Deceased
(12/76)*

Anthony Ritter, Jr.
5212 Villa Rd., Knoxville, Tenn. 37918
PT   1971   Active   1 emp.   MTO
Modern and historical   4/75 • Lute
1–10 to date   1–10 per year • Classical
guitar   1–10 to date   1–10 per year
• Appalachian dulcimer   1–10 to date   †

Frederick Ritter
2734 Russell St., Berkeley, Calif. 94705
FT   1974   Active   1 emp.   MTO
Historical   9/74 • Harpsichord   †
• Forte-piano   †

David Rivinus
715 College Ave., Richmond, Ind. 47374
FT   1973   Active   1 emp.   MTO
Modern and historical   11/74 • Violin
1–10 to date   † • Viola   1–10 to date   †
• Viola da gamba   1–10 to date   †

Samuel Rizzetta
Box 362A, Rt. 1, Barboursville, Va. 22923
FT   1959   Active   1 emp.   MTO
Modern   5/74 • Steel-string guitar   Over
50 to date   † • Appalachian dulcimer
10–25 to date   † • Psaltery-harp   10–25
to date   † • Mandolin   1–10 to date   †

Gene Paul Roach
1037 Cedar St., Lake Oswego, Ore. 97034
FT   1974   Active   1 emp.   IA/MTO
Modern and historical   Brochure   2/75
• Appalachian dulcimer   25–50 to date
† • *1980: Appalachian dulcimer   Over 50 to
date • Mandolin, Baroque guitar, and
hurdy-gurdy   25–50 to date*   † • *Repairs*

Ron Robbins
123 N. Cedar St., Traverse City, Mich. 49684
Maker of strings †   1/78

Zust Robbins
Richmond, Mass. 01254 †   4/77

Roberto-Venn School of Luthiery
5445 E. Washington, Phoenix, Ariz. 85034
FT   1969   Active   13 emp.   IA/MTO
Modern   Brochure   9/74 • Classical
guitar   Over 50 to date   25–50 per year
• Steel-string guitar   Over 50 to date
25–50 per year • Appalachian dulcimer
Over 50 to date   25–50 per year
• Mandolin   10–25 to date   25–50 per
year • Electric guitar   Over 50 to date
Over 50 per year • Resonator guitar   Over
50 to date   10–25 per year • Also known
as: John H. Roberts; Robert L. Venn • *1980: 4
emp. • Classical guitar   10–25 per year
• Steel-string guitar   Over 50 per year
• Appalachian dulcimer   10–25 per year
• Mandolin   10–25 per year*

Clifford Roberts
76 Toronto Ave., Massapequa, N. Y. 11758
FT   1971   Active   1 emp.   IA/MTO
Modern and historical   9/77 • Viola da
gamba   1–10 to date   † • Viola
d'amore   1–10 to date   † • Viola   1–10
to date   † • Cello   1–10 to date   †
• Violin   1–10 to date   † • *1980: Viola
25–50 to date*

James D. Roberts
2752 Cochese Rd., Memphis, Tenn. 38118   †
9/75

John H. Roberts
Also known as: Roberto-Venn School of
Luthiery

Donald Robertson
3003 Monte Vista N. E., Albuquerque, N. M.
87106
FT   1967   Inactive   3 emp.   IA
Historical   9/74 • Viola da gamba   1–10
to date   † • Primarily repairs

Bill Robinson
Sunnyland, Ill. 61571 †

Roland L. Robinson
P. O. Box 161, Mount Laguna, Calif. 92048
FT   1964   Active   1 emp.   IA/MTO
Modern and historical   Brochure   6/74
• Tara harp   25–50 to date • Paraguayan
harp   25–50 to date • Mexican harp
10–25 to date • Irish harp   Over 50 to date
• All instruments   25–50 per year

Trevor Robinson
65 Pine St., Amherst, Mass. 01002
PT   1964   Active   1 emp.   MTO
Historical   6/74 • Recorder   10–25 to
date • Flute   1–10 to date • Fife   1–10 to
date • Oboe   1–10 to date • Shawm
1–10 to date • Woodwinds   25–50 to date
• Brass   1–10 to date • All instruments
1–10 per year

Robin's Song
Also known as: Robin James McConnell

Roche Organ Co., Inc.
799 W. Water, Taunton, Mass. 02780
FT   1967   Active   5 emp.   MTO
Historical   10/75 • Pipe organ   10– 25 to
date   1– 10 per year

Rochester Folk Art Guild
Rochester, N. Y. 14600 †

Robert P. Rock
R. D. 1, Box 250, Everett, Pa. 15537
PT   1929   Active   1 emp.   MTO
Modern   6/74 • 5-string banjo   Over 50 to
date   10– 25 per year

B. J. Rockwood
617 Walsh St., Space 3, Grass Valley, Calif. 95945
FT   1956   Active   1 emp.   MTO
Modern   4/76 • Violin   1– 10 to date   †
• Viola   1– 10 to date   † • Primarily
repairs

Otis B. Rodeo
134 Rincon St., Santa Cruz, Calif. 95060
FT   1972   Active   1 emp.   IA/MTO
Modern and historical   6/78 • Steel-string
guitar   25– 50 to date   † • Mandolin
1– 10 to date   † • Mandola   1– 10 to
date   † • Also known as: Richard Hoover;
Santa Cruz Guitar Co.

Rodgers Organ Co.
1300 N. E. 25th Ave., Hillsboro, Ore. 97123
FT   1958   Active   325 emp.   IA
Modern   Brochure   6/74 • Electronic
organ   Over 50 to date   Over 50 per year
• 1980: 250 emp. • Pipe organ   Over 50 to
date   Over 50 per year • Also known as:
CBS Musical Instruments

Carlo A. Rodrigo
1518 W. Erie, Chicago, Ill. 60622
Maker of strings †   1/78

Manuel Rodriguez
8410 W. Third St., Los Angeles, Calif. 90048
Maker of strings †   2/76

Manuel E. Rodriguez
3455 Birch St., Denver, Colo. 80207
Maker of steel-string guitars   †   5/74

Don Rogers
28 Park Ave., Amityville, N. Y. 11701
PT   1971   Active   1 emp.   IA/MTO
Historical   5/74 • Harpsichord   1– 10 to
date • Virginal   1– 10 to date
• Clavichord   1– 10 to date • All
instruments   1– 10 per year

Joe Rogers, Jr.
627 W. State St., Redland, Calif. 92373
FT   1960   Active   1 emp.   IA/MTO
Modern   Brochure   4/76 • Steel-string
guitar   Over 50 to date   1– 10 per year
• Classical guitar   10– 25 to date   1– 10
per year

Keith Rogers
4803 Brian Rd., Mechanicsburg, Pa. 17055
Maker of strings †   3/78

Rogers Drum Co.
1300 E. Valencia, Box 4137, Fullerton, Calif.
92634
FT   1849   Active   60 emp.   IA
Modern   Brochure   2/78 • Marching
drum   Over 50 to date   Over 50 per year
• Tympani   Over 50 to date   Over 50 per
year • Concert drum   Over 50 to date
Over 50 per year • Also known as: CBS
Musical Instruments; Fender/Rogers/
Rhodes

W. E. Rohde
2612 E. 17th Pl., Tulsa, Okla. 74104
PT   1958   Active   1 emp.   IA
Historical   10/74 • Violin   25– 50 to
date   1– 10 per year • Viola   1– 10 to
date   1– 10 per year • Mandolin   1– 10 to
date   1– 10 per year • 1980: Violin   Over
50 to date • Viola   10– 25 to date • Cello
1– 10 to date   †

John R. Rohrbough
Also known as: Cytha-Harp Co.

Rolandcorp U. S.
2925 S. Vail Ave., Los Angeles, Calif. 90040
Maker of electronic pianos and synthesizers
†   1/78

John Rollins
1249 St. Paul, Bellingham, Wash. 98225
FT   1971   Active   1 emp.   MTO
Historical   5/74 • Lute   1– 10 to date

1– 10 per year • Vihuela   1– 10 to date   †
• Cittern   1– 10 to date   † • *1980:*
Brochure • Lute   25– 50 to date • Baroque
guitar   1– 10 to date   1– 10 per year
• Classical guitar   1– 10 to date   † • Not
making vihuelas

Charles Roman
5275 N. E. Fifth Ave., Miami, Fla. 33137
Maker of violins †   2/76 • *1980: FT*
1924   Active   1 emp.   IA/MTO
Historical   10/80 • Violin   Over 50 to date
• Viola   1– 10 to date • Cello   1– 10 to
date • All instruments   10– 25 per year

Ken Romans
13787 S. W. Farmington, #235, Beaverton, Ore.
97005
Maker of strings †   1/78

Don Romine
4724 N. W. 59th St., Oklahoma City, Okla. 73122
FT   1972   Active   2 emp.   IA/MTO
Modern   Brochure   3/75 • Steel-string
guitar   10– 25 to date   10– 25 per year
• Appalachian dulcimer   Over 50 to
date   10– 25 per year

Doug Roomian
1456 Haight St., San Francisco, Calif. 94117
FT   1971   Active   3 emp.   IA/MTO
Modern   11/74 • Appalachian dulcimer
Over 50 to date   Over 50 per year
• Steel-string guitar   1– 10 to date   1– 10
per year • Also known as: Acoustic Music

Del Roper
Also known as: Golden Bells Music Co.

Edward F. Rose
417 Rookwood Pkwy., Lexington, Ky. 40505
FT   1969   Active   1 emp.   IA/MTO
Modern   4/76 • Steel-string guitar   1– 10
to date   † • 5-string banjo   1– 10 to
date   † • Primarily repairs • Also known
as: The Workshop

Mike Rosen
287 W. College, Oberlin, Ohio 44074 †   5/78

Saul Rosenberg
375 E. 205th St., Bronx, N. Y. 10467
PT   1934   Active   1 emp.   IA
Modern   6/74 • Violin   25– 50 to date   †

Judy Rosenfeld
4532 Corliss North, Seattle, Wash. 98103
PT   1974   Active   1 emp.   IA/MTO
Modern and historical   Brochure   3/76
• Psaltery   1– 10 to date   †

Luthier Rosenthal and Son
507 Fifth Ave., New York, N. Y. 10017
Maker of strings †   2/76

Rosewood Guitar Shop
Also known as: Robert L. Wendt and Roy
Davis

Rosewood Lutherie
Also known as: Kirk Hogan

Bruce Ross
Also known as: Santa Cruz Guitar Co.

Stuart Ross
Phippsburg, Maine 04562 †   9/76

William Post Ross
Georgetown, Maine 04548
FT   1961   Active   1 emp.   IA
Historical   Brochure   5/74 • Virginal
10– 25 to date • Harpsichord   25– 50 to
date • Bows   25– 50 to date • All
instruments   1– 10 per year • *1980:*
IA/MTO • Virginal   25– 50 to date
• Harpsichord   Over 50 to date   10– 25
per year • Bows   Over 50 to date   1– 10
per year • Also known as: Ross
Harpsichords, Inc.; Annette Ellen Smith

Ronald D. Rossa
2915 31st Ave. N. E., Minneapolis, Minn. 55418
PT   1973   Active   1 emp.   MTO
Modern   6/74 • Steel-string guitar   †
• *1980: Hobbyist*

John L. Rossi, Ltd.
250 Fulton Ave., Hempstead, N. Y. 11550
FT   1959   Inactive   1 emp.   MTO
Historical   7/74 • Violin   1– 10 to date
† • Viola   1– 10 to date   † • Primarily
repairs

Heinz M. Rossner
11921 Allison Ct. N. E., Albuquerque, N. M.
87112
PT   1965   Active   1 emp.   MTO
Modern   1/76 • Classical guitar   Over 50

to date   1–10 per year • Steel-string
guitar   1–10 to date   †

Round Family Dulcimer Co.

6470 8th Ave., Grandville, Mich. 49418
PT   1971   Active   4 emp.   IA/MTO
Historical   Brochure   9/74
• Appalachian dulcimer   10–25 to date
† • Hammered dulcimer   Over 50 to
date   † • Also known as: Donald and Jay
Round • *1980: FT   6 emp.   Modern and
historical • Hammered dulcimer   Over 50
per year • Not making Appalachian
dulcimers*

Rowe Accordions

845 Gordon St., Atlanta, Ga. 30310
Maker of accordions †   2/75

Jan Rowland

Also known as: Visser-Rowland Associates

Steve Rowles

R. F. D. 1, Palmer, Mass. 01609
FT   1970   Active   1 emp.   IA/MTO
Modern and historical   Brochure   4/76
• Bamboo flute   Over 50 to date   † • Also
known as: Remarkable Flutes

James Rubin

Box 6, Jeffersonville, Vt. 05464
FT   1974   Active   1 emp.   IA/MTO
Modern   11/75 • Classical guitar   1–10
to date   † • Steel-string guitar   1–10 to
date   †

Philip Rubin

1319 Eaton Ave., San Carlos, Calif. 94070
Maker of strings †   2/76

George Rubino

Also known as: Lynn Hannings and George
Rubino

R. S. Ruck

7225 Hubbard Ave., Middleton, Wis. 53562
FT   1966   Active   1 emp.   MTO
Modern   6/74 • Classical guitar   Over 50
to date   10–25 per year • Flamenco
guitar   25–50 to date   1–10 per year
• Lute   1–10 to date   † • Vihuela   1–10
to date   †

Tim Rued

110 7th St., Santa Rosa, Calif. 95401
Maker of key fiddles †   12/76

Rugg and Jackel Music Co.

Box 389, Felton, Calif. 95018
FT   1969   Active   6 emp.   IA/MTO
Modern and historical   Brochure   5/75
• Appalachian dulcimer   Over 50 to
date   Over 50 per year • Kalimba   Over
50 to date   Over 50 per year • Also known
as: Capritaurus • *1980: Not affiliated with
Capritaurus • Also known as: Stephen Jackel
and Howard Rugg*

Matthew Ruggiero

40 Algonquin Rd., Chestnut Hill, Mass. 02167
Maker of violins †   2/76

Robert Allen Ruhl

206 S. Tally St., Wentzville, Mo. 63385
PT   1973   Inactive   1 emp.   MTO
Historical   4/76 • Harpsichord   1–10 to
date   1–10 per year

Ruhland Organ Co.

7715 Marlborough Ave., Cleveland, Ohio 44129
FT   1930   Active   4 emp.   MTO
Modern and historical   Brochure   9/75
• Pipe organ   Over 50 to date   1–10 per
year

L. R. Rumery Co.

1685 W. Cerritos Ave., Anaheim, Calif. 92802
PT   1969   Active   2 emp.   IA/MTO
Historical   2/76 • Harpsichord   1–10 to
date   † • Virginal   1–10 to date   †
• Psaltery   1–10 to date   †
• Appalachian dulcimer   1–10 to date †
• *1980: Guitar and harp   1–10 to date   †
• Early woodwinds   1–10 to date   †
• Early bowed strings   1–10 to date   †*

Henry D. Ruppel

2213 Bond St., Pittsburgh, Pa. 15237
PT   1972   Active   1 emp.   MTO
Modern and historical   1/77 • Steel-string
guitar   1–10 to date   1–10 per year

Rural Delights

Also known as: William J. Mitchell

Donald John Rusnak

Also known as: Vintage Banjo Co.

Roscoe Russell

Rt. 3, Box 317A, Galax, Va. 24333 †   2/76

William E. Russell

387 Harvard St., Cambridge, Mass. 02138
Maker of strings † 6/74

Mr. and Mrs. Pasquale Russo

Star Route, East Haven, Vt. 05837
FT 1970 Active 2 emp. IA
Historical 4/76 • Violin 10–25 to
date 1–10 per year • Mandolin 1–10 to
date 1–10 per year

Russo Accordions

1665 Bogart Ave., Bronx, N. Y. 10462
Maker of accordions † 2/75

Don Rust

314 W. Maple, Ursa, Ill. 62376
FT 1974 Active 1 emp. IA/MTO?
Modern ?/77 • Steel-string guitar †
• Primarily repairs

Judith Rutherford

292 W. 92d St., New York, N. Y. 10025
PT 1972 Active 1 emp. IA/MTO
Historical 7/74 • Viola 1–10 to date †

Rutkowski and Robinette

153 Center St., New York, N. Y. 10013
Maker of harpsichords † 2/76

Ned Rutland

1508 Market St., Opelousas, La. 70570
FT 1974 Active 3 emp. IA/MTO
Modern and historical 3/78 • Steel-string
guitar 10–25 to date † • 5-string
banjo 10–25 to date † • Mandolin
1–10 to date † • Appalachian dulcimer
25–50 to date †

David M. Rynerson

37 Park Trail, Croton-on-Hudson, N. Y. 10520
FT 1977 Active 1 emp. MTO
Modern 3/78 • Appalachian dulcimer
Over 50 to date 10–25 per year • Electric
mandolin 1–10 to date 1–10 per year
• Steel-string guitar 1–10 to date 1–10
per year • Electric guitar 1–10 to date
1–10 per year

Sacred Fire/Frogs Delight

R. D. 1, Box 2250, Plainfield, Vt. 05667
PT 1973 Active 1 emp. MTO
Modern 1/78 • Appalachian dulcimer

1–10 to date 1–10 per year • 5-string
banjo 1–10 to date 1–10 per year
• Vielle 1–10 to date 1–10 per year
• Steel-string guitar 1–10 to date 1–10
per year • *1980: Steel-string guitar 10–25
to date • Viola da gamba 1–10 to date
1–10 per year • Classical guitar 1–10 to
date 1–10 per year • Also known as: Fred
Carlson*

Roger Sadowsky

1041 Lancaster Ave., Bryn Mawr, Pa. 10910
FT 1972 Inactive 3 emp. MTO
Modern and historical 2/78 • Steel-string
guitar Over 50 to date † • Appalachian
dulcimer 10–25 to date † • Psaltery
10–25 to date † • Primarily repairs

Saga Banjos

325 Corey Way, Suite 11,
South San Francisco, Calif. 94080
Maker of 5-string banjos † 1/78

Saginaw Guitar Works

Also known as: William Colby

Sahara

303 E. 6th St., New York, N. Y. 10003
Maker of strings † 2/76

Eric Sahlin

Rt. 1, Box 157, Fairfield, Wash. 99012
PT 1975 Active 1 emp. IA
Modern 4/78 • Classical guitar 1–10 to
date † • Steel-string guitar 1–10 to
date † • Electric guitar 1–10 to date
† • *1980: FT MTO • Classical guitar
25–50 to date 10–25 per year*

St. Louis Music Supply Co.

1400 Ferguson Ave., St. Louis, Mo. 63133
Maker of electric guitars † 11/77 • Also
known as: Bently Guitars and Banjos • *1980:
FT 1922 Active ? emp. IA
Modern 10/80 • Violin, cello, guitar, banjo,
and electric guitar †*

William Salchow, Ltd.

1755 Broadway, New York, N. Y. 10019
FT 1960 Active 4 emp. IA/MTO
Modern and historical 9/74 • Bows
Over 50 to date 10–25 per year • *1980:
Brochure*

James R. Sambol
3436 N. Weil St., Milwaukee, Wis. 53212 †
2/78

Jack Samhat
3722 San Fernando Rd., Glendale, Calif. 91204
PT 1973 Active 3 emp. IA
Modern 11/75 • Drum Over 50 to
date † • Zil Over 50 to date † • Also
known as: Proto-Fab & Mfg. Co.

Howard Sams
Blowing Rock, N. C. 28605
Maker of strings † 12/74

Steve Samuels
Maker of Appalachian dulcimers †

Ulises Sanchez
2708 Walker, Berkeley, Calif. 94705
PT 1975 Active 1 emp. MTO
Historical 3/76 • Harpsichord 1–10 to
date †

Curt Sanders and Linda Foley
1217 Bemus S. E., Grand Rapids, Mich. 49506
FT 1975 Active 2 emp. IA
Modern 2/78 • Appalachian dulcimer
25–50 to date 10–25 per year • Also
known as: Linda Foley

John Sanders
2666 Tremont Rd., Columbus, Ohio 43221
PT 1962 Active 1 emp. IA/MTO
Modern and historical 3/78 • 5-string
banjo 10–25 to date 1–10 per year
• Mandolin 1–10 to date 1–10 per year
• Steel-string guitar 1–10 to date 1–10
per year • Electric bass guitar 1–10 to
date 1–10 per year

Robert Sanders
1918 Bridge St., Davenport, Iowa 52308
Maker of Baroque flutes †

Dave Sanderson
111 Briarcliff Pl., Danville, Va. 24541
Maker of strings † 1/78

Sano Corp.
49 Meeker St., Cranford, N. J. 07016
Maker of accordions † 1/78

Russell Sansom
2026 20th Ave., San Francisco, Calif. 94116
FT 1970 Active 1 emp. MTO
Modern and historical 4/76
• Clavichord 1–10 to date 1–10 per
year • Harpsichord 1–10 to date 1–10
per year • Appalachian dulcimer 10–25
to date 1–10 per year • Hammered
dulcimer 10–25 to date 1–10 per year
• 5-string banjo 1–10 to date 1–10 per
year • Autoharp 1–10 to date 1–10 per
year • *1980: Historical*

Michael T. Sansone, Jr.
1237 Main St. East, Rochester, N. Y. 14609
Maker of electric guitars and electric bass
guitars †

Santa Cruz Guitar Co.
328 Ingalls, P. O. Box 242, Santa Cruz, Calif.
95060
FT 1976 Active 3 emp. IA/MTO
Modern and historical 4/78 • Steel-string
guitar 25–50 to date 25–50 per year
• Also known as: William Davis; Richard
Hoover (Otis B. Rodeo); Bruce Ross • *1980: 2
emp. Brochure • Steel-string guitar Over
50 to date • Now known as: Richard Hoover
(Otis B. Rodeo); Bruce Ross*

Dave and Barbara Santo
513 Center, Costa Mesa, Calif. 92627
FT 1973 Active 2 emp. MTO
Modern and historical 3/75 • Steel-string
guitar † 1–10 per year • Also known as:
Barbara Santo • *1980: 1 emp. IA/MTO
• Steel-string guitar Over 50 to date
10–25 per year • Repairs • Now known as:
David Santo Guitars*

Sassman Harpsichords
Also known as: Gregoire Harpsichords

David Saunders
405 W. Galer, Seattle, Wash. 98119
FT 1955 Active 8 emp. MTO
Modern and historical 8/75 • Violin
10–25 to date 1–10 per year • Primarily
repairs

Sauter Pianos
813 Church St., Nashville, Tenn. 37203
Maker of pianos † 2/75

Kelvin Savell

1408 1st Ave. North, St. Petersburg, Fla. 33705
PT   1968   Active   1 emp.   IA
Modern   1/75 • Violin   10− 25 to date   †
• Viola   1− 10 to date   † • Cello   1− 10 to
date   † • Also known as: Bill Wasel

Louis Saverino

10616 Oliver St., Fairfax, Va. 22030
PT   1925   Active   1 emp.   MTO
Historical   6/75 • Bows   1− 10 to date   †

Saville Organ Corp.

2901 Shermer Rd., Northbrook, Ill. 60062
FT   1961   Active   50 emp.   IA/MTO
Modern   Brochure   4/76 • Pipe organ   †

Stephen M. Sawicki

1727 Lincoln Rd., Champaign, Ill. 61820
PT   1964   Active   1 emp.   MTO
Modern   7/74 • Classical guitar   1− 10 to
date   1− 10 per year • Steel-string guitar
1− 10 to date   1− 10 per year

Walter Sbanal

3819 Valencia Rd., Jacksonville, Fla. 32205 †
6/74

Joe Scalone

18390 Surrey Ln., Brookfield, Wis. 53005
FT   Year?   Inactive   1 emp.   MTO
Modern   3/78 • Appalachian dulcimer
1− 10 to date   † • Steel-string guitar
1− 10 to date   † • Electric guitar   1− 10 to
date   † • Primarily repairs · 1980: 1977

Schantz Organ Co.

Box 156, Orrville, Ohio 44667
FT   1873   Active   98 emp.   MTO
Modern   Brochure   4/75 • Pipe organ
Over 50 to date   25− 50 per year

David Schecter

P. O. Box 9783, North Hollywood, Calif. 91609
Maker of electric guitars †   11/77 • Also
known as: Charvel Mfg. Co.; Schecter Guitar
Research

Martha Schecter

97 School St., Belmont, Mass. 02178
PT   1968   Inactive   1 emp.   MTO
Modern   8/74 • Appalachian dulcimer
25− 50 to date   1− 10 per year

Otto K. Schenk

623½ N. Larchmont Blvd., Los Angeles, Calif.
90004
FT   1968   Active   1 emp.   IA/MTO
Modern   10/74 • Viola da gamba   1− 10
to date • Violin   1− 10 to date • Cello
1− 10 to date • Viola   1− 10 to date • All
instruments   1− 10 per year

Scherl and Roth, Inc.

1729 Superior Ave., Cleveland, Ohio 44114
Maker of violins, violas, cellos, and bass
violins †   2/76

E. L. Schertenlieb

93 W. William St., San Jose, Calif. 95110
FT   1939   Active   1 emp.   IA/MTO
Historical   7/74 • Viola   10− 25 to date
† • Violin   Over 50 to date   † • Cello
1− 10 to date   † • Bows   25− 50 to date
†

Milton Scheuerman, Jr.

1035 Eleonore St., New Orleans, La. 70115
PT   1970   Active   1 emp.   MTO
Historical   3/76 • Harpsichord   1− 10 to
date   1− 10 per year • Regal   1− 10 to
date   † • Portative organ   1− 10 to date
† • Psaltery   1− 10 to date   †

Schilke Co.

529 S. Wabash Ave., Chicago, Ill. 60605
FT   1950   Active   30 emp.   IA/MTO
Modern and historical   Brochure   6/75
• Trumpet   Over 50 to date   Over 50 per
year • Cornett   Over 50 to date   Over 50
per year • Fluegelhorn   Over 50 to date
Over 50 per year • Baroque trumpet   Over
50 to date   † • Renaissance trombone
Over 50 to date   †

Schiller Pianos

Also known as: Aeolian Corp.

Jean and Lee Schilling

P. O. Box 8, Cosby, Tenn. 37722
PT   1968   Active   2 emp.   MTO
Modern   Brochure   6/75 • Appalachian
dulcimer   Over 50 to date   10− 25 per
year • Also known as: Jean's Dulcimer Shop

Leonard Schilling

5088 W. 36th Terr., Indianapolis, Ind. 46224
Maker of strings †   1/78

Hardy Schlick
5335 S. Harper, Chicago, Ill. 60615
Maker of clavichords † 2/76

Schlicker Organ Co., Inc.
1530 Military Rd., Buffalo, N. Y. 14217
FT 1932 Active 40 emp. MTO
Modern Brochure 4/76 • Pipe organ
Over 50 to date 10–25 per year

Armin Schlieps
712 Warren North, Seattle, Wash. 98109
Maker of strings † 2/76

Sam Schliff
7037 Schroll, Lakewood, Calif. 90713
PT 1958 Active 2 emp. MTO
Modern and historical Brochure 2/76
• Harpsichord 25–50 to date †
• Piano 1–10 to date † • Violin 1–10
to date † • Also known as: Family Piano
Service

Richard and David Schlub
179 Arcadia Ave., Columbus, Ohio 43202
FT 1976 Active 2 emp. IA
Historical 1/77 • Viola da gamba 1–10
to date † • Violin 1–10 to date †
• Viola 1–10 to date † • Cello 1–10 to
date † • Primarily repairs • Also known
as: The Loft Violin Shop

Gerhart Schmeltekopf
1045 Garfield, Oak Park, Ill. 60304
PT 1976 Active 1 emp. MTO
Historical 2/78 • Rebec 1–10 to date
1–10 per year • Virginal 1–10 to date
1–10 per year • Clavichord 1–10 to
date 1–10 per year • Psaltery 1–10 to
date 1–10 per year

Herbert Schmelzer
Rt. 2, East Troy, Wis. 53120
Maker of strings † 2/76

K. C. Schmidt
1013C Michigan Ave., Sheboygan, Wis. 53081
FT 1977 Active 1 emp. MTO
Modern 2/78 • Electric guitar 1–10 to
date † • Steel-string guitar 1–10 to
date † • Primarily repairs • Also known
as: KCS Enterprises

Oscar Schmidt International
Garden State Rd., Union, N. J. 07083
FT 1879 Active 80 emp. IA
Modern Brochure 12/77 • Autoharp,
guitaro, zither, kalimba, steel-string guitar,
mandolin, ukulele, Appalachian dulcimer,
and drum †

Rudolph Schmoll
510 S. W. 5th St., Portland, Ore. 97204
Maker of strings † 2/76

Richard Schneider
326 W. Kalamazoo Ave., Kalamazoo, Mich. 49007
FT 1964 Active 3 emp. MTO
Modern 9/74 • Classical guitar Over 50
to date † • Flamenco guitar 10–25 to
date † • Steel-string guitar 10–25 to
date † • 12-string guitar 1–10 to
date †

Gunnar I. Schonbeck
8900 Bovie Hill Rd., Hoosick Falls, N. Y. 12090
FT 1940 Active 1 emp. MTO
Modern and historical 4/76
• Xylophone Over 50 to date Over 50
per year • Harp Over 50 to date Over 50
per year • Keyboard Over 50 to date
Over 50 per year • Brass Over 50 to date
Over 50 per year • Woodwinds Over 50 to
date Over 50 per year

Maurice Schoos
137 Douglas Rd., Warwick, R. I. 02886
PT 1971 Active 1 emp. MTO
Historical 4/75 • Rope-tensioned drum
1–10 to date † • *1980: Rope-tensioned
drum 10–25 to date*

Hank Schrieber
104 Deer Trail, P. O. Box 1434, Prescott, Ariz. 86301
PT 1970 Active 1 emp. MTO
Modern 6/74 • Classical guitar 1–10 to
date 1–10 per year • Steel-string guitar
25–50 to date 1–10 per year
• Appalachian dulcimer 10–25 to date
10–25 per year

Andrew Schroetter and Co., Inc.
303 Park Ave. South, New York, N. Y. 10010
Maker of violins † 12/77

Schuback Violin Shop
316 S. W. Alder St., Portland, Ore. 97204
FT 1970 Active 8 emp. IA/MTO
Modern and historical 4/76 • Violin
1–10 to date † • Viola 1–10 to date †
• Cello 1–10 to date † • Bass violin
1–10 to date †

Otto Schuff
92 Bakerdale Rd., Rochester, N.Y. 14614 †
2/76

Siegfried Schuh
854 Lakeside Pl., Chicago, Ill. 60640 † 12/74

Schulmerich Carillons, Inc.
Carillon Hill, Sellersville, Pa. 18960
Maker of carillons † 2/76 • *1980: FT
1934 Active 150 emp. IA/MTO
Modern Brochure 10/80 • Carillons,
cast bells, handbells, chimes, and electronic
bells †*

C. Eric Schulte
24 Buttonwood Ave., Malvern, Pa. 19355
FT 1958 Active 1 emp. MTO
Modern and historical 9/74 • Electric
guitar 25–50 to date † • Steel-string
guitar 10–25 to date † • Primarily
repairs

Severin G. Schurger
717 Disston St., P.O. Box 576, Crystal Beach, Fla.
33523
FT 1972 Active 1 emp. IA
Modern 10/76 • Violin 10–25 to date
1–10 per year • Viola 1–10 to date
1–10 per year • Viola da gamba 1–10 to
date † • Primarily repairs

Freddy Schwartz
1065 W. 7th St., Mesa, Ariz. 85201
Maker of strings † 2/76

Mark Schwartz
637½ S. Main, Ann Arbor, Mich. 48104
Maker of strings † 3/76

Heinz Schweinsberg
13329 Borgman, Huntington Wood, Mich. 48070
PT 1944 Active 1 emp. IA
Modern 4/76 • Violin Over 50 to date
† • Viola 1–10 to date † • Cello 1–10 to
date †

William E. Schweitzer
24221 San Jacinto St., Space 31, San Jacinto,
Calif. 92383
Maker of strings † 10/74

Scientific Music Industries
823 S. Wabash Ave., Chicago, Ill. 60605
Maker of orchestra bells and xylophones †
1/78

Alfred Scott
304 Charmian Rd., Richmond, Va. 23226
PT 1965 Inactive 1 emp. MTO
Modern 4/78 • Steel-string guitar 1–10
to date † • Autoharp 1–10 to date †
• Appalachian dulcimer 1–10 to date †

Allan Scott
110 Olsom St., New Bedford, Mass. 02749 †
6/75

George Scott
471½ E. Market St., Long Beach, Calif. 90805
Maker of strings † 2/76

James Scott
Box 24, El Cerrito, Calif. 94530
FT 1974 Active 1 emp. MTO
Historical Brochure 1/75 • Recorder
1–10 to date 1–10 per year

Roy Scott
2747 Woolsey St., Berkeley, Calif. 94705 † 2/76

Bruce Scotten
Also known as: The Apprentice Shop

Roy Seaman
2908 Tucson Hwy., Nogales, Ariz. 86521
FT 1946 Active 1 emp. IA/MTO
Modern 2/75 • Piccolo Over 50 to
date Over 50 per year • Fife Over 50 to
date Over 50 per year

Seamoon Co.
2802 10th, Berkeley, Calif. 94710 † 2/76

Lynn B. Sears
Star Route 1, Box 15A, Covelo, Calif. 95428
FT 1970 Active 1 emp. IA
Historical Brochure 8/75
• Appalachian dulcimer 25–50 to date
† • *1980: IA/MTO • Appalachian dulcimer
10–25 per year*

Thomas A. Sears
7 Frankwood Ave., Beverly, Mass. 01915
FT   1978   Active   1 emp.   MTO
Historical   11/78 • Recorder   1–10 to
date   1–10 per year

Jerry Secusa
380 S. Placentia, Fullerton, Calif. 92631 †   3/75

Jeremy Seeger
Box 117, Fassett Hill, Hancock, Vt. 05748
PT   1968   Active   1 emp.   IA/MTO
Modern and historical   5/76
• Appalachian dulcimer   25–50 to date
10–25 per year • *1980: Historical
Brochure • Appalachian dulcimer   Over 50
to date   25–50 per year • Hammered
dulcimer   1–10 to date*   †

Oliver Seeler
P.O. Box 686, Mendocino, Calif. 95460
Maker of woodwinds †   2/76

K. S. Seibert
Box 236, Remsenburg, N.Y. 11960 †   2/76

Christopher M. Sekerak
% Minnie Reece, Rt. 2, Booneville, N.C. 27011
PT   1974   Active   1 emp.   MTO
Modern and historical   4/76
• Appalachian dulcimer   10–25 to date
† • 5-string banjo   1–10 to date   †
• Mandolin   1–10 to date   †

Sekova Products
902 Broadway, New York, N.Y. 10003 †   2/75

George Sell
2210 Chicester Ave., Boothwyn, Pa. 19161 †
5/76

Selmer
Box 310, Elkhart, Ind. 46515
FT   1904   Active   999 emp.   IA
Modern   Brochure   4/76 • Woodwinds
Over 50 to date   Over 50 per year • Brass
Over 50 to date   Over 50 per year • Also
known as: Vincent Bach; Buescher Band
Instruments; Lesher Woodwind Co.; Signet
• *1980: 1,127 emp. • Strings   † • Now
known as: Vincent Bach; Buescher Band
Instruments; Bundy, Mercedes, and
Mercedes II; Glaesel Stringed Instruments;
Lesher Woodwind Co.; Signet*

Frank Semino
Rt. 1, Box 424, Three Rivers, Mich. 49093 †
4/76

Walt Senkow
4315 Sexton Ln., Dallas, Tex. 75229
PT   1938   Active   1 emp.   IA/MTO
Modern and historical   5/76 • Violin
Over 50 to date   † • Viola   Over 50 to
date   †

Sequoia Violin Shop
Also known as: William S. Pinches

Ben Setran
651 Lambrecht Ln., Billings, Mont. 59101 †
2/78

Dr. and Mrs. Michael Seyfrit
4752 Powder House Dr., Rockville, Md. 20853
PT   1975   Active   2 emp.   IA/MTO
Historical   10/75 • Baroque oboe   1–10
to date   † • Baroque flute   † • Piccolo   †
• Baroque bassoon   †

Shade Valley Instruments
Also known as: Bob White

Shady Grove Dulcimer Works
Also known as: David F. Darby

John H. Shal
316 Vine St., South Connellsville, Pa. 15425
FT   1964   Active   1 emp.   IA/MTO
Modern and historical   9/74 • Violin
Over 50 to date • Viola   1–10 to date
• Steel-string guitar   1–10 to date • All
instruments   1–10 per year • Primarily
repairs

Jon Shannon
870 Deer Trail, P.O. Box 1434, Prescott, Ariz.
86301
Maker of strings †   1/78

Peter Shapiro
Box 62, Rt. 5, Morgantown, W. Va. 26505
FT   1970   Active   1 emp.   MTO
Modern and historical   4/76 • Kalimba
Over 50 to date   Over 50 per year
• Xylophone   1–10 to date   1–10 per
year • Harp   1–10 to date   † • Ektar
1–10 to date   † • Steel drum   1–10 to
date   1–10 per year • *1980: IA/MTO • Not
making harps and ektars*

Carla Shapreau
Box 283, Arcata, Calif. 95521
FT   1972   Active   1 emp.   MTO
Modern and historical   8/75 • Violin
1–10 to date   † • Baroque violin   1–10 to
date   † • Viola   1–10 to date   †
• Division viol   1–10 to date   †

Karen Sharp
Also known as: Bob Wilhelm and Karen
Sharp

Shar Products
Box 1411, Ann Arbor, Mich. 48106
Maker of strings †   2/76

John Shaw
3028 Aviation, Miami, Fla. 33133 †   2/76

Owen Shaw
791 Tremont St., Suite W511, Boston, Mass.
02118
FT   1969   Active   1 emp.   MTO
Modern and historical   Brochure   8/75
• Viola da gamba   10–25 to date
• Violin   1–10 to date • Viola   1–10 to
date • Classical guitar   10–25 to date
• Vihuela   1–10 to date • Cello   1–10 to
date • Bass violin   1–10 to date • All
instruments   10–25 per year

Reginald Shaw
Wellesley, Mass. 02181 †

Tim Shaw
1008 Saratoga-Sunnyvale, San Jose, Calif. 95129
Maker of strings †   1/78 • Also known as:
Sunrise

Shawhan Pipe Organs
1901 Howell St., Fort Wayne, Ind. 46808
FT   1972   Active   1 emp.   MTO
Modern and historical   10/75 • Pipe
organ   1–10 to date   1–10 per year
• Primarily repairs

J. C. Shellnutt and Co.
Also known as: Magic Mountain
Instruments

Jesse Gordon Shepherd
225 Euclid Ave., Morgantown, W. Va. 26505
PT   1970   Active   1 emp.   MTO
Modern and historical   5/76

• Rebec-dulcimer   1–10 to date
• Kalimba   1–10 to date • All
instruments   1–10 per year • *1980: 258
Friday Creek Rd., Burlington, Wash. 98233
• Tamburitza   †   1–10 per year • Not
making kalimbas*

David B. Sheppard
1833 Spring Garden St., Greensboro, N.C. 27403
FT   1977   Active   1 emp.   MTO
Modern and historical   2/78 • Lute
1–10 to date   † • Hammered dulcimer
1–10 to date   † • Primarily repairs • *1980:
Steel-string guitar   1–10 to date   †*

Sid Sherman
226 S. Wabash Ave., Chicago, Ill. 60604
Maker of strings †   2/76

Michael P. Sherrick
6256 Belmar Ave., Reseda, Calif. 91335
PT   1972   Active   1 emp.   MTO
Historical   4/76 • Appalachian
dulcimer   1–10 to date   †

Roger Sherron
1509½ Grove St., Berkeley, Calif. 94709
FT   1973   Active   1 emp.   MTO
Historical   2/75 • Lute   1–10 to date   †

Shimmering Musical Instrument Co.
Also known as: Joellen Lapidus

Scott Shipley
1500 Hood Rd., Apt. N, Sacramento, Calif.
95815
Maker of strings †   1/78

Margaret Arlene Shipman
4954½ Beverly Blvd., Los Angeles, Calif. 90004
FT   1969   Active   1 emp.   IA
Modern   10/74 • Violin   1–10 to date   †
• Cello   1–10 to date   † • Viola   1–10 to
date   † • Primarily repairs

Robert Shlaer
2109 Alhambra S.W., Albuquerque, N.M. 87104
PT   1975   Active   1 emp.   MTO
Historical   11/74 • Baroque flute   10–25
to date   †

John and Linda Shortridge
P.O. Box 281, Rockport, Maine 04856
FT   1960   Active   2 emp.   MTO

Historical   Brochure   6/74
• Harpsichord   10–25 to date   1–10 per
year • Clavichord   1–10 to date   †

Linda Shortridge
Box 281, Rockport, Maine 04856
Maker of viols † • Also known as: John and
Linda Shortridge

Leonard Showalter
2249 Cardinal Dr., San Diego, Calif. 92123
PT   1972   Active   1 emp.   MTO
Modern   9/74 • Violin   1–10 to date
1–10 per year • Paraguayan harp   1–10
to date   1–10 per year

William Edward Shrum
1804 State, Big Spring, Tex. 79720
PT   1969   Active   1 emp.   IA
Modern   11/74 • Violin   1–10 to date   †
• Mandolin   1–10 to date   †

Dean L. Shultis
1533 29th Ave. West, Bradenton, Fla. 33505
FT   1974   Active   1 emp.   MTO
Modern and historical   12/74
• Steel-string guitar   1–10 to date   †
• Classical guitar   1–10 to date   †
• 5-string banjo   1–10 to date   †
• Primarily repairs

Don Shuttleworth
R.R. 3, Warren, Ind. 46792
Maker of strings †   2/76

Sid's Fingerboard Studio
Decatur Federal Bldg., Decatur, Ga. 30030
Maker of strings †   6/75

Lawrence S. Siegler
Box 107, Vienna, Maine 04360
FT   1967   Active   1 emp.   MTO
Modern and historical   10/76
• Appalachian dulcimer   25–50 to date
1–10 per year • Mandolin   1–10 to date
1–10 per year • 5-string banjo   1–10 to
date   1–10 per year • Steel-string guitar
1–10 to date   1–10 per year

Sierra Steel Guitars
530 N.E. Liberty, Gresham, Ore. 97030
Maker of pedal steel guitars †   5/76

Sigma Guitars
Also known as: C. F. Martin Organisation

Signet
Also known as: Selmer

Frank Silver
286 Laurel St., Hartford, Conn. 06105
PT   1977   Active   1 emp.   MTO
Modern   1/77 • Steel-string guitar   1–10
to date   1–10 per year • Mandolin   1–10
to date   1–10 per year

Steven Silverstein
Call Hollow Rd., Stony Point, N. Y. 10980
FT   1966   Active   1 emp.   IA
Modern and historical   Brochure   5/78
• Woodwinds   10–25 to date   †
• Renaissance flute   Over 50 to date   †
• Recorder   10–25 to date   † • Primarily
repairs • *1980: Renaissance flute   Over 50
per year • Recorder   Over 50 per year*

Roger H. Siminoff
37 Raynor Rd., Morristown, N. J. 07960
PT   1960   Active   3 emp.   IA/MTO
Historical   Brochure   12/74 • 5-string
banjo   10–25 to date   † • Mandolin
10–25 to date   †

Carmie Simon
2234 Sepulveda Blvd., Los Angeles, Calif. 90064
FT   1968   Active   1 emp.   MTO
Modern and historical   Brochure   12/75
• Appalachian dulcimer   Over 50 to
date   25–50 per year • Steel-string
guitar   10–25 to date   1–10 per year
• Electric guitar   10–25 to date   1–10
per year • Hammered dulcimer   †   1–10
per year • Mandolin   †   1–10 per year
• Autoharp   †   1–10 per year • Also
known as: Dulcimer Works

Mark Simon
54 Bryant Dr., Livingston, N. J. 07039
FT   1975   Active   1 emp.   IA/MTO
Historical   4/76 • 5-string banjo   1–10
to date   1–10 per year • Hammered
dulcimer   1–10 to date   1–10 per year
• Mandolin   1–10 to date   1–10 per year
• Primarily repairs

Richard Simons
724 S. Ridgeland Ave., Oak Park, Ill. 60304
PT   1976   Active   1 emp.   IA/MTO
Historical   9/77 • Viol   10–25 to date
10–25 per year • Vielle   10–25 to date

10–25 per year · *1980: Gothic harp*   *1–10 to date*   † · *Rebec*   *1–10 to date*   †
· *Psaltery*   †

John Sinclair

108 N. 2d Ave., Highland Park, N. J. 08904
FT   1976   Active   1 emp.   IA/MTO
Historical   2/78 · Lute   1–10 to date   †

M. K. Singleton

3828 36th St., San Diego, Calif. 92104
PT   1974   Inactive   2 emp.   MTO
Historical   9/74 · Wooden flute   1–10 to
date   † · Psaltery   1–10 to date   †
· Horn pipe   10–25 to date   †

John Sipe

708 Central Ave., Charlotte, N.C. 28204
FT   1964   Active   1 emp.   IA/MTO
Historical   6/74 · Violin   25–50 to
date   1–10 per year · Viola   10–25 to
date   1–10 per year

Steven Sirok

58513 Elm Rd., Mishawaka, Ind. 46544
PT   1971   Active   1 emp.   IA/MTO
Modern and historical   1/77 · Classical
guitar   1–10 to date   1–10 per year
· Violin   1–10 to date   1–10 per year
· Viola   1–10 to date   1–10 per year
· Appalachian dulcimer   1–10 to date
1–10 per year

Sistek Music Co.

5788 Linda Ln., Garfield Heights, Ohio 44125
†   2/76

Jeremiah Skarie

Rt. 3, Box 167, Independence, Va. 24348
PT   1974   Active   1 emp.   MTO
Modern   2/78 · Appalachian dulcimer
10–25 to date   † · Also known as:
Strum-Hollow Dulcimer Works

Patrick Sky

P.O. 349, Charlestown, R.I. 02813
PT   1972   Active   1 emp.   IA/MTO
Historical   10/75 · Uilleann pipes
10–25 to date   † · Also known as: Jon
Campbell

Skyland Musical Instrument Co.

Also known as: David A. Sturgill

William E. Slaby

1322 N. Vermont, Royal Oak, Mich. 48067
PT   1958   Active   1 emp.   IA/MTO
Modern   9/74 · Violin   1–10 to date
· Viola   1–10 to date · Cello   1–10 to
date · All instruments   1–10 per year
· *1980: Violin   10–25 to date*

Les Slaughter

740 Manitou Blvd., Manitou Springs, Colo.
80829 †   4/77
Also known as: Cornucopia, Ltd.; Larry
Gamble

Dave Sleeter

54790 N. Circle Dr., Idyllwild, Calif. 92349
Maker of strings †   2/78

Nolan Sleeth

542 Enderly, Apt. 6, Brownsburg, Ind. 46112
PT   1969   Active   1 emp.   MTO
Historical   12/74 · Appalachian
dulcimer   10–25 to date   1–10 per year
· Courting or double dulcimer   1–10 to
date   1–10 per year

Stanley Slejko

740 E. 236th St., Euclid, Ohio 44123
Maker of strings †   2/76

Slingerland Drum Co.

6633 N. Milwaukee Ave., Niles, Ill. 60648
FT   1919   Active   150 emp.   IA
Modern   Brochure   4/76 · Percussion
Over 50 to date   Over 50 per year

John Sloan

273 Maple Ave., South Chicago Heights, Ill.
60411
PT   1935   Active   1 emp.   IA/MTO
Modern   Brochure   4/75 · 5-string
banjo   25–50 to date   10–25 per year
· Also known as: Omar Mfg. Co.

Irving Sloane

Maker of strings †   11/74

Peter H. Smakula

6691 Thornapple Dr., Mayfield Village, Ohio
44143
PT   1974   Active   2 emp.   IA/MTO
Modern and historical   10/75 · 5-string
banjo   10/25 to date   10–25 per year

• Appalachian dulcimer   25– 50 to date
25– 50 per year • Mouth bow   25– 50 to
date   25– 50 per year • Kalimba   25– 50
to date   25– 50 per year • Also known as:
Goose Acres Thumbpiano Factory and
Dulcimer Works

Lawrence Smalts

4874 W. 125th St., Hawthorne, Calif. 90250 †
8/74

Anton Smith

352 Quince St., Salt Lake City, Utah 84103
Maker of strings †   6/76

Arthur E. Smith Banjo Co.

Box 825, Leverett Center, Mass. 01054
FT   1973   Active   4 emp.   IA/MTO
Modern   Brochure   9/74 • 5-string
banjo   25– 50 to date   † • Also known as:
Kathryn Spencer; Mark Surgies

Ed Smith

Also known as: Pinelands Dulcimer Shop

George A. Smith

1391 W. Broadway Dr., Portland, Ore. 97201
FT   1958   Active   1 emp.   IA/MTO
Modern and historical   7/74 • Classical
guitar   10– 25 to date   † • Flamenco
guitar   10– 25 to date   † • Steel-string
guitar   25– 50 to date   † • 12-string
guitar   25– 50 to date   † • Harpsichord
10– 25 to date   † • Lute   10– 25 to date
† • Primarily repairs

Jack F. Smith

909 Madison, Denver, Colo. 80206
PT   1965   Active   1 emp.   IA/MTO
Modern and historical   6/75 • Steel-string
guitar   1– 10 to date   † • Appalachian
dulcimer   25– 50 to date   †

Jack R. Smith, Jr.

1404 Deerfield Ln., Woodbridge, Va. 22191
PT   1965   Active   1 emp.   MTO
Modern and historical   1/78 • Steel-string
guitar, Appalachian dulcimer, 5-string
banjo, and mandolin   †

Jeffrey Lee Smith

P.O. Box 6816, Bellevue, Wash. 98007
Maker of strings †   1/78 • Also known as:
Bandwagon Repair

Joseph Smith

P.O. Box 201, Forestville, Calif. 95436 †   1/76

Larry Smith

Also known as: Pinelands Dulcimer Shop

Leon Smith

82 May St., Athens, Ohio 45701
PT   1972   Active   1 emp.   MTO
Modern and historical   3/75 • 5-string
banjo   1– 10 to date   † • Steel-string
guitar   1– 10 to date   † • Appalachian
dulcimer   1– 10 to date   †

Lonzo B. Smith

1001 Laird Ave., Parkersburg, W. Va. 26101
PT   1926   Active   1 emp.   IA/MTO
Modern   4/76 • 5-string banjo   10– 25 to
date   † • *1980: Inactive* • *5-string banjo
1– 10 per year*

M. G. Smith

3335 Fulton St., Saginaw, Mich. 48601
Maker of strings †   1/78

Michael Smith

Also known as: Great Lakes Banjo Co.

Rick Smith

36 High St., South Paris, Maine 04281
Maker of strings †   3/78

Robert Smith

R.F.D. 2, Box 99B, Raymond, N.H. 03077
PT   1969   Active   1 emp.   MTO
Historical   6/74 • Lute   1– 10 to date   †
• Vihuela 1– 10 to date • Sordonne   1– 10
to date   † • Krumhorn   1– 10 to date   †
• Also known as: Historical Stringed
Instruments

Robert E. Smith

20 Vernon St., Somerville, Mass. 02145
FT   1973   Active   1 emp.   IA/MTO
Historical   6/74 • Forte-piano   1– 10 to
date   † • Primarily repairs

Stephen O. Smith

432 S.W. 155th St., Seattle, Wash. 98166 †   2/76

Thomas Smith

626 S. Spencer Ave., Indianapolis, Ind. 46219
Maker of violins †   2/76 • *1980: Violin*

Over 50 to date † · *Viola Over 50 to date* † · *Deceased (7/80)*

Smith Guitars
Haysville, Kans. 67060
Maker of steel-string guitars † 10/75

John R. Snell
915 S. Maple, McPherson, Kans. 67460
PT 1971 Active 3 emp. IA
Modern 2/78 • Appalachian dulcimer
10– 25 to date 1– 10 per year • Also
known as: Acoustic Stringed Instruments

Don Snyder
13440 Hwy. 234, Gold Hill, Ore. 97525
Maker of strings † 1/78

Dr. Harold E. Snyder
17 Vineland Dr., Barrington, R.I. 02806
PT 1975 Active 1 emp. IA/MTO
Modern and historical Brochure 1/77
• Lute 25– 50 to date † · *Appalachian
dulcimer 1– 10 to date † · 1980:
Vihuela 1– 10 to date 1– 10 per year
· Baroque guitar 1– 10 to date 1– 10 per
year · Bandora 1– 10 to date † · Irish
harp 1– 10 to date † · Steel-string
guitar 1– 10 to date* †

Lawrence D. Snyder
P.O. Box 947, Davis, Calif. 95616
FT 1970 Active 2 emp. MTO
Historical 11/74 • Harpsichord 1– 10 to
date 1– 10 per year

Ed Sobansky
8102 Gorman Ave., Laurel, Md. 20810
Maker of Irish harps †

Dr. John Soderstrom
303 W. Casa Linda Dr., Woodland, Calif. 95695
PT 1960 Active 1 emp. MTO
Historical 10/75 • Classical guitar
10– 25 to date • Recorder 1– 10 to date
• Appalachian dulcimer 1– 10 to date
• All instruments 1– 10 per year

Sohmer and Co., Inc.
31 W. 57th St., New York, N.Y. 10019
FT 1872 Active 110 emp. IA
Modern Brochure 5/74 • Piano Over
50 to date Over 50 per year

C. Soistman
Gladway Rd., Baltimore, Md. 21220 † 2/76

Ervin Somogyi
3052 Telegraph Ave., Berkeley, Calif. 94705
FT 1970 Active 1 emp. IA/MTO
Modern and historical 4/74 • Lute
10– 25 to date 1– 10 per year
• Steel-string guitar Over 50 to date
1– 10 per year • Appalachian dulcimer
25– 50 to date 1– 10 per year • Also
known as: Guitar and Lute Workshop
· *1980: Brochure · Flamenco, classical,
12-string, and electric guitars and zithers
Over 50 to date 1– 10 per year · Now
known as: The Acoustic Guitar*

Songbird
Also known as: Larry English

Sonola Accordion Co., Inc.
300 Observer Hwy., Hoboken, N.J. 07030
Maker of accordions † 2/75

Sorkin Music Co.
370 Motor Pkwy., Hauppauge, N.Y. 11787
Maker of electric organs † 2/76

Steven W. Sorli
1081 Westford St., Carlisle, Mass. 01741
FT 1973 Active 1 emp. MTO
Historical 2/75 • Harpsichord 1– 10 to
date 1– 10 per year

John Soto
35 Dayton Ln., Englishtown, N.J. 07726
PT 1973 Active 1 emp. MTO
Modern and historical 6/74 • Classical
guitar 1– 10 to date †

Sound Guitar Co.
82 Suffolk St., Holyoke, Mass. 01040
*1980: FT 1975 Active 2 emp.
IA/MTO Modern 10/80 · Electric guitar,
electric mandolin, electric bass guitar,
steel-string guitar, 12-string guitar 25– 50
to date † · Also known as: Frank E.
Lucchesi; Paul J. Rasmussen*

Steven V. Sowers
204 Brownwood, Columbia City, Ind. 46725
Maker of strings † 1/78

Southern-Highland-Dulcimers
Also known as: Stinsen R. Behlen

Gabriel Souza
41888 Vargas Rd., Fremont, Calif. 94538
Maker of strings †   1/78

Space Banjo Co.
Also known as: Dennis Reed

Fred Spafford
400 Willnondaga St., Syracuse, N. Y. 13202
FT   1933   Inactive   1 emp.   IA
Modern and historical   10/74 • Violin
10–25 to date   † • Viola   1–10 to date
† • Primarily repairs

Earl Sparks
1942 Quebec Rd., Cincinnati, Ohio 45214
PT   1975   Active   1 emp.   IA
Modern   4/76 • 5-string banjo   1–10 to
date   † • Appalachian dulcimer   1–10 to
date   †

David T. Specht
1840 Seavy Rd., Corvallis, Ore. 97330
PT   1965   Active   1 emp.   MTO
Modern and historical   4/76 • 5-string
banjo   1–10 to date   † • Mandolin
1–10 to date   † • Steel-string guitar
1–10 to date   † • Primarily repairs

John Cordell Spence
4710 Southern S.E., Albuquerque, N. M. 87108
PT   1976   Active   1 emp.   MTO
Modern   1/77 • Steel-string guitar   1–10
to date   1–10 per year • *1980: Hobbyist*

Kathryn Spencer
Also known as: Arthur E. Smith Banjo Co.

William S. Spigelsky
1020 Wilson St., Monessen, Pa. 15062
FT   1940   Inactive   1 emp.   MTO
Modern and historical   4/76 • Classical
guitar   1–10 to date   † • Flamenco
guitar   1–10 to date   † • Tamburitza
1–10 to date   † • Primarily repairs

Bennet Spielvogel
South Acworth, N. H. 03607 †   2/76

Spirit of Jubal
Also known as: Paul J. Rasmussen

J. M. Springfield III
7413 Cedar Ave., Tacoma Park, Md. 20012 †
2/76

Edgar F. Sprouse
P. O. Box 963, Bloomfield, N. M. 87413
PT   1975   Active   1 emp.   MTO
Modern and historical   10/75 • 5-string
banjo   1–10 to date   †

Alan A. Stack
P. O. Box 192, Vergennes, Vt. 05491
FT   1973   Inactive   ? emp.   IA
Modern   12/77 • Steel-string guitar
Over 50 to date   † • Electric guitar   Over
50 to date   † • Electric bass guitar   1–10
to date   † • Appalachian dulcimer   Over
50 to date   † • Also known as: Time
Guitars

Stadler Guitars
924 S. Scales St., Reidsville, N. C. 27320
FT   1960   Active   1 emp.   IA/MTO
Modern   Brochure   5/76 • Pedal steel
guitar   Over 50 to date   Over 50 per year

Stadler Music Co.
Also known as: Marlen Guitar Co.

Standel Co.
4935 Double Dr., Temple City, Calif. 91780
Maker of electric guitars †   2/75

Mr. and Mrs. Peter Stanley
Box 67, Rapidan, Va. 22733
FT   1977   Active   2 emp.   IA/MTO
Modern and historical   2/78 • Steel-string
guitar   1–10 to date   †

Walter Stanul
15 Green St., #1, Cambridge, Mass. 02139
PT   1972   Active   1 emp.   MTO
Modern and historical   6/74 • Classical
guitar   1–10 to date   1–10 per year
• *1980: IA/MTO • Classical guitar   25–50
to date*

Craig N. Stapley
34 Scotch Ln., Rochester, N. Y. 14617
FT   1972   Active   1 emp.   MTO
Modern and historical   Brochure   12/75
• Classical guitar   25–50 to date   10–25
per year • Steel-string guitar   25–50 to

date   10– 25 per year • Appalachian
dulcimer   Over 50 to date   25– 50 per
year • Viola   1– 10 to date   †

P. A. Starch Piano Co.
299 Northfield Rd., Northfield, Ill. 60093
Maker of pianos †   2/75

Martin Starkman
19 Knollwood Dr., Larchmont, N. Y. 10538
PT   1958   Active   1 emp.   IA
Historical   7/74 • Violin   10– 25 to
date   1– 10 per year • Viola   1– 10 to
date   †

George Steck and Co., Inc.
Also known as: Aeolian Corp.

Henry Steele
Rt. 2, Box 20B, Belvidere, Tenn. 37306
PT   1923   Inactive   1 emp.
IA/MTO   Modern   5/74 • Appalachian
dulcimer   †

Sandy Stehling
3436 N. Cramer, Milwaukee, Wis. 53211
PT   1972   Active   1 emp.   MTO
Modern and historical   12/74
• Appalachian dulcimer   25– 50 to date †

Bert Stein
826 Woodworth Ave., Pittsburgh, Pa. 15221
FT   1960   Active   1 emp.   IA/MTO
Modern and historical   Brochure   4/76
• Flamenco guitar   25– 50 to date   †
• Classical guitar   Over 50 to date   †
• Lute   25– 50 to date   † • Strings
10– 25 to date   †

Steiner Organs, Inc.
P. O. Box 895, Louisville, Ky. 40201
FT   1957   Active   6 emp.   MTO
Modern   Brochure   4/75 • Pipe organ
25– 50 to date   1– 10 per year • *1980: 10*
emp. • Pipe organ   Over 50 to date

Steiner-Parker Synthesizers
2734 S. 2700 West, Salt Lake City, Utah 84119
Maker of synthesizers †   1/78

Steinway and Sons
Steinway Pl., Long Island City, N. Y. 11105
FT   1853   Active   400 emp.   IA
Modern   Brochure   6/74 • Piano   Over

50 to date   Over 50 per year • Also known
as: CBS, Inc.

Stelling Banjo Works
8815 Kenwood Dr., Spring Valley, Calif. 92077
FT   1974   Active   5 emp.   MTO
Modern   Brochure   10/75 • 5-string
banjo   Over 50 to date   † • *1980: 8 emp.*
• 5-string banjo   Over 50 per year
• Mandolin   Over 50 to date   Over 50 per
year

Sterling Piano Co., Inc.
Also known as: Aeolian Corp.

Doc Steudle
208 Ash Ave., Pewee Valley, Ky. 40056
PT   1968   Active   1 emp.   IA
Historical   6/74 • Appalachian
dulcimer   25– 50 to date   †

D. W. Stevens
16500 W. 63d Pl., Golden, Colo. 80401
FT   1965   Active   1 emp.   MTO
Modern   6/74 • Steel-string guitar
25– 50 to date • Mandolin   1– 10 to date
• 5-string banjo   1– 10 to date • Ukulele
1– 10 to date • All instruments   10– 25 per
year

Larry Stevens
7003 W. Mt. Hope Rd., R. R. 3, Lansing, Mich.
48917
FT   1975   Active   1 emp.   IA
Modern   2/78 • Classical guitar   1– 10 to
date   † • Steel-string guitar   1– 10 to
date   † • Primarily repairs

E. P. Stevenson
217 Garden St., Hoboken, N. J. 07030
Maker of harpsichords †   2/76

Stewart-MacDonald Mfg. Co.
Box 900, Athens, Ohio 45701
1980: FT   Year?   Active   15 emp.   IA
Modern   Brochure   10/80 • 5-string
banjo (kit)   Over 50 to date   Over 50 per
year • Mandolin (kit)   Over 50 to date
Over 50 per year • Also known as: Eagle
Banjos

Stick Enterprises, Inc.
8320 Yucca Trail, Los Angeles, Calif. 90046
FT   1974   Active   4 emp.   IA

Modern Brochure 8/75 • Strings Over 50 to date   Over 50 per year • Also known as: Emmett Chapman • *1980: Touchboard   Over 50 to date   Over 50 per year*

Duane Stigen
306 E. Vasa, Fergus Falls, Minn. 56537
Maker of strings †   1/78

G. L. Stiles
4925 E. 10th Ct., Hialeah, Fla. 33013
FT   1957   Active   1 emp.   MTO
Modern   4/76 • Electric guitar   Over 50 to date   † • Jazz guitar   10−25 to date   † • Steel-string guitar   Over 50 to date   †

Phillip J. Stiles
417 Nayatt Rd., Barrington, R. I. 02806
PT   1975   Active   1 emp.   MTO
Historical   2/76 • Rackett   1−10 to date   † • Sordonne   1−10 to date   †

George Stilphen
Box 242, Center Ossipee, Effingham Falls, N. H. 03814
FT   1970   Active   1 emp.   MTO
Historical   Brochure   5/74
• Harpsichord   1−10 to date   1−10 per year • Virginal   1−10 to date   1−10 per year • Piano   1−10 to date   †

Daniel Stimmerman
71 Gainsborough St., #1, Boston, Mass. 02115
Maker of strings †   5/74

Burt Stimson
10401 Burnt Ember Dr., Silver Spring, Md. 20903
PT   Year?   Active   1 emp.   MTO
Modern   4/78 • Steel-string guitar   †

Sting Player-Piano
Also known as: Aeolian Corp.

Glen Terry Stockton
911 First, Rm. 10, Spokane, Wash. 99204
FT   1964   Active   2 emp.   IA/MTO
Modern   Brochure   9/76 • Violin   10−25 to date   †

Randy Stockwell
2819 E. 5th Ave., Columbus, Ohio 43219
FT   1964   Active   1 emp.   MTO

Modern and historical   6/76 • 5-string banjo   1−10 to date   † • Mandolin   1−10 to date   † • Steel-string guitar   1−10 to date   †

Peter Stoffel
Elks Club, Redlands, Calif. 92373
Maker of strings †   2/76

David Stoller
14 Summit Ln., New Hyde Park, N. Y. 11040
FT   1962   Active   1 emp.   MTO
Modern   4/76 • Violin   1−10 to date   † • Mandolin   1−10 to date   † • Primarily repairs • *1980: 1957*

Robert W. Stoltenberg
1405 W. Belden, Chicago, Ill. 60614
FT   1974   Active   1 emp.   MTO
Modern   Brochure   6/74 • Violin   10−25 to date   † • Viola   10−25 to date   † • Cello   10−25 to date   † • Bass violin   10−25 to date   † • *1980: Violin   1−10 per year • Viola   1−10 per year • Cello   1−10 per year • Bass violin   1−10 per year • Bows   †   1−10 per year*

Mike Stoetzer
22961 Carolina, St. Clair Shores, Mich. 48080
Maker of strings †   1/78

Gregory A. Stojkov
5711 Forest Ave., Parma, Ohio 44129
Maker of strings †   1/78

Benjamin Stone
Rt. 10, Orford, N. H. 03777
FT   1973   Active   1 emp.   IA/MTO
Modern and historical   1/75
• Appalachian dulcimer   10−25 to date   † • Hammered dulcimer   1−10 to date   †

Dennis Stone
9901 Mariner Ct., Oxon Hill, Md. 20022
Maker of violins †

Stoney Lonesome Bazaar
Also known as: Jack Brubaker

Ben Storch Corp.
257 E. 46th St., Brooklyn, N. Y. 11203
Maker of violins †   3/76

Story and Clark Piano Co.
100 Fulton St., Grand Haven, Mich. 49417

FT 1857 Active 220 emp. IA Modern Brochure 6/74 • Piano Over 50 to date Over 50 per year • Also known as: Hobart M. Cable Co.; Kingsbury Pianos • *1980: Also known as: Norlin Music, Inc.*

Harry Stoutenbourgh
West Hurley, N. Y. 11491
Maker of violins † 2/76

Stradivarius Studios
Also known as: Vahakn Nigogosian

Stradivarius Violin Shop
111 W. 57th St., New York, N. Y. 10019
Maker of violins † 2/76

Stradi-Varni Co.
8542 Georgetown Pike, McLean, Va. 22101
FT 1952 Active 1 emp. IA/MTO
Historical 7/74 • Violin Over 50 to
date † • *1980: Violin, viola, and cello
Over 50 to date 10–25 per year • Also
known as: Harry Lebovit*

Natale Armando Strafaci
13 Thomas St., Charlestown, R. I. 02813
FT 1974 Active 2 emp. MTO
Modern and historical 12/75 • Electric
guitar 1–10 to date • Steel-string
guitar 1–10 to date • Classical guitar
1–10 to date • All instruments 10–25 per
year • Also known as: Charlestown Guitar
Shop

Steve Strait
R. R. #4, Corning, Iowa 50841
Maker of strings † 12/77

Robert Stratton
416 Hune Ave., Alexandria, Va. 22301
Maker of harpsichords † 5/74

Strider Systems, Inc.
P. O. Box 2934, Norman, Okla. 73070
FT 1975 Active 2 emp. IA
Modern Brochure 1/78 • Synthesizer
1–10 to date 1–10 per year

Stringed Instrument Woodcrafting Shop
Also known as: Jerry Werhner

Stringfellow Guitars
121 Union St., North Adams, Mass. 01247

FT 1969 Active 1 emp. IA/MTO
Modern and historical Brochure 10/75
• Steel-string guitar 10–25 to date
1–10 per year • Appalachian dulcimer
25–50 to date 10–25 per year
• Psaltery 25–50 to date 10–25 per
year • Wind harp 25–50 to date 10–25
per year • Also known as: William Richard
Cumpiano

The String Shop
Also known as: William R. Belles

H. A. Strobel
27 Kristy Ct., Novato, Calif. 94947
PT Year? Active 1 emp. MTO
Modern 10/74 • Violin 1–10 to date †
• Strings 1–10 to date †

Strum-Hollow Dulcimer Works
Also known as: Jeremiah Skarie

Stuart Organ Co.
P. O. Box 1844, Springfield, Mass. 01101
FT 1973 Active 3 emp. MTO
Modern and historical 6/74 • Pipe
organ 1–10 to date 1–10 per year

Mike Stuber
823 S. Minnesota St., Shakopee, Minn. 55379
PT 1976 Active 1 emp. MTO
Modern 2/78 • Steel-string guitar
10–25 to date † • Dobro 1–10 to date
† • Mandolin 1–10 to date † • Electric
guitar 1–10 to date †

Studio City Music
Also known as: Paul Toenniges

Stumpf Fiddle
Also known as: Fiddle Factory, Inc.

David A. Sturgill
Rt. 1, Box 87, Piney Creek, N. C. 28663
FT 1971 Active 2 emp. IA/MTO
Modern and historical Brochure 6/74
• Violin 25–50 to date 1–10 per year
• Mandolin 25–50 to date 10–25 per
year • Steel-string guitar Over 50 to
date Over 50 per year • 5-string banjo
25–50 to date Over 50 per year • Also
known as: Skyland Musical Instrument Co.
• *1980: 1930 • Violin Over 50 to date
• Mandolin Over 50 to date • 5-string*

banjo   Over 50 to date · Appalachian
dulcimer   Over 50 to date   † · Hammered
dulcimer   10–25 to date   † · All
instruments   Over 50 per year

Mark Sugar
4516 N. Monticello, Chicago, Ill. 60625
PT   1973   Inactive   1 emp.   MTO
Modern   4/76 · Steel-string guitar   1–10
to date · Classical guitar   1–10 to date
· Flamenco guitar   1–10 to date
· Mandolin   1–10 to date · All
instruments   1–10 per year

Sugar Loaf Folk Instruments
Woods Rd., Sugar Loaf, N. Y. 10981
FT   1972   Active   2 emp.   IA
Modern   Brochure   7/74 · Appalachian
dulcimer   Over 50 to date   25–50 per
year · Steel-string guitar   1–10 to date
1–10 per year · Also known as: Dick Manley
· 1980: 1 emp. · Classical guitar   1–10 to
date   1–10 per year · Wood kazoo   Over
50 to date   Over 50 per year · Wood
shepherd's flute   Over 50 to date   Over 50
per year · Not making steel-string guitars

Daniel T. Sullivan
44 Round Hill Rd., Northampton, Mass. 01060
Maker of strings †

Lisle Sultzbaugh
25795 Lomas Verdes, Loma Linda, Calif. 92373
Maker of strings †   2/76

Seth Summerfield
635 Aberdeen Rd., Hampton, Va. 23661
PT   1960   Active   1 emp.   MTO
Modern   9/74 · Steel-string guitar
25–50 to date   1–10 per year · 5-string
banjo   10–25 to date   1–10 per year
· Mandolin   10–25 to date   1–10 per
year · Violin   10–25 to date   1–10 per
year · 1980: Steel-string guitar   Over 50 to
date

Sunflower Music Shop
632 Portage Ave., South Bend, Ind. 46616
PT   1973   Active   2 emp.   IA/MTO
Modern   10/75 · Electric guitar   10–25
to date   1–10 per year · Steel-string
guitar   10–25 to date   1–10 per year
· 5-string banjo   1–10 to date   1–10 per
year

Sunhearth Musical Instruments
Also known as: Walter P. Martin

Sunrise
131 E. Kalamazoo Ave., Kalamazoo, Mich.
49006
Also known as: Pat Murphy; Tim Shaw

Sunshine Woodworks
N. Wintzel, Tucson, Ariz. 85700 †   5/74

Debbie Suran
P. O. Box 223, Deer Isle, Maine 04627
FT   1977   Active   1 emp.   MTO
Modern   2/78 · Steel-string guitar   1–10
to date   † · 5-string banjo   1–10 to
date   † · Hammered dulcimer   1–10 to
date   † · 1980: PT · Hammered dulcimer
10–25 to date · Not making guitars and
banjos

Mark Surgies
Also known as: Arthur E. Smith Banjo Co.

David A. Sutherland
637½ S. Main St., Ann Arbor, Mich. 48104
FT   1974   Active   1 emp.   IA
Historical   4/76 · Virginal   1–10 to
date   † · Harpsichord   1–10 to date   †
· Primarily repairs

Sweeney Banjo Mfg. Co.
Box 5104, Long Beach, Calif. 90805
Maker of 5-string banjos †   6/74

Charles S. Sweet
4920 S. Jamaica Way, Tucson, Ariz. 85706
PT   1950   Active   1 emp.   IA
Historical   11/74 · Violin   1–10 to
date   † · Viola   1–10 to date   †

Ralph Sweet
32 S. Maple St., Enfield, Conn. 06082
PT   1973   Active   1 emp.   IA/MTO
Modern and historical   1/75 · Tabor
pipe   10–25 to date   † · Fife   Over 50 to
date   † · Flageolette   Over 50 to date   †
· 1980: 2 emp.   Brochure · Tabor pipe
Over 50 to date   25–50 per year · Fife
Over 50 per year · Flageolette   Over 50 per
year · Baroque and Irish flutes   Over 50 to
date   Over 50 per year · Tin whistle   Over
50 to date   Over 50 per year · Also known
as: Sweetheart Flute Co.

Dr. William Swettman

710 Fairview Ave., Salem, Ore. 97302
FT 1965 Active 1 emp. IA
Historical 9/74 • Violin 10– 25 to
date 1– 10 per year • Viola 1– 10 to
date 1– 10 per year • Primarily repairs
• Also known as: Violin Shop

Michael H. Swinger

8565 Benson Rd., Carroll, Ohio 43112
FT 1970 Active 1 emp. MTO
Modern and historical Brochure 5/74
• Portative organ 1– 10 to date †
• Positive organ 1– 10 to date †

J. Dean Swisher

325 Central Pl., Kirkwood, Mo. 63122
FT 1969 Active 1 emp. MTO
Modern 5/76 • Violin 1– 10 to date †
• Bass violin 1– 10 to date † • Primarily
repairs

Julius Switra

1248 12th Ave., San Diego, Calif. 92101
Maker of strings † 10/74

Syn-Cordion Musical Instrument Corp.

Also known as: Octave Electronics, Inc.

Syndrum

Also known as: Pollard Industries, Inc.

W. T. Szaborn

1224 Cedar, Ponca City, Okla. 74601 † 2/76

Wally Szwajda

2464 William, Buffalo, N. Y. 14206
Maker of strings †

Takoma Banjo Works

308 Boyd Ave., Takoma Park, Md. 20012
Maker of 5-string banjos † 2/76

C. Garo Takoushian

112 Commander Black Dr., Oradell, N. J. 02649
FT 1946 Active 1 emp. MTO
Modern and historical 4/76 • Steel-string
guitar 1– 10 to date † • Lute 1– 10 to
date † • Oud 1– 10 to date †
• Violin 1– 10 to date † • Primarily
repairs

Tama Guitars

Also known as: Elger Co.

Peter Taney

1005 S. 46th St., Philadelphia, Pa. 19104
Maker of Appalachian dulcimers † 2/76

Pietro Tatar

149 W. 57th St., New York, N. Y. 10019
FT 1960 Inactive 2 emp. MTO
Historical 4/76 • Viola 1– 10 to date †
• Primarily repairs

Tatay and Son

655 Horseblock Rd., Farmingville, N. Y. 11738
FT 1940 Active 1 emp. IA/MTO
Modern 10/74 • Classical guitar Over
50 to date Over 50 per year • *1980:
Steel-string guitar Over 50 to date Over
50 per year*

Marjorie Tayloe

4527 Kraft Ave., North Hollywood, Calif. 91602
FT 1960 Active 3 emp. IA
Modern and historical Brochure 7/74
• Welsh triple harp † 1– 10 per year
• Harp 1– 10 to date † • Irish harp
Over 50 to date 10– 25 per year • Wind
harp † 10– 25 per year • Also known as:
Irish Harp Center • *1980: PT • Welsh triple
harp 25–50 to date • Harp 1– 10 to
date • Not making wind harps • Now known
as: Musical Arts Academy*

David Taylor

106 Montgomery Blvd., Norwich, Ohio 43767
PT 1973 Active 1 emp. MTO
Historical 3/75 • Steel-string guitar
1– 10 to date †

Ed Taylor

Box 263, Main St., Plaistow, N. H. 03865
FT 1972 Active 1 emp. MTO
Modern and historical 9/74 • 5-string
banjo 1– 10 to date † • Mandolin
1– 10 to date 1– 10 per year • Primarily
repairs • Also known as: Mignon-Loew Mfg.
Co.: Uncle Banjo

J. Bradley Taylor, Inc.

390 Commonwealth Ave., Suite 701, Boston,
Mass. 02215
Maker of violins † 11/76 • *1980: FT
1964 Active 4 emp. MTO
Historical 10/80 • Violin, viola, and
bows †*

Tut Taylor Music
500 Arlington Ave., Nashville, Tenn. 37210
FT   1950   Active   12 emp.   IA
Historical   Brochure   4/76 • 5-string
banjo   Over 50 to date   † • Mandolin   †
• Dobro   † • Also known as: Tennessee
Dulcimer Works

W. Bruce Taylor
4831 Willett Pkwy., Chevy Chase, Md. 20015 †
1/78
Also known as: John Yerxa

Taylor Guitars
Also known as: Kurt R. Listug

Don E. Teeter
Also known as: Don's Guitar Shop

Telegraph Music Works
1000 Harris, Bellingham, Wash. 98225
FT   1970   Active   3 emp.   MTO
Modern   4/76 • Appalachian dulcimer
1–10 to date   † • 5-string banjo   1–10 to
date   † • Primarily repairs • Also known
as: Jack Hanson • *1980: 2 emp. • Now known
as: Clifford Perry*

Teleguitars
100 Grove Rd., Frederick, Md. 21701
Maker of steel-string guitars †   5/76

Tempo Band Instruments
Also known as: King Musical Instruments
• *1980: No longer affiliated with King
Musical Instruments*

Tennessee Dulcimer Works
Also known as: Tut Taylor Music

David Templing
R. R. 2, Box 70, Hoistington, Kans. 67544
PT   1950   Inactive   1 emp.   MTO
Modern   10/74 • Cello   1–10 to date   †
• Violin   1–10 to date   † • Viola   1–10
to date   † • Appalachian dulcimer
10–25 to date   †

T. Burdell Tenney
968 Kevin, Redlands, Calif. 92373
FT   1962   Active   1 emp.   IA/MTO
Modern and historical   4/76 • Bows
Over 50 to date   †

Deborah Teplow
8741 Brook, P. O. Box 662, Kings Beach, Calif.
95719
PT   1972   Active   1 emp.   MTO
Historical   4/76 • Recorder   25–50 to
date   10–25 per year • Baroque flute
1–10 to date   1–10 per year

Paul Tester
5606 Eastwood Ct., Clinton, Md. 20735 †   1/76

Lucille Tewell
235 E. 7th St., Hastings, Neb. 68901
PT   1970   Active   1 emp.   IA
Modern   5/74 • Violin   1–10 to date
1–10 per year • Viola   1–10 to date
1–10 per year

John Thierman
2406 N. 4th St., Columbus, Ohio 43202
FT   1973   Active   1 emp.   MTO
Modern and historical   6/76 • 5-string
banjo   10–25 to date   † • Autoharp
1–10 to date   † • Steel-string guitar
1–10 to date   † • Appalachian dulcimer
1–10 to date   † • Also known as: Chandler
Instruments

Thomas
[?], Ky. 00000
Maker of Appalachian dulcimers †

Harry Thomas
8648 N. Mercer Way, Mercer Island, Wash.
98040
Maker of strings †   1/78

Robert A. Thomas
Holiday Meadow Apts., #A-7, Hamburg, N. Y.
14075
PT   1970   Active   1 emp.   MTO
Modern   5/75 • Jazz guitar   1–10 to
date   † • Mandolin   1–10 to date   †
• Appalachian dulcimer   1–10 to date   †

Dr. Thomas Thomas
5445 E. Washington, Phoenix, Ariz. 85034
PT   Year?   Active   1 emp.   IA/MTO
Modern   Brochure   6/74 • 12-string
guitar   1–10 to date   † • Classical
guitar   1–10 to date   † • Mandolin
1–10 to date   † • Appalachian dulcimer
1–10 to date   †

Thomas International Corp.
7310 N. Lehigh Ave., Chicago, Ill. 60648
Maker of electric organs †   2/76

Carl Thompson
Court St., Brooklyn, N. Y. 11200
Maker of strings †

Earl Thompson
13145 Triadelphia Rd., Clarksville, Md. 21029
FT   1956   Active   3 emp.   IA
Modern   Brochure   5/74 • Irish harp
Over 50 to date   1–10 per year • Minstrel
harp   Over 50 to date   Over 50 per year
• Also known as: Linrud Harp Co.

Dr. Oliver Thompson
13261 Triadelphia Mill Rd., Clarksville, Md.
21029
PT   1967   Active   1 emp.   IA
Modern and historical   9/74 • Violin
25–50 to date   1–10 per year • Viola
1–10 to date   †

Robert G. Thompson
Rt. 1, Sandyville, W. Va. 25275 †   1/76

William Thompson
313 N. Wabach, Walton, Kans. 67151 †   11/74

Roger Thurman
900 Franklin Ave., Kent, Ohio 44240
Maker of strings †   2/76 • Also known as:
Music Workshop

Florian Thurston
Rt. 6, Box 8, Leslie, Ark. 72645
PT   1922   Active   1 emp.   IA
Historical   4/76 • Violin   10–25 to
date   † • *1980: Violin   25–50 to date
1–10 per year*

John Tignor
Rt. 7, Frankfort, Ky. 40601
PT   1954   Active   1 emp.   IA
Historical   10/74 • Appalachian
dulcimer   Over 50 to date   Over 50 per
year

Time Guitars
Also known as: Alan A. Stack

J. W. Tippets
5445 Castle Hills Dr., San Diego, Calif. 92109
Maker of strings †   2/76

Titano Accordion Co.
P. O. Box 608, 230 Herricks Rd., Mineola, N. Y.
11501
Maker of accordions †   2/76

Paul Toenniges
11340 Ventura Blvd., Studio City, Calif. 91604
PT   1953   Active   2 emp.   IA
Modern and historical   4/76 • Violin   †
• Bass violin   † • Also known as: Studio
City Music

Toledo Pipe Organ Co.
Also known as: Julian E. Bulley

Bennett Tolliver
160 Main St., Northampton, Mass. 01060
FT   1967   Active   1 emp.   IA/MTO
Modern and historical   1/75 • Steel-string
guitar   25–50 to date   †

Tone Cone Electronics
Box 91, Little Rock, Ark. 72203 †   2/76

Toneline Mfg. Co.
1812 S. Halsted St., Chicago, Ill. 60608 †   2/76

Tone-Master
114 S. Ninth St., Lincoln, Neb. 68508
Maker of drums †   2/76

Bob Tool
Chesterfield, N. J. 07900
Maker of Appalachian dulcimers †

Howard Toplansky
559 Winthrop Rd., Union, N. J. 07083 †   2/76

Torma Violin
14021 Madison, Lakewood, Ohio 44107
Maker of violins †   2/76

Daniel and Dawne Torres
14567 Big Basin Way, Saratoga, Calif. 95070
Maker of strings †   1/78 • *1980: FT
1975   Active   5 emp.   IA/MTO
Modern   Brochure   10/80 • Electric
guitar and electric bass guitar   Over 50 to
date   10–25 per year • Also known as:
Torres Guitars*

Ray Torstenson
301 S. Plymouth Rd., Huntsville, Ala. 35811 †
2/76

Total Technology
1346 Bayport Ave., San Carlos, Calif. 94070
FT 1970 Active 10 emp. IA/MTO
Modern Brochure 4/76 • Synthesizer
Over 50 to date Over 50 per year • Also
known as: George A. Gluck, Jr.

Peter Tourin
Box 575, Duxbury, Vt. 05676
FT 1967 Active 1 emp. MTO
Historical Brochure 9/77
• Harpsichord 1–10 to date † • Viola da
gamba 1–10 to date † • *1980: Viola da
gamba 10–25 to date 10–25 per year*

Thomas H. Tower
640 Center N. E., Salem, Ore. 97301
PT 1972 Active 1 emp. MTO
Modern and historical Brochure 11/74
• 5-string banjo 1–10 to date 1–10 per
year • Appalachian dulcimer 10–25 to
date 10–25 per year

Traditional Musical Instrument Co.
21322 Lopez St., Woodland Hills, Calif. 91364
† 2/76

Charles Traeger
115 Christopher St., New York, N. Y. 10014
PT 1968 Active 1 emp. MTO
Modern and historical 4/76 • Bass
violin 1–10 to date 1–10 per year

Warren Transue
834 N. Kenmore Ave., Los Angeles, Calif. 90029
Maker of strings † 2/76

Dake Traphagen
Rt. 3, Box 499 H-2, Grass Valley, Calif. 95945
FT 1972 Active 1 emp. IA/MTO
Modern and historical 10/75 • Classical
guitar 10–25 to date 10–25 per year
• Lute 1–10 to date 1–10 per year
• Vihuela 1–10 to date 1–10 per year
• Appalachian dulcimer 25–50 to date
25–50 per year

Chris Trautwein
88 Cypress Ave., Mill Valley, Calif. 94941
PT 1971 Active 1 emp. IA/MTO
Modern 7/74 • Appalachian dulcimer
25–50 to date †

**Tree & Anchor Musical Instrument
Works**
Also known as: Mikael Carstanjen

Tree Frog Music
6201 Geary Blvd., San Francisco, Calif. 94121
† 2/76

Otto R. Trefz, Jr., and Co.
1305 N. 27th St., Philadelphia, Pa. 19121
FT 1913 Active 12 emp. IA
Modern Brochure 2/75 • Piano Over
50 to date 10–25 per year • Primarily
repairs

Collins Robb Trier
714 Central Ave., Wilmette, Ill. 60091
PT 1972 Active 1 emp. MTO
Modern 5/76 • Hammered dulcimer
1–10 to date 1–10 per year • Psaltery
1–10 to date †

Tringas String Instruments and Repair
2501 N. Pace Blvd., Pensacola, Fla. 32505
FT 1975 Active 1 emp. MTO
Modern 2/78 • Electric guitar †
• Electric bass guitar † • *1980: 3 emp.*
• *5-string banjo and steel-string guitar †*
• *Also known as: Greg Tringas*

Martha Trolin
636 Millwood, Los Angeles, Calif.
Maker of wooden drums † 9/75

Mike Troovich
288 S. Wabash, Chicago, Ill. 60604
Maker of strings † 2/76

Warren Trumbo
2941 Fried Ave., San Diego, Calif. 92122
Maker of strings † 3/78

Lynette Tsiang
Davisville Rd., Wilton, N. H. 03086
FT 1974 Active 1 emp. MTO
Historical 5/76 • Spinet 1–10 to date
† • Clavichord 1–10 to date †

Floyd Tubbs
319 E. Southfield Rd., Shreveport, La. 71105
PT 1952 Active 1 emp. IA/MTO
Historical 10/74 • Violin 10–25 to
date 1–10 per year • Viola 1–10 to
date 1–10 per year • *1980: FT • Violin*

25–50 to date · Cello   1–10 to date
1–10 per year · Repairs

Andrew Tucker
56 Baskin Rd., Lexington, Mass. 02173
PT   1974   Active   1 emp.   IA/MTO
Historical   4/75 · Rebec   1–10 to date
† · Psaltery   1–10 to date   †
· Appalachian dulcimer   1–10 to date   †
· Steel-string guitar   1–10 to date   †
· Cornett   1–10 to date   † · *1980:*
Inactive

Judy Tucker
722 N. W. 21st St., Portland, Ore. 97209 †   2/76

Kristine Tuckerman
25929 Woodfield Rd., Damascus, Md. 20750 †
9/76

Ake Tugel
264–266 Sea Cliff Ave., Sea Cliff, N. Y. 11579
PT   1955   Active   2 emp.   IA/MTO
Modern and historical   Brochure   8/75
· Appalachian dulcimer   Over 50 to
date   10–25 per year · Steel-string
guitar   10–25 to date   1–10 per year
· Vihuela   1–10 to date   1–10 per year

Robert S. Tuller
1290 Cavanagh S. E., Grand Rapids, Mich.
49508 †   2/76

Tulsa Music Center
Also known as: Allan J. Rapp

Dave Tupper
2150 Camino de los Robles, Menlo Park, Calif.
94025
Maker of strings †   1/78

Rick Turner
P. O. Box 568, Cotati, Calif. 94928
FT   1970   Active   6 emp.   IA/MTO
Modern   Brochure   10/74 · Electric bass
guitar   Over 50 to date   † · Electric
guitar   25–50 to date   † · Strings
10–25 to date   † · Also known as:
Alembic, Inc.

Robert M. Turner
53 Railroad Pl., Hopewell, N. J. 08525
FT   1969   Active   3 emp.   MTO

Modern   4/75 · Pipe organ   10–25 to
date   1–10 per year

William P. Turner
P. O. Box 161, West Union, Ohio 45693 †   2/76

Turner Corp.
401 E. Main St., P. O. Box 1461, Charlottesville,
Va. 22902
Maker of harpsichords †   5/74

Enas Turney
601 N. Pine St., Harrison, Ark. 72601
FT   1944   Active   1 emp.   IA
Historical   5/74 · Violin   25–50 to
date   1–10 per year · Viola   1–10 to
date   1–10 per year · Steel-string guitar
1–10 to date   1–10 per year
· Appalachian dulcimer   10–25 to date
1–10 per year · 5-string banjo   1–10 to
date   †

Lawrence M. Tuttle
380 Broadway, Cambridge, Mass. 02139
PT   Year?   Active   1 emp.   MTO
Modern   4/78 · Steel-string guitar   1–10
to date   †

Kip Tweedie †

Twelfth Street Guitars
322 Tulane Pl. N. E., Albuquerque, N. M. 87106
Maker of steel-string guitars †   2/76

B. R. Twyman
4114 W. 140th St., Cleveland, Ohio 44135
PT   1964   Active   1 emp.   IA/MTO
Historical   6/74 · Appalachian
dulcimer   25–50 to date   †

F. Scott Tygert
P. O. Box 28, Deer Hill Rd., Cornwall, N. Y.
12518
PT   1973   Active   1 emp.   MTO
Modern   1/78 · Classical guitar   1–10 to
date   † · Steel-string guitar   1–10 to
date   † · Primarily repairs

Lawrence S. Tyk
7613 Asbury Ct., Spring Grove, Ill. 60081
PT   1975   Inactive   1 emp.   MTO
Historical   2/78 · Lute   1–10 to date   †
· Harpsichord   1–10 to date   †

• Steel-string guitar   1–10 to date   †
• Clavichord   1–10 to date   †

Clyde Tyndale
Box 522, North Falmouth, Mass. 02556
PT   1964   Active   1 emp.   MTO
Modern   Brochure   5/74 • Steel-string
guitar   1–10 to date   1–10 per year
• 12-string guitar   1–10 to date   1–10
per year • Euterpe harp   10–25 to date
1–10 per year • Mouth bow   10–25 to
date   1–10 per year • Appalachian
dulcimer   1–10 to date   1–10 per year
• Also known as: Euturpe Instruments

W. C. Tyson
76 Lawrence St., New Haven, Conn. 06511
Maker of strings †   1/78

Carl Ulmschneider
1945 26th Ave. East, Seattle, Wash. 98112
FT   1971   Active   1 emp.   IA/MTO
Modern and historical   9/74
• Appalachian dulcimer   Over 50 to
date   1–10 per year • Kantele   1–10 to
date   1–10 per year • Kalimba   Over 50
to date   10–25 per year • Epinette   1–10
to date   † • *1980: PT • Kit   Over 50 to
date   Over 50 per year • Not making
kanteles, kalimbas, and epinettes*

Uncle Banjo
Also known as: Ed Taylor

Uncle Bob's Dulcimers
Also known as: Robert P. Bryan

Doug Unger
5437 Walnut St., Pittsburgh, Pa. 15232
PT   1972   Active   1 emp.   IA/MTO
Historical   10/74 • 5-string banjo   1–10
to date   † • Mandolin   1–10 to date   †

Unicord, Inc.
89 Frost St., Westbury, N. Y. 11590
Maker of synthesizers and electronic pianos
†   1/78 · *1980: Inactive*

Unicorn Musical Instruments
337 W. Josephine, San Antonio, Tex. 78212
FT   1971   Active   1 emp.   MTO
Modern   Brochure?   1/75 • Lute   1–10
to date   † • Appalachian dulcimer   1–10

to date   † • Steel-string guitar   1–10 to
date   † • 5-string banjo   1–10 to date   †
• Mandolin   10–25 to date   † • Also
known as: Ralph Garhardt

Union Grove Village Guitar Shop
227 N. Santa Cruz Ave., Los Gatos, Calif. 95030
Maker of strings †   2/76

Unique Strings
Also known as: Peter Kyvelos

United Guitar Co.
278 Johnstone Ave., Jersey City, N. J. 07304
Maker of steel-string guitars †   2/76

Universal Accordion
3080 W. Main, Alhambra, Calif. 91801
Maker of accordions †   2/75

Upper Cumberland Craft Center
545 E. 20th St., Cookeville, Tenn. 38501
Maker of Appalachian dulcimers †   2/76

David Usher
5067 Westminster Pl., St. Louis, Mo. 63108
PT   1974   Inactive   1 emp.   MTO
Modern and historical   4/77 • Hammered
dulcimer   1–10 to date   † • *1980: Active
· Hammered dulcimer   10–25 per year*

Valco Guitars, Inc.
2717 N. Normandy St., Chicago, Ill. 60635
Maker of steel-string guitars †   2/75

Thomas Valenti
14 Morton Ave., Hempstead, N. Y. 11550
Maker of steel-string guitars and
Appalachian dulcimers †   2/76

Valje Drums
3312 W. Sunset, Los Angeles, Calif. 90026
Maker of congas and bongos †   2/76

John L. Valterza
16273 Old Mehama Rd., Stayton, Ore. 97383
Maker of strings †   1/78

Van Bergen Foundry
P. O. Box 607, Greenwood, S. C. 29646
FT   1940   Active   ? emp.   IA
Historical   Brochure   5/76 • Carillon   †

M. W. Vance and Stanley P. Miller

P. O. Box 461, 315 Commercial St., Nevada City, Calif. 95959
PT   1972   Active   2 emp.   IA/MTO
Modern and historical   Brochure   5/74
• Appalachian dulcimer   25–50 to date
10–25 per year • Mandolin   1–10 to
date   † • Also known as: Stanley P. Miller;
Nevada City Dulcimers

Jan Van Daalen

6809 Medicine Lake Rd., Golden Valley, Minn. 55427
Maker of organs †   2/76

Diederik Van Hamel

6 Lower Byrdcliffe Rd., Woodstock, N. Y. 12498
Maker of strings †   2/76 • *1980: FT
1972   Active   1 emp.   IA/MTO
Modern and historical   10/80 • Violin and
viola   †*

Johan Van Leer

520 W. Belden Ave., Chicago, Ill. 60614
Maker of harpsichords †   5/74

Joel R. Van Lennep

21 Harvard St., Charlestown, Mass. 02129
FT   1969   Active   1 emp.   MTO
Historical   6/74 • Lute   1–10 to date   †
• Clavichord   1–10 to date   †
• Virginal   1–10 to date   †

Phil Van West

91 Meredith St., Springfield, Mass. 01108 †
1/77

Harry Vas Dias

2519 McCurdy Way, Decatur, Ga. 30033
FT   1974   Active   1 emp.   MTO
Historical   6/74 • Baroque oboe   10–25
to date   †

Zoltan Vashli

Box 69, Sheffield, Mass. 01257
FT   1970   Active   1 emp.   MTO
Modern and historical   2/76
• Appalachian dulcimer   25–50 to date
10–25 per year • Steel-string guitar   1–10
to date   1–10 per year

D. Ross Vaughan and Steven K. Gustafson

491 Ryan Rd., Duluth, Minn. 55802

PT   1976   Active   2 emp.   MTO
Modern   4/78 • Steel-string guitar
25–50 to date   10–25 per year
• Mandolin   1–10 to date   1–10 per year
• Classical guitar   1–10 to date   † • Also
known as: Steven K. Gustafson; Zenith
Guitar Works

Mark Vaughan

3870 Wawona St., Los Angeles, Calif. 90065
Maker of strings †   3/78

John B. Vaughn

611 4th Ave., Holdredge, Neb. 68949
FT   1962   Active   3 emp.   MTO
Modern   Brochure   2/75 • Pipe organ
10–25 to date   1–10 per year

Mr. and Mrs. Ralph J. Vaughn

Brasstown, N. C. 28902
FT   1963   Active   2 emp.   MTO
Historical   11/76 • Harpsichord   †
1–10 per year

Alfons Vavra

2147 Hudson Terr., Fort Lee, N. J. 07024
FT   1957   Active   1 emp.   MTO
Modern and historical   7/74 • Violin
Over 50 to date • Viola   10–25 to date
• Cello   1–10 to date • All instruments
1–10 per year

Alberto W. Vazquez

Rt. 1, Box 176, Free Union, Va. 22940
PT   1960   Active   1 emp.   MTO
Modern and historical   4/76
• Appalachian dulcimer   1–10 to date   †
• 5-string banjo   10–25 to date   †

Vega Instrument Co.

155 Reservoir St., Needham Heights, Mass. 02194
Also known as: C. F. Martin Organisation

Joseph and Jane Veillette

848 McDonald Ave., Brooklyn, N. Y. 11218
FT   1970   Active   2 emp.   IA
Modern   11/75 • Steel-string guitar
10–25 to date   † • Classical guitar   1–10
to date   † • Electric guitar   1–10 to
date   † • Appalachian dulcimer   1–10 to
date   †

Manuel Velasquez
31-07 90th St., Jackson Heights, N. Y. 11369
Maker of steel-string guitars †   5/74

Veleno Guitars
Box 20247, St. Petersburg, Fla. 33702
Maker of steel-string guitars †   5/76

Veneman Music Co.
8429 Georgia Ave., Silver Spring, Md. 20910 †
2/76

Venice Dulcimer Works
Venice, Calif. 90291
Maker of Appalachian dulcimers †

Robert L. Venn
5545 E. Washington, Phoenix, Ariz. 85034
FT   Year?   Active   ? emp.   IA/MTO
Modern and historical   Brochure   6/74
• Steel-string guitar   Over 50 to date   †
• Electric bass guitar   Over 50 to date   †
• Mandolin   25– 50 to date   † • Violin
25– 50 to date   † • Also known as:
Roberto-Venn School of Luthiery

Ventura Guitars
55 Marais Dr., Melville, N. Y. 11746
Maker of steel-string guitars †   5/76

Knight Vernon
525 White Pigeon St., Constantine, Mich. 49042
FT   1972   Active   1 emp.   MTO
Historical   Brochure   7/74
• Harpsichord   1– 10 to date   †
• Spinet   1– 10 to date   † • *1980:*
Harpsichord   10– 25 to date • Not making
spinets

Vespe Drum Shop
435 Spruce St., Camden, N. J. 08103
Maker of drums †   2/76

Jake Vile
121 Duncan Ave., Westville, N. J. 08093
PT   1974   Active   1 emp.   MTO
Modern   2/75 • Steel-string guitar
10– 25 to date • 12-string guitar   1– 10
to date • Classical guitar   1– 10 to date
• All instruments   1– 10 per year

The Village Luthier
Also known as: Roger A. Benedict

Lawrence Vineyard
W. 605 1st Ave., Spokane, Wash. 99204
FT   1974   Active   1 emp.   IA/MTO
Modern and historical   1/77
• Appalachian dulcimer   25– 50 to date
† • Steel-string guitar   1– 10 to date   †
• Mandolin   1– 10 to date   †

Vintage Banjo Co.
618 N. Jefferson St., Arlington, Va. 22205
FT   1966   Active   1 emp.   IA
Historical   10/75 • 5-string banjo   10– 25
to date   10– 25 per year • Appalachian
dulcimer   1– 10 to date   1– 10 per year
• Mandolin   1– 10 to date   1– 10 per year
• Also known as: Donald John Rusnak

Violin Shop
Also known as: Dr. William Swettman

Pieter Visser
Also known as: Visser-Rowland Associates,
Inc.

Visser-Rowland Associates, Inc.
2033 Johanna, B, Houston, Tex. 77055
FT   1973   Active   5 emp.   MTO
Modern and historical   10/75
• Mechanical-action organ   1– 10 to
date   1– 10 per year • Electric organ
1– 10 to date   1– 10 per year • Also known
as: Jan Rowland; Pieter Visser • *1980: 12*
emp. • Mechanical-action organ   25– 50 to
date • Not making electric organs

Vito Woodwinds
Also known as: G. LeBlanc Corp.

Robert Vogel
12401 Alba Rd., Ben Lomond, Calif. 95005
PT   1962   Inactive   1 emp.   MTO
Modern   Brochure   8/75 • Appalachian
dulcimer   25– 50 to date   †

Friedrich Von Huene
65 Boylston St., Brookline, Mass. 02146
FT   1958   Active   3 emp.   MTO
Modern and historical   Brochure   9/74
• Renaissance flute   Over 50 to date
Over 50 per year • Baroque flute   Over 50
to date   Over 50 per year • Recorder
Over 50 to date   Over 50 per year
• Baroque oboe   Over 50 to date   †

• Tabor pipe   Over 50 to date   † • *1980: 5 emp.*

Clark Voorhees
Weston, Vt. 05161
PT   1946   Active   1 emp.   IA/MTO
Historical   6/75 • Appalachian
dulcimer   Over 50 to date   1– 10 per year

Vose & Sons
Also known as: Aeolian Corp.

Judy Waddle
Fox, Ark. 72051 †   4/76
1980: Inactive

Donnie Wade
2522 Oak Lawn at South, Dallas, Tex. 70749
FT   1971   Active   4 emp.   MTO
Modern and historical   12/75 • Resonator
guitar   1– 10 to date   1– 10 per year
• Electric guitar   1– 10 to date   1– 10 per
year • Primarily repairs • Also known as:
BMC Guitars

Mark Wade
Box 124, Ivy Hill Rd., Cockeysville, Md. 21030
Maker of strings †   1/78

Richard S. Wade
R. D. 3, Box 170 FPG, Export, Pa. 15632
Maker of strings †   1/78

Wager Music
Winchester, Mass. 01890 †

Ronald Wahl
804 E. South St., Appleton, Wis. 54911
FT   1966   Active   4 emp.   MTO
Modern   Brochure   2/78 • Organ   1– 10
to date   †

H. S. Wake
4171 Stettler Way, San Diego, Calif. 92122
PT   1960   Active   1 emp.   IA
Historical   Brochure   9/78 • Violin
25– 50 to date   1– 10 per year • Viola
10– 25 to date   1– 10 per year • Cello
1– 10 to date   1– 10 per year • Classical
guitar   1– 10 to date   1– 10 per year

John Homer Wakefield
Brigham Young University, Provo, Utah 84601
PT   Year?   Active   1 emp.   IA

Historical   5/76 • Recorder   10– 25 to
date   † • Clavichord   1– 10 to date   †
• Rebec   1– 10 to date   †

Earl Wakeman
R.F.D. 4, Kattelville Rd., Binghamton, N. Y.
13901
PT   1970   Active   1 emp.   MTO
Historical   4/76 • Violin   25– 50 to
date   1– 10 per year

David Wald
1062 Larch, Moraga, Calif. 94556 †   2/76

Gene Walker
Eugene, Ore. †

Kim Walker
Rt. 2, Box 138, Cosby, Tenn. 37722
FT   1974   Active   1 emp.   MTO
Modern and historical   4/76
• Appalachian dulcimer   25– 50 to date
† • 5-string banjo   10– 25 to date   †
• Steel-string guitar   1– 10 to date   †

William P. Walker
Elkhorn, Ky. 42733
FT   1969   Active   2 emp.   IA
Modern   Brochure   11/74 • Appalachian
dulcimer   Over 50 to date   Over 50 per
year • Also known as: Green River
Dulcimers

Conrad Wall
5428 Hobart St., Pittsburgh, Pa. 15217
PT   1960   Inactive   1 emp.   MTO
Historical   6/74 • Lute   1– 10 to date   †
• 12-string guitar   1– 10 to date   †

Andrew Wallace
Also known as: Grassroots Productions

Joseph H. Wallace
985 Bay Rd., West Webster, N. Y. 14850 †   2/76

William Wallace
863 Toulon Dr., Pacific Palisades, Calif. 92247
†   6/75

Joseph F. Wallo
1319 F St. N. W., Washington, D. C. 20004
FT   1950   Inactive   1 emp.
IA/MTO   Modern and historical
Brochure   6/74 • Violin   10– 25 to date

† • Viola   1–10 to date   † • Steel-string guitar   Over 50 to date   † • Appalachian dulcimer   25–50 to date   † • Primarily repairs

Mark Walsh
Also known as: Associated Luthiers

Gilbert Walter
648 W. Fairhaven, Roseburg, Ore. 97470 †
2/76

Walter Piano Co., Inc.
700 W. Beardsley Ave., Elkhart, Ind. 46514
FT   1970   Active   27 emp.   IA
Modern   Brochure   4/76 • Piano   Over 50 to date   Over 50 per year

W and W Harp Co.
Chicago, Ill.
Maker of harps †   2/76

Robert Warburton
2489 E. Lake Rd., Skaneateles, N. Y. 13152
PT   1976   Active   1 emp.   MTO
Historical   2/78 • Appalachian dulcimer   1–10 to date   †

Ben T. Ward, Jr.
Vilas, N. C. 28692
Maker of Appalachian dulcimers †   2/76

John R. Ware
11908 Bayswater Rd., Gaithersburg, Md. 20760
PT   1972   Active   1 emp.   MTO
Modern   11/74 • Appalachian dulcimer   10–25 to date   1–10 per year

Charles Wark
2999 E. Ocean Blvd., Long Beach, Calif. 90803
PT   1968   Inactive   1 emp.
IA/MTO?   Historical   10/74 • Violin   1–10 to date   †

Caleb Warner
Also known as: The Instrument Guild, Inc.

Chris Warner
10 Eichelberger St., Hanover, Pa. 17331
FT   1974   Active   1 emp.   MTO
Historical   6/74 • Mandolin   10–25 to date   1–10 per year • 5-string banjo   †
1–10 per year • *1980: IA/MTO   Modern*

and historical   Brochure • Mandolin Over 50 to date   10–25 per year • 5-string banjo   Over 50 to date   10–25 per year • Also known as: Warner String Works

Donald Warnock
P. O. Box 265, Wilton, N. H. 03086
FT   1960   Active   1 emp.   MTO
Historical   9/77 • Lute   Over 50 to date • Archlute   1–10 to date • Vihuela   1–10 to date • Viola da gamba   1–10 to date • Baroque guitar   1–10 to date • Rebec 1–10 to date • Vielle   1–10 to date • All instruments   1–10 per year

Kenneth Warren and Son, Ltd.
28 E. Jackson Blvd., Chicago, Ill. 60604
FT   1942   Active   10 emp.   MTO
Modern   6/74 • Cello   10–25 to date 1–10 per year • Violin   1–10 to date   † • Primarily repairs • *1980: 1926 • Repairs only*

Kenneth Warsh
6313 Sandy St., Laurel, Md. 20810
Maker of strings †   1/78 • *1980: Inactive*

Steven F. Warshaw
426 Broadway, Cambridge, Mass. 02138
FT   1973   Active   1 emp.   MTO
Modern   6/74 • Steel-string guitar   1–10 to date   † • Primarily repairs

Bill Wasel
1435 4th St. South, St. Petersburg, Fla. 33701
FT   1961   Active   2 emp.   IA/MTO
Modern   Brochure   4/76 • Appalachian dulcimer   25–50 to date   10–25 per year • Steel-string guitar   1–10 to date   † • Limber Jim   25–50 to date   † • Mouth bow   1–10 to date   † • Primarily repairs • Also known as: Kelvin Savell

Washburn Guitars
1234 Sherman Ave., Evanston, Ill. 60202
Maker of steel-string guitars †   11/77 • Also known as: Fretted Industries, Inc.

Otis Waterville
Star Route, Newport, Tenn. 37821 †   1/76

Claude H. Watson
318 E. 10th Ave., Escondido, Calif. 92025
FT   1942   Active   1 emp.   IA/MTO

Modern Brochure 10/74 • Violin
25–50 to date 1–10 per year • Viola
10–25 to date 1–10 per year
• Steel-string guitar 1–10 to date 1–10
per year • Mandolin 10–25 to date
1–10 per year • Also known as: The
Emmanuel Guitar Shop

Jimmy Watson
2569 Legion St., Bellmore, N. Y. 11710
Maker of strings † 2/76

John R. Watson
4508 Oxford Pl., Binghamton, N. Y. 13903
FT 1972 Active 1 emp. MTO
Historical Brochure 6/74
• Clavichord 1–10 to date †
• Harpsichord 1–10 to date †

Keith Watson
108 Mulberry Ln., Newtown Square, Pa. 19073
Maker of strings † 3/78

R. P. Watson
4303 Maybelle, Austin, Tex. 78756
Maker of strings † 1/78

Theodore Watson
2513 N. Country Club, Tucson, Ariz. 85716 †
4/78

William D. Watson
145-02 108th Ct. East, Puyallup, Wash. 98371
PT 1959 Active 1 emp. IA/MTO
Modern 10/75 • Violin Over 50 to
date 1–10 per year • Viola 10–25 to
date 1–10 per year

Watters Distributing Co.
2219 E. 42d St., Minneapolis, Minn. 55407 †
2/75

Tom Wattington
Box 164, Hokana Zia, University of New Mexico,
Albuquerque, N. M. 87131
PT 1973 Active 1 emp. MTO
Historical 2/75 • Appalachian
dulcimer 10–25 to date †

Donald Watts
Rt. 1, Monroe, Va. 24574
PT 1960 Active 1 emp. IA/MTO
Historical 11/76 • Violin 10–25 to
date 1–10 per year • Steel-string guitar

1–10 to date 1–10 per year
• Appalachian dulcimer 10–25 to date
1–10 per year • Harp 1–10 to date
1–10 per year • Primarily repairs

David J. Way
P. O. Box 121, Storington, Conn. 06378 † 2/76

Maxwell Weaner
Dicktown Rd., Carmel, N. Y. 10512
FT 1958 Active 1 emp. IA
Modern 6/74 • Viola 1–10 to date †
• Violin 1–10 to date † • Primarily
repairs • *1980: 1967 Inactive MTO*

Andrew Weaver
3320 Nakora Dr., Tampa, Fla. 33618
PT 1976 Inactive 1 emp. MTO
Modern 3/78 • Steel-string guitar 1–10
to date † • Mandolin 1–10 to date †

M. A. and William A. Weaver
1319 F St. N. W., Suite 808, Washington, D. C.
20004
FT 1898 Active 7 emp. IA/MTO
Modern and historical 5/74 • Violin
Over 50 to date † • Viola 25–50 to
date † • Cello 10–25 to date † • Bass
violin 1–10 to date †• Primarily repairs

Scott Webb
330 Sixth Ave., San Diego, Calif. 92101
Maker of strings † 10/74

The Weber Piano Co.
Also known as: Aeolian Corp.

William Webster
17240 Fairport, Detroit, Mich. 48205
PT 1970 Active 1 emp. MTO
Historical 3/78 • Hammered dulcimer
25–50 to date † • 5-string banjo 10–25
to date † • Mandolin 1–10 to date †

Dr. Robert Weedle
5721 Breton Way, San Diego, Calif. 92120
Maker of strings † 2/76

Weehutty Industries
P. O. Box 98, Turtletown, Tenn. 37391 † 2/76
Also known as: Otto Pietz

Roelof Weertman
90 Alma Rd., Falmouth, Mass. 02540

FT 1965 Active 1 emp. IA/MTO
Modern and historical 9/75 • Violin
25– 50 to date 1– 10 per year • Viola
10– 25 to date 1– 10 per year • Cello
1– 10 to date 1– 10 per year • *1980:
1915 MTO • Violin Over 50 to date
• Viola Over 50 to date • Cello Over 50 to
date • Not making cellos*

Thomas M. Weideman
497 La Connor, #2, Sunnyvale, Calif. 94087
Maker of strings † 1/78

John P. Weir
#10 Brighton Ct., Gathersburg, Md. 20760 †
2/76

Hans Weisshaar
627 N. Larchmont Blvd., Hollywood, Calif.
90004
FT 1947 Active 8 emp. IA
Modern and historical Brochure 6/74
• Violin Over 50 to date † • Viola
25– 50 to date † • Cello 10– 25 to date
† • Primarily repairs

Mark Welch
Box 29, Avalon, Wis. 53505
Maker of strings † 1/78

Pete Welker
912 27th St., Parkersburg, W. Va. 26101
PT 1966 Inactive 1 emp.
IA/MTO Modern and historical 9/75
• Appalachian dulcimer 25– 50 to date
† • 5-string banjo 1– 10 to date †
• Steel-string guitar 1– 10 to date †

Robert Welland
627 Library Pl., Evanston, Ill. 60201
Maker of strings † 1/78

Susan Welsh
81 Pine St., Cambridge, Mass. 02139
Maker of virginals † 1/76

Weltron, Inc.
Durham, N. C. 27702 † 2/76

Robert L. Wendt and Roy Davis
629 E. Green St., Champaign, Ill. 61820
FT 1974 Inactive 2 emp. MTO
Historical 4/76 • 5-string banjo †
• Primarily repairs • Also known as: Roy
Davis; Rosewood Guitar Shop

Stanley Werbin
1309 E. Oakland, Lansing, Mich. 48906
Maker of strings † 1/78 • *1980: Not
making instruments*

Jerry Werhner
P. O. Box 47, Goshen, Mass. 01032
Maker of strings † 2/76 • Also known as:
Stringed Instrument Woodcrafting Shop

Craig and Elizabeth Werth
Box 11, Hancock, N. H. 03449
FT 1974 Active 2 emp. MTO
Historical Brochure 4/76 • Harp
25– 50 to date 10– 25 per year
• Psaltery 1– 10 to date 1– 10 per year
• Rebec 10– 25 to date 1– 10 per year
• Vielle 1– 10 to date 1– 10 per year
• Organ 1– 10 to date †

Weser Piano Co.
524 W. 43d St., New York, N. Y. 10036
Maker of pianos † 2/76

Wesner Recorders
823 S. Wabash, Chicago, Ill. 60605
Maker of recorders and harps † 2/76
• Also known as: David Wexler & Co.

Pearl West
1212 5th St., Coralville, Iowa 52241
FT 1967 Active 2 emp. MTO
Modern Brochure 6/74 • Oboe Over
50 to date † • Modern flute 25– 50 to
date † • Also known as: Westwind Flutes

Bob Westbrook
Also known as: The Pickin' Post

Rich Westerman
R. R. 1, Box 279, St. Anne, Ill. 60964
FT 1976 Active 1 emp. IA
Modern and historical 2/77 • Steel-string
guitar 1– 10 to date † • Appalachian
dulcimer 1– 10 to date † • Bouzoukee
1– 10 to date † • Hammered dulcimer
1– 10 to date †

Westheimer Sales Co.
1414 S. Wabash Ave., Chicago, Ill. 60605 †
2/75

Westland Music Co.
Also known as: Kurt R. Listug

Westminster Dulcimers

R.F.D. 3, Putney, Vt. 05346
FT   1971   Active   2 emp.   IA
Modern and historical   Brochure   5/74
• Appalachian dulcimer   Over 50 to
date   † • Psaltery   Over 50 to date   †
• Also known as: Marnie Barbers; Mitchell
Komisar • *1980: 1 emp.   MTO
• Appalachian dulcimer   25–50 per year
• Mandolin   1–10 to date   † • Not
making psalteries • Now known as: Marnie
Barberi MacLean*

Harold and Allene Westover

Box 304, Westminster & Elm Sts., Walpole,
N. H. 03608
FT   1961   Active   3 emp.   MTO
Historical   4/76 • Harp   Over 50 to
date   Over 50 per year • Psaltery   Over 50
to date   Over 50 per year • Viol   Over 50
to date   10–25 per year • Vielle   Over 50
to date   10–25 per year • Rebec   Over 50
to date   10–25 per year • Portative
organ   Over 50 to date   1–10 per year
• Positive organ   Over 50 to date   1–10
per year • Strings   Over 50 to date
25–50 per year

Westwind Flutes

Also known as: Pearl West

David Wexler & Co.

Also known as: Wesner Recorders

Margaret Whaley

Box 7069, Santa Rosa, Calif. 95401
Also known as: Larry Cottingham

J. W. Whatley

1908 W. 35th, Austin, Tex. 78703 †   3/78

Wheeler Ped-All

1038 N. Killingsworth St., Portland, Ore. 97217
Maker of strings †   5/76

Whippany Electronics, Inc.

1275 Bloomfield Ave., Fairfield, N. J. 07006
FT   1962   Active   20 emp.   IA
Modern   Brochure   6/74 • Electronic
organ   Over 50 to date   Over 50 per year

Ladd Whitcher

Olympia, Wash. 98502 †

Charles G. Whitcomb

144 Madison S.E., Grand Rapids, Mich. 49503
PT   1976   Active   1 emp.   IA
Modern   2/78 • Appalachian dulcimer
10–25 to date   10–25 per year • Also
known as: Grassroots Music Shop

Bob White

Rt. 2, Box 100, Coolville, Ohio 45723
Maker of strings †   2/76 • Also known as:
Shade Valley Instruments

David White

Box 626, Williams Bay, Wis. 53191
Maker of strings †   2/76

Glenn White

318 N. 36th St., Seattle, Wash. 98103
PT   1968   Active   1 emp.   MTO
Historical   1/75 • Harpsichord   10–25 to
date   1–10 per year • Also known as:
Olympic Organ Builders

Hayward Gerald White

1360 Waqstaff Rd., Paradise, Calif. 95969
PT   1939   Inactive   1 emp.   MTO
Modern and historical   2/78 • Violin
Over 50 to date   † • Steel-string guitar
10–25 to date   1–10 per year • Primarily
repairs

Ken and Jim White

Rt. 4, Box 182-D, Hillsboro, Ore. 97123
Maker of strings †   1/78

Matthew White

Rt. 1, Box 125, Piney Creek, N. C. 28663
Maker of strings †   2/76

Odd White

Asheville, N. C. 28800 †

Warren H. White

3110 Impala Dr., San Jose, Calif. 95117 †

William White

1820 Hamilton Rd., Apt. G12, Okemos, Mich.
48864 †   4/76

The H. N. White Co.

33999 Curtis, Eastlake, Ohio 44094
Maker of woodwinds †   3/76 • Also known
as: King Musical Instruments, Inc.

Michael Whitebook
2997 Reseda Blvd., Tarzana, Calif. 91356
Maker of strings † 2/76

Kenneth Wicker
35-100 Date Palm Dr., 30, Palm Springs, Calif. 92262
Maker of strings † 2/76

G. H. Wickham
Box 492, Talent, Ore. 97540
PT 1976 Active 1 emp. MTO Historical Brochure 5/76 • 5-string banjo †

Wicks Organ Co.
Highland, Ill. 62249
FT 1906 Active 116 emp. IA Modern Brochure 6/74 • Organ Over 50 to date † • *1980: MTO*

Felix Wickstrom
2947 Mackin Rd., Flint, Mich. 48504
FT 1955 Active 1 emp. IA Modern 4/75 • Violin Over 50 to date † • Viola 1–10 to date † • Cello 1–10 to date †

David Wiebe
715 4th St., David City, Neb. 68632
FT 1973 Active 2 emp. IA Modern Brochure 2/78 • Violin 1–10 to date † • Viola 10–25 to date 1–10 per year • Cello 1–10 to date 1–10 per year • Bass violin 1–10 to date 1–10 per year • *1980: 1 emp. MTO No brochure • Violin 1–10 per year • Viola 25–50 to date • Not making bass violins*

Henry and Adolph Wiegand
Tenino, Wash. 98589 † 4/76

Karl D. Wienand
Also known as: David Hummer and Karl D. Wienand

Mark Wightbook
Los Angeles, Calif. 90000 †

Donald Wilcox
903 Spring, Ann Arbor, Mich. 48104 † 2/76

Wild Edible Dulcimers
North Pomfret, Vt. 05053
Maker of Appalachian dulcimers † 1/76

Wild Flower Musical Instrument Co.
Also known as: Robert Lindner

Wildwood Music
1027 I St., Arcata, Calif. 95521
FT 1970 Active 1 emp. IA/MTO Historical Brochure 10/75 • 5-string banjo 1–10 to date † • Steel-string guitar 1–10 to date † • Also known as: Mark Platin

David Wiles
216 W. Grove, Midland, Mich. 48640
FT 1978 Active 2 emp. MTO Modern Brochure 4/78 • Ceramic bells Over 50 to date Over 50 per year • Percussion 1–10 to date 1–10 per year • Marimba 1–10 to date 1–10 per year • *1980: Not making marimbas*

Bob Wilhelm and Karen Sharp
1040 Natoma, San Franciso, Calif. 94103
FT 1973 Active 2 emp. IA Modern Brochure 6/74 • Troubador harp 25–50 to date 25–50 per year

Richard Wilkinson
Ponder, Tex. 76259
Maker of strings † 3/78

Byron J. Will
1577 Scheuber Rd. South, Centralia, Wash. 98531
Maker of strings † 1/78 • *1980: FT 1975 Active 1 emp. MTO Historical 10/80 • Harpsichord 10–25 to date 1–10 per year*

Robert J. Willcutt
443 S. Ashland Ave., Lexington, Ky. 40502
FT 1969 Active 3 emp. IA/MTO Modern 6/77 • Steel-string guitar 1–10 to date † • Appalachian dulcimer Over 50 to date † • Electric violin 1–10 to date †

Jack Williams
Rt. 4, Box 543A, North Wilksboro, N.C. 28659
† 2/78

Joe Williams
Rensselaer Polytechnic Institute, Troy, N.Y. 12181
PT   1968   Active   1 emp.   MTO
Modern and historical   6/74 • 5-string banjo   1–10 to date   1–10 per year • Steel-string guitar   1–10 to date   1–10 per year • Appalachian dulcimer   10–25 to date   †

John B. Williams
520 N. University, Norman, Okla. 73069
Maker of strings †   1/78

Michael S. Williams
Also known as: Crow Peak Music

S. R. Williams
1229 Olancha Dr., Los Angeles, Calif. 90065
FT   1962   Active   2 emp.   MTO
Modern and historical   Brochure   5/74 • Harpsichord   †   1–10 per year • Clavichord   †   1–10 per year • Spinet   †   1–10 per year

Williamsburg Restoration
Williamsburg, Va. 23185 †   2/76
Also known as: George Wilson

Williamson's Violin Shop
722 Greenleaf, Richardson, Tex. 75080
FT   1968   Inactive   3 emp.   MTO
Historical   4/76 • Violin   † • Primarily repairs

Alan Willis
122 Berrian Rd., Stamford, Conn. 06905
Maker of violins †   2/76

Willow Glen Crafts
Also known as: J. Ralph Campbell

Denise and Richard Wilson
1729 N. Prospect, Ypsilanti, Mich. 48197
FT   1975   Active   1 emp.   IA/MTO
Historical   4/78 • Appalachian dulcimer   Over 50 to date   Over 50 per year

George Wilson
Also known as: Williamsburg Restoration

Max G. Wilson
R.R. 1, Box 114C, Spencer, Ind. 47460

PT   1961   Active   1 emp.   MTO
Historical   5/74 • Steel-string guitar   1–10 to date   † • Appalachian dulcimer   Over 50 to date   25–50 per year

Minor Wilson
415 Evergreen, Stinson Beach, Calif. 94970 †   1/75

Richard Wilson
Also known as: Denise and Richard Wilson

Edward Winslow
Rt. 11, Potter Pl., Andover, N.H. 03265
PT   1972   Active   1 emp.   MTO
Modern and historical   5/76 • Harpsichord   1–10 to date   1–10 per year • Appalachian dulcimer   1–10 to date   †

Julian Winston
6 University Mews, Philadelphia, Pa. 19104
PT   1962   Active   1 emp.   MTO
Modern   4/76 • 5-string banjo   1–10 to date   † • Pedal steel guitar   1–10 to date   † • *1980: 1957*

Winter & Co.
Also known as: Aeolian Corp.

Stephen L. Wise
601 A Bellevue Pl., Austin, Tex. 78705
FT   1971   Active   1 emp.   IA/MTO
Modern   3/78 • Classical guitar   1–10 to date   1–10 per year • Steel-string guitar   1–10 to date   † • Appalachian dulcimer   10–25 to date   †

Steve Wishnevsky
Bedford, Tenn. 37100 †   1/77

Jay Witcher
759 Petaluma, Sebastopol, Calif. 95472
FT   1969   Active   4 emp.   IA
Modern and historical   Brochure   9/75 • Harp   Over 50 to date   Over 50 per year • Also known as: Ancient Instruments; Harps Unlimited

E. O. Witt
12298 Hoffman Rd., Three Rivers, Mich. 49093
FT   1964   Active   1 emp.   IA/MTO?
Historical   Brochure   ?/77 • Harpsichord, clavichord, spinet, and

virginal   † · *1980: 1950   Modern and
historical · All instruments   Over 50 to date*

W. M. I. Corp.
3725 W. Lunt Ave., Lincolnwood, Ill. 60645 †
2/76

George Woddail
4392 Ogden Ave., Beaumont, Tex. 77705
PT   1970   Active   1 emp.   MTO
Modern   7/74 · Classical guitar   1–10 to
date   1–10 per year

M. Wolf
116 8th St. N.E., Washington, D.C. 20002 †
2/76

Thomas and Barbara Wolf
P.O. Box 40572, Washington, D.C. 20016
FT   1975   Active   2 emp.   MTO
Historical   5/76 · Harpsichord   1–10 to
date   † · Clavichord   1–10 to date   †
· *1980: Brochure · Harpsichord   10–25 to
date · Virginal   1–10 to date
· Forte-piano   1–10 to date · All
instruments   1–10 per year*

John W. Wood
102 Madison St., Maplewood, La. 70663 †
2/76

Randy Wood
105 2d Ave. North, Nashville, Tenn. 37201
FT   1965   Active   5 emp.   MTO
Modern and historical   6/75 · Steel-string
guitar   1–10 to date   † · Mandolin
10–25 to date   † · 5-string banjo   10–25
to date   † · Also known as: Old Time
Pickin' Parlor

Wood & Sound
420 Pine St., Burlington, Vt. 05401
FT   1973   Active   1 emp.   IA/MTO
Modern   2/78 · Appalachian dulcimer
1–10 to date   † · Steel-string guitar
1–10 to date   1–10 per year · Primarily
repairs · *1980: Steel-string, arch-top, electric,
classical, tenor, and 12-string guitars
25–50 to date   10–25 per year · Not
making Appalachian dulcimers · Also
known as: Roger Borys*

Wooden Music
Also known as: Joan Applequist

Jack Woods
Also known as: Allison Stringed
Instruments

The Wood Shop
Also known as: Will Norwood

Woodwind Co.
111 Fourth Ave., New York, N.Y. 10003
Maker of woodwinds †

Woodworks
306 E. Bee Caves Rd., Austin, Tex. 78746 †
2/76

The Wood Works
Also known as: Geoffrey Bishop

William Devoe Woolf
1022 S.W. Morrison, Portland, Ore. 97205
PT   1977   Active   1 emp.   MTO
Modern   1/77 · Appalachian dulcimer
1–10 to date   † · Mandolin   1–10 to
date   † · Violin   10–25 to date   1–10
per year · Cello   1–10 to date   †
· Viola   1–10 to date   † · Steel-string
guitar   1–10 to date   †

John Workman
711 Locust, Kalamazoo, Mich. 49007 †   2/76

The Workshop
Also known as: Edward F. Rose

Workshop of Historical Instruments
Also known as: George Kelishek

World of Strings
Also known as: R. L. Mattingly

Albert W. Worthen, Jr.
Box 44, Rt. 28, Old Forge, N.Y. 13420
PT   1970   Active   1 emp.   MTO
Modern and historical   6/74 · 5-string
banjo   25–50 to date   1–10 per year
· Tenor banjo   1–10 to date   1–10 per
year · Appalachian dulcimer   1–10 to
date   1–10 per year · *1980: Brochure
· 5-string banjo   Over 50 to date · Also
known as: The Banjo Shop*

Jerry Wray
R.R. 2, Box 1891, 118th Ave., Allegan, Mich.
49010 †   2/78

Rossco Wright
866 Hawkins Ct., St. Louis, Mo. 63126
Maker of strings † 1/78

Tad Wright Woodworks
Box 111, Rt. 1, Horse Shoe, N.C. 28742
FT 1975 Active 2 emp. IA/MTO
Modern 2/78 • Steel-string guitar 1–10
to date † • Appalachian dulcimer
10–25 to date † • 5-string banjo 1–10
to date † • *1980: PT 1 emp. Modern and
historical • Steel-string guitar 1–10 per
year • Not making Appalachian dulcimers*

Keith P. Wrigley
Rt. 1, Box 122, Lake George, N.Y. 12845
FT 1977 Active 1 emp. MTO
Modern 2/78 • Steel-string guitar 1–10
to date † • Also known as: Zephyr Guitars

Curt Wunderlich
Dearborn, Mich. † 12/76

Wurlitzer Co.
105 W. Adams St., Chicago, Ill. 60603
FT 1856 Active 3,000 emp. IA
Modern Brochure 2/75 • Piano Over
50 to date Over 50 per year • Organ
Over 50 to date Over 50 per year
• Electronic piano Over 50 to date Over
50 per year

Howard Wurtz
2503 Medcliff Rd., Santa Barbara, Calif. 93109
PT 1967 Active 1 emp. MTO
Historical 8/75 • Psaltery 10–25 to
date 1–10 per year • Clavichord 1–10
to date 1–10 per year • Appalachian
dulcimer 25–50 to date 10–25 per year
• Hammered dulcimer 1–10 to date
1–10 per year • Steel-string guitar 10–25
to date 1–10 per year • Folk harp 1–10
to date 1–10 per year

Lenny Wurtzel
R.D. 2, Box 224, Pennsylvania Ave., Binghamton,
N.Y. 13903
PT 1972 Active 1 emp. MTO
Modern 7/74 • Appalachian dulcimer
10–25 to date † • 5-string banjo 1–10
to date † • Also known as: Bill Crume
Memorial Workshop

Xinde International, Inc.
Walker Dr., Upton, Mass. 01568
Maker of electronic violins † 1/78

Yamaha International Corp.
Also known as: Everett Piano Co.

Rual Yarbrough
2211 Woodward Ave., Muscle Shoals, Ala. 35660
Maker of strings † 2/76

Jim Yasutome
630 N.E. 106 Pl., Portland, Ore. 97220
Maker of strings † 1/78

Charles L. Yates
1027 Abington Pike, Richmond, Va. 47374
PT 1972 Active 1 emp. IA
Modern 6/74 • Steel-string guitar 1–10
to date 1–10 per year • Mandolin
10–25 to date 1–10 per year

Henry Yeaton
3230 Ellis St., Berkeley, Calif. 94703 † 5/74

Peter Michael Yelda
146 Santa Fe, Shell Beach, Calif. 93449
PT 1974 Active 1 emp. MTO
Modern 3/78 • Steel-string guitar 1–10
to date 1–10 per year

John Yerxa
Also known as: Telegraph Music Works

Lee Yoder
1113 E. Mission, Escondido, Calif. 92025
PT 1974 Active 1 emp. MTO
Modern Brochure 11/74 • Irish harp
1–10 to date † • Also known as: Hidden
Valley Harps

York Band Instrument Co.
1600 Division Ave. South, Grand Rapids, Mich.
49502 † 2/75

Phil Yost
314 Oregon St., Santa Cruz, Calif. 95060
PT 1955 Active 1 emp. MTO
Modern 6/76 • Electric guitar 1–10 to
date † • Electric bass guitar 1–10 to
date † • Bass violin 1–10 to date †
• *1980: FT IA/MTO Brochure • Bass
violin 10–25 to date 1–10 per year*

· Not making electric guitars and electric bass guitars

Henry S. Younce
4124 T St., Sacramento, Calif. 95819
PT 1973 Active 1 emp. MTO
Modern and historical 4/76 • Steel-string guitar 1– 10 to date † • Electric guitar 1– 10 to date † • Mandolin 1– 10 to date † • 5-string banjo 1– 10 to date † • Primarily repairs

Arthur W. Young II
1516 Ferris, P.O. Box 2547, Lawton, Okla. 73501
FT 1968 Active 2 emp. MTO
Modern 3/78 • Electric guitar 1– 10 to date † • Lute 1– 10 to date †
• Harpsichord 1– 10 to date †
• Primarily repairs · *1980: Electric guitar 1– 10 per year · Steel-string guitar † · Not making harpsichords · Also known as: Young's Trading Co.*

David Russell Young
7134 Balboa Blvd., Van Nuys, Calif. 91406
PT 1965 Active 1 emp. MTO
Modern and historical 10/75
• Steel-string guitar Over 50 to date †
• Lute 1– 10 to date † • Violin 1– 10 to date †

Jerry and Deborah Young
R.F.D. 1, Box 46A, Robbinston, Maine 04671
PT 1971 Active 2 emp. MTO
Modern 4/76 • Appalachian dulcimer Over 50 to date †

Keith Young
3815 Kendale Rd., Annandale, Va. 22003
PT 1971 Active 1 emp. IA/MTO
Historical Brochure 10/74
• Appalachian dulcimer Over 50 to date 25– 50 per year • Autoharp 1– 10 to date 1– 10 per year · *1980: Appalachian dulcimer Over 50 per year · Autoharp 10– 25 to date*

Roger Young
1800 Brewton Ct., District Heights, Md. 20028
PT 1969 Active 1 emp. IA/MTO
Historical Brochure 10/74
• Appalachian dulcimer Over 50 to date 10– 25 per year • Hammered

dulcimer 1– 10 to date 1– 10 per year
• 5-string banjo 1– 10 to date 1– 10 per year

William Henry Young
153 W. Warren, Germantown, Ohio 45327
PT 1962 Inactive 1 emp. MTO
Historical 8/75 • Appalachian dulcimer 25– 50 to date 1– 10 per year

R. David Youngberg
711 S. Illinois Ave., Carbondale, Ill. 62901
FT 1973 Active 1 emp. IA/MTO
Modern Brochure 6/74 • 5-string banjo 10– 25 to date 10– 25 per year

Michael Yursco
1321 Walnut St., Monessen, Pa. 15062
PT 1961 Active 1 emp. MTO
Historical 4/76 • Classical guitar 1– 10 to date † • Lute 1– 10 to date †
• Harpsichord 1– 10 to date †
• Balalaika 1– 10 to date †
• Appalachian dulcimer 1– 10 to date †

Yuta Musical Instruments
210 W. 83d St., New York, N.Y. 10024 †

Mirror Zabala
2022 Sheridan Rd., Leucadia, Calif. 92024
PT 1976 Active 1 emp. MTO
Modern 1/77 • Classical guitar 1– 10 to date †

Zack Fifes
Also known as: Zachariah Fisher

Zachary Organ Co.
5 Eastmans Rd., Parsippany, N.J. 07054
FT 1972 Active 20 emp. IA
Modern Brochure 5/75 • Auto-chord Over 50 to date Over 50 per year · *1980: 40 emp.*

Michael Zadro
State University College, New Paltz, N.Y. 12561
PT 1970 Active 1 emp. IA/MTO
Historical 5/74 • Renaissance flute 10– 25 to date † • Primarily repairs

Bob Zatzman Guitar Studio
6655 McCallum St., Apt. 100, Philadelphia, Pa. 19119

FT 1959 Active 1 emp. MTO
Modern 6/74 • Steel-string guitar 1—10
to date † • Primarily repairs • *1980:
Steel-string guitar 25—50 to date
• Classical, electric, and electric bass
guitars* †

Jim Zdunek
1016 S. Humphrey, Oak Park, Ill. 60304
PT 1972 Inactive 1 emp. MTO
Modern 1/78 • 5-string banjo 10—25 to
date • Appalachian dulcimer 1—10 to
date • Strings 1—10 to date • All
instruments 1—10 per year

Mickie Zekley
Also known as: Lark in the Morning

Yaris Zeltins
3233 Midway Dr., San Diego, Calif. 92110
Maker of strings † 2/76 • Also known as:
The Blue Guitar

Zenith Guitar Works
Also known as: D. Ross Vaughan and Steven
K. Gustafson

Zephyr Guitars
Also known as: Keith Wrigley

Wm. Zeswitz String Repair Shop
5550 Philadelphia Pike, Reading, Pa. 19606
FT 1923 Active 2 emp. IA/MTO
Modern and historical Brochure 6/75
• Viola 1—10 to date † • Violin 1—10
to date † • Bass violin 1—10 to date †
• Primarily repairs • *1980: No brochure
• Violin 25—50 to date • Not making bass
violins*

Ivan Zgradic
4951 Greenbush Ave., Sherman Oaks, Calif.
91423
FT 1967 Active 1 emp. MTO
Modern 9/74 • Violin, viola, and cello †
• Primarily repairs • *1980: 1950
IA/MTO Brochure • Violin Over 50 to
date 1—10 per year • Viola 10—25 to
date 1—10 per year • Cello 25—50 to
date 1—10 per year*

Zickos Corp.
11844 W. 85th St., Lenexa, Kans. 66214
Maker of drums † 12/77

Ziedler and Quagliata Harpsichords
Box 103, Flemington, N.J. 08822
PT 1969 Active 2 emp. MTO
Historical Brochure 8/75
• Harpsichord 1—10 to date 1—10 per
year • Also known as: Russell Quagliata

Avedis Zildjian Co.
Box 198, Accord, Mass. 02018
FT 1623 Active 35 emp. IA
Modern Brochure 6/75 • Cymbals
Over 50 to date Over 50 per year

W. Zimmer and Sons
P.O. Box 11024, Charlotte, N.C. 28209
FT 1964 Active 13 emp. MTO
Modern Brochure 4/75 • Pipe organ
Over 50 to date 10—25 per year

Mark Zimmerman
Also known as: Great Lakes Banjo Co.

Robert Zink
3376 30th St., San Diego, Calif. 92014
FT 1972 Active 1 emp. MTO
Modern and historical 3/78 • 5-string
banjo 25—50 to date 10—25 per year
• Also known as: The New Expression

Rich Ziven
1607 Carver Ln., Appleton, Wis. 54911
PT Year? Active 2 emp. MTO
Modern and historical 4/76
• Appalachian dulcimer 10—25 to date
• Steel-string guitar 1—10 to date
• Electric guitar 1—10 to date
• 5-string banjo 1—10 to date • Lute
1—10 to date • All instruments 1—10 per
year

Harold Zussin
Little Deer Isle, Maine 04650
PT 1957 Active 1 emp. IA
Modern 1/78 • Violin 10—25 to date
1—10 per year • Viola 1—10 to date
1—10 per year • Cello 1—10 to date
1—10 per year

2. List of Instrument Makers by Instrument

Strings

Strings (unspecified)

Bahr-Schall Music Co.
Baily, Harry
Baity, Harvey
Banjo and Fiddle Shop
Baystate Stringed
    Instrument Co.
Beach, John
Beaujolais, Mr.
Becker, Tim
Beckman, Alan T.
Beehler, Raymond
Behrns, Harold E.
Bennett, Dave
Best, John E.
Billiris, J. Charles
Blackwell, M. Robert
Blair, R. B.
Blozen, Tony
Blue Grass Farm
Boardman, Olcott
Boomhower, H. E.
Born, Mary Lucille
Botnick, Norman W.
Bouslaugh, William
Bozo Music Gallery
Brady's Violin Shop
Brakmanis, Zigfrid S.
Briskey, Dale
Broekhuizen, Elaine
Brown, Robin
Brown, Steve
Budapest String Shop
Burdick, Lynn
Burks, Herbert M., Jr.
Burning Water Instruments
Buss, Graydon
Cantrell, David
Carll, Willis
Carroll, Randy
Castellano, Robert M.
Caton, Donald
Cellino, Chuck
Chelys
Cherin, Milton
Christensen, Royce
Ciano, John

Cichonovich, Nicholas
Clark, Paul S.
Clark, T.
Collingsworth, W. J.
Conner, Karl
Conrad, Robert, III
Corsale, Leonard
Cottingham, Larry
Cowan, John
Crader, Lee
Crawford, Andrew E.
Crowder, V. C.
Crump, P. W.
Curtin, Stephen H.
Daniels, Arthur
Danko, Karen J.
Dauphinais, George
Davidson, Keith S.
Davis, Carroll
Davis, E. David
Davis, Keith
Delgado, Candelario
Delmarto, John
DeLuccia and Son
De Mano Guitars
DeRose and Co.
Desmond, Bob
Diaz, David Demetrius
Dickinson, Arthur S.
Disend, Nadya
Dunning, James
Ebert, L. Allen
Edkford, E. B.
Ekland, Donald
Electro String
    Instrument Corp.
Elwell, Michael
Fahey, Kevin M.
Fallon, Joe
Fawcett, Matthew
Feinman, Ronald
Finn, Emit
Fisher, David B.
Fleming, C. H.
Flynn, Ovie
Fortune, Abel
Frank, Ray
Fret Shop
Fricker, John N.
Gabbanelli, John
Galloway, Russell

Gannuck, Don
Garrison, Craig
Gar-Zim
Gasser, Gordon A.
Gendron, Mark Steven
Gerlach, Fred
Gertner, John
Girard, Neal K.
Givens, Bob
Glemann, Walter C.
Goodrich, David C.
Gordon, Russell
Gould, Jan
Graham, John S., Jr.
Gray, Chester
Gray, John
Griffin, W. T.
Grossman Music Corp.
Guitar and Banjo Workshop
Guitar Workshop
Haensel, Frank
Haldon, Charles
Hales, Mike
Hall, Don E., Jr.
Halvorsen, Oscar
Hanks, Larry
Hanover Stringed
    Instrument Co.
Harlos, Leonard
Harmon, Ted
Harris, Alan
Hart, Richard
Hart, Dr. William
Hartley, John, III
Hathaway, Dale C.
Hebert, Dan
Hewitt, Al
Hicks, Jim D.
Hild, David G.
Hill, Barney
Hinton, J. Steele, III
Hoeber, Tony
Hofmann, Willy
Hog Fiddle Music Co.
Holick, Ed
Holt, Alan
Holt, Stan
Hood, Robert T.
Hoppe, John
Horine, Dave
Horn, Guy

Huang, Ben
Hubert, Carl W.
Hudd, Peter
Hunt, David
Hunter, Fred
Huvard, Anthony J.
Hyndman, Max
Izzo, Richard
Jacks, Richard L.
Jamison, Cliff
Jannotti, John
Janofsky, Stephen
Johnson, Brian and
    Mary Lou
Jones, Glenn L.
Jorgenson, David
Kahn, Bruce R.
Kakos, Stephen
Kalb, Steve
Kamimoto, Hideo
Kamps, Jeff
Kaster, Thomas J.
Kelly, Ritch
Kent, Maurice
Kenyon, Richard Lee
Kepley, John C.
Kettle, Rupert
Kiersten, John
Kinderman, Paul D.
Klein, Richard
Koenig, Al
Koontz, Sam
Korechoff, J. D.
Kortier, David
Kramer, Ira B.
Kreutziger, John W., Jr.
Kroon, Lambert
Kuehnert, T. A.
Kuniche, George F.
Kuspa, James
LaGrandeur Music
LaMay, L.
Lamont, Peter
Landis, Felix
Landry, Robert F.
Larsen, John M.
Lawrence, Bill
LeCler, Rose
Lee, Steven D.
Lehmann, Jeff
Lehrer, John A.
Lennard, Arthur
Lenzi, Joseph
Leslie, Michael D.

Lesmeister, Lauren A.
Levin, Henry
Lindberg, Dick
Lipnick, William
Littleboy, Henry, and Son
Litwin Luthiers
Lobdill, Jerry
Lohman, Craig F.
Lomax, John A.
London Stringed
    Instrument Repairs
Long, Robbie
Lostumo, Larry
Luedeke, Tim
Luffman, B. E.
Mabry, Jeff
McCrimmon, Dan
McGreevy, Don
McInturff, Terry
Macnak, Andrew
McNeese, Lee
McQuen, Dennis
Madsen, Erling
Maier, Howard A.
Maliha, Ernest J.
Mandl, Otto W.
Mari, E. and O.
Marquardt, Bill, Jr.
Marshall, John
Marshall Music Co.
Martin, Charles T.
Martin, Christian F., IV
Matheson, Rod
Mazza Guitar Shop
Meador, John
Mejia, Fredrico
Mellobar
Meramec Handcrafts
Messer, Casimer
Milian, Jeffrey
Miller, H. Burritt
Miller, James
Millhouse, Steven
Millstein, Bernie
Mind Dust Music
Misuriello, Harry P.
Moe, Edwin
Moore, Howard
Moore, Thomas L.
Morris, William V.
Morrison, Chuck
Mortenson, Mark
Moskow, Wayne
Moulton, Peter

Muehl, Philip
Music Factory
Nealon, William A.
Newcomb, Larry
Newman, B. E.
New Orleans Banjo Sales
Nicksic, Milan S.
Nick's Music Store
Noble, Tim
Norman's Rare Guitars
Norton, William F.
Norwood, Tom
O'Donnell, Roger
Olsen, Cheston
Olsen, Richard S.
Orren, R. S., Jr.
Ortiz, Oscar
Page, Gilbert Owen
Palis, Charles A.
Palmason, Victor
Park, Joe
Parson, Charles
Partridge, David
Pausic, Frank
Pease, Don
Peoples, Richard Douglas
Perryman, Daniel B.
Peterson, Jon
Petrulis, Stanly and Lou
Pickin' Post, The
Pigman, John
Pinkham, Ron
Pinter, Lazlo
Plant, Stanley
Plott, Robert F.
Polla, David
Pollard, Gary
Polts, Allan
Prevo, B. W.
Pyle, Harry
Ramblin' Conrad's Guitar
    Shop
Rayman, Kent
Reeck, Rick
Reeve, Harry J.
Reeves, Bill
Reitz, Albert
Rembrand Co.
Ridge Runner Music
Robbins, Ron
Rodrigo, Carlo A.
Rodriguez, Manuel
Rogers, Keith
Romans, Ken

Rosenthal, Luthier, and Son
Rubin, Philip
Russell, William E.
Sahara
Sams, Howard
Sanderson, Dave
Schilling, Leonard
Schlieps, Armin
Schmelzer, Herbert
Schmoll, Rudolph
Schwartz, Freddy
Schwartz, Mark
Schweitzer, William E.
Scott, George
Shannon, Jon
Shar Products
Shaw, Tim
Sherman, Sid
Shipley, Scott
Shuttleworth, Don
Sid's Fingerboard Studio
Sleeter, Dave
Slejko, Stanley
Sloane, Irving
Smith, Anton
Smith, Jeffrey Lee
Smith, M. G.
Smith, Rick
Snyder, Don
Sowers, Steven V.
Sound Guitar Co.
Souza, Gabriel
Stein, Bert
Stick Enterprises, Inc.
Stigen, Duane
Stimmerman, Daniel
Stoetzer, Mike
Stoffel, Peter
Stojkov, Gregory A.
Strait, Steve
Strobel, H. A.
Sullivan, Daniel T.
Sultzbaugh, Lisle
Switra, Julius
Szwajda, Wally
Thomas, Harry
Thompson, Carl
Thurman, Roger
Tippets, J. W.
Torres, Daniel and Dawne
Transue, Warren
Troovich, Mike
Trumbo, Warren
Tupper, Dave

Turner, Rick
Tyson, W. C.
Union Grove Village Guitar
    Shop
Valterza, John L.
Van Hamel, Diederik
Vaughan, Mark
Wade, Mark
Wade, Richard S.
Warsh, Kenneth
Watson, Jimmy
Watson, Keith
Watson, R. P.
Webb, Scott
Weedle, Dr. Robert
Weideman, Thomas M.
Welch, Mark
Welland, Robert
Werbin, Stanley
Werhner, Jerry
Westover, Harold and
    Allene
Wheeler Ped-All
White, Bob
White, David
White, Ken and Jim
White, Matthew
Whitebook, Michael
Wicker, Kenneth
Wilkinson, Richard
Will, Byron J.
Williams, John B.
Wright, Rossco
Yarbrough, Rual
Yasutome, Jim
Zdunek, Jim
Zeltins, Yaris

Archlute

Warnock, Donald

Autoharp

Bodd, Roy, and Ken Eye
Colby, Peter
Gotzmer, Carl
Gravelin, Tom
Hauser, Scott
Hollifield, Clyde
Millard, Michael
Morgan, Tom and Mary
Sansom, Russell
Schmidt, Oscar,
    International

Scott, Alfred
Simon, Carmie
Thierman, John
Young, Keith

Bajo Sexto

Hennig, Arnold

Balalaika

Belles, William R.
Chrapkiewicz, David
    Ludvik
Diapason Guitar Shop
Eppler, Alexander Illitch
Huttig, H. E.
Huzela, Andrew
Yursco, Michael

Bandurria

Gido, Julius

5-string Banjo

Adams, Paul
Allen, Richard C.
Allison, Michael
Ampeg Co.
Ariail, James
Associated Luthiers
Aydlett, Raymond Clifton
Bailey, Q. J.
Banjos by Richelieu
Barker Brothers
Bartolomeo, Carl
Bartow, Clarence Nolan
Beacon Banjo Co., Inc.
Becker, George
Becvar, Bruce R.
Bland, William
Blaylock, Bill
Blue Lion
Boarman, Andrew
Bodd, Roy, and Ken Eye
Boyer, William
Bradley, Don
Branhut, Mike
Brodrick, Daniel L.
Brown, Lawrence
Bryan, C. Alex
Buck, Henry L., Jr.
Buck Musical Instrument
    Products
Carstanjen, Mikael

Chacey, Ron
Chester, Wayland C.
Chromey, Joe
Colby, Peter
Cottrell, Jenes
Cox, Jimmy
C. R. Banjo Co.
Creager, Marcus O.
Creamer, Anthony J.
Creed, Kyle
Crow Peak Music
Dailey, Tom
David, Herbert
Deering Banjo Co.
Dickinson, L. Eugene
Dillman, Warren
Dixon, Robert T.
Eckhaus, Joel
Eklund, Karl
Elgin, Pico
Elliott, Ernest Lee
Elliott, Jeffrey R.
Ellis Mandolins
Erickson, Charles W.
Essex Banjo Co.
Fearn, Cabell J.
Ferguson, Ren
Fisher, Alfred L.
Flavell, Stuart H.
Florence, Ed
Folkstore, The
Fretted Industries, Inc.
Furgason, Rodney J.
Gaudette, Arthur
Gawley, Bob
Gerke, Randy
Gibson, Inc.
Gilbert, James H.
Gillespie, Thomas
Gilmour, John Tunnoch, III
Glenn, Charlie Monroe
Glenn, Clifford
Glenn, Leonard
Goose Nest Prairie Banjos
Gooze, Tom
Gotzmer, Carl
Grassroots Productions
Gravelin, Tom
Great Lakes Banjo Co.
Gretsch, The Fred, Co.
Greven, John
Griffith, Owen E.
Gryphon Stringed
    Instruments
Hagler Banjo Craftsmen

Haile, Thomas Vose
Hall, James Newell
Hall, Merle
Hamblin, Ken
Hash, Albert
Hauser, Scott
Hawkins, Lt. Frank J.
Henderson, Wayne
Hendrickson, S. J.
Here, Inc.
Hicks, Floyd
Hicks, Stanley
Hoffman Guitars
Hosmer, Tom
Hughes Co.
Imperial Banjo Co.
Intermountain Guitar
    and Banjo
Irwin, Lew
Iverson, Capt. Derek
Janzegers, John
Johnson, Frank A.
Jones, Danny R.
Jones, Sam
Kardos, Andy
Kemnitzer, Michael
Kendall, Wayman A.,
    and Son
Kepner, Gil
King Banjos
Kingan, John
Kirk's Musical Instruments
Krimmel, Max
Lafoy, John B.
Lane, Harris
Ledford, Homer
Liberty Banjo Co.
Limbursky, Richard
Lipton, Walter
Lissant, Kenneth J.
Low, Douglas A.
Lynch, Steve
McConnell, Cecil A., Sr.
McCormick Strings
McDevitt, Mr. and Mrs. John
McDonald, Zeke
McSpadden, Lynn
Marks, David
Martin, C. F., Organisation
Martin, Walter P.
Mason, Robert M.
Massey, Richard
Maxson, Charles
Michael, Jan D.
Milligan, Weldon Eugene

Moats, Douglas
Montefuso, Marc
Monteleone, John
Morgan, Tom and Mary
Moudy, L. W.
Mt. Lebanon Banjo Co.
Murphy, Michael
Needham, Howard
Newman, Richard Scott
New Traditions Banjo Co.
Nichols, David R.
Norwood, Will
O'Brian, Frank S.
Ode Banjos
OME Banjo Co., Inc.
Oosting, Jan
Original Musical
    Instrument Co., Inc.
Orthey Dulcimers
Park, Joe
Pelton, Clifford
Perkins, Latham
Phillips, Bill
Phil-Lu Inc.
Pierce, R. Brent
Pinelands Dulcimer Shop
Piper, Ty
Polifka, Donald K., Jr., and
    Judy Polifka
Presnell, Edd
Prior, Jim
Privratsky, Bruce
Proffitt, Frank, Jr.
Quality Banjo Co.
Raimi, Richard
Ramsey, John
Reed, David
Reed, Dennis
Rees, Harold S.
Resek, Thomas Lee
Reuter, Ronald Lee
Richelieu, C. C.
Riportella, Ken
Rock, Robert P.
Rose, Edward F.
Rutland, Ned
Sacred Fire/Frogs Delight
Saga Banjos
Sanders, John
Sansom, Russell
Sekerak, Christopher M.
Shultis, Dean L.
Siegler, Lawrence S.
Siminoff, Roger H.
Simon, Mark

Sloan, John
Smakula, Peter H.
Smith, Arthur E., Banjo Co.
Smith, Jack R., Jr.
Smith, Leon
Smith, Lonzo B.
Sparks, Earl
Specht, David T.
Sprouse, Edgar F.
Stelling Banjo Works
Stevens, D. W.
Stewart-MacDonald
    Mfg. Co.
Stockwell, Randy
String Instrument
    Workshop
Sturgill, David A.
Summerfield, Seth
Sunflower Music Shop
Suran, Debbie
Sweeney Banjo Mfg. Co.
Takoma Banjo Works
Taylor, Ed
Taylor Guitars
Telegraph Music Works
Thierman, John
Tower, Thomas H.
Turney, Enas
Tut Taylor Music
Unger, Doug
Unicorn Musical
    Instruments
Vazquez, Alberto W.
Vega Instrument Co.
Vintage Banjo Co.
Walker, Kim
Warner, Chris
Webster, William
Welker, Pete
Wendt, Robert L., and Roy
    Davis
Wickham, G. H.
Wildwood Music
Williams, Joe
Winston, Julian
Wood, Randy
Worthen, Albert W., Jr.
Wright, Tad, Woodworks
Wurtzel, Lenny
Younce, Henry S.
Young, Roger
Youngberg, R. David
Zdunek, Jim
Zink, Robert
Ziven, Rich

Tenor Banjo

Diapason Guitar Shop
Dillman, Warren
O'Brian, Frank S.
Worthen, Albert W., Jr.

Banjo-guitar

Kepner, Gil

Banjolin

Dodson, Ivan

Baryton

Cassis, George B.

Bass Violin

Anderson, Arvil
Ashley, Hammond,
    Associates
Atchley, E. V.
Bartow, Clarence Nolan
Beck, John
Camille Violin Shop
DePaul, Clive Andy Vincent
Engelhardt-Link
Hockenberry, William N.
Hutchins, Carleen
Jansma, Timothy
Kolstein, Samuel, and Son
Lyman, Fred, Jr.
Maestro, Edward
Meisel, K. Lothar
Prier, Peter
Scherl and Roth, Inc.
Schuback Violin Shop
Shaw, Owen
Stoltenberg, Robert W.
Swisher, J. Dean
Toenniges, Paul
Traeger, Charles
Weaver, M. A. and
    William A.
Wiebe, David
Yost, Phil
Zeswitz, Wm., String Repair
    Shop

Bouzoukee

Gleaves, William Russell
Huzela, Andrew
Kyvelos, Peter
Westerman, Rich

Bows

Balint, Geza
Bolander, John A.
Boucha, Parnell
Callier, Paul Joseph
Cassis, George B.
Crocker, Derwood
Frosali, Mario
Hannings, Lynn, and
    George Rubino
Henderson, Frank V.
Hendricks, Neil
Johnston, Neil M.
Liu, Lloyd
Minnerly, Donald
Ross, William Post
Salchow, William, Ltd.
Saverino, Louis
Schertenlieb, E. L.
Tenney, T. Burdell

Cello

Anderson, Arnold Dean
Anderson, Arvil
Artindale, Fred H.
Ashley, Hammond,
    Associates
Atchley, E. V.
Bartow, Clarence Nolan
Bearden Violin Shop
Beck, John
Beckman, Wayne
Bischofberger, Herman
Boucha, Parnell
Briggs, David Byron
Burt, Chris
Camille Violin Shop
Clifford, Roger
Cole, Anne
Conrad, A. G.
Cornelissen, Marten
Curry, Dr. Hiram
Damin, Rik
D'Attili, Dario
Dornhelm, Solomon
Engelhardt-Link
Eppler, Alexander Illitch
Evans, Ruth Esther
Fairbanks, Harvey
Freeman, S. D., Jr.
Frosali, Mario
Fry, William
Gault's Violin Shop
Giardinieri, Vittore E.

Hart, Paul
Henderson, Frank V.
Hooker, Basil J.
Hutchins, Carleen
Jansma, Timothy
Kapfhammer, Wilhelm
Keller, Helmuth A.
Knapik, Eugene
Kyvelos, Peter
Liu, Lloyd
Malgi, Meeme
Masters Violin Shop
Miller, H. Burritt
Morel, Rene
Mueller, Albert
Nebel, Hans
Nigogosian, Vahakn
O'Brien, Vincent
Papazian, Manouk
Petesh, Zenon W.
Prier, Peter
Puskas, Joseph
Rashid, Joseph G.
Roberts, Clifford
Savell, Kelvin
Schenk, Otto K.
Scherl and Roth, Inc.
Schertenlieb, E. L.
Schlub, Richard and David
Schuback Violin Shop
Schweinsberg, Heinz
Shaw, Owen
Shipman, Margaret Arlene
Slaby, William E.
Stoltenberg, Robert W.
Templing, David
Vavra, Alfons
Wake, H. S.
Warren, Kenneth, and
    Son, Ltd.
Weaver, M. A. and
    William A.
Weertman, Roelof
Weisshaar, Hans
Wickstrom, Felix
Wiebe, David
Woolf, William Devoe
Zgradic, Ivan
Zussin, Harold

Chitarrone

Brown, Lawrence D.
Hachez, Daniel
Lundberg, Robert

Citera

Magyar, Kalman, Sr.

Cittern

Blasius, John
Bryan, C. Alex
Carstanjen, Mikael
Gilmore, George
Hampton, James
Hart, Paul
Hess, Stanley
Kottick, Edward L.
Myers, Herb
Rollins, John

Crwth

Foster, Charles C.

Cuatro

Garabieta, Ignacio
Huttig, H. E.

Dobro

Hoeffgen, Thomas E.
Hoffman, Mark
Original Musical
    Instrument Co., Inc.
Stuber, Mike
Tut Taylor Music

Dombra

Eppler, Alexander Illitch

Appalachian Dulcimer

Ackley, Dennis
Adams, Paul
Albin, R. Kent
Alpine Dulcimer Co.
Anderson, Robert S.
Anderson, Steven
Antes, Scott E.
Apollonio, Nicholas
Appleseed John's
Apprentice Shop
Arkenberg, John
Associated Luthiers
Autorino, Mike
Bailey, Keith
Bailey, Q. J.
Balderose, George

Bartolomeo, Carl
Battershell, Frederick
Beall, J. R.
Becvar, Bruce R.
Bednark, Tom
Behlen, Stinsen R.
Belles, William R.
Bidne, Leo L.
Bishop, Geoffrey
Blair, Bobby L.
Blair Dulcimers
Blake, Basil
Blake, Ronald
Bland, William
Blue Lion
Bodd, Roy, and Ken Eye
Bonnie Carol Ducilmer Co.
Bostard, Kenneth
Boulding, Philip
Bourgeois, Dana W.
Bradley, Don
Brewer, George
Broekhuizen, John
Brosnac, Donald
Brown, Edwin A.
Bryan, C. Alex
Bryan, Robert P.
Buck Musical Instrument
    Products
Burke, William
Burnside, Richard
Bush, Edwin E.
Carpenter, Lane O.
Carpenter, Robert
Carrell, Sam
Carriveau, Ron
Carruth, Alan E.
Carstanjen, Mikael
Cassis, George B.
Chacey, Ron
Chertok, Alan
Childs Family Mt.
    Dulcimers
Ching, Douglas, Luthier
Chouteau, Jane
Chromey, Joe
Claxton, Edward
Clifford, Roger
Colburn, David
Colby, William
Cole, Kenneth Reagan
Cone, Michael
Conner, David R.
Corwin, Stuart
Cottingham, Larry

Cox, Jacob
Creamer, Anthony J.
Cripple Creek Dulcimers
Crocker, Jennifer
Crow Peak Music
Dahlgren, William
Dailey, Tom
Damin, Rik
Damm, Edward A., and
    Anne Damm
Dan Doty's Dulcimers
Darby, David F.
David, Herbert
Davidson, F. R.
Davis, Bill
Deering Banjo Co.
DePaul, Clive Andy Vincent
Diamond, Morton S. and
    Louise
Dickinson, L. Eugene
Dickson, Rev. Gordon
Dillman, Warren
Dixon, Arthur
Dixon, Robert T.
Don's Guitar Shop
Dorogi, Dennis
D'Ossche, Al
Dover, Daniel
Downeast Dulcimer Shop
Dudley, Charles
Dulcimer Shop
Dunkle, Robert E.
Eckerworks
Eklund, Karl
Elliott, J. C.
English, Larry
Epler, Raymond
Farrell, Susan Caust
Felder, Mark
Field, David
Fitzsimons, Bill
Fleming, H. A.
Fletcher, Richard
Florence, Ed
Foley, Linda
Folkstore, The
Force, Robert Lewis, Jr.
Frederick, Peach
Gaiennie, Clark
Garfield, Harry, II
Geiger, Paul
Gemza, Bela
Gillespie, Thomas
Gilmore, George
Gilmour, John Tunnoch, III

Giuttari, Glenn
Glenn, Charlie Monroe
Glenn, Clifford
Glenn, Leonard
Godfried, Robert
Good, Jimmy L.
Goodrich, Theodore O.
Gordon, William B., Jr.
Gotzmer, Carl
Gravelin, Tom
Greene, Blaine
Gryphon Stringed
    Instruments
Haile, Thomas Vose
Hall, Jack Reed
Hall, James Newell
Hall, Wesley
Ham, Roy
Hamblin, Ken
Hampton, James
Hardy, Jay
Harmon, Robert Wilson, IV
Harris, Rodger
Harris, William Reed
Hartsell, Jim
Hash, Albert
Hauser, Scott
Hendricks, Daniel
Hendricks, Neil
Hendrickson, S. J.
Here, Inc.
Heritage Dulcimers
Herman, Bruce
Hess, Stanley
Hicks, Floyd
Hicks, Stanley
Hill, Kenny
Hines, Chet
Hoeffgen, Thomas E.
Hoffman, David
Hoffman, Mark
Hogan, Kirk
Hogue, Ben
Hollifield, Clyde
Hudgens, A. D.
Hughes Dulcimer Co., Inc.
Humphrey, Scott
Ingraham, Kermit
Iverson, Capt. Derek
Jackson, M. Eli
Jeffreys, A. W., Inc.
Jenks, J. P.
Jensen, Dane
J-Folks Dulcimers
Johnson, Thomas F.

Johnston, David
Jones, Freeman
Jones, Danny R.
Joseph, Eugene
Kardos, Andy
Katz, Robert
Keith, J. B.
Kelishek, George
Kelly, Ritch
Kemnitzer, Michael
Kennedy, Bill
Kepner, Gil
Kern, Dr. Evan
Kimball, Dean
King Banjos
Kingsley, Craig
Kish, Charles N.
Kleske, John
Knatt, Thomas
Kottick, Edward L.
Koucky, William
Kraft, Roger
Kramer-Harrison, William
Krieg, Russell
Krimmel, Max
Kyvelos, Peter
Lamoreaux, Cal
Lapidus, Joellen
Lasky, Howard
Latham, Joe
Latray, Carl
Layne, Raymond
Ledford, Homer
Lee, Melvin D.
Lehmann, Bernard E.
Levelle, W. Robert
Limbursky, Richard
Lipiczky, Thom
Lissant, Kenneth J.
Logan, Kitty
Long, Robbie
Low, Douglas A.
Luke Dulcimers
Luther, James D.
Lynch, Steve
McConnell, Robin James
McCormick Strings
McDevitt, Mr. and Mrs. John
McDonald, Zeke
McElroy, Jeremiah T.
McGlincy, L. Edward
McGuire, Bruce
McSpadden, Lynn
Mager, Martin
Magic Mountain Instruments

Marks, David
Martin, Edsel
Martin, James D.
Martin, Walter P.
Martindale, Howard
Masasso, William Louis
Mason, Steve
Massey, Richard
Maxson, Charles
Maxwell, John
Meads, James H., II
Medearis, Douglas W.
Melton, Raymond W.
Millard, Michael
Miller, Audrey Hash
Mintz, Anne
Mitchell, Howard
Mixon, Bill
Mize, Robert R.
Montague, Fred
Montefuso, Marc
Moore, S. Brook
Moore, Thomas B.
Moore, Timothy
Moroz, John
Moudy, L. W.
Muelrath, Dave
Mumford, Brian
Murdock, Robert L.
Murdock, Tom
Murphy, Barry
Murphy, Dennis
Murphy, Michael
Murray, Dave
Musco, Thomas Guy
Myers, McAllen C.
Neff, Rusty
Nicholas, General Custer,
    and Sons
Nolte, Mr. and Mrs. Jerome
North Country Music Store
Norton, Jesse
Norwood, Will
Olds, Dr. John
Olsen, Timothy
Oosting, Jan
O'Riordan, Patrick
Orthey Dulcimers
Oster, Doran
Park, Joe
Parks, Gary C.
Patterson, James E.
Payne, Thomas
Peacewood Dulcimer
Peacock, George

Pelton, Clifford
Pergram, Wallace
Perkins, Latham
Perlman, Alan
Perry, William
Petros, Bruce
Phillips, Bill
Pierce, R. Brent
Pietz, Otto
Pinelands Dulcimer Shop
Pizzini, Mr. and
    Mrs. David S.
Pizzo, Tony, and Laura
    Fontana Pizzo
Polifka, Donald K., Jr., and
    Judy Polifka
Popelka, Ray E.
Presnell, Edd
Price, Rodney
Privratsky, Bruce
Proffitt, Frank, Jr.
Putnam, John F.
Pyle, Mr. and Mrs. Paul
Ramsey, John
Reed, David
Rein, Thomas G.
Reis, Irvin
Reisler, Paul
Reiter, Bart
Rembrand Co.
Resek, Thomas Lee
Reuter, Ronald Lee
Rickert, Bradford
Riesenberger, James A.
Riportella, Ken
Ritchie, Jean
Ritter, Anthony, Jr.
Rizzetta, Samuel
Roach, Gene Paul
Roberto-Venn School of
    Luthiery
Romine, Don
Roomian, Doug
Round Family Dulcimer Co.
Rugg and Jackel Music Co.
Rumery, L. R., Co.
Rutland, Ned
Rynerson, David M.
Sacred Fire/Frogs Delight
Sadowsky, Roger
Samuels, Steve
Sanders, Curt, and Linda
    Foley
Sansom, Russell
Scalone, Joe

Schecter, Martha
Schilling, Jean and Lee
Schmidt, Oscar,
    International
Schrieber, Hank
Scott, Alfred
Sears, Lynn B.
Seeger, Jeremy
Sekerak, Christopher M.
Sherrick, Michael P.
Siegler, Lawrence S.
Simon, Carmie
Sirok, Steven
Skarie, Jeremiah
Sleeth, Nolan
Smakula, Peter H.
Smith, Jack F.
Smith, Jack R., Jr.
Smith, Leon
Snell, John R.
Snyder, Dr. Harold E.
Soderstrom, Dr. John
Somogyi, Ervin
Sound Guitar Co.
Sparks, Earl
Stack, Alan A.
Stapley, Craig N.
Steele, Henry
Stehling, Sandy
Steudle, Doc
Stone, Benjamin
Stringfellow Guitars
String Instrument
    Workshop
Sugar Loaf Folk Instruments
Taney, Peter
Taylor Guitars
Telegraph Music Works
Templing, David
Thierman, John
Thomas
Thomas, Robert A.
Thomas, Dr. Thomas
Tignor, John
Tool, Bob
Tower, Thomas H.
Traphagen, Dake
Trautwein, Chris
Tucker, Andrew
Tugel, Ake
Turney, Enas
Twyman, B. R.
Tyndale, Clyde
Ulmschneider, Carl
Unicorn Musical

Instruments
Upper Cumberland Craft
    Center
Valenti, Thomas
Vance, M. W., and Stanley P.
    Miller
Vashli, Zoltan
Vazquez, Alberto W.
Veillette, Joseph and Jane
Venice Dulcimer Works
Vineyard, Lawrence
Vintage Banjo Co.
Vogel, Robert
Voorhees, Clark
Walker, Kim
Walker, William P.
Wallo, Joseph F.
Warburton, Robert
Ward, Ben T., Jr.
Ware, John R.
Wasel, Bill
Wattington, Tom
Watts, Donald
Welker, Pete
Westerman, Rich
Westminster Dulcimers
Whitcomb, Charles G.
Wild Edible Dulcimers
Willcutt, Robert J.
Williams, Joe
Wilson, Denise and Richard
Wilson, Max G.
Winslow, Edward
Wise, Stephen L.
Wood and Sound
Woolf, William Devoe
Worthen, Albert W., Jr.
Wright, Tad, Woodworks
Wurtz, Howard
Wurtzel, Lenny
Young, Jerry and Deborah
Young, William Henry
Young, Keith
Young, Roger
Yursco, Michael
Zdunek, Jim
Ziven, Rich

Courting or Double Dulcimer

Bryan, Robert P.
Ledford, Homer
Reisler, Paul
Sleeth, Nolan

Hammered Dulcimer

Adams, Paul
Antes, Scott E.
Apollonio, Nicholas
Armanino, Peter A.
Autorino, Mike
Bailey, Q. J.
Balderose, George
Beall, J. R.
Benson, Harold
Bieker, Robert Lee
Blasius, John
Boulding, Philip
Breyre, Brian
Bryan, C. Alex
Burke, William
Bush, Edwin E.
Campbell, J. Ralph
Carpenter, Lane O.
Carstanjen, Mikael
Cox, Eugene A.
Crocker, Jennifer
Crow Peak Music
Dalglish, Malcolm
Damm, Edward A., and
    Anne Damm
Darby, David F.
Dickinson, L. Eugene
Dixon, Robert T.
Dorogi, Dennis
Eckerworks
Elton, Fred
Field, David
Gardner, Asel
Gifford, Paul
Hardy, Jay
Hughes Dulcimer Co., Inc.
Humphrey, Scott
Jackson, M. Eli
Keith, J. B.
Kramer-Harrison, William
Lamoreaux, Cal
Latray, Carl
Limbursky, Richard
McDevitt, Mr. and Mrs. John
Marks, David
Martin, James D.
Martin, Walter P.
Maxson, Charles
Mitchell, Howard
Montague, Fred
Moore, Timothy
Mumford, Brian
Murphy, Dennis

Murphy, Michael
Musco, Thomas Guy
Nehil, Tom
North Country Music Store
Oosting, Jan
O'Riordan, Patrick
Orthey Dulcimers
Oster, Doran
Patterson, James E.
Pinelands Dulcimer Shop
Pippin, Sylvia
Pizzo, Tony, and Laura
    Fontana Pizzo
Privratsky, Bruce
Redfern, Robert F.
Reisler, Paul
Rembrand Co.
Rizzetta, Samuel
Round Family Dulcimer Co.
Sansom, Russell
Sheppard, David B.
Simon, Carmie
Simon, Mark
Stone, Benjamin
Suran, Debbie
Trier, Collins Robb
Usher, David
Webster, William
Westerman, Rich
Wurtz, Howard
Young, Roger

Dulcitar

Ledford, Homer

Ectero

Cone, Michael

Ektar

Pizzo, Tony, and Laura
    Fontana Pizzo
Shapiro, Peter

Epinette

Hollifield, Clyde
Mitchell, William J.
Mumford, Brian
Ulmschneider, Carl

Key Fiddle

Rued, Tim

Medieval Fiddle

Foster, Charles C.

Gadulka

Flexer, J. Robert

Gourdamer

Hollifield, Clyde

Acoustic Bass Guitar

Breslin, Larry Pohl
Fox, Charles
Sound Guitar Co.

Baroque Guitar

Hachez, Ronald J.
Higgins, Larry
Hill, Richard
Warnock, Donald

Classical Guitar

Aberle, Hank
Adams, Andy
Albin, R. Kent
Allison Stringed
    Instruments
Anderson, Robert S.
Apprentice Shop
Ariail, James
Arkenberg, John
Barney, Carl
Bearden, Sherid Sailer
Becvar, Bruce R.
Beeder, Lee
Beeston, Thomas
Benedict, Roger A.
Bland, William
Blanton, Ron
Booth, Newton J.
Bourgeois, Dana W.
Bradley, Wesley
Breslin, Larry Pohl
Brune, R. E.
Buckel, Thomas R.
Burkhart, Daniel R.
Burns, Brian
Callister, Jan E.
Campbell, Richard A.
Carriveau, Ron
Carruth, Alan E.
Cassidy, Stewart
Chester, Charles Allen

Ching, Douglas, Luthier
Christie, Robert
Clark, Gene
Clifton, Harrold C.
Cone, Michael
Corwin, Stuart
Cox, James, Jr.
Damler, Fritz
Davenport, Roy
Davis, Tom
DePaul, Clive Andy Vincent
DeVeto, Charles
Diapason Guitar Shop
Dickens, Fred T.
Dippold, Timothy W.
Don's Guitar Shop
Dover, Daniel
Eckhardt, Martin
Elliott, J. C.
Elliott, Jeffrey R.
Erdman, John P.
Farrar, Paul
Finck, Henry
Fish, Troy
Fletcher, Richard
Fox, Charles
Fraguela, Manuel
Furgason, Rodney J.
Gemza, Bela
Gibson, Inc.
Gido, Julius
Gilbert, James H.
Gilbert, John M.
Gleaves, William Russell
Goose Nest Prairie Banjos
Gordon, William B., Jr.
Guitar Hospital
Gurian, Michael
Hachez, Ronald J.
Hagstrom Guitars
Haile Guitars
Hennig, Arnold
Herman, Bruce
Hettinger Guitars, Ltd.
Higgins, Larry
Hill, Kenny
Hill, Richard
Hills, Norman L.
Hoeffgen, Thomas E.
Hoffman, Mark
Holsclaw, Raymond
Hom, Tom
Hood, Robert T.
Horowitz, William
Horvath, Marian

Hudgens, A. D.
Humphrey, Thomas
Iverson, Capt. Derek
Johnson, Louis
Johnson, Thomas F.
Kimball, Dean
King, Geoffrey
Kingan, John
Kingsley, J. William
Knatt, Thomas
Knight, Tom
Korenvaes, Herman
Kramer-Harrison, William
Kukick, Nicholas
Kyvelos, Peter
LaPlant, Lloyd G.
Ledbetter, Joseph
Lenz, Richard L., Jr.
Leonard, Rose-Ellen
Levelle, W. Robert
McGuire, Bruce
MacLerran, Frank L.
Martin, C. F., Organisation
Martone, Leo J.
Mattingly, R. L.
Mello, John F.
Menkevich, Michael
Michael, Jan D.
Mills, Scott
Moze Guitars
Murphy, Barry
Murray, Anthony
Neff, Rusty
Norwood, Will
Ogawa, Albert
Oribe, Jose
Papazian, Manouk
Patchen, Josef
Patterson, James E.
Peacock, George
Perlman, Alan
Perry, Douglas M.
Peterson, Jesper
Petros, Bruce
Phil-Lu Inc.
Piasecki, Michael
Pierce, R. Brent
Pimentel, Lorenzo,
    and Sons
Plumbo, Phillip S.
Porter, Steve
Reed, Abijah
Reeder, Duane
Reints, John
Rembrand Co.

Restivo, Dr. Andrew Philip
Ritter, Anthony, Jr.
Roberto-Venn School of
   Luthiery
Rogers, Joe, Jr.
Rossner, Heinz M.
Rubin, James
Ruck, R. S.
Sahlin, Eric
Sawicki, Stephen M.
Schneider, Richard
Schrieber, Hank
Shaw, Owen
Shultis, Dean L.
Sirok, Steven
Smith, George A.
Soderstrom, Dr. John
Soto, John
Spigelsky, William S.
Stanul, Walter
Stapley, Craig N.
Stein, Bert
Stevens, Larry
Strafaci, Natale Armando
Sugar, Mark
Tatay and Son
Thomas, Dr. Thomas
Traphagen, Dake
Tygert, F. Scott
Vaughan, D. Ross, and
   Steven K. Gustafson
Veillette, Joseph and Jane
Vile, Jake
Wake, H. S.
Wise, Stephen L.
Woddail, George
Yursco, Michael
Zabala, Mirror

Electric Guitar

Allen, Richard C.
Allison, Michael
Alper, Charles D.
Antes, Scott E.
Bailey, Keith
Bean, Travis
Becvar, Bruce R.
Benson, Harold
Bland, William
Blanton, Ron
Bradley, Walter, Jr.
Buckel, Thomas R.
Burda, Jan
Campbell, Jon
Carvin Mfg. Co.

Chaney, Garrett B.
Chester, Charles Allen
Childs, Steve
Colby, William
Cooper, Gary
DiSalvo, Frank
Elliott, J. C.
Elliott, Jeffrey R.
Ellis Mandolins
Enright, Bryan
Erlewine Guitars
Farrar, Paul
Fearn, Cabell J.
Fender/Rogers/Rhodes
Fish, Troy
Geiger, Paul
Gibson, Inc.
Goodrich, Theodore O.
Grant, Robert S., Jr.
Gruhn, George
Guitar Hospital
Hagstrom Guitars
Hall, James Newell
Harris, William Reed
Hayes, Stephen
Heitzman, David
Hoeffgen, Thomas E.
Hoffman, Mark
Ingraham, Kermit
Irving, Howard
Irwin, Douglas
Johnston, David
Kauffman, C. O.
Kharma Bodies
Kraft, Roger
Kramer Guitar Co.
Latham, Joe
Lenz, Richard L., Jr.
Lo Bue, Charles
Micro-Frets
Miller, Raymond
Moss, Edward B.
Moze Guitars
Murdock, Robert L.
Music Man, Inc.
Olsen, Timothy
Ovation Instruments, Inc.
Parker, Kenneth
Phil-Lu Inc.
Price, Rodney
Rainbow Electric Guitars
Rampulla, Jim
Reiter, Bart
Rickenbacker, Inc.
Rico, Bernardo C.

Roberto-Venn School of
   Luthiery
Rynerson, David M.
Sahlin, Eric
St. Louis Music Supply Co.
Sansone, Michael T., Jr.
Scalone, Joe
Schecter, David
Schmidt, K. C.
Schulte, C. Eric
Simon, Carmie
Sound Guitar Co.
Stack, Alan A.
Standel Co.
Stiles, G. L.
Strafaci, Natale Armando
Stuber, Mike
Sunflower Music Shop
Tringas String Instruments
   and Repair
Turner, Rick
Veillette, Joseph and Jane
Wade, Donnie
Yost, Phil
Younce, Henry S.
Young, Arthur W., II
Ziven, Rich

Electric Bass Guitar

Becvar, Bruce R.
Bradley, Don
Clifford, Roger
Cooper, Gary
Curlee, S. D., Mfg. Co.
DiSalvo, Frank
Fender/Rogers/Rhodes
Hagstrom Guitars
Hayes, Stephen
Irwin, Douglas
Kramer Guitar Co.
Lenz, Richard L., Jr.
Micro-Frets
Musiconics International,
   Inc.
Ovation Instruments, Inc.
Parker, Kenneth
Sanders, John
Sansone, Michael T., Jr.
Stack, Alan A.
Tringas String Instrument
   and Repair
Turner, Rick
Venn, Robert L.
Yost, Phil

Flamenco Guitar

Adams, Andy
Allison Stringed
    Instruments
Arkenberg, John
Beeder, Lee
Beeston, Thomas
Blackshear, Tom
Bradley, Wesley
Branhut, Mike
Brune, R. E.
Burns, Brian
Campbell, Richard A.
Damler, Fritz
Don's Guitar Shop
Draves, Peter Sargent
Elliott, Jeffrey R.
Fox, Charles
Gemza, Bela
Hachez, Daniel
Hachez, Ronald J.
Hill, Richard
Hood, Robert T.
Huzela, Andrew
Johnson, Thomas F.
Knatt, Thomas
Korenvaes, Herman
Kyvelos, Peter
Levelle, W. Robert
Oribe, Jose
Perez, Allen
Peterson, Jesper
Ruck, R. S.
Schneider, Richard
Smith, George A.
Spigelsky, William S.
Stein, Bert
Sugar, Mark

Jazz Guitar

Enright, Bryan
Kopp, David E.
Olsen, Timothy
Parker, Kenneth
Stiles, G. L.
Thomas, Robert A.

Octave Guitar

Hayes, Stephen

Pedal Steel Guitar

Dekley Corp.
Emmons Guitar Co.
Marlen Guitar Co.

Multi-Kord Factory
Sierra Steel Guitars
Stadler Guitars
Winston, Julian

Resonator Guitar

Roberto-Venn School of
    Luthiery
Wade, Donnie

Steel-string Guitar

Adams, Andy
Albin, R. Kent
Allen, Dale
Allison, Michael
Allison Stringed
    Instruments
Ampeg Co.
Anderson, Arvil
Anderson, Steven
Antes, Scott E.
Apache Guitars
Apollonio, Nicholas
Apprentice Shop
Ariail, James
Arkenberg, John
Armanino, Peter A.
Armstrong, Patrick
Arvin, Dan
Associated Luthiers
Audio Western Corp.
Aydlett, Raymond Clifton
Bailey, Keith
Barbero Guitars
Barger, Newcomb
Barker Brothers
Barnes, Lucien, IV
Barrons Harpsichords
Bartolomeo, Carl
Bartow, Clarence Nolan
Beall, J. R.
Becvar, Bruce R.
Bednark, Tom
Beeston, Thomas
Benedetto Guitars
Berger, Paul
Bishop, Geoffrey
Bland, William
Blasius, John
Blue Guitar Workshop
Bodd, Roy, and Ken Eye
Bogue, Rex
Boling, Rick
Borromey, Andrew J.

Boston String Instrument
    Co.
Boucha, Parnell
Boulding, Philip
Bourgeois, Dana W.
Boyce, James C.
Boyd, Michael
Bradley, Don
Bradley, Walter, Jr.
Branhut, Mike
Breslin, Larry Pohl
Brodrick, Daniel L.
Brosnac, Donald
Brunetti Guitar Factory
Buckel, Thomas R.
Burda, Jan
Burke, William
Callister, Jan E.
Carpenter, Lane O.
Carpenter, Robert
Carriveau, Ron
Caudy, Michael A.
Chacey, Ron
Chaney, Garrett B.
Chapman, Alan
Chapple, Jeffrey
Chester, Charles Allen
Ching, Douglas, Luthier
Christie, Robert
Chromey, Joe
Cigledy, Richard S.
Claxton, Edward
Cloutier, Steve
Cobb, Greg
Code Corp.
Colby, William
Cole, Kenneth Reagan
Coleman, Harry A.
Collings, William, II
Conner, David R.
Contessa Guitars
Cornelissen, Marten
Corwin, Stuart
Cowan, James
Cox, Jimmy
Creamer, Anthony J.
Crucianelli Guitars
Curlee, S. D., Mfg. Co.
Daly, Tom, Jr.
Damler, Fritz
Daniels, Sam W.
D'Aquisto, James
David, Herbert
Day, Harley A., Jr., and
    Michael Batell

DeCavage, John
Dempsey, Trish
DeNeve, Richard J.
DePaul, Clive Andy Vincent
D'Georgio Guitars
Dippold, Timothy W.
DiSalvo, Frank
D'Merle Guitars
Don's Guitar Shop
Drews Custom Guitars
Earthwood, Inc.
Eckhardt, Martin
Ekstedt, John R.
Elcombe, Art
El Degas Guitars
Elgin, Pico
Elliott, Jeffrey R.
Emperador Guitars
English, Larry
Enright, Bryan
Ensenada Guitars
Estes, Peter
Farrell, Eugene
Favilla Guitars
Fearn, Cabell J.
Ferguson, Ren
Fish, Troy
Fisher, Alfred L.
Flavell, Stuart H.
Fleming, H. A.
Folkstore, The
Foster, Douglas
Fox, Charles
Framus of Nashville
Franklin Guitars
Fretted Industries, Inc.
Furgason, Rodney J.
Gaiennie, Clark
Galaxie Guitars
Gallagher, J. W., and Son
Garabieta, Ignacio
Geiger, Paul
Gemza, Bela
Gerke, Randy
Gibson, Inc.
Gilbert, James H.
Gillespie, Thomas
Gilmore, George
Goldzweig, Robert
Goodrich, Theodore O.
Goose Nest Prairie Banjos
Gotzmer, Carl
Grace, Dennis
Grant, Robert S., Jr.
Grassroots Productions

Gravelin, Tom
Greene, Blaine
Gretsch, The Fred, Co.
Green, John
Griffith, Owen E.
Gronning, Richard
Gruhn, George
Gryphon Stringed
    Instruments
Guild Musical Instruments
Guitar Hospital
Guitar Works, The
Hagstrom Guitars
Haile Guitars
Haile, Thomas Vose
Hall, James Newell
Ham, Roy
Hampton, James
Hardy, Jay
Harris, William Reed
Hartley, Steven H.
Hauser, Scott
Hayes, Stephen
Heitzman, David
Henderson, Wayne
Hendricks, Daniel
Hendrickson, S. J.
Hennig, Arnold
Herman, Bruce
Hettinger Guitars, Ltd.
Higgins, Larry
Hill, Richard
Hoffman Guitars
Hoffman, Mark
Hoffses, Virgil
Hogue, Ben
Hondo Guitar Co.
Humphrey, Scott
Humphrey, Thomas
Huttig, H. E.
Huzela, Andrew
Ingraham, Kermit
Irving, Howard
Irwin, Douglas
Irwin, Lew
Iverson, Capt. Derek
Janke, John
Jensen, Dane
Jirousek, Charles
Johnson, D. Ray
Johnson, Erik A., II
Johnson, Thomas F.
Johnston, David
Jones, Danny R.
Jones, Sam

Kantele Guitars
Kapa Guitars
Kauffman, C.O.
Kay Musical Instrument Co.
Kelly, Ritch
Kendall, Wayman A.,
    and Son
Kepner, Gil
Kern, Dr. Evan
King Banjos
King, Geoffrey
Kingan, John
Kirk's Musical Instruments
Klein Custom Guitars
Klepper, Howard
Knight, Tom
Kopp, David E.
Kottick, Edward L.
Koucky, William
Kraft, Roger
Kramer-Harrison, William
Krieg, Russell
Krimmel, Max
Kukick, Nicholas
Laney, Peter
Langejans, Delwyn J.
LaPlant, Lloyd G.
Lasky, Howard
Latray, Carl
Ledford, Homer
Lee, Billy
Lehmann, Bernard E.
Lenz, Richard L., Jr.
Levin, Jeff
Lipton, Walter
Lissant, Kenneth J.
LoMonaco, Joseph
Long, Robbie
LoPrinzi, A., Guitars, Inc.
LoPrinzi, Augustine
Low, Douglas A.
Luke Dulcimers
Lyman, Fred, Jr.
Mabry, Mr. and Mrs. Eppes
McConnell, Robin James
McCormick Strings
McDonald, Zeke
McElroy, Jeremiah T.
McGlincy, L. Edward
McGuire, Bruce
McSpadden, Lynn
Madison, Christopher
Marston, Walter
Martin, C. F., Organisation
Mason, Robert M.

Mason, Steve
Matheson, Ron D.
Meek, Jimmie
Mello, John F.
Michael, Jan D.
Millard, Michael
Miller, Don R.
Miller, Exmar
Miller Guitars
Miller, Raymond
Milligan, Weldon Eugene
Mills, Scott
Minnerly, Donald
Minstrel Guitars
Monari, Jay H.
Montefuso, Marc
Monteleone, John
Moroz, John
Morris, George
Moss, Edward B.
Mossman, S. L., Co., Inc.
Moze Guitars
Muelrath, Dave
National Guitars
Nattelson, John
NBN Guitars
Nebel, Hans
Needham, Howard
Newton, David A.
Nichols, David R.
Nigogosian, Vahakn
Noble, Mr. and Mrs. Roy
Olsen, Timothy
O'Riordan, Patrick
Orozco, Juan
Orthey Dulcimers
Osborne, Foy D.
Ovation Instruments, Inc.
Overholtzer, A. E.
Park, Joe
Patterson, Etoyse
Patterson, James E.
Peacock, George
Pedulla/Orsini Guitars
Pelton, Clifford
Perez, Allen
Perfect, John
Perkins, Latham
Perlman, Alan
Perry, Douglas M.
Peterson, Thomas
Petros, Bruce
Phil-Lu Inc.
Pierce, R. Brent

Pimentel, Lorenzo,
    and Sons
Piper, Ty
Polifka, Donald K., Jr., and
    Judy Polifka
Porter, Steve
Price, Rodney
Privratsky, Bruce
Raimi, Richard
Ramos, Agustin, Jr.
Rampulla, Jim
Randall, Thomas R., Jr.
Reeder, Duane
Rein, Thomas G.
Reisler, Paul
Reiter, Bart
Resek, Thomas Lee
Reuter, Ronald Lee
Rickert, Bradford
Rico, Bernardo C.
Riesenberger, James A.
Riportella, Ken
Rizzetta, Samuel
Roberto-Venn School of
    Luthiery
Rodeo, Otis B.
Rodriguez, Manuel E.
Rogers, Joe, Jr.
Romine, Don
Roomian, Doug
Rose, Edward F.
Rossa, Ronald D.
Rossner, Heinz M.
Rubin, James
Ruppel, Henry D.
Rust, Don
Rutland, Ned
Rynerson, David M.
Sacred Fire/Frogs Delight
Sadowsky, Roger
Sahlin, Eric
Sanders, John
Santa Cruz Guitar Co.
Santo, Dave and Barbara
Sawicki, Stephen M.
Scalone, Joe
Schmidt, K. C.
Schmidt, Oscar,
    International
Schneider, Richard
Schrieber, Hank
Schulte, C. Eric
Scott, Alfred
Shal, John H.

Shultis, Dean L.
Siegler, Lawrence S.
Silver, Frank
Simon, Carmie
Smith, George A.
Smith Guitars
Smith, Jack F.
Smith, Jack R., Jr.
Smith, Leon
Somogyi, Ervin
Sound Guitar Co.
Specht, David T.
Spence, John Cordell
Stack, Alan A.
Stanley, Mr. and Mrs. Peter
Stapley, Craig N.
Stevens, D. W.
Stevens, Larry
Stiles, G. L.
Stimson, Burt
Stockwell, Randy
Strafaci, Natale Armando
Stringfellow Guitars
String Instrument
    Workshop
Stuber, Mike
Sturgill, David A.
Sugar Loaf Folk
    Instruments
Sugar, Mark
Summerfield, Seth
Sunflower Music Shop
Suran, Debbie
Takoushian, C. Garo
Taylor, David
Taylor Guitars
Teleguitars
Thierman, John
Tolliver, Bennett
Tucker, Andrew
Tugel, Ake
Turney, Enas
Tuttle, Lawrence M.
Twelfth Street Guitars
Tygert, F. Scott
Tyk, Lawrence S.
Tyndale, Clyde
Unicorn Musical
    Instruments
United Guitar Co.
Valco Guitars, Inc.
Valenti, Thomas
Vashli, Zoltan

Vaughan, D. Ross, and
    Steven K. Gustafson
Veillette, Joseph and Jane
Velasquez, Manuel
Veleno Guitars
Ventura Guitars
Vile, Jake
Vineyard, Lawrence
Walker, Kim
Wallo, Joseph F.
Warshaw, Steven F.
Wasel, Bill
Washburn Guitars
Watson, Claude H.
Watts, Donald
Weaver, Andrew
Welker, Pete
Westerman, Rich
White, Hayward Gerald
Wildwood Music
Willcutt, Robert J.
Williams, Joe
Wilson, Max G.
Wise, Stephen L.
Wood and Sound
Wood, Randy
Woolf, William Devoe
Wright, Tad, Woodworks
Wrigley, Keith P.
Wurtz, Howard
Yates, Charles L.
Yelda, Peter Michael
Younce, Henry S.
Young, David Russell
Zatzman, Bob, Guitar
    Studio
Ziven, Rich

Tenor Guitar

Bocheneck, Doc
Martin, C. F., Organisation

12-string Guitar

Adams, Andy
Anderson, Steven
Boyd, Michael
Childs, Steve
DeNeve, Richard J.
Don's Guitar Shop
Farrar, Paul
Gemza, Bela
Jirousek, Charles

Klein Custom Guitars
Langejans, Delwyn J.
LoPrinzi, A., Guitars, Inc.
McCormick Strings
Martin, C. F., Organisation
Michael, Jan D.
Millard, Michael
Neff, Rusty
Perkins, Latham
Schneider, Richard
Smith, George A.
Thomas, Dr. Thomas
Tyndale, Clyde
Vile, Jake
Wall, Conrad

Guitar-lute

Maxson, Charles

Guitaro

Schmidt, Oscar,
    International

Guitar-organ

Govox, Inc.
Musiconics International,
    Inc.

Harp (unspecified)

Bartolomeo, Carl
Bishop, Walter H.
Bostard, Kenneth
Damm, Edward A., and
    Anne Damm
David, Herbert
Ekstedt, John R.
English, Larry
Hooker, Basil J.
Kepner, Gil
Lindner, Robert
Lyon-Healy
Moore, S. Brook
Pietz, Otto
Riportella, Ken
Schonbeck, Gunnar I.
Shapiro, Peter
Tayloe, Marjorie
Watts, Donald
Werth, Craig and Elizabeth
Wesner Recorders
Westover, Harold and
    Allene

Witcher, Jay
W and W Harp Co.

Aeolian Harp

Chacey, Ron
Hughes, Richard P., Jr.
Pizzo, Tony, and Laura
    Fontana Pizzo

Bardic Harp

Nonamaker, Brian

Celtic Harp

Nonamaker, Brian

Cytha Harp

Cytha-Harp Co.

Door Harp

Lissant, Kenneth J.

Euterpe Harp

Tyndale, Clyde

Folk Harp

Hughes Dulcimer Co., Inc.
Wurtz, Howard

Gothic Harp

Day, Harley A., Jr., and
    Michael Batell
Nonamaker, Brian

Gourd Harp

Merrifield, Edward

Horizontal Sash Harp

Brechin, Gray

Irish Harp

Adams, Parker
Albin, R. Kent
Bishop, Geoffrey
Bostard, Kenneth
DePaul, Clive Andy Vincent
Dixon, Robert T.
Eckerworks
Latray, Carl

McDevitt, Mr. and Mrs. John
O'Brien, Vincent
O'Riordan, Patrick
Robinson, Roland L.
Sobansky, Ed
Tayloe, Marjorie
Thompson, Earl
Yoder, Lee

Lap Harp

Carstanjen, Mikael
Pietz, Otto

Medieval Harp

Bostard, Kenneth

Memling Harp

Lewandowski, Lynne

Mexican Harp

Robinson, Roland L.

Minstrel Harp

Foster, Charles C.
Merrifield, Edward
Thompson, Earl

Paraguayan Harp

Pietz, Otto
Robinson, Roland L.
Showalter, Leonard

Tara Harp

Robinson, Roland L.

Troubador Harp

Gault's Violin Shop
Wilhelm, Bob, and Karen
    Sharp

Welsh Triple Harp

Tayloe, Marjorie

Wind Harp

Stringfellow Guitars
Tayloe, Marjorie

Hummel

Mumford, Brian

Hurdy-gurdy

Bailey, Q. J.
Brush, Bart
Cox, James, Jr.
Damin, Rik
Elder, Lyn
Gravelin, Tom
Humphrey, Scott
Joseph, Eugene
Kelishek, George
Kepner, Gil
Montgomery, John
Prihoda, Cheryl

Kantele

Damm, Edward A., and
    Anne Damm
Ulmschneider, Carl

Kit

Blasius, John
Hess, Stanley
Jeffreys, A. W., Inc.

Langaleik

Force, Robert Lewis, Jr.

Lanspil

Force, Robert Lewis, Jr.

Lute

Adams, Andy
Aydlett, Raymond Clifton
Bartolomeo, Carl
Battershell, Frederick
Beeston, Thomas
Betz, Alan
Blasius, John
Brown, Douglas R.
Brown, Lawrence D.
Brune, R. E.
Bump, James
Butler, Mark William
Carpenter, Robert
Chase, Hal
Ching, Douglas, Luthier
Cooper, Robert
Corwin, Stuart
Cox, James, Jr.
Crocker, Derwood
Damin, Rik
David, Herbert

Day, Harley A., Jr., and
    Michael Batell
Elder, Lyn
Eppler, Alexander Illitch
Estenson, Paul S.
Farrell, Eugene
Fletcher, Richard
Gemza, Bela
Gido, Julius
Gilmore, George
Gleaves, William Russell
Greene, Edward R.
Gronning, Richard
Gurian, Michael
Hachez, Daniel
Hachez, Ronald J.
Hart, Paul
Hennig, Arnold
Higgins, Larry
Hom, Tom
Janke, John
Johnson, Erik A., II
Kelishek, George
Kern, Dr. Evan
Knatt, Thomas
Knight, Tom
Kottick, Edward L.
Kyvelos, Peter
Lehmann, Bernard E.
Low, Douglas A.
Lundberg, Robert
Lundy, Lawrence
Malgi, Meeme
Manderen, Michael
Maynard, Judson
Meadow, Robert
Middleton, Art
Miller, H. Burritt
Murphy, Barry
Murray, Anthony
Musco, Thomas Guy
Noble, Mr. and Mrs. Roy
Ostberg, Neil
Papazian, Manouk
Peterson, Jesper
Phillips, John M.
Pimentel, Lorenzo, and
    Sons
Reints, John
Renaissance Gilde
Ritter, Anthony, Jr.
Rollins, John
Ruck, R. S.
Sheppard, David B.
Sherron, Roger

Sinclair, John
Smith, George A.
Smith, Robert
Snyder, Dr. Harold E.
Somogyi, Ervin
Stein, Bert
Takoushian, C. Garo
Traphagen, Dake
Tyk, Lawrence S.
Unicorn Musical
    Instruments
Van Lennep, Joel R.
Wall, Conrad
Warnock, Donald
Young, Arthur W., II
Young, David Russell
Yursco, Michael
Ziven, Rich

Lute-zither

Ariail, James

Lyra da Braccia

Minnerly, Donald

Lyre

Crocker, Jennifer
Florence, Ed
Lindner, Robert
Malmquist, Milton G.
Merrifield, Edward
Mitchell, William J.

Mando-cello

Cole, Kenneth Reagan

Mandola

Johnson, Frank A.
Rodeo, Otis B.

Mandolin

Ampeg Co.
Apprentice Shop
Armanino, Peter A.
Aydlett, Raymond Clifton
Bartow, Clarence Nolan
Beeston, Thomas
Benson, Harold
Borromey, Andrew J.
Bourgeois, Dana W.
Brunetti Guitar Factory
Bryan, C. Alex

Bush, Edwin E.
Carpenter, Robert
Carstanjen, Mikael
Chacey, Ron
Chaney, Garrett B.
Collings, William, II
Conner, David R.
Cooper, Gary
Cowan, James
Cox, Jimmy
Crow Peak Music
Crozier, Bill
David, Herbert
DePaul, Clive Andy Vincent
Dorenz, David
Eckhaus, Joel
Ellis Mandolins
Estenson, Paul S.
Ferguson, Ren
Fleming, H. A.
Folkstore, The
Frankel, Dr. Emanuel
Fretted Industries, Inc.
Gemza, Bela
Gibson, Inc.
Gilbert, James H.
Greven, John
Griffith, Owen E.
Grimes, Stephen
Gryphon Stringed
    Instruments
Hagler Banjo Craftsmen
Hash, Albert
Hauser, Scott
Heitzman, David
Henderson, Wayne
Hendrickson, S. J.
Hogue, Ben
Hollifield, Clyde
Huzela, Andrew
Irwin, Lew
Jeffreys, A. W., Inc.
Johnston, David
Kemnitzer, Michael
Kendall, Wayman A.,
    and Son
Kepner, Gil
Kirk's Musical Instruments
Lafoy, John B.
Ledford, Homer
Lee, Billy
Lehmann, Bernard E.
McSpadden, Lynn
Manderen, Michael
Marks, David

Massey, Richard
Milligan, Weldon Eugene
Montefuso, Marc
Monteleone, John
Morgan, Tom and Mary
Neff, Rusty
Newton, David A.
Nichols, David R.
Nolte, Mr. and Mrs. Jerome
Original Musical
    Instrument Co., Inc.
Paganoni, John A., and Sons
Park, Joe
Patterson, Etoyse
Perez, Allen
Perfect, John
Peterson, Jesper
Phil-Lu Inc.
Polifka, Donald K., Jr., and
    Judy Polifka
Prior, Jim
Rees, Harold S.
Reints, John
Reisler, Paul
Riportella, Ken
Rizzetta, Samuel
Roberts, John
Rodeo, Otis B.
Rohde, W. E.
Russo, Mr. and Mrs.
    Pasquale
Rutland, Ned
Sanders, John
Schmidt, Oscar,
    International
Sekerak, Christopher M.
Shrum, William Edward
Siegler, Lawrence S.
Silver, Frank
Siminoff, Roger H.
Simon, Carmie
Simon, Mark
Smith, Jack R., Jr.
Specht, David T.
Stevens, D. W.
Stockwell, Randy
Stoller, David
String Instrument
    Workshop
Stuber, Mike
Sturgill, David A.
Sugar, Mark
Summerfield, Seth
Taylor, Ed
Taylor Guitars

Hayden, Nick
Markusic, Frank
Spigelsky, William S.

Theorbo

Brown, Lawrence D.
Lundberg, Robert

Tromba Marina

Bishop, Walter H.
Hoover, Edgar
Kramer-Harrison, William
Latray, Carl
Mitchell, William J.

Ukulele

Ampeg Co.
Booth, Newton J.
Ching, Douglas, Luthier
Cowan, James
Favilla Guitars
Garabieta, Ignacio
Ledford, Homer
Martin, C. F., Organisation
Newton, David A.
Perfect, John
Schmidt, Oscar,
    International
Stevens, D. W.
String Instrument
    Workshop

Veena

Garrison, David William

Vielle

Cassis, George B.
Cox, James, Jr.
Crocker, Derwood
Day, Harley A., Jr., and
    Michael Batell
Hart, Richard
Myers, Herb
Renaissance Workshop
Sacred Fire/Frogs Delight
Simons, Richard
Warnock, Donald
Werth, Craig and Elizabeth
Westover, Harold
    and Allene

Vihuela

Brune, R. E.

Carriveau, Ron
Day, Harley A., Jr., and
    Michael Batell
Farrell, Eugene
Gido, Julius
Gilmore, George
Hachez, Ronald J.
Higgins, Larry
Manderen, Michael
Papazian, Manouk
Pimentel, Lorenzo, and
    Sons
Rollins, John
Ruck, R. S.
Shaw, Owen
Smith, Robert
Traphagen, Dake
Tugel, Ake
Warnock, Donald

Viol

Battershell, Frederick
Bishop, Walter H.
Cox, James, Jr.
Foster, Daniel
Gaiennie, Clark
Gault's Violin Shop
Hart, Paul
Knatt, Thomas
Shortridge, Linda
Simons, Richard
Westover, Harold and
    Allene

Division Viol

Bishop, Walter H.
Burt, Chris
Shapreau, Carla

Viola

Anderson, Arnold Dean
Anderson, Arvil
Artindale, Fred H.
Atchley, E. V.
Balter, Joan
Bartow, Clarence Nolan
Batts, Jack
Bearden Violin Shop
Benning, Hans
Bishop, Walter H.
Blaas, Dr. Karl
Boerner, Lawrence
Bonito, Dr. Fedele
Borromey, Andrew J.

Boucha, Parnell
Brock, Myron
Brownell, David
Burt, Chris
Callier, Paul Joseph
Camille Violin Shop
Caron, David
Cilecek, Joseph
Clark, Julian
Cole, Anne
Conrad, A. G.
Cornelissen, Marten
Craig, Fred
Curry, Dr. Hiram
Damin, Rik
Daniels, Sam W.
D'Attili, Dario
Davidson, F. R.
Davis, Al
Dodson, Ivan
Dornhelm, Solomon
Eppler, Alexander Illitch
Evans, Ruth Esther
Fairbanks, Harvey
Foster, Douglas
Freeman, S. D., Jr.
Frosali, Mario
Fry, William
Gandy, T. G.
Gault's Violin Shop
Giardinieri, Vittore E.
Grand, Dr. Louis L.
Harrison, Benjamin F., Jr.
Hart, Paul
Henderson, Frank V.
Hickerson, Vern
Hird, Martin
Hirsch, Harold
Hockenberry, William N.
Hooker, Basil J.
Hutchins, Carleen
Jansma, Timothy
Kapfhammer, Wilhelm
Keller, Helmuth A.
Knapik, Eugene
Kob, Martin
Liu, Lloyd
Lyman, Fred, Jr.
Malgi, Meeme
Mann, Ivie W.
Martin, Henry
Masters Violin Shop
Meisel, K. Lothar
Meissner, Henry, and Son
Miller, H. Burritt

Morel, Rene
Moss, Edward B.
Mueller, Albert
Nagy, Sando Alex
Nebel, Hans
O'Brien, Vincent
Papazian, Manouk
Petesh, Zenon W.
Petrula, Stephen J.
Pirtle, R. Alva
Prier, Peter
Puskas, Joseph
Ramey, Harry
Rashid, Joseph G.
Rivinus, David
Roberts, Clifford
Rockwood, B. J.
Rohde, W. E.
Rossi, John L., Ltd.
Rutherford, Judith
Savell, Kelvin
Schenk, Otto K.
Scherl and Roth, Inc.
Schertenlieb, E. L.
Schlub, Richard and David
Schuback Violin Shop
Schurger, Severin G.
Schweinsberg, Heinz
Senkow, Walt
Shal, John H.
Shapreau, Carla
Shaw, Owen
Shipman, Margaret Arlene
Sipe, John
Sirok, Steven
Slaby, William E.
Spafford, Fred
Stapley, Craig N.
Starkman, Martin
Stoltenberg, Robert W.
Sweet, Charles S.
Swettman, Dr. William
Tatar, Pietro
Templing, David
Tewell, Lucille
Thompson, Dr. Oliver
Tubb, Floyd
Turney, Enas
Vavra, Alfons
Wake, H. S.
Wallo, Joseph F.
Watson, Claude H.
Watson, William D.
Weaner, Maxwell

Weaver, M. A. and
    William A.
Weertman, Roelof
Weisshaar, Hans
Wickstrom, Felix
Wiebe, David
Woolf, William Devoe
Zeswitz, Wm., String
    Repair Shop
Zgradic, Ivan
Zussin, Harold

Viola da Gamba

Adams, Andy
Bastarache, Clarence
Benning, Hans
Bryant, Curtis
Cassis, George B.
Damin, Rik
Day, Harley A., Jr., and
    Michael Batell
Dell, Albert Hampson
Gault's Violin Shop
Germer, John
Gilmore, George
Gootnick, David
Hart, Richard
Hendricks, Neil
Hoover, Edgar
Janke, John
Kelishek, George
Maynard, Judson
Miller, H. Burritt
Moore, S. Brook
Nebel, Hans
O'Brien, Vincent
Ramey, Harry
Renaissance Gilde
Rivinus, David
Roberts, Clifford
Robertson, Donald
Schenk, Otto K.
Schlub, Richard and David
Schurger, Severin G.
Shaw, Owen
Tourin, Peter
Warnock, Donald

Viola d'Amore

Bonito, Dr. Fedele
Burt, Chris
Damin, Rik
Dell, Albert Hampson

Eppler, Alexander Illitch
Evans, Ruth Esther
Gault's Violin Shop
Hart, Paul
Hart, Richard
Hoover, Edgar
O'Brien, Vincent
Ramey, Harry
Roberts, Clifford

Vertical Viola

Ashley, Hammond,
    Associates

Violin

Anderson, Arnold Dean
Anderson, Arvil
Arensburg, Ted J.
Artindale, Fred H.
Atchley, E. V.
Balter, Joan
Bartow, Clarence Nolan
Batts, Jack
Bearden Violin Shop
Becker
Beckman, Wayne
Benning, Hans
Benson, Harold
Bertucca, Thomas
Bicknell, Dr. Stuart
Bischofberger, Herman
Blaas, Dr. Karl
Bodor, Janos
Boerner, Lawrence
Bolton, John
Bonito, Dr. Fedele
Borromey, Andrew J.
Boston String Instrument
    Co.
Boucha, Parnell
Breyre, Brian
Briggs, David Byron
Brobst Violin Shop
Brock, Myron
Brownell, David
Brullo, Lawrence R.
Bryan, Clarence L.
Burgess, David
Burt, Chris
Callier, Paul Joseph
Camille Violin Shop
Caron, David
Cigledy, Richard S.

Cilecek, Joseph
Clark, Julian
Cole, Anne
Collier's Violin Shop
Conn, C. G., Ltd.
Conrad, A. G.
Cornelissen, Marten
Cowan, James
Craig, Fred
Curry, Dr. Hiram
Damin, Rik
Daniels, Sam W.
D'Attili, Dario
Davenport, Roy
Davidson, F. R.
Davis, Al H.
DeCavage, John
DeLuccia, Gennara
DePaul, Clive Andy Vincent
Derek, Stephen
Dodson, Ivan
Dornhelm, Solomon
Eastman Violin Shop
Edson, Harold
Eisenstein, Samuel
Eppler, Alexander Illitch
Erbel, Art
Erwin, John Bruce
Evans, Ruth Esther
Fairbanks, Harvey
Fischer, Albert W.
Fisher, Alfred L.
Flexer, J. Robert
Flynn, Clifford J.
Forestiere, Jerry G.
Foster, Douglas
Freeman, S. D., Jr.
Frirsz, Max
Frosali, Mario
Fry, William
Fullenwider, John, and Sons
Fulton, William
Gadd, Charles W.
Gandy, T. G.
Gault's Violin Shop
Gemza, Bela
Giardinieri, Vittore E.
Gootnick, David
Gorish Violin Shop
Graber, John T.
Grand, Dr. Louis L.
Greene, Blaine
Griffith, Owen E.
Guthrie, Marvin L.

Guttenberg, John
Haenel, Frederick
Hagler Banjo Craftsmen
Haile, Thomas Vose
Ham, Roy
Harrison, Benjamin F., Jr.
Hart, Paul
Hash, Albert
Hegedus, Louis V.
Henderson, Frank V.
Hendrickson, Floyd
Hendrickson, S. J.
Henn, Eugene E.
Hertel, Erwin
Hickerson, Vern
Hirsch, Harold
Hockenberry, William N.
Hoerster, John Henry
Holm, Dan
Honeycutt, John T.
Hood, Robert T.
Hooker, Basil J.
Hutchins, Carleen
James, Lester L.
Janke, John
Jansma, Timothy
Johnson, Charles V.
Johnston, Neil M.
Kapfhammer, Wilhelm
Kaston, Henryk
Katz, Robert
Keller, Helmuth A.
Kendall, Wayman A.,
    and Son
Kimball, Dean
Kloss, Horst L.
Knapik, Eugene
Knapp, Richard V.
Kolstein, Samuel, and
    Son, Ltd.
Koscak, John
Koster, John
Kunz, Ulrich
Kuriloff, Arthur
Kyvelos, Peter
Lee, Billy
Liu, Lloyd
Luderer, Otto
Lyman, Fred, Jr.
Malgi, Meeme
Mann, Ivie W.
Markusic, Frank
Martin, Henry
Mason, Robert M.

Masters Violin Shop
Meek, Jimmie
Meisel, K. Lothar
Meissner, Henry, and Son
Miller, A. A.
Miller, H. Burritt
Miller, Joseph Bernard
Moglie, Albert
Mondragon
Moore, S. Brook
Morel, Rene
Moss, Edward B.
Mueller, Albert
Murphy, Dennis
Nebel, Hans
Nielsen Violin Shop
Nigogosian, Vahakn
O'Brien, Vincent
Olsen, Rudolf
Papazian, Manouk
Patashne, Theodore
Patterson, Etoyse
Peresson, Sergio
Perez, Allen
Perfect, John
Peterson, Jesper
Petesh, Zenon W.
Petrula, Stephen J.
Pinches, William S.
Pirtle, R. Alva
Polsinelli, P. Gio.
Ponziani Violin
Porter, Leonard V.
Prier, Peter
Puskas, Joseph
Ramey, Harry
Rapp, Allan J.
Rashid, Joseph G.
Rasmussen, Aage,
    Violin Shop
Rees, Harold S.
Reuter, Fritz, and Sons
Riegel, Terenzio
Rivinus, David
Roberts, Clifford
Rockwood, B. J.
Rohde, W. E.
Roman, Charles
Rosenberg, Saul
Rossi, John L., Ltd.
Ruggiero, Matthew
Russo, Mr. and Mrs.
    Pasquale
Saunders, David

Savell, Kelvin
Schenk, Otto K.
Scherl and Roth, Inc.
Schertenlieb, E. L.
Schliff, Sam
Schlub, Richard and David
Schroetter, Andrew, and
    Co., Inc.
Schuback Violin Shop
Schurger, Severin G.
Schweinsberg, Heinz
Senkow, Walt
Shal, John H.
Shapreau, Carla
Shaw, Owen
Shipman, Margaret Arlene
Showalter, Leonard
Shrum, William Edward
Sipe, John
Sirok, Steven
Slaby, William E.
Smith, Thomas
Spafford, Fred
Starkman, Martin
Stockton, Glen Terry
Stoller, David
Stoltenberg, Robert W.
Stone, Dennis
Storch, Ben, Corp.
Stoutenbourgh, Harry
Stradivarius Violin Shop
Stradi-Varni Co.
Strobel, H. A.
Sturgill, David A.
Summerfield, Seth
Sweet, Charles S.
Swettman, Dr. William
Swisher, J. Dean
Takoushian, C. Garo
Taylor, J. Bradley, Inc.
Templing, David
Tewell, Lucille
Thompson, Dr. Oliver
Thurston, Florian
Toenniges, Paul
Torma Violin
Tubbs, Floyd
Turney, Enas
Vavra, Alfons
Venn, Robert L.
Wake, H. S.
Wakeman, Earl
Wallo, Joseph F.
Wark, Charles

Warren, Kenneth, and
    Son, Ltd.
Watson, Claude H.
Watson, William D.
Watts, Donald
Weaner, Maxwell
Weaver, M. A. and
    William A.
Weertman, Roelof
Weisshaar, Hans
White, Hayward Gerald
Wickstrom, Felix
Wiebe, David
Williamson's Violin Shop
Willis, Alan
Woolf, William Devoe
Young, David Russell
Zeswitz, Wm., String
    Repair Shop
Zgradic, Ivan
Zussin, Harold

Alto Violin

Cole, Anne

Baroque Violin

Hoover, Edgar
Shapreau, Carla

Electric Violin

Albin, R. Kent
Willcutt, Robert J.

Electronic Violin

Dodson, Ivan
Xinde International, Inc.

New (catgut) Violin

Ashley, Hammond,
    Associates
Hutchins, Carleen

Tenor Violin

Cole, Anne

Zither

Allen, Laura Rachel
Associated Luthiers
Balderose, George
Fearn, Cabell J.

Force, Robert Lewis, Jr.
Hollifield, Clyde
Lapidus, Joellen
Reuter, Ronald Lee
Schmidt, Oscar,
    International

Zither-harp

Martindale, Howard

Woodwinds

Woodwinds (unspecified)

Baime, Thomas C.
Connelly, W. H.
Cundy-Bettoney Co.
Denzer, R. H.
Lamont Band Instruments
Lemberg, Sandy
McLellan, Michael
Maheu, Richard
Robinson, Trevor
Schonbeck, Gunnar I.
Seeler, Oliver
Selmer
Silverstein, Steven
Woodwind Co.

Aulos

Platz, Joseph

Bagpipe

Hornpipe, Michael

Bansuri

King, Eric

Basset Horn

Elo, Arpad, Jr.

Bassoon

Berdon Co.
Fox Products Corp.
King Musical Instruments
Linton Mfg. Co.
MacGibbon, R. W.
Polisi Bassoon Corp.

Baroque Bassoon

Levin, Phillip

Seyfrit, Dr. and Mrs.
Michael

Bladder Pipe

Neuman, Phil and Gayle

Chalumeaux

Bosworth and Hammer
Historical Woodwinds

Chanter

Hornpipe, Michael

Clarinet

Armstrong, W. T., Co., Inc.
Artley, Inc.
Auch, Frederick E.
DEG Music Products, Inc.
King Musical Instruments
LeBlanc, G., Corp.
Linton Mfg. Co.
McIntyre Clarinet Co.
McLaughlin, Leo
Mazzeo, Rosario

Baroque Clarinet

Elo, Arpad, Jr.
Gentle Winds Flute Co.
Prescott, Thomas M.,
Workshop

Contrabassoon

Berdon Co.
Fox Products Corp.

Cornett

Grossman, James
Kelishek, George
McCann, John R.
Miller, Janet

Duoinitza

Kasik, Joseph and Nancy

Dulcian

Cameron, Roderick

English Horn

Berdon Co.
Laubin, A., Inc.
Linton Mfg. Co.

Fife

American Plating and Mfg.
Co.
Auch, Frederick E.
Brass City Fifecraft
Cooperman, Patrick
Ferrary, Henry E.
Fisher, Zachariah
Gentle Winds Flute Co.
Hornpipe, Michael
Kirby, Russell P.
Landell, Jonathon
Lindner, Robert
O'Riordan, Patrick
Pope, Martin A.
Robinson, Trevor
Seaman, Roy
Sweet, Ralph

Flageolette

Sweet, Ralph

Flute (unspecified)

Aldridge, Alan
Burning Water Instruments
Celestial Flute Co.
Davenport, Ken J.
DEG Music Products, Inc.
Forrester, Kent
Gentle Winds Flute Co.
Kilpatrick, J. R.
King, Eric
LeBlanc, G., Corp.
Lindner, Robert
Melody Flute Co.
Molvai, Manocher
Ohrstrom, Thomas
O'Riordan, Patrick
Oster, Doran
Payne, Dr. Richard W.
Robinson, Trevor

Bamboo Flute

Deihl, Douglas
Ingalls, John T.
Kanner, Michael Barry
Kasik, Joseph and Nancy
Platz, Joseph

Baroque Flute

Auch, Frederick E.

B and G Instrument
Workshop
Boehm, Thomas C.
Brooks, David R.
Cameron, Roderick
Dell, Albert Hampson
Elo, Arpad, Jr.
Folkers, Catherine E.
Ingalls, John T.
Prescott, Thomas M.,
Workshop
Rowles, Steve
Sanders, Robert
Seyfrit, Dr. and
Mrs. Michael
Shlaer, Robert
Teplow, Deborah
Von Huene, Friedrich

Cane Flute

Lipiczky, Thomas

Ceramic Flute

Crowl and Hook
Ingalls, John T.
Minnerly, Donald
Reliable Brothers

Copper Flute

Blackburn, David
Coll Divine Flutes
Fisher, Zachariah

Modern Flute

Aitkins, Reginald
Armstrong, W. T., Co., Inc.
Artley, Inc.
Brannon, Bickford
and Robert
DeFord Flutes
Gemeinhardt, K. G., Co.
Gyld, The
Hardy, P. J., Musical
Instruments
Haynes, William S., Flute
Co., Inc.
Lamberson, N. D.
Landell, Jonathon
Linton Mfg. Co.
Lorello, Eugene E.
Opperman, George,
Woodwinds

Powell, Verne Q.
West, Pearl

North and South Indian Flute

Bauer, Fred
Ingalls, John T.

Renaissance Flute

Aardvark Fluteworks
Bartram, James F., Jr.
Brooks, David R.
Cameron, Roderick
Ingalls, John T.
Landell, Jonathon
Silverstein, Steven
Von Huene, Friedrich
Zadro, Michael

Wooden Flute

Blackburn, David
Coll Divine Flutes
Collier, Charles
Deihl, Douglas
Eppler, Alexander Illitch
Lipiczky, Thomas
Platz, Joseph
Singleton, M. K.

Gaida

Eppler, Alexander Illitch

Gemshorn

Bump, James

Highland Pipes

Cushing, Mark

Horn Pipe

Singleton, M. K.

Irish War Pipe

Hornpipe, Michael

Kaval

Eppler, Alexander Illitch

Krumhorn

Forrester, Kent

Kelishek, George
Smith, Robert

Mute Cornetto

Auch, Frederick E.
Collier, Charles
Cook, Richard

Oboe

Berdon Co.
Ford Platz Oboe Co.
Fox Products Corp.
King Musical Instruments
Larilee Oboe Co.
Laubin, A., Inc.
Lindner, Robert
Linton Mfg. Co.
MacGibbon, R. W.
Markle, Cecil
Pedler, Sid
West, Pearl

Baroque Oboe

Bosworth and Hammer
 Historical Woodwinds
Damin, Rik
Dell, Albert Hampson
Elo, Arpad, Jr.
Marteney, Eugene R.
Moore, Grant
Robinson, Trevor
Seyfrit, Dr. and Mrs.
 Michael
Vas Dias, Harry
Von Huene, Friedrich

Classical Oboe

Moore, Grant

Oboe da Caccia

Moore, Grant

Oboe d'Amore

Marteney, Eugene R.

Occarina

Bassing, Carolyn
Johnson, Paul

Penny Whistle

Bok, Gordon
Goodfellow, Ted

Piccolo

Aitkins, Reginald
Armstrong, W. T., Co., Inc.
Artley, Inc.
DEG Music Products, Inc.
Gemeinhardt, K. G., Co.
Hardy, P. J., Musical
 Instruments
Haynes, William S., Flute
 Co., Inc.
Kilpatrick, J. R.
King Musical Instruments
Seaman, Roy
Seyfrit, Dr. and Mrs.
 Michael

Rackett

Neuman, Phil and Gayle
Stiles, Phillip J.

Rauschpfeifer

Foster, Charles C.

Recorder

Bartram, James F., Jr.
Cameron, Roderick
Clifford, Roger
Damin, Rik
Dayan, Stanley
Dell, Albert Hampson
Dushkin, David
Forrester, Kent
Hess, Stanley
James, Clarence R.
Koch Recorders
Ohannesian, David
Palm, Richard
Platz, Joseph
Prescott, Thomas M.,
 Workshop
Robinson, Trevor
Scott, James
Sears, Thomas A.
Silverstein, Steven
Soderstrom, Dr. John
Teplow, Deborah
Von Huene, Friedrich
Wakefield, John Homer
Wesner Recorders

Saxophone

Armstrong, W. T., Co., Inc.

Blessing, E. K., Co., Inc.
Conn, C. G., Ltd.
DEG Music Products, Inc.
King Musical Instruments
LeBlanc, G., Corp.
Linton Mfg. Co.

Shakuhachi

Kasik, Joseph and Nancy
King, Eric
Levenson, Monty

Shawm

Cassis, George B.
Collier, Charles
Hornpipe, Michael
Robinson, Trevor

Sordonne

Neuman, Phil and Gayle
Smith, Robert
Stiles, Phillip J.

Tabor Pipe

Bosworth and Hammer
    Historical Woodwinds
Sweet, Ralph
Von Huene, Friedrich

Uilleann Pipes

Campbell, Jon
Henly, Patrick
Konzak, Ron
Sky, Patrick

Voice Flute

Ohannesian, David

Brass

Brass (unspecified)

Lamont Band Instruments
Robinson, Trevor
Schonbeck, Gunnar I.
Selmer

Alto Horn

DEG Music Products, Inc.
LeBlanc, G., Corp.

Altonium

King Musical Instruments

Baritone Horn

Blessing, E. K., Co., Inc.
DEG Music Products, Inc.
Getzen Co.
King Musical Instruments
LeBlanc, G., Corp.

Bass Horn

King Musical Instruments

Bugle

Buglecraft, Inc.

Cornet

Blessing, E. K., Co., Inc.
Conn, C. G., Ltd.
DEG Music Products, Inc.
Getzen Co.
King Musical Instruments
LeBlanc, G., Corp.
Schilke Co.
Tucker, Andrew

Euphonium

DEG Music Products, Inc.
King Musical Instruments

Fluegelhorn

Blessing, E. K., Co., Inc.
DEG Music Products, Inc.
Getzen Co.
King Musical Instruments
LeBlanc, G., Corp.
Schilke Co.

French Horn

Blessing, E. K., Co., Inc.
Conn, C. G., Ltd.
DEG Music Products, Inc.
King Musical Instruments
LeBlanc, G., Corp.

Mellophone

LeBlanc, G., Corp.

Sousaphone

Conn, C. G., Ltd.
DEG Music Products, Inc.
King Musical Instruments
LeBlanc, G., Corp.

Alto Trombone

Auch, Frederick E.

Renaissance Trombone

Schilke Co.

Rotor Trombone

Blessing, E. K., Co., Inc.

Slide Trombone

Blessing, E. K., Co., Inc.
Conn, C. G., Ltd.
DEG Music Products, Inc.
Getzen Co.
King Musical Instruments
LeBlanc, G., Corp.

Valve Trombone

Blessing, E. K., Co., Inc.
Getzen Co.

Trombonium

King Musical Instruments

Trumpet

Blessing, E. K., Co., Inc.
Conn, C. G., Ltd.
DEG Music Products, Inc.
Getzen Co.
King Musical Instruments
LeBlanc, G., Corp.
Schilke Co.

Baroque Trumpet

Schilke Co.

Herald Trumpet

Blessing, E. K., Co., Inc.
Damin, Rik

Tuba

Blessing, E. K., Co., Inc.
LeBlanc, G., Corp.

Keyboard

Keyboard (unspecified)

Beall, J. R.
Groethe, Russell

Kantor, Jay
Schonbeck, Gunnar I.

Accordion

Ace Accordion Co.
Bell Accordion Corp.
Bianco Accordions
Castiglione Accordion Co.
Empire Accordion Corp.
Giulietti Accordion Corp.
Imperial Accordion
  Mfg. Co.
Iorio Accordion Corp.
Italo-American Accordion
  Mfg. Co.
Karpek Accordion Mfg. Co.
LaPrima Accordions, Inc.
Melodiana Accordion Co.
Mussi Accordions
Penzel Mueller, Inc.
Petosa Accordions
Pollina Accordion Mfg. Co.
Rowe Accordions
Russo Accordions
Sano Corp.
Sonola Accordion Co., Inc.
Titano Accordion Co.
Universal Accordion

Clavichord

Bakeman, Ken
B and G Instrument
  Workshop
Bannister Harpsichords
Beckman, Wayne
Benn, Bradley W. M.
Bishop, Walter H.
Broekman, Hendrik
Brosnac, Donald
Brown, Tom
Brueggeman, John
Buecker and White
Burhans, Ralph W.
Cone, Michael
De Angeli, Maurice
Feder, Yves Albert
Fudge, Carl
Germann, Sheridan
Germer, John
Gotzmer, Carl
Gough, Roger D.
Greene, Edward R.
Haas, Ron
Heitzman, David

Herz, Eric, Harpsichords,
  Inc.
Hill, Kenny
Kern, Dr. Evan
Kottick, Edward L.
Meyer, Kenton
Middleton, Art
Osborne, Joseph
Peters, Jack
Poulton, Curt A.
Ratajak, W. P.
Redstone, Peter and
  Kathryn
Reed, Abijah
Rogers, Don
Sansom, Russell
Schlick, Hardy
Schmeltekopf, Gerhart
Shortridge, John and Linda
Tsiang, Lynette
Tyk, Lawrence S.
Van Lennep, Joel R.
Wakefield, John Homer
Watson, John R.
Williams, S. R.
Witt, E. O.
Wolf, Thomas and Barbara
Wurtz, Howard

Digi-vox

Burhans, Ralph W.

Forte-piano

Bakeman, Ken
Bannister Harpsichords
Belt, Philip, and Maribel
  Meisel
Gough, Roger D.
Redstone, Peter and
  Kathryn
Ritter, Frederick
Smith, Robert E.

Harpsichord

Adams, Jeremy
Adler, Mark
Alexander, Richard
Allen, John W.
Bakeman, Ken
B and G Instrument
  Workshop
Bannister Harpsichords
Barrons Harpsichords
Barry, Wilson

Batchelder, Charles
Battershell, Frederick
Beckman, Wayne
Bell, Donald
Belt, Philip, and Maribel
  Meisel
Benn, Bradley W. M.
Bishop, Walter H.
Blood, William
Brodersen, Christopher
Brody, M.
Broekman, Hendrik
Brown, Tom
Brueggeman, John
Brune, R. E.
Buecker and White
Burhans, Ralph W.
Burr, Walter
Calhoun, David Charles
Cannon, James H.
Chapline Organs
Chiasson, Claude
Cigledy, Richard S.
Cucciara Harpsichord
  Co., Inc.
Day, Harley A., Jr., and
  Michael Batell
De Angeli, Maurice
Dell, Albert Hampson
Diehl, T. Pieter
Dowd, William
Dowling, William F.,
  and Co.
Draves, Peter Sargent
Eckstein, Larry G.
Everngam, Howard
Farrell, Eugene
Feder, Yves Albert
Flowers, James
Fontwit, Sandy
Fudge, Carl
Germann, Sheridan
Germer, John
Giuttari, Glenn
Gotzmer, Carl
Gough, Hugh, Inc.
Gough, Roger D.
Greenberg, Robert
Greene, Edward R.
Gregoire Harpsichord
Greven, John
Haas, Ron
Heitzman, David
Herz, Eric,
  Harpsichords, Inc.

Hill, Keith
Hill, Kenny
Hubbard, Frank
Instrument Guild, The, Inc.
Jeffreys, A. W., Inc.
Jones-Clayton
 Harpsichords, Inc.
Katz, Don
Kern, Dr. Evan
Kingston, Richard
Kottick, Edward L.
Lee, Richard J.
Lehigh Organ Co.
Lignell, Anton
Lockard, Barry
Maynard, Judson
Mercer, Thomas
Merz, Richard
Middleton, Art
Minnerly, Donald
Monette, Louis Gayle
Myrvaagnes, Rodney
Nargesian, John
Newman, William
Norris, Joseph
O'Brien, Walter F.
Orthey Dulcimers
Osborne, Joseph
Parmelee, Clyde H., Jr.
Peters, Jack
Phillips, John M.
Postol, Elliott
Poulton, Curt A.
Ratajak, W. P.
Redstone, Peter
 and Kathryn
Reed, Abijah
Reed, John M.
Ritter, Frederick
Rogers, Don
Ross, William Post
Ruhl, Robert Allen
Rumery, L. R., Co.
Rutkowski and Robinette
Sanchez, Ulises
Sansom, Russell
Scheuerman, Milton, Jr.
Schliff, Sam
Shortridge, John and Linda
Smith, George A.
Snyder, Lawrence D.
Sorli, Steven W.
Stevenson, E. P.
Stilphen, George
Stratton, Robert

Sutherland, David A.
Tourin, Peter
Turner Corp.
Tyk, Lawrence S.
Van Leer, Johan
Vaughn, Mr. and Mrs.
 Ralph J.
Vernon, Knight
Watson, John R.
White, Glenn
Williams, S. R.
Winslow, Edward
Witt, E. O.
Wolf, Thomas and Barbara
Young, Arthur W., II
Yursco, Michael
Ziedler and Quagliata
 Harpsichords

Organ (unspecified)

Adams, Jeremy
Akright, James
Barry, Wilson
Bozeman-Gibson and Co.
Burger and Shafer
Carey Organ Co.
Casavent Organs
Cunningham, Tom
Estey Division of Miner
 Industries, Inc.
Gress-Miles Organ Co., Inc.
McRuggles, Charles
Magnus Organ Corp.
Mudler-Hunter Co.
Noack Organ Co., Inc., The
Opsonar Organ Co.
Reuter Organ Co.
Van Daalen, Jan
Wahl, Ronald
Werth, Craig and Elizabeth
Wicks Organ Co.
Wurlitzer Co.

Auto-chord Organ

Zachary Organ Co.

Band Organ

Johnson Organ Co., Inc.

Chord Organ

GTR Products, Inc.

Electric Organ

Artisan Electronics Corp.

Sorkin Music Co.
Thomas International Corp.
Visser-Rowland
 Associates, Inc.
Zachary Organ Co.

Electronic Organ

Allen Organ Co.
Alpha Omega Corp.
General Electro Music
Gulbransen Industries, Inc.
Halifax Musical
 Instruments, Ltd.
Holland Organ Co., Inc.
Kimball Piano and
 Organ Co.
LoDuca Brothers Musical
 Instruments, Inc.
Rodgers Organ
Whippany Electronics, Inc.

Electro-pneumatic Organ

Brandt, A. W., Co.
McManis Organs, Inc.

Mechanical-action Organ

Chapline Organs
Visser-Rowland
 Associates, Inc.

Pipe Organ

Abbott and Sieker
Andover Organ Co., Inc.
Austin Organs, Inc.
Beaudry, Philip A., Co.
Berkshire Organ Co., Inc.
Bulley, Julian E.
Cannarsa Organs, Inc.
Delaware Organ Co., Inc.
Emola, Albert
Fisk, C. B., Inc.
Frels, Rubin S., Co.
Greenwood Organ Co.
Holloway Pipe Organs
Holtkamp Organ Co.
Johnson Organ Co., Inc.
Lehigh Organ Co.
Lima Pipe Organ Co.
Ludden, James
Moller, M. P., Inc.
Noack Organ Co., Inc., The
Outerbridge, Thaddeus, III
Phelps, Lawrence,
 and Associates

Redman Organ Co.
Roche Organ Co., Inc.
Ruhland Organ Co.
Saville Organ Corp.
Schantz Organ Co.
Schlicker Organ Co., Inc.
Shawhan Pipe Organs
Steiner Organs, Inc.
Stuart Organ Co.
Turner, Robert M.
Vaughn, John B.
Zimmer, W., and Sons

Portative Organ

Crocker, Derwood
Ebert Organ Co.
Hummer, David, and Karl
    D. Wienand
McManis Organs, Inc.
Scheuerman, Milton, Jr.
Swinger, Michael H.
Westover, Harold
    and Allene

Positive Organ

Crocker, Derwood
Swinger, Michael H.
Westover, Harold and
    Allene

Reed Organ

LoDuca Brothers Musical
    Instruments, Inc.

Tracker Organ

Brombaugh, John
McManis Organs, Inc.
Moore, A. David

Piano

Adams Piano Factory
Aeolian American
Aeolian Corp.
Astin Weight Pianos
Bach Piano Co.
Baldwin Piano Co.
Belt, Philip, and
    Maribel Meisel
Currier Piano Co.
Estey Piano Corp.
Everett Piano Co.
Grand Piano Co., Inc.
Griffith Piano Co.

Hammond Organ Co.
Irwin and Son Piano Co.
Kimball Piano and
    Organ Co.
Knight Royale Pianos
Kohler and Campbell, Inc.
Krakauer Brothers
Laughead Co.
Lester Piano Mfg. Co.
Lindner Pianos
Sauter Pianos
Schliff, Sam
Sohmer and Co., Inc.
Starch, P. A., Piano Co.
Steinway and Sons
Stilphen, George
Story and Clark Piano Co.
Trefz, Otto R., Jr., and Co.
Walter Piano Co., Inc.
Weser Piano Co.
Wurlitzer Co.

Electric Piano

Fender/Rogers/Rhodes
Music Technology, Inc.
Octave Electronics, Inc.
Rhodes Keyboard
    Instruments

Electronic Piano

Allen Organ Co.
Beckman Musical
    Instrument Co., Inc.
Burhans, Ralph W.   *
Chamberlin Instrument
    Co., Inc.
General Electro Music
LoDuca Brothers Musical
    Instruments, Inc.
Multivox
Novaline, Inc.
Rolandcorp U. S.
Unicord, Inc.
Wurlitzer Co.

Reed Pipes

Brown, Don

Regal

Scheuerman, Milton, Jr.

Spinet

Bakeman, Ken

Bannister Harpsichords
Batchelder, Charles
Benn, Bradley W. M.
Buecker and White
Cassis, George B.
De Angeli, Maurice
Gregoire Harpsichord
Martin, James D.
Merrifield, Edward
Tsiang, Lynette
Vernon, Knight
Williams, S. R.
Witt, E. O.

Synthesizer

ARP Industries, Inc.
Barney, Carl
Beckman Musical
    Instrument Co., Inc.
Moog Music, Inc.
Multivox
Oberheim Electronics, Inc.
Octave Electronics, Inc.
Rolandcorp U. S.
Steiner-Parker Synthesizers
Strider Systems, Inc.
Total Technology
Unicord, Inc.

Virginal

Batchelder, Charles
Bell, Donald
Benn, Bradley W. M.
Bishop, Walter H.
Broekman, Hendrik
Brueggeman, John
Calhoun, David Charles
Fudge, Carl
Germann, Sheridan
Greene, Edward R.
Knight, Tom
Mercer, Thomas
Minnerly, Donald
Newman, William
O'Brien, Walter F.
Parmelee, Clyde H., Jr.
Ratajak, W. P.
Rogers, Don
Ross, William Post
Rumery, L. R., Co.
Schmeltekopf, Gerhart
Stilphen, George
Sutherland, David A.
Van Lennep, Joel R.

Welsh, Susan
Witt, E. O.

Percussion

Percussion (unspecified)

Beckman Musical
    Instrument Co,. Inc.
Logi-Rhythm, Inc.
Slingerland Drum Co.
Wiles, David

Amphion Chimes

Mayland Co.

Ceramic Bells

Wiles, David

Lyra Bells

Deagan, J. C., Inc.

Orchestra Bells

Deagan, J. C., Inc.
Decatur Instruments, Inc.
Mayland Co.
Scientific Music Industries

Bodhran

Dixon, Robert T.
Lark in the Morning

Bongo

Gon-Bops
Latin Percussion
Valje Drums

Boomagong

Golden Bells Music Co.

Cabasa/a Fuche

Latin Percussion

Carillon

Maas-Rowe Carillons, Inc.
Schulmerich Carillons, Inc.
Van Bergen Foundry

Orchestra Chimes

Deagan, J. C., Inc.

Decatur Instruments, Inc.
Ludwig Industries

Conga

Gon-Bops
Latin Percussion
Valje Drums

Cow Bell

Gon-Bops
Latin Percussion

Cymbals

Camber Cymbal
Zildjian, Avedis, Co.

Drum (unspecified)

Beckman Musical
    Instrument Co., Inc.
Drumland
Fender/Rogers/Rhodes
Frank's Drum Shop
Gretsch, The Fred, Co.
Kelly, Ritch
Leedy Drum Co.
Ludwig Industries
Mandile, Michael
Martin, C. F., Organisation
Noble and Cooley Co.
Ohrstrom, Thomas
Pollard Industries, Inc.
Republic Drums
Samhat, Jack
Schmidt, Oscar,
    International
Tone-Master
Vespe Drum Shop
Zickos Corp.

African Drum

Crescent Moon Drums

American Indian Drum

Indian Jim

Caluba Drum

Plektron Corp.

Concert Drum

Rogers Drum Co.

Hand Drum

Natraj
Plektron Corp.

Log Drum

Kuistad, Garry
Pizzo, Tony, and Laura
    Fontana Pizzo

Marching Drum

Rogers Drum Co.

Rope-Tensioned Drum

Cooperman, Patrick
Eames Drum Co.
Hollwedel, Henry, Jr.
L'Heureux, Larry
Schoos, Maurice

Snare Drum

Andress Mfg. Co.
Hinger Touch-Tone Corp.

Steel Drum

Shapiro, Peter

Wooden Drum

Bardin, Charles, and Sean
    Maroney
Cottingham, Larry
Evans, Linda
Lewis, Juno
Trolin, Martha

Early Percussion

Lark in the Morning

English Handbell

Malmark, Inc.

Glockenspiel

Pizzo, Tony, and Laura
    Fontana Pizzo

Harmonica

Kratt, William, Co.

Jew's Harp

Bilyeu, Thomas P.

Jingle Rings

Natraj

Kalimba

Adams, Paul
Bishop, Geoffrey
Burning Water Instruments
Cottingham, Larry
Elliott, J. C.
Gray, Gary
Here, Inc.
Kramer-Harrison, William
Marks, David
Rugg and Jackel Music Co.
Schmidt, Oscar,
  International
Shapiro, Peter
Shepherd, Jesse Gordon
Smakula, Peter H.
Ulmschneider, Carl

Limber Jim

Damm, Edward A., and
  Anne Damm
Wasel, Bill

Marimba

Bardin, Charles, and Sean
  Maroney
Deagan, J. C., Inc.
Decatur Instruments, Inc.
Golden Bells Music Co.
Wiles, David

Monochord

Ackley, Dennis

Mouth Bow

Blair, Bobby L.
Lamoreaux, Cal
Mitchell, Howard
Mitchell, William J.
Smakula, Peter H.
Tyndale, Clyde
Wasel, Bill

Musical Saw

Mussehl and Westphal

Pickin' Bow

Mabry, Mr. and Mrs. Eppes

Stumpf Fiddle

Fiddle Factory, Inc.

Tabor

Frieg, Stephen
Natraj

Tambourine

Frieg, Stephen
Micoa, Inc.
Natraj
Plektron Corp.

Temple Blocks

Plektron Corp.

Timbales

Latin Percussion

Tympani (unspecified)

Hinger Touch-Tone Corp.
Ludwig Industries
Rogers Drum Co.

Chain Tympani

Goodman Drum Co.

Pedal Tympani

Goodman Drum Co.

Vibra-harp

Deagan, J. C., Inc.
Decatur Instruments, Inc.

Vibra-slap

Latin Percussion

Wooden Blocks

Kuistad, Garry

Xylophone

Balderose, George
Deagan, J. C., Inc.
Decatur Instruments, Inc.
Frieg, Stephen
Golden Bells Music Co.
Mayland Co.
Schonbeck, Gunnar I.
Scientific Music Industries
Shapiro, Peter

Zil

Samhat, Jack

Table 1. Strings

Instrument	No. of Makers	Instrument	No. of Makers	Instrument	No. of Makers
Strings (unspecified)	497	Guitar (pedal steel)	7	Mandola	2
Archlute	1	Guitar (tenor)	2	Mandolin	133
Autoharp	14	Guitar (jazz)	6	Mandolin (electric)	3
Bajo sexto	1	Guitar (steel-string)	447	Mandolin-banjo	1
Balalaika	7	Guitar (12-string)	24	Mandora	1
Bandurria	1	Guitar-lute	1	Medialuna	1
Banjo (5-string)	238	Guitar-organ	2	Orpharion	2
Banjo (tenor)	4	Guitaro	1	Oud	3
Banjo-guitar	1	Harp (unspecified)	23	Pandora	1
Banjolin	1	Harp (Aeolian)	3	Porta-bass	1
Baryton	1	Harp (bardic)	1	Psaltery	48
Bass violin	27	Harp (Celtic)	1	Psaltery-harp	2
Bouzoukee	4	Harp (cytha)	1	Qanun	2
Bows	18	Harp (door)	1	Rebec	18
Cello	78	Harp (Euterpe)	1	Rebec-dulcimer	1
Chitarrone	3	Harp (folk)	2	Renquinto	1
Citara	1	Harp (Gothic)	2	Salterio	1
Cittern	10	Harp (gourd)	1	Santouri	2
Crwth	1	Harp (horizontal sash)	1	Sitar	1
Cuatro	2	Harp (Irish)	16	Tambouritza	5
Dobro	5	Harp (lap)	2	Theorbo	2
Dombra	1	Harp (medieval)	1	Tromba marina	5
Dulcimer (Appalachian)	431	Harp (Memling)	1	Ukulele	13
Dulcimer (courting or		Harp (Mexican)	1	Veena	1
double)	4	Harp (minstrel)	3	Vielle	12
Dulcimer (hammered)	82	Harp (Paraguayan)	3	Vihuela	18
Dulcitar	1	Harp (tara)	1	Viol	11
Ectero	1	Harp (troubadour)	2	Viol (division)	3
Ektar	2	Harp (Welsh triple)	1	Viola	132
Epinette	4	Harp (wind)	2	Viola da gamba	33
Fiddle (key)	1	Hummel	1	Viola d'amore	13
Fiddle (medieval)	1	Hurdy-gurdy	12	Viola (vertical)	1
Gadulka	1	Kantele	2	Violin	265
Gourdamer	1	Kit	3	Violin (alto)	1
Guitar (acoustic bass)	3	Langaleik	1	Violin (Baroque)	2
Guitar (Baroque)	4	Lanspil	1	Violin (electric)	2
Guitar (classical)	175	Lute	91	Violin (electronic)	2
Guitar (double resonator)	2	Lute-zither	1	Violin (new catgut)	2
Guitar (electric)	95	Lyra da braccia	1	Violin (tenor)	1
Guitar (electric bass)	23	Lyre	6	Zither	9
Guitar (flamenco)	36	Mando-cello	1	Zither-harp	1
Guitar (octave)	1				

Table 2. Woodwinds

Instrument	No. of Makers	Instrument	No. of Makers	Instrument	No. of Makers
Woodwinds (unspecified)	15	Flute (unspecified)	18	Oboe	11
Aulos	1	Flute (bamboo)	5	Oboe (Baroque)	10
Bagpipe	1	Flute (Baroque)	16	Oboe (classical)	1
Bansuri	1	Flute (cane)	1	Oboe da caccia	1
Basset horn	1	Flute (ceramic)	4	Oboe d'amore	1
Bassoon	5	Flute (copper)	3	Occarina	2
Bassoon (Baroque)	2	Flute (modern)	16	Penny whistle	2
Bladder pipe	1	Flute (North and South		Piccolo	10
Chalumeaux	1	Indian)	2	Rackett	2
Chanter	1	Flute (Renaissance)	9	Rauschpfeifer	1
Clarinet	10	Flute (wooden)	8	Recorder	25
Clarinet (Baroque)	3	Gaida	1	Saxophone	6
Contrabassoon	2	Gonassi flute	1	Shakuhachi	4
Cornett	5	Highland pipes	1	Shawm	4
Duoinitza	1	Horn pipe	1	Sordonne	3
Dulcian	1	Irish war pipe	1	Tabor pipe	3
English horn	3	Kaval	2	Uilleann pipes	4
Fife	16	Krumhorn	3	Voice flute	2
Flageolette	1	Mute cornetto	3		

Table 3. Brass

Instrument	No. of Makers	Instrument	No. of Makers	Instrument	No. of Makers
Brass (unspecified)	4	French horn	4	Trombone (slide)	5
Alto horn	2	Mellophone	1	Trombone (valve)	2
Baritone horn	4	Sousaphone	3	Trumpet	6
Bugle	1	Trombone (alto)	1	Trumpet (Baroque)	1
Cornet	7	Trombone (Renaissance)	1	Trumpet (herald)	2
Euphonium	1	Trombone (rotor)	1	Tuba	2
Fluegelhorn	5				

Table 4. Keyboard

Instrument	No. of Makers	Instrument	No. of Makers	Instrument	No. of Makers
Keyboard (unspecified)	4	Organ (chord)	1	Organ (tracker)	3
Accordion	22	Organ (electric)	5	Piano	31
Clavichord	49	Organ (electronic)	10	Piano (electric)	4
Digi-vox	1	Organ (electro-pneumatic)	3	Piano (electronic)	11
Forte-piano	7	Organ (mechanical-action)	2	Reed pipes	1
Harpsichord	128	Organ (pipe)	34	Regal	1
Organ	21	Organ (portative)	7	Spinet	14
Organ (auto-chord)	1	Organ (positive)	3	Synthesizer	11
Organ (band)	1	Organ (reed)	1	Virginal	28

Table 5. Percussion

Instrument	No. of Makers	Instrument	No. of Makers	Instrument	No. of Makers
Percussion (unspecified)	4				
Amphion chimes	1	Drum (concert)	1	Mouth bow	7
American Indian drum	1	Drum (hand)	1	Pickin' bow	1
Bells (ceramic)	1	Drum (log)	2	Saw (musical)	1
Bells (lyra)	1	Drum (rope-tensioned)	5	Stumpf fiddle	1
Bells (orchestra)	4	Drum (snare)	2	Tabor	2
Bodhran	2	Drum (steel)	1	Tambourine	4
Bongo	3	Drum (wooden)	5	Temple blocks	1
Boomagong	1	Early percussion	1	Timbales	1
Cabasa/a fuche	1	English handbell	1	Tympani (unspecified)	3
Carillon	3	Glockenspiel	1	Tympani (chain)	1
Chimes (orchestra)	3	Harmonica	1	Tympani (pedal)	1
Conga	3	Jew's harp	1	Vibra-harp	2
Cow bell	2	Jingle rings	1	Vibra-slap	1
Cymbals	2	Kalimba	15	Wood blocks	1
Drum (unspecified)	19	Limber Jim	2	Xylophone	9
Drum (African)	1	Marimba	5	Zil	1
Drum (caluba)	1	Monochord	1		

3. List of Instrument Makers by State

Alabama

Cantrell, David
Coleman, Harry A.
Kirk's Musical Instruments
Torstenson, Ray
Yarbrough, Rual

Alaska

Alper, Charles D.
Lenzi, Joseph
Perkins, Latham

Arizona

Anderson, Steven
Artley, Inc.
Aydlett, Raymond Clifton
Beach, John
Beeston, Thomas
Bland, William
Carriveau, Ron
Cassidy, Stewart
Cellino, Chuck
Coin Art, Inc.
Eaton, Bill
Flynn, Clifford J.
Hood, W. G.
James, Chester
Jones, Freeman
Kingan, John
Manne, Diane
Moore, Dave
Oppedal, G. K.
Plant, Stanley
Rainbow Electric Guitars
Rasmussen, Paul J.
Rayburn, Ray
Reeder, Duane
Roberto-Venn School of
    Luthiery
Schrieber, Hank
Schwartz, Freddy
Seaman, Roy
Shannon, Jon
Sunshine Woodworks
Sweet, Charles S.
Thomas, Dr. Thomas
Watson, Theodore

Arkansas

Black, Dude
Blair, Bobby L.
Bolton, John
Cole, Kenneth Reagan
Evans, Linda
Hall, Don E., Jr.
Klemmedson, Gene
McSpadden, Lynn
Mabry, Mr. and Mrs. Eppes
Massey, Richard
Reeve, Harry J.
Thurston, Florian
Tone Cone Electronics
Turney, Enas
Waddle, Judy

California

Abbott and Sieker
Albin, R. Kent
Alexander, Richard
Allen, Laura Rachel
Allen, Richard C.
Anger, Darrol
Applequist, Joan
Armanino, Peter A.
Armstrong, Patrick
Artindale, Fred H.
Aslanian, Dan
Auch, Frederick E.
Audio Western Corp.
Avila, Victor N.
Bagley, Lynn
Balter, Joan
Bardin, Charles, and Sean
    Maroney
Bardin, Lester F.
Barrons Harpsichords
Batelli, Alfio
Bauer, Fred
Baum, John
Bay, Dr. Charles
Bean, Travis
Beckman Musical
    Instrument Co., Inc.
Becvar, Bruce R.
Beeder, Lee
Beehler, Raymond

Behrns, Harold E.
Benge Trumpet Co.
Benning, Hans
Berg, Jon
Bicknell, Dr. Stuart
Bishop, Geoffrey
Blackman, Martha
Blackwell, M. Robert
Blanton, Ron
Blue Guitar Workshop
Blue Lion
Bocheneck, Doc
Boerner, Lawrence
Bogue, Rex
Bolander, John A.
Borbeck, Robert W.
Botnick, Norman W.
Boyer, William
Bozo Music Gallery
Bradley, Don
Bradley, Walter, Jr.
Bradley, Wesley
Brechin, Gray
Breyre, Brian
Brosnac, Donald
Brown, Don
Brown, Lawrence
Brown, Tom
Brullo, Lawrence R.
Burgess, David
Burgess, Dennis
Burkhart, Daniel R.
Burning Water Instruments
Burns, Brian
Callier, Paul Joseph
Cameron, Roderick
Camille Violin Shop
Campbell, Richard A.
Capritaurus
Carvin Mfg. Co.
CBS Musical Instruments
Chamberlin Instrument
    Co., Inc.
Chase, Hal
Chester, Wayland C.
Childs Family Mt.
    Dulcimers
Cigledy, Richard S.
Clark, Gene
Clark, T.

Clarke, Paul
Cobb, Greg
Collier, Charles
Collier's Violin Shop
Conrad, A. G.
Cooper, Gary
Corsale, Leonard
Corwin, Stuart
Cos, Emile
Cottingham, Larry
Crawford, James
Creager, Marcus O.
Crowder, V. C.
Crowl and Hook
Crown
Crucianelli Guitars
Crump, P. W.
Cytha-Harp Co.
Dahlgren, William
Damin, Rik
Davenport, Roy
Davis, Carroll
Davis, E. David
Deering Banjo Co.
Delgado, Candelario
DePaul, Clive Andy Vincent
Derderian, Lynn
Derek, Stephen
D'Georgio Guitars
Dickinson, Arthur S.
DiSalvo, Frank
Doan, L. C.
Dodson, Ivan
Drum City–Guitar Town
DuPont, Brad
Earthwood, Inc.
Edkford, E. B.
Edson, Harold
Elder, Lyn
Electro String Instrument
    Corp.
English, Larry
Epcor, Inc.
Erickson, Charles W.
Evans, Ruth Esther
Fawcett, Matthew
Feidelberg, Roy
Fender/Rogers/Rhodes
Ferguson, Ren
Fischer, Albert W.
Fisher, David B.
Flexer, J. Robert
Flowers, James
Fontwit, Sandy

Freegard, Stephen
Freeman, Morris
Frosali, Mario
Fulton, William
Furey, James
Gariepy, Joseph H.
Gasser, Gordon A.
Gautz, William A.
Gerlach, Fred
Germer, John
Gido, Julius
Gilbert, James H.
Gilbert, John M.
Givens, Bob
Golden Bells Music Co.
Goldzweig, Robert
Gon-Bops
Gonzales, Joseph
Goodfellow, Ted
Grace, Dennis
Greenberg, Robert
Greenstein, Sidney
Gryphon Stringed
    Instruments
Guitar Works, The
Haas, Ron
Habekoss, Stephan
Hachez, Ronald J.
Haldon, Charles
Hanks, Larry
Harmolin, Inc.
Harris, William Reed
Hart, Dr. William
Heitzman, David
Hewitt, Al
Hicks, Jim D.
Higgins, Larry
Hill, Kenny
Hill, Richard
Hines, Chet
Hirsch, Harold
Holsman Instruments
Hooker, Basil J.
Hoover, Edgar
Horn, Guy
Hunter, Fred
Indian Jim
Irwin, Douglas
J and D Resonator Co.
Janke, John
Johnson, Brian and
    Mary Lou
Johnson, Charles V.
Johnston, David

Jones-Clayton
    Harpsichords, Inc.
Jones, Glenn L.
Kaiserling, McWilliam
Kamimoto, Hideo
Kanner, Michael Barry
Kantele Guitars
Katz, Robert
Kauffman, C. O.
Kenyon, Richard Lee
Kerson, Michael C. O.
King, Eric
Klein Custom Guitars
Klepper, Howard
Knapp, Richard V.
Kob, Martin
Kovanda, Frank
Kuriloff, Arthur
LaGrandeur Music
Lamont, Peter
Landis, Felix
Landry, Robert F.
Lanini, Henry
Lapidus, Joellen
Lark in the Morning
Lasky, Howard
LeCler, Rose
Lee Music Mfg. Co.
Lee, Richard J.
Lee, Steven D.
Lennard, Arthur
Leonard, Rose-Ellen
Levenson, Monty
Lewis, Juno
Lipnick, William
Lohberg, Ernst
Long, Robbie
Loughton, Robert A.
Lynch, Steve
Maas-Rowe Carillons, Inc.
McCabes Guitar Shop
McGreevy, Don
McGuire, Bruce
McLellan, Michael
McWillis and Strauss
Mages, Andreas
Magic Mountain
    Instruments
Maheu, Richard
Main, Lewis
Mandl, Otto W.
Martin, Henry
Masasso, William Louis
Mattingly, R. L.

Mazzeo, Rosario
Meador, John
Meissner, Henry, and Son
Mejia, Frederico
Mello, John F.
Merz, Richard
Messer, Casimer
Miller, Russ
Millstein, Bernie
Minnerly, Donald
Mitchael, Danlee
Mitchell, William J.
Moe, Edwin
Mondragon
Montz, Lowell
Moore, Howard
Moran, Arlie
Mortenson, Mark
Moskow, Wayne
Mosrite of California
Moudy, L. W.
Moze Guitars
Mueller, Albert
Mumford, Brian
Murdock, Tom
Murphy, Dennis
Music Factory
Music Man, Inc.
Myers, Herb
Natraj
Newman, B. E.
Noble, Mr. and Mrs. Roy
Nonamaker, Brian
Norman's Rare Guitars
Norris, Paul E.
Norwood, Tom
Oberheim Electronics, Inc.
O'Donnell, Roger
Ohannesian, David
Olds, Dr. John
Olson, Daniel R.
Oribe, Jose
Original Musical
    Instrument Co., Inc.
Ortiz, Oscar
Overholtzer, A. E.
Palm, Richard
Parmelee, Clyde H., Jr.
Patterson, James E.
Pausic, Frank
Peacock, George
Pedit, Byrne
Peoples, Richard Douglas
Perez, Allen

Perkins, C. B.
Perryman, Daniel B.
Peterson, Thomas
Petrula, Stephen J.
Phillips, John M.
Phillips, Todd
Piasecki, Michael
Pinches, William S.
Pippin, Sylvia
Plektron Corp.
Plott, Robert F.
Pollard, Gary
Pollard Industries, Inc.
Popelka, Ray E.
Porter, Steve
Poulsen, Boyd
Prager, Jerome
Prince, Ralph
Puskas, Joseph
Pyle, Harry
Rashid, Joseph G.
Read, Robert
Rees, Harold S.
Reliable Brothers
Remo, Inc./Pro-Mark
Rheem Mfg. Co.
Rhodes Keyboard
    Instruments
Rickenbacker, Inc.
Rico, Bernardo C.
Ritter, Frederick
Robinson, Roland L.
Rockwood, B. J.
Rodeo, Otis B.
Rodriguez, Manuel
Rogers Drum Co.
Rogers, Joe, Jr.
Rolandcorp U.S.
Roomian, Doug
Rubin, Philip
Rued, Tim
Rugg and Jackel Music Co.
Rumery, L. R., Co.
Saga Banjos
Samhat, Jack
Sanchez, Ulises
Sansom, Russell
Santa Cruz Guitar Co.
Santo, Dave and Barbara
Schecter, David
Schenk, Otto K.
Schertenlieb, E. L.
Schliff, Sam
Schweitzer, William E.

Scott, George
Scott, James
Scott, Roy
Seamoon Co.
Sears, Lynn B.
Secusa, Jerry
Seeler, Oliver
Shapreau, Carla
Shaw, Tim
Sherrick, Michael P.
Sherron, Roger
Shipley, Scott
Shipman, Margaret Arlene
Showalter, Leonard
Simon, Carmie
Singleton, M. K.
Sleeter, Dave
Smalts, Lawrence
Smith, Joseph
Snyder, Lawrence D.
Soderstrom, Dr. John
Somogyi, Ervin
Souza, Gabriel
Standel Co.
Stelling Banjo Works
Stick Enterprises, Inc.
Stoffel, Peter
Strobel, H. A.
Sultzbaugh, Lisle
Sweeney Banjo Mfg. Co.
Switra, Julius
Tayloe, Marjorie
Taylor Guitars
Tenney, T. Burdell
Teplow, Deborah
Tippets, J. W.
Toenniges, Paul
Torres, Daniel and Dawne
Total Technology
Traditional Musical
    Instrument Co.
Transue, Warren
Traphagen, Dake
Trautwein, Chris
Tree Frog Music
Trumbo, Warren
Tupper, Dave
Turner, Rick
Union Grove Village
    Guitar Shop
Universal Accordion
Valje Drums
Vance, M. W. and
    Stanley P. Miller

Vaughan, Mark
Venice Dulcimer Works
Vogel, Robert
Wake, H. S.
Wald, David
Wallace, William
Wark, Charles
Watson, Claude H.
Webb, Scott
Weedle, Dr. Robert
Weideman, Thomas M.
Weisshaar, Hans
Whaley, Margaret
White, Hayward Gerald
White, Warren H.
Whitebook, Michael
Wicker, Kenneth
Wildwood Music
Wilhelm, Bob, and Karen
    Sharp
Williams, S. R.
Wilson, Minor
Witcher, Jay
Wurtz, Howard
Yeaton, Henry
Yelda, Peter Michael
Yoder, Lee
Yost, Phil
Younce, Henry S.
Young, David Russell
Zabala, Mirror
Zeltins, Yaris
Zgradic, Ivan
Zink, Robert

Colorado

Alpine Dulcimer Co.
Appleseed John's
Becker, George
Bennett, Dave
Bieker, Robert Lee
Bonnie Carol Dulcimer Co.
Briskey, Dale
Burdick, Lynn
Clifton, Harrold C.
Cowan, John
Cripple Creek Dulcimers
Davenport, Ken J.
Dulcimer Shop
Gamble, Larry
Goodrich, David C.
Hathaway, Dale C.
Hughes Dulcimer Co., Inc.

Hummer, David, and Karl
    D. Wienand
Jamison, Cliff
Kaster, Thomas J.
Kemnitzer, Michael
Krimmel, Max
Lemberg, Sandy
Milligan, Weldon Eugene
Morrison, Chuck
Murdock, Robert L.
NBN Guitars
OME Banjo Co., Inc.
Payne, Thomas
Rodriguez, Manuel E.
Slaughter, Les
Smith, Jack F.
Stevens, D. W.

Connecticut

Atwell, Robert
Austin Organs, Inc.
Barger, Newcomb
Barney, Carl
Batchelder, Charles
Belt, Philip, and Maribel
    Meisel
Brass City Fifecraft
Bringe, John
Carstanjen, Mikael
Castellano, Robert M.
Curtin, Stephen H.
Dekley Corp.
Desola, W.
Essex Banjo Co.
Feder, Yves Albert
Ferrary, Henry E.
Guitar and Banjo Workshop
Haenel, Frederick
Hollwedel, Henry, Jr.
Hughes, Richard P., Jr.
Kinsolving, Pitt
L'Heureux, Larry
Liberty Banjo Co.
McIntyre Clarinet Co.
Mayland Co.
Ovation Instruments, Inc.
Page, Gilbert Owen
Reed, David
Republic Drums
Rickert, Bradford
Silver, Frank
Sweet, Ralph
Tyson, W. C.

Way, David J.
Willis, Alan

Delaware

Brakmanis, Zigfrid S.
Erdman, John P.

District of Columbia

Christie, Robert
Garfield, Harry, II
Haynes, Robert
Mitchell, Howard
Moglie, Albert
Wallo, Joseph F.
Weaver, M. A. and
    William A.
Wolf, M.
Wolf, Thomas and Barbara

Florida

Arvin, Dan
Benedetto Guitars
Berger, Paul
Boling, Rick
Breslin, Larry Pohl
Bucheck, Joseph, Sr. and Jr.
Caton, Donald
Chester, Charles Allen
Curry, Donald L., Jr.
Day, Harley A., Jr., and
    Michael Batell
DeLuccia, Gennara
Drumland
Ekland, Donald
Elliott, Ernest Lee
Fernandez, Jose A.
Fleming, C. H.
Fraguela, Manuel
Gandy, T. G.
Gentle Winds Flute Co.
Govox, Inc.
Graber, John T.
Halback, Bill
Hartley, John, III
Hartley, Steven H.
Hendrickson, Floyd
Hutchinson, Frank
Huttig, H. E.
Kopp, David E.
Korenvaes, Herman
Kuspa, James
Larsen, William

McDevitt, Mr. and Mrs. John
Madsen, Erling
Mayo, Salvador
Minnerly, Percy
Oster, Doran
Roman, Charles
Savell, Kelvin
Sbanal, Walter
Schurger, Severin G.
Shaw, John
Shultis, Dean L.
Stiles, G. L.
Tringas String Instrument
  and Repair
Veleno Guitars
Wasel, Bill
Weaver, Andrew

Georgia

Adams Piano Factory
Aull, Louis
Barrows, David
Bishop, Walter H.
Blaylock, Bill
Buck, Henry L., Jr.
Cohen, Don
Cooper, Robert
Diapason Guitar Shop
Galloway, Russell
Izzo, Richard
Lane, Harris
Myers, McAllen C.
New Traditions Banjo Co.
Patchen, Josef
Rowe Accordions
Sid's Fingerboard Studio
Vas Dias, Harry

Hawaii

Booth, Newton J.
Ching, Douglas, Luthier
Gilmore, George
Marienthal, Donald C.
Ogawa, Albert

Idaho

Craft, John
Craig, Fred
Daniels, Sam W.
Elwell, Michael
Evergreen Mt.

Florence, Ed
Franklin Guitars
Guthrie, Marvin L.
Larsen, John M.
MacLerran, Frank L.
Matheson, Ron D.
Mellobar
Nolte, Mr. and Mrs. Jerome
Perfect, John
Ramsey, Henry

Illinois

Adams, Paul
Allison Stringed
  Instruments
Alpha Omega Corp.
American Plating and Mfg.
  Co.
American Rawhide Mfg. Co.
Barbero Guitars
Barker Brothers
Batts, Jack
Beaujolais, Mr.
Becker
Brune, R. E.
Bryan, C. Alex
Carpenter Co.
Conn, C. G., Ltd.
C. R. Banjo Co.
Curlee, S. D. Mfg. Co.
Dauphinais, George
Deagan, J. C., Inc.
Decatur Instruments, Inc.
Delmarto, John
Dushkin, David
Elo, Arpad, Jr.
Emperador Guitars
Engelhardt-Link
Ensenada Guitars
Frank's Drum Shop
Fretted Industries, Inc.
Fret Shop
Goose Nest Prairie Banjos
Gray, John
Griffith, Owen E.
Gulbransen Industries, Inc.
Hammond Organ Co.
Henly, Patrick
Holt, Stan
Horowitz, William
Horvath, Marian
Huang, Ben
Hudd, Peter

Irving, Howard
Irwin, Lew
Italo-American Accordion
  Mfg. Co.
Jannotti, John
Johnson, Carl Albanus
Kamps, Jeff
Kay Musical Instrument Co.
Kent, Maurice
Kitching, B. F., and Co.
Krasicki, Walter
Kreutziger, John W., Jr.
Krupp Music Co.
Leedy Drum Co.
Limbursky, Richard
Little, Homer
Lostumo, Larry
Ludwig Industries
Lyon-Healy
McQuen, Dennis
Markle, Cecil
Medearis, Douglas W.
Merlin Mfg. Corp.
Micoa, Inc.
Milian, Jeffrey
Miller Guitars
Minstrel Guitars
Moore, Thomas L.
National Guitars
Norlin Music, Inc.
Petesh, Zenon W.
Pinter, Lazlo
Prihoda, Cheryl
Rasmussen, Aage, Violin
  Shop
Reeves, Bill
Reuter, Fritz, and Sons
Robinson, Bill
Rodrigo, Carlo A.
Rust, Don
Saville Organ Corp.
Sawicki, Stephen M.
Schilke Co.
Schlick, Hardy
Schmeltekopf, Gerhart
Schuh, Siegfried
Scientific Music Industries
Sherman, Sid
Simons, Richard
Slingerland Drum Co.
Sloan, John
Starch, P. A., Piano Co.
Stoltenberg, Robert W.
Sugar, Mark

Thomas International Corp.
Toneline Mfg. Co.
Trier, Collins Robb
Troovich, Mike
Tyk, Lawrence S.
Valco Guitars, Inc.
Van Leer, Johan
Warren, Kenneth, and Son, Ltd.
Washburn Guitars
Welland, Robert
Wendt, Robert L., and Roy Davis
Wesner Recorders
Westerman, Rich
Westheimer Sales Co.
White Eagle Rawhide Mfg. Co.
Wicks Organ Co.
W. M. I. Corp.
Wurlitzer Co.
Youngberg, R. David
Zdunek, Jim

Indiana

Ampeg Co.
Armstrong, W. T., Co., Inc.
Associated Luthiers
Belles, William R.
Blessing, E. K., Co., Inc.
Bremer, Wil
Brubaker, Jack
Bush, Edwin E.
Conner, Karl
Dahl, Ole
Danner, John
DeFord Flutes
Eckstein, Larry G.
Eversole, Ron and Nancy
Flynn, Ovie
Ford Platz Oboe Co.
Fox Products Corp.
Frederick, Franz
Garland, Becky
Gemeinhardt, K. G., Co.
Gerke, Randy
Hall, Wesley
Hardy, P. J., Musical Instruments
Harlin Brothers
H. E. Products, Inc.
Holloway Pipe Organs
Jackson, M. Eli
Jasper Corp.

Kamp, Wayne
Kimball Piano and Organ Co.
Knapik, Eugene
Kraft, Roger
Larilee Oboe Co.
Linton Mfg. Co.
Macnak, Andrew
Multi-Kord Factory
Opperman, George, Woodwinds
O'Riordan, Patrick
Parks, Gary C.
Pedler, Sid
Petrulis, Stanly and Lou
Pizzini, Mr. and Mrs. David S.
Rivinus, David
Schilling, Leonard
Selmer
Shawhan Pipe Organs
Shuttleworth, Don
Sirok, Steven
Sleeth, Nolan
Smith, Thomas
Sowers, Steven V.
Sunflower Music Shop
Walter Piano Co., Inc.
Wilson, Max G.

Iowa

Aardvark Fluteworks
Boyd, Michael
Foster, Daniel
Gillespie, Thomas
Gray, Gary
Gyld, The
Hall, Merle
Hess, Stanley
Hills, Norman L.
Jacks, Richard L.
Kottick, Edward L.
Lamberson, N. D.
Michael, Jan D.
Middleton, Art
Rembrand Co.
Sanders, Robert
Strait, Steve
West, Pearl

Kansas

Arensburg, Ted J.
Arkenberg, John

Blaas, Dr. Karl
Eckhardt, Martin
Furgason, Rodney J.
Hoeffgen, Thomas E.
Holick, Ed
Kustom Gretsch
McManis Organs, Inc.
Mason, Steve
Mossman, S. L., Co., Inc.
Pierce, R. Brent
Pickin' Post, The
Reuter Organ Co.
Smith Guitars
Snell, John R.
Templing, David
Thompson, William
Zickos Corp.

Kentucky

Butler's Music Instrument Repair
Dixon, Arthur
Forrester, Kent
Green, Gerald, Jr.
Haile Guitars
Haile, Thomas Vose
Hall, Jack Reed
Hinton, J. Steele, III
LaMay, L.
Layne, Raymond
Ledford, Homer
Maluda, John
Miller, Joseph Bernard
Parson, Charles
Ramey, Harry
Rein, Thomas G.
Reuter, Ronald Lee
Rose, Edward F.
Steiner Organs, Inc.
Steudle, Doc
Tignor, John
Walker, William P.
Willcutt, Robert J.

Louisiana

Diaz, David Demetrius
Foster, Charles C.
Gannuck, Don
New Orleans Banjo Sales
Olsen, Cheston
Rutland, Ned
Scheuerman, Milton, Jr.

Tubbs, Floyd
Wood, John W.

Maine

Apollonio, Nicholas
Baily, Harry
Bartolomeo, Carl
Bass, Peter
Bok, Gordon
Bourgeois, Dana W.
Carll, Willis
Ciano, John
Clifford, Roger
Cone, Michael
Cox, Jimmy
Damm, Edward A., and
    Anne Damm
Dowling, William F., and
    Co.
Downeast Dulcimer Shop
Farrar, Paul
Farrell, Susan Caust
Felder, Mark
Finlayson, Scott
Frederick, Peach
Gertner, John
Golze, Tom
Gooze, Tom
Greene, Edward R.
Hannings, Lynn, and
    George Rubino
Harris, Alan
Hathaway, Eric
Hoffses, Virgil
Holt, Alan
Kendrick, Jim
Kingsley, Craig
Lamb, Neil
Lignell, Anton
Maestro, Edward
Mann, Ivie W.
Martin, James D.
Newcomb, Larry
Pinkham, Ron
Redfern, Robert F.
Ross, Stuart
Ross, William Post
Shortridge, John and Linda
Shortridge, Linda
Siegler, Lawrence S.
Smith, Rick
String Instrument
    Workshop
Suran, Debbie

Young, Jerry and Deborah
Zussin, Harold

Maryland

Adams, Andy
Adler, Mark
Akright, James
Armitage, Kenneth
Barnes, Warring
Bassing, Carolyn
Brock, Myron
Bumgardener, Jim
Butler, Mark William
Carpenter, Lane O.
Cassis, George B.
Cox, Jacob
Cox, James, Jr.
Diamond, Morton S. and
    Louise
Fisher, Zachariah
Fitzsimons, Bill
Garrison, Craig
Gault's Violin Shop
Gotzmer, Carl
Hegedus, Louis V.
Hendrickson, S. J.
Herman, Bruce
Holzapfel, Carl C.
Janzegers, John
Kapa Guitars
Kelly, Ritch
Leiva, Manuel
Melody Flute Co.
Micro-Frets
Moller, M. P., Inc.
Moore, S. Brook
Muehl, Philip
Neecker, Otto, and Sons
Niebell, Paul
Payne, G. L.
Pigman, John
Poynor, George V.
Price, Rodney
Putnam, John F.
Quality Banjo Co.
Seyfrit, Dr. and Mrs.
    Michael
Sobansky, Ed
Soistman, C.
Springfield, J. M., III
Stimson, Burt
Stone, Dennis
Takoma Banjo Works
Taylor, W. Bruce

Teleguitars
Tester, Paul
Thompson, Earl
Thompson, Dr. Oliver
Tuckerman, Kristine
Veneman Music Co.
Wade, Mark
Ware, John R.
Warsh, Kenneth
Weir, John P.
Young, Roger

Massachusetts

Adams, Jeremy
Aeolian Workshop
Aitkins, Reginald
Andover Organ Co., Inc.
Armstrong, Tom
ARP Instruments, Inc.
Ascrizzi, Anthony
Barry, Wilson
Baystate Stringed
    Instrument Co.
Beacon Banjo Co., Inc.
Beaudry, Philip A., Co.
Bednark, Tom
Berkshire Organ Co., Inc.
Betz, Alan
Boston String
    Instrument Co.
Bosworth and Hammer
    Historical Woodwinds
Boyce, James C.
Bozeman-Gibson and Co.
Brannon, Bickford and
    Robert
Brewer, George
Bryant, Curtis
Bump, James
Burke, William
Cannon, James H.
Carruth, Alan E.
Casey, Jack
Chapman, Alan
Chertok, Alan
Childs, Steve
Colby, Peter
Cook, Richard
Cornelissen, Marten
Creamer, Anthony J.
Cundy-Bettoney Co.
Deihl, Douglas
Desmond, Bob

Dillman, Warren
Dowd, William
Eames Drum Co.
Eckerworks
Engels, John
Enright, Bryan
Exinde Corp.
Fahey, Kevin M.
Fallon, Joe
Farrell, Eugene
Ferry, Frank
Fisk, C. B., Inc.
Freeman, David
Fudge, Carl
Gaiennie, Clark
Garabieta, Ignacio
Gaudette, Arthur
Germann, Sheridan
Giuttari, Glenn
Gootnick, David
Gorey, Herb
Gregoire Harpsichord
Guitar Workshop
Guttenberg, John
Hamel, Leo
Harlos, Leonard
Hart, Richard
Haynes, William S., Flute
  Co., Inc.
Herz, Eric, Harpsichords,
  Inc.
Houtsma, Adrianus J. M.
Hubbard, Frank
Ingalls, John T.
Instrument Guild, Inc.
Joseph, Eugene
Kepner, Gil
Kirby, Russell P.
Knatt, Thomas
Koenig, Al
Koster, John
Kyvelos, Peter
Landell, Jonathon
Laney, Peter
Lee, Lorraine
Lehmann, Bernard E.
Lipiczky, Thomas
Littleboy, Henry, and Son
Mandile, Michael
Mandrake Music
Marteney, Eugene R.
Merwin, Deborah
Mixon, Bill
Montague, Fred
Mt. Lebanon Banjo Co.

Musco, Thomas Guy
Myrvaagnes, Rodney
Nargesian, John
Nattelson, John
Noack Organ Co., Inc., The
Noble and Cooley Co.
Novaline, Inc.
Outerbridge, Thaddeus, III
Owen, Barbara
Pedulla/Orsini Guitars
Platz, Joseph
Pope, Martin A.
Powell, Verne Q.
Prescott, Thomas M.,
  Workshop
Reed, Abijah
Reed, John M.
Renaissance Workshop
Robbins, Zust
Robinson, Trevor
Roche Organ Co., Inc.
Rowles, Steve
Ruggiero, Matthew
Russell, William E.
Schecter, Martha
Scott, Allan
Sears, Thomas A.
Shaw, Owen
Shaw, Reginald
Smith, Arthur E., Banjo Co.
Smith, Robert E.
Sorli, Steven W.
Sound Guitar Co.
Stanul, Walter
Stimmerman, Daniel
Stringfellow Guitars
Stuart Organ Co.
Sullivan, Daniel T.
Taylor, J. Bradley, Inc.
Tolliver, Bennett
Tucker, Andrew
Tuttle, Lawrence M.
Tyndale, Clyde
Van Lennep, Joel R.
Van West, Phil
Vashli, Zoltan
Vega Instrument Co.
Von Huene, Friedrich
Wager Music
Warshaw, Steven F.
Weertman, Roelof
Welsh, Susan
Werhner, Jerry
Xinde International, Inc.
Zildjian, Avedis, Co.

Michigan

Andress Mfg. Co.
Bartow, Clarence Nolan
Bastarache, Clarence
Battershell, Frederick
Blasius, John
Blood, William
Borromey, Andrew J.
Boucha, Parnell
Briggs, David Byron
Brodersen, Christopher
Brownell, David
Budapest String Shop
Burda, Jan
Burks, Herbert M., Jr.
Byl, Robert J.
Carle, Richard B., Jr.
Castiglione Accordion Co.
Cichonovich, Nicholas
Colby, William
Cox, Eugene A.
David, Herbert
Electro-Voice, Inc.
Elton, Fred
English Sales, Inc.
Erbel, Art
Everett Piano Co.
Foley, Linda
Folkers, Catherine E.
Foster, Douglas
Gadd, Charles W.
Gibson, Inc.
Gifford, Paul
Gilmour, John Tunnoch, III
Great Lakes Banjo Co.
Harrison, Benjamin F., Jr.
Hennig, Arnold
Hill, Keith
Hitter, John
Imperial Accordion
  Mfg. Co.
Jansma, Timothy
Jenks, J. P.
J-Folks Dulcimers
Johnston, Woodie
Jorgenson, David
Kepley, John C.
Kettle, Rupert
Koucky, William
Kroon, Lambert
Kukick, Nicholas
Lamoreaux, Cal
Langejans, Delwyn J.
Laughead Co.

Lourdley, E.
Marshall Music Co.
Moore, Grant
Moore, Timothy
Nehil, Tom
Peacewood Dulcimer
Pirtle, R. Alva
Polla, David
Pollina Accordion Mfg. Co.
Prokopow, Brad
Reiter, Bart
Riesenberger, James A.
Ritchie, Raymond
Robbins, Ron
Round Family Dulcimer Co.
Sanders, Curt, and Linda
    Foley
Schneider, Richard
Schwartz, Mark
Schweinsberg, Heinz
Semino, Frank
Shar Products
Slaby, William E.
Smith, M. G.
Stevens, Larry
Stoetzer, Mike
Story and Clark Piano Co.
Sunrise
Sutherland, David A.
Tuller, Robert S.
Vernon, Knight
Webster, William
Werbin, Stanley
Whitcomb, Charles G.
White, William
Wickstrom, Felix
Wilcox, Donald
Wiles, David
Wilson, Denise and Richard
Witt, E. O.
Workman, John
Wray, Jerry
York Band Instrument Co.

Minnesota

Anderson, Arnold Dean
Benn, Bradley W. M.
Brown, Robert
Brown, Robin
Brown, Steve
Cloutier, Steve
Davis, Al H.
Gravelin, Tom
Gronning, Richard

Hall, James Newell
Here, Inc.
Hickerson, Vern
Hoffman Guitars
Hubert, Carl W.
Jirousek, Charles
Kakos, Stephen
LaPlant, Lloyd G.
Malmquist, Milton G.
Meisel, K. Lothar
Patashne, Theodore
Plumbo, Phillip S.
Poulton, Curt A.
Reeck, Rick
Rossa, Ronald D.
Stigen, Duane
Stuber, Mike
Van Daalen, Jan
Vaughan, D. Ross, and
    Steven K. Gustafson
Watters Distributing Co.

Mississippi

Keith, J. B.

Missouri

Atchley, E. V.
Bearden Violin Shop
Beckman, Alan T.
Chouteau, Jane
Darby, David F.
Elgin, Pico
Fuchs, Ed
Hofmann, Willy
Hogan, Kirk
Krieg, Russell
Lee, Billy
Lissant, Kenneth J.
Meramec Handcrafts
Palis, Charles A.
Porter, Leonard V.
Ruhl, Robert Allen
St. Louis Music Supply Co.
Swisher, J. Dean
Usher, David
Wright, Rossco

Montana

Anderson, Arvil
Beckman, Wayne
Bitterroot Music
Christensen, Royce

Crow Peak Music
Polts, Allan
Setran, Ben

Nebraska

Bahr-Schall Music Co.
Carroll, Randy
Davis, Keith
Drews Custom Guitars
London, Dale
London Stringed
    Instrument Repairs
McConnell, Robin James
McCormick Strings
Nielsen Violin Shop
Tewell, Lucille
Tone-Master
Vaughn, John B.
Wiebe, David

Nevada

Geiger, Paul
Hendricks, Neil
James, Lester L.
Lenz, Richard L., Jr.
Nicksic, Milan S.

New Hampshire

Broekman, Hendrik
Capadestria, Denis
Chelys
Colburn, David
Dover, Daniel
Girard, Neal K.
Gurian, Michael
Hanover Stringed
    Instrument Co.
Hettinger Guitars, Ltd.
Koch Recorders
Lipton, Walter
LoMonaco, Joseph
Ludden, James
Mager, Martin
Marston, Walter
Millard, Michael
Paganoni, John A., and Sons
Perry, William
Smith, Robert
Spielvogel, Bennet
Stilphen, George
Stone, Benjamin
Taylor, Ed

Tsiang, Lynette
Warnock, Donald
Werth, Craig and Elizabeth
Westover, Harold and
    Allene
Winslow, Edward

New Jersey

Accorgan Corp.
Artisan Electronics Corp.
Bannister Harpsichords
Beach Instrument Corp.
Bearden, Sherid Sailer
Berkshire Instruments, Inc.
Billiris, J. Charles
Blozen, Tony
Carroll Sound
Chiasson, Claude
Code Corp.
Danelectro Corp.
Denzer, R. H.
Dickens, Fred T.
Donnan, Mark
Estey Piano Corp.
Field, David
Frankel, William
Galanti Brothers, Inc.
General Electro Music
Glaubitz, H. G.
Glemann, Walter C.
Gress-Miles Organ Co., Inc.
Griffith Piano Co.
GTR Products, Inc.
Guild Musical Instruments
Guitar Hospital
Hardy, Jay
Hayes, Stephen
Hinger Touch-Tone Corp.
Holland Organ Co., Inc.
Hutchins, Carleen
Kiersten, John
King, Geoffrey
Klein, John O.
Koontz, Sam
Kramer Guitar Co.
Kramer, Ira B.
Kratt, William, Co.
Kuniche, George F.
Kuntz, Samuel
Kunz, Ulrich
Latin Percussion
LoPrinzi, A., Guitars, Inc.
LoPrinzi, Augustine
Lyman, Fred, Jr.

McGlincy, L. Edward
McLaughlin, Leo
Madison, Christopher
Magnus Organ Corp.
Magyar, Kalman, Sr.
Melodiana Accordion Co.
Monari, Jay H.
Montefuso, Marc
Morel, Rene
Murza, Jeff
Nebel, Hans
Olsen, Rudolf
Peresson, Sergio
Phil-Lu Inc.
Pinelands Dulcimer Shop
Pratt, Samuel O., Co.
Reints, John
Restivo, Dr. Andrew Philip
Reynoso, Nicholas
Sano Corp.
Schmidt, Oscar,
    International
Siminoff, Roger H.
Simon, Mark
Sinclair, John
Sonola Accordion Co., Inc.
Soto, John
Stevenson, E. P.
Takoushian, C. Garo
Tool, Bob
Toplansky, Howard
Turner, Robert M.
United Guitar Co.
Vavra, Alfons
Vespe Drum Shop
Vile, Jake
Whippany Electronics, Inc.
Zachary Organ Co.
Ziedler and Quagliata
    Harpsichords

New Mexico

Berkov, Christopher A.
Brown, Douglas R.
Bryan, Clarence L.
Cole, Anne
Damler, Fritz
De Mano Guitars
Dempsey, Trish
Gould, Jan
Hachez, Daniel
Honeycutt, John T.
Kendall, Wayman A.,
    and Son

Lancaster, Don
Pimentel, Lorenzo,
    and Sons
Robertson, Donald
Rossner, Heinz M.
Shlaer, Robert
Spence, John Cordell
Sprouse, Edgar F.
Twelfth Street Guitars
Wattington, Tom

New York

Abbate, Frank
Aberle, Hank
Ace Accordion Co.
Adams, G. F.
Aeolian American
Albright, Alan
Aldridge, Alan
Allerton, Steven
Ames, Archer
Apache Guitars
Arcieri, Carlos
Autorino, Mike
Avery, Eugene E.
Bach Piano Co.
Barnes, Lucien, IV
Bell Accordion Corp.
Benedict, Roger A.
Benson, Harold
Bertucca, Thomas
Blake, Ronald
Bonito, Dr. Fedele
Brody, M.
Brush, Bart
Buecker and White
Buglecraft, Inc.
Burger, Chris
Burr, Walter
Camber Cymbal
Carey Organ Co.
Celestial Flute Co.
Chapple, Jeffrey
Cherin, Milton
Chrapkiewicz, David
    Ludvik
Cilecek, Joseph
Clarke, Greg, III
Cohen, Michael J.
Colby, Dr. T. E.
Contessa Guitars
Cooperman, Patrick
Crabtree, James
Crocker, Derwood

Crocker, Jennifer
Cushing, Mark
Daimaru New York Corp.
Daly, Tom, Jr.
Daniels, Arthur
D'Aquisto, James
D'Attili, Dario
Dayan, Stanley
Delaware Organ Co., Inc.
Delpilar, William
DeNeve, Richard J.
Dickson, Rev. Gordon
Diehl, T. Pieter
Disend, Nadya
Dishaw, Daniel
D'Merle Guitars
Dorenz, David
Dornhelm, Solomon
Dorogi, Dennis
Dudley, Charles
Dunham, Harold
Dunning, James
Dynastar
Eastern Musical Instrument Co.
Edmon, Emul P.
Eisenstein, Samuel
Eklund, Karl
El Degas Guitars
Emola, Albert
Empire Accordion Corp.
Estey Division of Miner Industries, Inc.
Everngam, Howard
Fairbanks, Harvey
Favilla Guitars
Fearn, Cabell J.
Feinman, Ronald
Fiber Age Products
Fleisher, H.
Frank, Ray
Frankel, Dr. Emanuel
Fricker, John N.
Frirsz, Max
Galizi and Sordoni
Gar-Zim
Giardinelli Band Instrument Co.
Giulietti Accordion Corp.
Gleaves, William Russell
Godfried, Robert
Goodman Drum Co.
Gough, Hugh, Inc.
Grand, Dr. Louis L.
Grassroots Productions

Gregory Musical Instrument Corp.
Grossman, James
Guglielmo, Dennis
Haensel, Frank
Hagstrom Guitars
Halifax Musical Instruments, Ltd.
Hebert, Dan
Henderson, Guy Fred
Heritage Dulcimers
Hertel, Erwin
Hird, Martin
Hom, Tom
Hosmer, Tom
Humphrey, Thomas
Ingraham, Kermit
Iorio Accordion Corp.
Irwin and Son Piano Co.
Janofsky, Stephen
Kahn, Bruce R.
Kalb, Steve
Kantor, Jay
Kaston, Henryk
Kelly, James
Kharma Bodies
Kimbel, James
Kinhaven
Kish, Charles N.
Kleske, John
Knight, Tom
Kolstein, Samuel, and Son, Ltd.
Korechoff, J. D.
Krakauer Brothers
Kramer-Harrison, William
Kriskey, Charles J.
Lamont Band Instruments
LaPrima Accordions, Inc.
Latray, Carl
Laubin, A., Inc.
Levin, Henry
Levin, Jeff
Levin, Phillip
Lewandowski, Lynne
Lifton Mfg. Co.
Lindner Pianos
Lo Bue, Charles
Lockard, Barry
Logi-Rhythm, Inc.
Lorello, Eugene E.
Low, Douglas A.
Maier, Howard A.
Malgi, Meeme
Maliha, Ernest J.

Manderen, Michael
Marcantonio, Michael
Mari, E. and O.
Martindale, Howard
Matusewitch, Boris
Meadow, Robert
Meyer Brothers
Miller, Janet
Misuriello, Harry P.
Molvai, Manocher
Monteleone, John
Montgomery, John
Moog Music, Inc.
Moroz, John
Moulton, Peter
Multivox
Music Technology, Inc.
Mussi Accordions
Nagy, Sando Alex
Needham, Howard
Newman, Brett
Newman, Richard Scott
Nichols, David R.
Nigogosian, Vahakn
Nordenholz
O'Brian, Frank S.
O'Brien, Vincent
Octave Electronics, Inc.
Olyslager, Robert
Oosting, Jan
Orozco, Juan
Osco Mfg. Corp.
Palco Products Corp.
Pancordion, Inc.
Papazian, Manouk
Parker, Kenneth
Pease, Don
Pelton, Clifford
Penzel, Mueller, Inc.
Peripole, Inc.
Pizzi, Enzo
Pizzo, Tony, and Laura Fontana Pizzo
Polisi Bassoon Corp.
Postol, Elliott
Ramos, Agustin, Jr.
Randall, Thomas R., Jr.
Ritchie, Jean
Roberts, Clifford
Rochester Folk Art Guild
Rogers, Don
Rosenberg, Saul
Rosenthal, Luthier, and Son
Rossi, John L., Ltd.

Russo Accordions
Rutherford, Judith
Rutkowski and Robinette
Rynerson, David M.
Sahara
Salchow, William, Ltd.
Sansone, Michael T., Jr.
Schlicker Organ Co., Inc.
Schonbeck, Gunnar I.
Schroetter, Andrew, and
　　Co., Inc.
Schuff, Otto
Seibert, K. S.
Sekova Products
Silverstein, Steven
Sohmer and Co., Inc.
Sorkin Music Co.
Spafford, Fred
Stapley, Craig N.
Starkman, Martin
Steinway and Sons
Stoller, David
Storch, Ben, Corp.
Stoutenbourgh, Harry
Stradivarius Violin Shop
Sugar Loaf Folk
　　Instruments
Szwajda, Wally
Tatar, Pietro
Tatay and Son
Thomas, Robert A.
Thompson, Carl
Titano Accordion Co.
Traeger, Charles
Tugel, Ake
Tygert, F. Scott
Unicord, Inc.
Valenti, Thomas
Van Hamel, Diederik
Veillette, Joseph and Jane
Velasquez, Manuel
Ventura Guitars
Wakeman, Earl
Wallace, Joseph H.
Warburton, Robert
Watson, Jimmy
Watson, John R.
Weaner, Maxwell
Weser Piano Co.
Williams, Joe
Woodwind Co.
Worthen, Albert W., Jr.
Wrigley, Keith P.
Wurtzel, Lenny

Yuta Musical Instruments
Zadro, Michael

North Carolina

Baity, Harvey
Best, John E.
Bryan, Robert P.
Conrad, Robert, III
Currier Piano Co.
Dell, Albert Hampson
Emmons Guitar Co.
Gawley, Bob
Gendron, Mark Steven
Glenn, Charlie Monroe
Glenn, Clifford
Glenn, Leonard
Grand Piano Co., Inc.
Greenwood Organ Co.
Ham, Roy
Harmon, Robert Wilson, IV
Harmon, Ted
Hicks, Floyd
Hicks, Stanley
Hollifield, Clyde
International Musical
　　Instruments, Inc.
Johnson, D. Ray
Kelishek, George
Kohler and Campbell, Inc.
McCrimmon, Dan
McInturff, Terry
Marlen Guitar Co.
Martin, Edsel
Miller, Don R.
Murray, Dave
Norton, Jesse
Osborne, Foy D.
Peck, Elizabeth
Pennington, Ralph
Phillips, Bill
Porter, Bill
Presnell, Edd
Proffitt, Frank, Jr.
Ramsey, John
Sams, Howard
Sekerak, Christopher M.
Sheppard, David B.
Sipe, John
Stadler Guitars
Sturgill, David A.
Vaughn, Mr. and Mrs.
　　Ralph J.
Ward, Ben T., Jr.

Weltron, Inc.
White, Matthew
White, Odd
Williams, Jack
Wright, Tad, Woodworks
Zimmer, W., and Sons

North Dakota

Estenson, Paul S.
Holm, Dan
Johnson Organ Co., Inc.
Lehmann, Jeff
Lesmeister, Lauren A.

Ohio

Antes, Scott E.
Baker, Dennis
Baldwin Piano Co.
Balint, Geza
Beall, J. R.
Blair, R. B.
Bodd, Roy, and Ken Eye
Brandt, A. W., Co.
Brombaugh, John
Brown, Edwin A.
Brown, Lawrence D.
Brueggeman, John
Brunetti Guitar Factory
Bulley, Julian E.
Burger and Shafer
Burhans, Ralph W.
Caudy, Michael A.
Chacey, Ron
Clark, Paul S.
Crader, Lee
Cucciara Harpsichord Co.,
　　Inc.
Cunningham, Tom
Dalglish, Malcolm
Davidson, F. R.
Davis, Tom
DeRose and Co.
DeVeto, Charles
Dunkle, Robert E.
Eastman Violin Shop
Forestiere, Jerry G.
Frieg, Stephen
Gemza, Bela
Gray, Chester
Gretsch, The Fred, Co.
Grossman Music Corp.
Guldan, Jackson
Henn, Eugene E.

Hild, David G.
Hill, Barney
Hog Fiddle Music Co.
Holtkamp Organ Co.
Hoppe, John
Horine, Dave
Horvath, Joe
Humphrey, Scott
Isaac, Norman E.
Isenbanger, Robert
James, Clarence R.
Kimball, Dean
King Musical Instruments
Kortier, David
Kuistad, Garry
Ledbetter, Joseph
Lehrer, John A.
Leonard, D. A.
Lima Pipe Organ Co.
Luderer, Otto
Luedeke, Tim
McRuggles, Charles
Martin, Charles T.
Mason, Robert M.
Masters Violin Shop
Matheny, Herman Edmond
Mathews, C. Weldon
Mazza Guitar Shop
Mind Dust Music
Murphy, Michael
Nealon, William A.
Neff, Rusty
Nicholas, General Custer,
    and Sons
O'Brien, Walter F.
Ode Banjos
Pergram, Wallace
Plesnicar, D. B.
Polsinelli, P. Gio.
Ponziani Violin
Protexorgan Co.
Rosen, Mike
Ruhland Organ Co.
Sanders, John
Schantz Organ Co.
Scherl and Roth, Inc.
Schlub, Richard and David
Sistek Music Co.
Slejko, Stanley
Smakula, Peter H.
Smith, Leon
Sparks, Earl
Stewart-MacDonald Mfg.
    Co.

Stockwell, Randy
Stojkov, Gregory A.
Swinger, Michael H.
Taylor, David
Thierman, John
Thurman, Roger
Torma Violin
Turner, William P.
Twyman, B. R.
White, Bob
Young, William Henry

Oklahoma

Don's Guitar Shop
Elcombe, Art
Harris, Rodger
Imperial Banjo Co.
Kemper, Bob
Kuehnert, T. A.
Layton, Tom
Moss, Edward B.
Payne, Dr. Richard W.
Piper, Ty
Rapp, Allan J.
Rohde, W. E.
Romine, Don
Strider Systems, Inc.
Szaborn, W. T.
Williams, John B.
Young, Arthur W., II

Oregon

Adams, Parker
Akin, David
Anderson, Robert S.
Ariail, James
Banjo and Fiddle Shop
Bianco Accordions
Bilyeu, Thomas P.
Burt, Chris
Collinsworth, W. J.
Daniellson, Jim
Elliott, Jeffrey R.
Finn, Emit
Galaxie Guitars
Giardinieri, Vittore E.
Gordon, William B., Jr.
Hagler Banjo Craftsmen
Hampton, James
Hauser, Scott
Hoeber, Tony
Hoerster, John Henry

Kasik, Joseph and Nancy
Kinch, Don
Leslie, Michael D.
Lundberg, Robert
McNeese, Lee
Merrifield, Edward
Musicraft, Inc.
Neuman, Phil and Gayle
Olsen, Richard S.
Palmason, Victor
Partridge, David
Prior, Jim
Ratajak, W. P.
Roach, Gene Paul
Rodgers Organ
Romans, Ken
Schmoll, Rudolph
Schuback Violin Shop
Sierra Steel Guitars
Smith, George A.
Snyder, Don
Specht, David T.
Swettman, Dr. William
Tower, Thomas H.
Tucker, Judy
Valterza, John L.
Walter, Gilbert
Wheeler Ped-All
White, Ken and Jim
Wickham, G. H.
Woolf, William Devoe
Yasutome, Jim

Pennsylvania

Allen Organ Co.
Bailey, Keith
Bailey, Q. J.
Balderose, George
Bernardo, Fred
Bodor, Janos
Boyer, Curt
Branhut, Mike
Buckel, Thomas R.
Buck Musical Instrument
    Products
Campbell, Edward
Cannarsa Organs, Inc.
Chaney, Garrett B.
Chapline Organs
Cindrich, John
Crawford, Andrew E.
Danko, Karen J.
De Angeli, Maurice

DeCavage, John
DeLuccia and Son
Dippold, Timothy W.
Ebert Organ Co.
Estes, Peter
Estey Musical Instrument
    Corp.
Finck, Henry
Fletcher, Richard
Framus-Phila Music Co.,
    Inc.
Freeman, S. D., Jr.
Givens-Gourley, Inc.
Goodrich, Theodore O.
Graham, John S., Jr.
Hayden, Nick
Hockenberry, William N.
Hornpipe, Michael
Huber, John R.
Huzela, Andrew
Keller, Helmuth A.
Kern, Dr. Evan
Knight Royale Pianos
Lehigh Organ Co.
Lester Piano Mfg. Co.
Lomax, John A.
Malmark, Inc.
Markusic, Frank
Marshall, John
Martin, C. F., Organisation
Martin, Christian FMN
    IVFMartin, Walter P.
Menkevich, Michael
Mercer, Thomas
Miller, H. Burritt
Miller, James
Moats, Douglas
Mudler-Hunter Co.
NHF Musical Merchandise
    Corp.
Noble, Tim
Norris, Joseph
North Country Music Store
Ohrstrom, Thomas
Opsonar Organ Co.
Orthey Dulcimers
Osborne, Joseph
Phelps, Lawrence, and
    Associates
Prall, Rusty
Rampulla, Jim
Reitz, Albert
Riegel, Terenzio
Rock, Robert P.

Rogers, Keith
Ruppel, Henry D.
Sadowsky, Roger
Schulmerich Carillons, Inc.
Schulte, C. Eric
Sell, George
Shal, John H.
Spigelsky, William S.
Stein, Bert
Taney, Peter
Trefz, Otto R., Jr., and Co.
Unger, Doug
Wade, Richard S.
Wall, Conrad
Warner, Chris
Watson, Keith
Winston, Julian
Yursco, Michael
Zatzman, Bob, Guitar
    Studio
Zeswitz, Wm., String Repair
    Shop

Rhode Island

Allison, Michael
Bartram, James F., Jr.
Campbell, Jon
Crozier, Bill
Flavell, Stuart H.
Gadoury, Norman
Gotjen, J. T.
Leis, Alfred C.
Schoos, Maurice
Sky, Patrick
Snyder, Dr. Harold E.
Stiles, Phillip J.
Strafaci, Natale Armando

South Carolina

Curry, Dr. Hiram
Holsclaw, Raymond
Lafoy, John B.
Luffman, B. E.
Van Bergen Foundry

South Dakota

None

Tennessee

Aeolian Corp.

Albright, Capt. Cliff
Apprentice Shop
Bradbury Piano Co., Inc.
Broekhuizen, Elaine
Carrell, Sam
Dan Doty's Dulcimers
Davis, Bill
Dixon, Robert T.
Fleming, H. A.
Framus of Nashville
Fraser, Rod
Gallagher, J. W., and Son
Greene, Blaine
Greven, John
Gruhn, George
Hartsell, Jim
Hood, Robert T.
Hurley, F. Jack
Lawrence, Bill
Logan, Kitty
Luther, James D.
McDonald, Zeke
Maxwell, John
Mize, Robert R.
Morgan, Tom and Mary
Murphy, Barry
Park, Joe
Peterson, Jesper
Pietz, Otto
Pyle, Mr. and Mrs. Paul
Ritter, Anthony, Jr.
Roberts, James D.
Sauter Pianos
Schilling, Jean and Lee
Steele, Henry
Tut Taylor Music
Upper Cumberland Craft
    Center
Walker, Kim
Waterville, Otis
Weehutty Industries
Wishnevsky, Steve
Wood, Randy

Texas

Abernathy, Dr. Peter
APP Electronics
Behlen, Stinsen R.
Blackburn, David
Blackshear, Tom
Brady's Violin Shop
Buss, Graydon

Caron, David
Chapman, Harold
Claxton, Edward
Coll Divine Flutes
Collings, William, II
Elliott, J. C.
Ellis Mandolins
Erlewine Guitars
Erwin, John Bruce
Fels, Rubin S., Co.
Gabbanelli, John
Gordon, Russell
Gorish Violin Shop
Grant, Robert S., Jr.
Hales, Mike
Hogue, Ben
Hondo Guitar Co.
Hudgens, A. D.
Johnson, Paul
Jones, Danny R.
Jones, Sam
Kilpatrick, J. R.
Kingsley, J. William
Kingston, Richard
Kloss, Horst L.
Lindberg, Dick
Lobdill, Jerry
McElroy, Jeremiah T.
Marquardt, Bill, Jr.
Maynard, Judson
MCI, Inc.
Meek, Jimmie
Miller, A. A.
Musiconics International,
    Inc.
Newton, David A.
Orren, R. S., Jr.
Pettitt, Denver L.
Prevo, B. W.
Redman Organ Co.
Reis, Irvin
Ridge Runner Music
Senkow, Walt
Shrum, William Edward
Unicorn Musical
    Instruments
Visser-Rowland Associates,
    Inc.
Wade, Donnie
Watson, R. P.
Whatley, J. W.
Wilkinson, Richard
Williamson's Violin Shop
Wise, Stephen L.

Woddail, George
Woodworks

Utah

Astin Weight Pianos
Callister, Jan E.
Hart, Paul
Intermountain Guitar and
    Banjo
Kapfhammer, Wilhelm
Prier, Peter
Smith, Anton
Steiner-Parker Synthesizers
Wakefield, John Homer

Vermont

Baker, Ralph W.
Broekhuizen, John
Eckhaus, Joel
Flagg, Russell
Fox, Charles
Groethe, Russell
Heineman, Chris
Hoffman, Mark
Hunter, Clyde H.
Katz, Don
Litwin Luthiers
Liu, Lloyd
Marks, David
Moore, A. David
Morris, George
Perlman, Alan
Riportella, Ken
Rubin, James
Russo, Mr. and Mrs.
    Pasquale
Sacred Fire/Frogs Delight
Seeger, Jeremy
Stack, Alan A.
Tourin, Peter
Voorhees, Clark
Westminster Dulcimers
Wild Edible Dulcimers
Wood and Sound

Virginia

Allen, Dale
Allen, John W.
Blair Dulcimers
Blue Grass Farm
Boomhower, H. E.

Brobst Violin Shop
Brooks, David R.
Burnside, Richard
Butten, Clifton H.
Creed, Kyle
Darnell, John
Dingus, Otto B.
Dunovan, Jay
Ebert, L. Allen
Garrison, David William
Gough, Roger D.
Hamblin, Ken
Hash, Albert
Hawkins, Lt. Frank J.
Henderson, Wayne
Hendrickson, George
Hoffman, David
Hohman, Paul
Jeffreys, A. W., Inc.
Korpal, M. L.
Largen, William
Latham, Joe
Lee, Melvin D.
Luke Dulcimers
McCann, John R.
McConnell, Cecil A., Sr.
Macoy and Masonic
Martone, Leo J.
Melton, Raymond W.
Miller, Audrey Hash
Miller, Raymond
Millhouse, Steven
Minnich, Larry
Murray, Anthony
Patterson, Etoyse
Perry, Darell
Polifka, Donald K., Jr., and
    Judy Polifka
Privratsky, Bruce
Ramblin' Conrad's Guitar
    Shop
Redstone, Peter and
    Kathryn
Rizzetta, Samuel
Russell, Roscoe
Sanderson, Dave
Saverino, Louis
Scott, Alfred
Skarie, Jeremiah
Smith, Jack R., Jr.
Stanley, Mr. and Mrs. Peter
Stradi-Varni Co.
Stratton, Robert
Summerfield, Seth

Turner Corp.
Vazquez, Alberto W.
Vintage Banjo Co.
Watts, Donald
Williamsburg Restoration
Yates, Charles L.
Young, Keith

Washington

Ackley, Dennis
Ashley, Hammond,
    Associates
Bakeman, Ken
B and G Instrument
    Workshop
Bell, Donald
Berdon Co.
Bidne, Leo L.
Bischofberger, Herman
Boardman, Olcott
Born, Mary Lucille
Bostard, Kenneth
Boulding, Philip
Bouslaugh, William
Calhoun, David Charles
Carpenter, Robert
Chromey, Joe
Clark, Julian
Connelly, W. H.
Conner, David R.
Cowan, James
Davidson, Keith S.
Dorris, Brian N.
D'Ossche, Al
Ekstedt, John R.
Eppler, Alexander Illitch
Erickson, Lyle J.
Fish, Troy
Fisher, Alfred L.
Folkstore, The
Force, Robert Lewis, Jr.
Fortune, Abel
Fullenwider, John, and Sons
Griffin, W. T.
Grimes, Stephen
Grout, Gary
Hacker, Richard
Henderson, Frank V.
Hunt, David
Huvard, Anthony J.
Hyndman, Max
Iverson, Capt. Derek
Jensen, Dane
Johnson, Frank A.

Johnson, Louis
Johnston, Neil M.
Kinderman, Paul D.
Konzak, Ron
Levelle, W. Robert
Lindner, Robert
Lyons, Jim
McCarthy, R. J.
Matheson, Rod
Mitchell, Henry
Moore, Thomas B.
Morris, William V.
Newman, William
Norwood, Will
Olsen, Timothy
Oosting, Marilije
Peters, Jack
Peterson, Jon
Petosa Accordions
Prang, Larry
Raimi, Richard
Rayman, Kent
Reed, Dennis
Resek, Thomas Lee
Rollins, John
Rosenfeld, Judy
Sahlin, Eric
Saunders, David
Schlieps, Armin
Smith, Jeffrey Lee
Smith, Stephen O.
Stockton, Glen Terry
Telegraph Music Works
Thomas, Harry
Ulmschneider, Carl
Vineyard, Lawrence
Watson, William D.
Whitcher, Ladd
White, Glenn
Wiegand, Henry and
    Adolph
Will, Byron J.

West Virginia

Blake, Basil
Boarman, Andrew
Bridges, Jim
Campbell, J. Ralph
Cottrell, Jenes
Dailey, Tom
Dickinson, L. Eugene
Epler, Raymond
Gardner, Asel
Gardner, Worley

Good, Jimmy L.
Kardos, Andy
Kennedy, Bill
Kennedy, Davis E.
King Banjos
Lohman, Craig F.
Maxson, Charles
Meads, James H., II
Miller, Exmar
Mills, Scott
Muelrath, Dave
Nick's Music Store
Reisler, Paul
Shapiro, Peter
Shepherd, Jesse Gordon
Smith, Lonzo B.
Thompson, Robert G.
Welker, Pete

Wisconsin

Baime, Thomas C.
Banjos by Richelieu
Beck, John
Becker, Tim
Boehm, Thomas C.
Brodrick, Daniel L.
DEG Music Products, Inc.
Draves, Peter Sargent
Fiddle Factory, Inc.
Fry, William
Getzen Co.
Gunn, Shannon
Hendricks, Daniel
Johnson, Thomas F.
Karpek Accordion Mfg. Co.
Keans, Robert
Klein, Richard
Koscak, John
LeBlanc, G., Corp.
LoDuca Brothers Musical
    Instruments, Inc.
Lundy, Lawrence
MacGibbon, R. W.
Meyer, Kenton
Monette, Louis Gayle
Mussehl and Westphal
Norton, William F.
Ostberg, Neil
Pascoe, Bob, and Doug Perry
Perry, Douglas M.
Petros, Bruce
Renaissance Gilde
Reppert, Robert
Ruck, R. S.

Sambol, James R.
Scalone, Joe
Schmelzer, Herbert
Schmidt, K. C.

Stehling, Sandy
Wahl, Ronald
Welch, Mark
White, David

Ziven, Rich

Wyoming

Johnson, Erik A., II

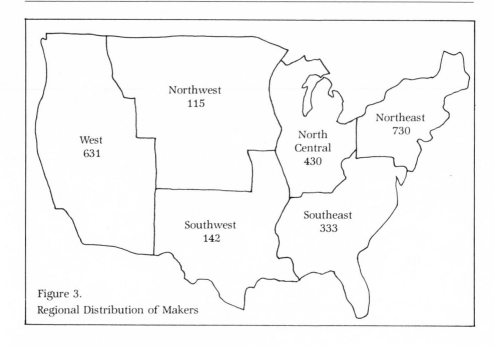

Figure 3.
Regional Distribution of Makers

Table 6. Number of Instrument Makers by State

	Number	Rank		Number	Rank
Alabama	5	41	Montana	7	40
Alaska	3	46	Nebraska	1	48
Arizona	34	21	Nevada	5	43
Arkansas	15	34	New Hampshire	28	24
California	423	1	New Jersey	85	8
Colorado	34	22	New Mexico	20	29
Connecticut	35	20	New York	262	2
Delaware	2	47	North Carolina	53	14
District of Columbia	9	37	North Dakota	5	44
Florida	49	16	Ohio	102	5
Georgia	18	32	Oklahoma	17	33
Hawaii	5	42	Oregon	52	15
Idaho	15	35	Pennsylvania	88	7
Illinois	111	4	Rhode Island	13	36
Indiana	56	13	South Carolina	5	45
Iowa	18	31	South Dakota	0	51
Kansas	20	28	Tennessee	43	18
Kentucky	23	27	Texas	62	11
Louisiana	9	38	Utah	9	39
Maine	48	17	Vermont	27	26
Maryland	59	12	Virginia	64	10
Massachusetts	142	3	Washington	85	9
Michigan	95	6	West Virginia	27	25
Minnesota	29	23	Wisconsin	43	19
Mississippi	1	49	Wyoming	1	50
Missouri	19	30			

Table 7. Types of Instruments Made by State

State	Strings	Woodwinds	Brass	Percussion	Keyboard
Alabama	4				
Alaska	5				
Arizona	15	4			
Arkansas	9			3	
California	60	20	2	25	14
Colorado	11	2			1
Connecticut	16	4		5	7
Delaware	1				
District of Columbia	8			1	2
Florida	26	3		3	1
Georgia	14	1			5
Hawaii	9				
Idaho	10				
Illinois	24	8	8	11	10
Indiana	20	11	11		4
Iowa	12	5		1	2
Kansas	11			1	4
Kentucky	15	3			1
Louisiana	11	1			3
Maine	24	2			4
Maryland	29	8		1	6
Massachusetts	39	22	2	4	9
Michigan	24	4	6		6
Minnesota	18			1	5
Mississippi	2				
Missouri	13				1
Montana	11				2
Nebraska	9			1	1
Nevada	10				
New Hampshire	19	3			9
New Jersey	24	2		11	13
New Mexico	16	1			
New York	37	12	2	9	15
North Carolina	20	5			3
North Dakota	4				2
Ohio	24	2		8	13
Oklahoma	12	1			2
Oregon	26	6		1	6
Pennsylvania	25	6		4	11
Rhode Island	7	5		1	
South Carolina	7			1	
South Dakota					
Tennessee	17			1	2
Texas	18	4		1	5
Utah	12	1			3
Vermont	20			1	3
Virginia	17	3			3
Washington	37	11		2	6
West Virginia	13			3	
Wisconsin	15	8	12	1	7
Wyoming	2				

The Apprentice Shop
Box 267
Spring Hill, Tenn. 37174

The Hoosick Institute
The Windsor Mills
North Adams, Mass. 01247

Northwest School of Instrument Design
P.O. Box 30698
Seattle, Wash. 98103

N.E. School of Stringed Instrument
Technology
William E. Garlick, Director
P.O. Box 8307
Boston, Mass. 02114

William Cumpiano
c/o Stringfellow Guitars
121 Union St.
North Adams, Mass. 02147

Arthur E. Smith Banjo Co.
Box 825
Leverett Center, Mass. 01054

Guitar Building
Craftsbury Center
Craftsbury Center, Vt. 05827

Earthworks
South Strafford, Vt. 05827

Mr. Roy
University of New Hampshire
Durham, N.H.

Hofstra University
West Hempstead, N.Y.

The Guitar Works
c/o Nick Apollonio
Tenants Harbor, Maine

Kenneth Warren & Son School of Violin
Making
28 E. Jackson Blvd.
Chicago, Ill. 60604

D.A. Smith
Lute Society—Practical and Theoretical Lute
Construction
2151 Princeton
Palo Alto, Calif. 94306

Bartrow Institute of Professional Violin
Making
329-1/2 S. Washington
Lansing, Mich.

Peter Prier School of Violin Making
308 E. Second South
Salt Lake City, Utah 84111

Roberto-Venn School of Lutherie
5445 E. Washington
Phoenix, Ariz. 85034

Accordion Teacher's Guild, Inc.
George Cailooto, President
12626 W. Creek Rd.
Minnetonka, Minn. 55343

American Academy of Organologists
Roy Anderson, Secretary
P.O. Box 714
Mount Vernon, N.Y. 10551

American Accordionists' Association, Inc.
Maddalena Belfiore, President
37 W. Eighth St.
New York, N.Y. 10011

American Banjo Fraternity
c/o W.C. Kentner
2665 Woodstock Rd.
Columbus, Ohio 43221

American Guild of English Handbell Ringers,
Inc.
100 W. 10th St.
Wilmington, Del. 19899

American Guild of Organists
Charles Dodsley Walker, President
630 Fifth Ave.
New York, N.Y. 10020

American Guitar Society
Vandah Olcott Bickford, Secretary
2031 Holly Hill Terr.
Hollywood, Calif. 90028

American Harp Society
Catherine Gotthoffer, President
43748 N. Waddington Ave.
Lancaster, Calif. 93534

American Institute of Organ Builders
c/o F. Robert Roche
P.O. Box 971
Taunton, Mass. 02780

American Musical Instrument Society
Membership Office
University of South Dakota
Box 194
Vermillion, S. Dak. 57069

American Organists International
6877 Washington Ave. South
Eding, Minn. 55435

American Society of Ancient Instruments
Mrs. Colgate W. Darden, Jr., President
7445 Devon St.
Philadelphia, Pa. 19119

Associated Pipe Organ Builders of America
c/o Schantz Organ Co.
Box 156
Orrville, Ohio 44667

Catgut Acoustical Society
112 Essex Ave.
Montclair, N.J. 07042

Choristers Guild
P.O. Box 38188
Dallas, Tex. 75238

The Company of Fifers and Drummers
Horse Hill
Westbrook, Conn. 06498

Guild of American Luthiers
8222 S. Park Ave.
Tacoma, Wash. 98408

The Guild of Carilloneurs in North America
c/o Margo Halsted
6231 Monero Dr.
Palos Verdes
Penninsula, Calif. 90274

Guitar Foundation of America
P.O. Box 4323
Santa Barbara, Calif. 93103

The International Clarinet Society
Dept. of Music
Idaho State University
Pocatello, Idaho 83209

International Harpsichord Society
Box 4323
Denver, Colo. 80204

International Horn Society

Barry Tuckwell, President
P.O. Box 161
Interlocken, Mich. 49643

International Society of Bassists
University of Cincinnati
College Conservatory of Music
Cincinnati, Ohio 45221

International Society of Violin and Bow
   Makers
no address

International Trombone Association
c/o T.G. Everett, President
Harvard University
Cambridge, Mass.

International Violin and Guitar Makers
   Association
560 S. 3d St.
Louisville, Ky. 40202

Lute Society of America
P.O. Box 194
Topanga, Calif. 90290

Mountaineer Dulcimer Club
c/o Russell Fluharty, President
R.D. no. 3, Box 119
Mannington, W. Va. 26582

National Association of Band Instrument
   Manufacturers
c/o H.H. Slingerland, Jr.
6633 N. Milwaukee Ave.
Niles, Ill. 60648

National Association of College Wind and
   Percussion Instruments
Thomas Ayres
Dept. of Music
University of Iowa
Iowa City, Iowa 52240

National Association of Electronic Organ
   Manufacturers
c/o Rodger W. Jenkins, President
Rodgers Organ Co.
Hillsboro, Ore. 97123

National Association of Musical Merchandise
   Wholesalers
Edward Davidoff, President

111 E. Wacker Dr.
Chicago, Ill. 60601

National Association of Organ Teachers, Inc.
Dorothy S. Grieg, President
7938 Bertram Ave.
Hammond, Ind. 46324

National Association of Rudimental
   Drummers
Wm. F. Ludwig, Sr., President
1728 N. Damen Ave.
Chicago, Ill. 60647

National Band Association
George S. Howard, President
Purdue University Bands
Lafayette, Ind. 47907

National Flute Association
c/o Harry Moskowitz
P.O. Box 222
Forest Hills, N.Y. 11375

National Organization of Pipe Organ Mfgs.
no address

National Piano Manufacturers Association of
   America, Inc.
George M. Otto, Executive Secretary
435 N. Michigan Ave.
Chicago, Ill. 60611

National Society of the Classic Guitar
P.O. Box 19290
Washington, D.C. 20036

Organ Historical Society
Thomas Cunningham, President
250 E. Market St.
York, Pa. 17403

Organ and Piano Teachers Association, Inc.
William Irwin, President
436 Via Media
Palos Verdes Estates, Calif. 90274

Percussive Arts Society, Inc.
Saul Feldstein, President
130 Carol Dr.
Terre Haute, Ind. 47805

The Queens Mandolin and Guitar Society
Joe Goffery

110-15 Myrtle Ave.
Richmond Hill, N.Y. 11418

The Society for Old Music
719 Wheaton Ave.
Kalamazoo, Mich. 49008

Society of the Classic Guitar
V. Bobri, President
409 E. 50th St.
New York, N.Y. 10022

Southern California Association of Violin
  Makers
no address

Viola da Gamba Society
John A. Whistler
2009 Peabody, Apt. 5
Memphis, Tenn. 38104

Violin and Guitar Makers Association
403 W. Maple St.
Jeffersonville, Ind. 47130

Violin and Guitar Makers' Association of
  Arizona
Sam Waddle, President
1446 E. 1st Pl.
Mesa, Ariz. 85203

Violincello Society, Inc.
Lillian Rehberg Goodman, President
140 W. 57th St.
New York, N.Y. 10019

Violin Society of America
c/o Herbert Goodman
25 Helena Ave.
Larchmont, N.Y. 10538

Stringed Instruments

Classic Guitar Makers Guide by H. E. Brown. Distributed by Scott E. Antes, 236 Lincoln St., Hartville, Ohio 44632.

How to Make a Classic Guitar by Joseph F. Wallo, 1319 F St., N.W., Washington, D.C. 20004.

Complete Guitar Repair by Hideo Kamimoto. Oak Publication, Embassy Music Corp., 33 W. 60th St., New York, N.Y.

The Classical Guitar: Design and Construction by Donald McLeod and Robert Welford. The Dryad Press, Northgates, Leicester, England.

Classic Guitar Making by Arthur E. Overholtzer, 618 Orient St., Chico, Calif. 95926.

Guitar Repair Manual by Guitar Player Magazine, P.O. Box 615, Saratoga, Calif. 95070.

The Steel String Guitar: Construction and Repair by David Russell Young. Chilton Book Co., Radnor, Pa.

The Steel String Guitar: Its Construction, Origin and Design by Donald Brosnac. Panjandrum Press, 99 Sanchez, San Francisco, Calif.

The Electric Guitar: Its History and Construction by Donald Brosnac. Panjandrum Press, 99 Sanchez, San Francisco, Calif.

Guitar Repair by Irving Sloane. E. P. Dutton & Co., New York, N.Y.

Steel String Guitar Construction by Irving Sloane. E. P. Dutton & Co., New York, N.Y.

Classic Guitar Construction by Irving Sloane. E. P. Dutton & Co., New York, N.Y.

The Acoustic Guitar by Don Teeter. University of Oklahoma Press, Norman, Okla.

Making Your Own Spanish Guitar, Balalaika and Violin. Distributed by Caldwell Industries, Luling, Tex.

Fix Your Axe—Easy Guitar Repairs You Can Do at Home by Guitar Player Magazine, P.O. Box 615, Saratoga, Calif. 95070.

The Mountain Dulcimer: How to Make It and Play It by Howard W. Mitchell. Folk-Legacy Records, Inc., Sharon, Conn. (book and record).

The Hammered Dulcimer: How to Make It and Play It by Howard W. Mitchell. Folk-Legacy Records, Inc., Sharon, Conn. (book and record).

How to Make and Play the Dulcimore by Chet Hines. Stackpole Books, Cameron and Kelker Sts., Harrisburg, Pa. 17105.

Notes on Dulcimer Building by Rodger Harris, 9607 Stratford, Oklahoma City, Okla., 73120.

How to Build a Hammered Dulcimer by Phillip Mason, P.O. Box 157, Front Royal, Va. 22630.

Violin Making as It Was and Is by Ed. Heron-Allen. Ward Lock, Ltd., 116 Baker St., London W1M 2BB, England.

Making a Simple Violin and Viola by Ronald Roberts. David and Charles Newton, North Pomfret, Vt.

Folk Harp Journal, P.O. Box 161, Mount Laguna, Calif. 92048.

Folk Harps by Gildas Jaffrenou. Distributed by *Folk Harp Journal*, P. O. Box 161, Mount Laguna, Calif. 92048.

Lute Construction by Robert Cooper. The Carriage House, 105 W. Perry St., Savannah, Ga. 31401.

Musical Instruments Made to Be Played by Ronald Roberts. The Dryad Press, Northgates, Leicester, England.

How to Make a Banjo and a Banjo-Guitar by Stamm Industries. Distributed by Warehouse Music Sales, P.O. Box 11449, Fort Worth, Tex. 76109.

Country Instruments—Makin' Your Own by Andy DePaule. Oliver Press, Willits, Calif.

Making Musical Instruments: Strings and Keyboard, edited by Charles Ford. Pantheon Books, New York, N.Y.

Constructing a Bluegrass Mandolin by Roger Siminoff. Colonial Press, 46 Ford Rd., Denville, N.J. 07834.

Wind Instruments

The Amateur Wind Instrument Maker by Trevor Robinson. University of Massachusetts Press, Amherst, Mass.

Woodwinds for Schools by Peter Tomlin. The Dryad Press, Northgates, Leicester, England.

Making and Playing Bamboo Pipes by Margaret Galloway. The Dryad Press, Northgates, Leicester, England.

The Northumbrian Bagpipes by W. A. Cocks and J. F. Bryan. Northumbrian Pipers' Society, c/o W. E. Hume, 15 Parkside Cres., Seaham Co., Durham, England.

Miscellaneous

Home Made Musical Instruments by Tom Kenyon. Drake Publications.

Make Your Own Musical Instruments by Muriel Mandell and Robert E. Wood. Sterling.

The Making of Musical Instruments by Thomas Campbell Young. Books for Libraries Press, Plainview, N.Y.

Making Musical Instruments by Irving Sloane. E. P. Dutton & Co., New York, N.Y.

Bow Making: 1000 Bows and a Tribute by John Alfred Bolander, 2814 Alum Rock Ave., San Jose, Calif. 95127.

HUME LIBRARY
SHENANDOAH COLLEGE &
CONSERVATORY OF MUSIC
WINCHESTER, VA.

781.91   71997
F247d

781.91   71997
F247d
Farrell, Susan Caust
Directory of contemporary
American musical instru-
ment makers

OCT 27 82

S 1136